THE ENGLISH CHURCH
AND NATION

THE
ENGLISH CHURCH
AND NATION

by

R. H. MALDEN

formerly Dean of Wells

LONDON

S · P · C · K

1952

First published in 1952
by S.P.C.K.
Northumberland Avenue, London, W.C. 2

(

It was the wish of my husband to dedicate this, which proved to be his last book, to the Bishop of London, and since Dr Wand has kindly accepted the dedication, I have the great honour of endorsing it, with gratitude, affection, and admiration from us both.

THEODORA MALDEN.

April 1952.

PREFACE

THE greater part of what appears in the following pages formed the substance of a course of lectures which I delivered at Wells during the years 1945–6–7. The origin of the lectures was in a sense almost fortuitous. On Sunday, 7 January 1945, it fell to me to preach in the Cathedral Church. Since the Wednesday following was the three hundredth anniversary of the execution of Archbishop Laud, who had held the See of Bath and Wells from 1626 to 1628, I made him the theme of my sermon. A few days later some members of the congregation asked whether I would deliver a course of six lectures on English Church History during the forthcoming Lent. The notice was short, but I agreed to do what I could, though I felt very doubtful whether more than a handful of people at the most would come to hear them. The Wells Natural History and Archaeological Society kindly placed their lecture room at my disposal. It can seat about eighty persons, and when I arrived to give the first lecture it was full. This attendance was maintained until the end of the course, and I was asked to continue the lectures during the Lent of the following year.

In the summer the Theological College, which had been closed for about two years, was reopened, and the then Principal, Canon H. B. Salmon, now rector of Weston-super-Mare and sub-dean of the Cathedral Church, invited me to lecture to the students. This course lasted for some months, and the interest of the audience seemed to be well sustained throughout. The shorter courses which I gave during Lent 1946 and 1947 appeared to be equally successful. This led me to think that there was some real demand for historical lectures of this kind, and that it might be worth while to try to get them published. The task of writing them out has been delayed by the fact that I was ill for some months during the first half of 1948 and not much more than convalescent during the second.

Throughout I have tried to link the history of the Church with the general history of the nation. I have been at pains to avoid overloading my pages with detail, such as can be studied better elsewhere. When lecturing I had to remember that most of the

v

members of my audiences had very little background of general ecclesiastical or historical knowledge, and did not understand either Latin or Greek. Probably similar considerations will apply to most of the readers I can expect, and I have tried to keep this in mind whilst writing out the lectures.

My debt to the writings of Lord Acton, Bishops Lightfoot and Creighton, and Dr G. M. Trevelyan has been so large that there may be some instances in which it has not been duly recorded. I hope this general acknowledgment may be considered to cover such inadvertent omissions. At times I have had to rely on note-books which I filled some forty years ago when the University Library at Cambridge was readily accessible to me. I have been unable to verify all the references with the resources within my reach now. Those which I have tested have proved to be accurate.

I am indebted to the Rev. Canon Charles Smyth, Rector of St Margaret's and Canon of Westminster, for very generous help in correcting mistakes in my MS, and for making many valuable suggestions.

In a course of lectures delivered at irregular intervals during a period of three years some repetition is almost bound to occur. I have tried to eliminate this when writing out in full what I had said.

It is the recognized privilege of any lecturer to be at times personal, discursive and even colloquial. If I have exceeded my rights in any of these respects, perhaps a little additional latitude may be conceded to a dean lecturing (literally) in the shadow of his own Cathedral Church, especially if he happens to be known personally, and in some cases intimately, to most of those whom he is addressing.   R. H. M.

WELLS, *Christmas* 1948.

I would like to apologize for any faults or inaccuracies in this book, which are due to my inexperience in preparing it for the press.

Also I wish to express my most grateful thanks to Canon Charles Smyth for so kindly finding time in his busy life to write the Foreword.   T. M.

January 1952.

FOREWORD

*T*HE *English Church and Nation* meets a real need. For it is difficult to think offhand of any other book of comparable size and scope which can be recommended with equal confidence to any educated layman who is conscious of the patchiness of his knowledge of the history of the Church of England and wishes to improve his mind. What he wants is an introduction to the subject—not too technical, not too elementary, and not too insular—which he can read for pleasure as well as for instruction at the end of a day's work. For such a purpose H. O. Wakeman's classic *History of the Church of England* (1896: 8th edition, revised by S. L. Ollard, 1914) is too much of a student's textbook: Gordon Crosse's *Short History of the English Church* (1947) is perhaps a little too slight: G. R. Balleine's *The Layman's History of the Church of England* (1923), though brilliantly conceived and executed in terms of an imaginary Kentish parish, is probably too simplified. Canon E. W. Watson's *The Church of England* (Home University Library, 1914) is a skilful outline, but of the kind that assumes a certain amount of previous knowledge: and *The Anglican Tradition in the Life of England* (1947), by the Bishop of Durham (Dr A. T. P. Williams), though highly valuable and suggestive, does not go back behind the Elizabethan Settlement. In short, no other writer known to me has attempted to do what the late Dean of Wells has done in this book; and it is safe to add that no other writer could have done it with quite the same touch. For *The English Church and Nation* is, in a very real sense, a personal document, stamped with the author's vigorous and forthright personality.

Admirers of the late Stanley Casson's enlightened venture in detective fiction, *Murder by Burial* (1938), will recall that Inspector Meatyard's library included ten years' issues of Crockford's Clerical Directory. "Few people", he explained, "know

that the annual introduction to *Crockford* is one of the few remaining delights of literature. Read it, and you will see. There, en-
shrined under the name of Editor, is each year as masterly a
piece of prose invective as has ever been penned since the time of
Samuel Johnson. It purports to be a summary of the year's work
in Christianity. In effect it is a superb study in the higher
criticism of the clergy." The description is not, of course,
entirely accurate, and should be checked by reference to the
modest volume of collected *Crockford Prefaces* (1921–44),
published by the Oxford University Press in 1947: but the
Inspector's tribute was as intelligent as it was appreciative. And,
although the editorship is always officially concealed behind the
veil of anonymity, it was in fact for many years an open secret—
a secret indeed so open that when it was divulged in various of
the obituary notices of the late Dean of Wells, the writers
appeared to be quite unconscious that they were referring to
anything that was not public knowledge.

Readers of *The English Church and Nation* will recognize in its
pages many of the literary qualities that distinguished the prefaces
to *Crockford*. Here, as there, nobody will agree with all the
author's prejudices, but everybody will enjoy his blunt expression of them. Here is the same magisterial faculty of crisp and
trenchant judgement, the slightly staccato style, the dry caustic
humour, the mastery of understatement, and the unexpected
scraps of curious learning. (Who was the last Archbishop of
Canterbury, and the first graduate of the University of Oxford,
to be canonized as a saint? The answer will be found on p. 92.)

This book, as the author himself informs us, had its origin in
a course of popular lectures on English Church History which
he delivered at Wells during the years 1945–47. Malden had a
natural gift for popularizing the results of historical study, and he
greatly enjoyed that kind of work. In its printed form, his
survey of the history of the English Church and Nation does not
pretend to cover every inch of the ground: it is rather in the
nature of a running commentary, although the material is not
arbitrarily selected or manipulated. It is not, in the technical
sense, a work of scholarship, though it is a work that only a

scholar (with a classical education) could have written. It is
robust, racy, confident, and contains many intriguing details
such as do not ordinarily occur in history books and are not very
generally known. It is also thoughtful and suggestive. Here are
two or three illustrations, chosen almost at random:

> The most terrible lesson of history is that almost all the
> deeds which posterity condemns as wicked or foolish were
> regarded at the time as good and wise; if not absolutely, at
> least as the best and wisest course open in the circumstances.
>
> (p 16.)
>
> The efficacy of a moral penalty must depend almost entirely
> upon the moral level of the person upon whom it is imposed.
>
> (p. 75)
>
> [The history of indulgences] shows what may happen,
> what indeed is bound to happen, if the clergy do not really
> understand the principles of the Church, and rely on their
> natural kindness of heart to guide them through the difficulties
> and perplexities which arise in the course of pastoral work.
>
> (p. 119)

There are other characteristics of this book which may also be
singled out for honourable mention: and among them I would
include the skilful and judicious use of local history and antiquities
(e.g. pp. 70, 149, 279); of personal observation (e.g. pp. 28,
37, 46, 147); and of secondary authorities—Lightfoot, Creighton,
Benson, Church. It may be remembered that Dr J. P. Whitney,
in his Inaugural Lecture as Dixie Professor of Ecclesiastical
History in the University of Cambridge (1919), pleaded very
cogently for "the use of great secondary writers. . . . It is
sometimes thought enough to say that History must be written
from original authorities. But we should add the rider that it
cannot be written solely from them. . . . We cannot afford to
neglect our predecessors, and we learn even from their mistakes"
(The Study of Ecclesiastical History To-day, pp. 17, 19–20).

But, when all is said and done, the most engaging feature of
The English Church and Nation derives from the obvious enjoyment
which its author found in writing it. There is a vigour and fresh-

ness, not to say gusto, about his treatment which, more than anything else, is calculated to commend it to the kind of public to which it is addressed. Yet underlying the delivery of these popular lectures there was a deeper purpose, which is best described in the words of the lecturer himself:

> I have tried to give you a series of pictures of our Church in relation to the national life as a whole and to show how and why it has come to be as we know it now. My aim has been to give you a better understanding of the real character of our unique spiritual inheritance, and a deeper appreciation of its value. It is the best thing which we have to offer to the world to-day, and there can never have been a time when there was greater need of it.   (p. 380)

It remains only to say something about the author of this book.

Richard Henry Malden was born on 19 October 1879, and died on Sunday 19 August 1951. The eldest son of Charles Edward Malden, Recorder of Thetford, he was educated at Eton and at King's College, Cambridge. He graduated with a double first in Classics, and was ordained in 1904 to a curacy at St Peter's, Swinton, Manchester. In 1907 he returned to Cambridge as a lecturer at Selwyn College: but three years later he was appointed Principal of Leeds Clergy School, and Lecturer at Leeds Parish Church. He retained these appointments until 1919, though for two years during the first World War he served as a Naval Chaplain, and in that capacity was present at the Battle of Jutland in H.M.S. *Valiant*. After the war he became vicar of St Michael's, Headingley, a residential suburb of Leeds, in succession to Canon G. A. Hollis (who became Principal of Wells Theological College, and then Bishop of Taunton).

Malden remained at Headingley for fifteen years. In 1926 he was made Chaplain to the King and an honorary canon of Ripon. From 1924 to 1933 he was a Proctor in Convocation, and in the early days of the Church Assembly distinguished himself as an outspoken champion of the rights of the parochial clergy. His contributions to the debates were marked by his habitual

forthrightness and independence, and were not always relished
by Archbishop Davidson. At the Church Assembly of February
1929, his proposal that there should be a black list of hymns that
"ought never to be sung in any self-respecting place of worship"
attracted a good deal of attention. He pointed out that the
Church of England was in the anomalous position of having no
authorized hymn-book of its own, which is still the case.

In 1933 he succeeded Dr Armitage Robinson as Dean of Wells.
His first major task, and one for which his hereditary connection
with the legal profession gave him taste and aptitude, was to
draft new statutes under the Cathedrals Measure. He was a good
administrator and a careful guardian of the fabric and of the
finances of what he loved to describe as "our Cathedral",
and he initiated "The Friends". He improved the ceremonial,
and organized a guild of embroiderers: and, although no
musician himself, he was tenacious of the musical traditions of
the Cathedral services, which were maintained daily throughout
the second World War. He resigned in 1950, on grounds of
health: but, despite the breakdown of his physical frame, which
he accepted with great fortitude, his mind remained robust
and vigorous to the last.

Malden was a versatile and prolific author of great range and
considerable learning. Of his theological publications, *The
Promise of the Father* (1937), a contribution to the problem of
Reunion, is probably the best remembered. His other works
include a history of the church of Headingley (1923) and
The Story of Wells Cathedral (1934). He was President of the
Somerset Archaeological Society (1943–4) and Chairman of the
Somerset Record Society. He also wrote ghost stories, some of
which he published in 1942: and in his Headingley days he
showed himself a comic actor of very considerable power in
private amateur theatricals.

He had a natural and somewhat old-fashioned dignity of person
and of mind. He always wore a top-hat when he came to London.
He was proud of being an Old Etonian. He never courted popularity, and was outspoken and sometimes devastating both in
public and private. Some of his more Johnsonian utterances are

remembered: "Sir, you may dissent from my opinions, but you must not contradict my facts": and, when a fellow-member of the Leeds Ruridecanal Chapter remarked with some complacency that he made little or no use of libraries, preferring to buy his own books and mark them, Malden commented tersely, "Mr —— must be either a very wealthy man or a very small reader." Yet in his personal relations with his brother clergy he was greatly valued for his ready sympathy and wise counsel. His manner was sometimes a little brusque, and he lacked that facile affability which puts strangers and casual acquaintances at their ease: but this was due largely to the fact that he was by nature a very shy man. He certainly did not wear his heart upon his sleeve: but he cared for people much more than they sometimes imagined; and those who knew him well not only respected him as a shrewd judge of character, but loved him as a just, straightforward, generous, and very loyal friend.

It may be suspected that the role of Elder Churchman was one which he found especially congenial. Endowed with a talent for discerning and incisive criticism of the follies of mankind, he disliked intensely and explicitly bad manners, lack of thought, and anything in the least degree unreal and untrue; and he was instinctively suspicious of emotionalism and artificiality in matters of religion. His ecclesiastical outlook was conservative: he abominated the Revised Prayer Book of 1928. His opinions were expressed with verbal economy and precision. There was never any doubt as to what he thought and meant. He had a powerful rather than a subtle intellect: indeed his mind, like his voice, was a little lacking in flexibility. As a priest, he was a dutiful, diligent, and conscientious pastor. As a preacher, he was lucid and instructive, without any of the tricks of oratory. Throughout the whole course of his ministry, the three outstanding notes of his character were simplicity, honesty, and complete courage.

CHARLES SMYTH

St Margaret's Rectory,
20 Dean's Yard, Westminster, S.W.1.

CONTENTS

APPENDIXES

1

The Study of Ecclesiastical History

A SUCCESSFUL manufacturer of motor vehicles is credited with having said, "History is bunk." Whatever may be the precise meaning of the last word, the general sense of the aphorism is unmistakable. It is, perhaps, not altogether surprising that a man who is more familiar with machinery than with ideas should think that the past has no lessons for us.

On the other hand, Bishop Lightfoot (Bishop of Durham 1879–89) once wrote, "History is an excellent cordial for the drooping courage."[1] The remark is often misquoted, and fathered upon more recent authors. Sometimes also it appears to be misunderstood. I think that the bishop meant that a knowledge of history will save us from the despondency into which we are liable to fall if we indulge in imaginary pictures of an idealized past.

It is of real value to recognize that there never was a time when there were not difficulties to be faced and failures to be repaired, if possible. There never was a time when human society in any part of the world ran, as it were, on oiled wheels—when everybody was honest and truthful, contented and prosperous, and did his duty from day to day as well as lay in him. Naturally the story of the past is chequered. History records periods of advance, periods of stagnation, periods of decline and periods of recovery. But I doubt whether it records any period during which men did not think that the difficulties and dangers which they had to meet were the worst with which mankind had ever been confronted, and did not sigh (at times with more justice than at others) for

[1] *Historical Essays*, p. 73.

the return of the good old days. And therefore I should venture to interpret Bishop Lightfoot's remark by appending, "because it gives us a true perspective".

We shall understand the present much better, and are less likely to allow our judgment to be perverted either by optimism or by pessimism, if we can see our world against the background of the past.

It is possible to study history with a view to discovering precedents which may prove useful. But this is really a waste of time. It would seldom be difficult to unearth a historical precedent of such a nature as to be entitled to some respect, which could be used to justify almost any course of action which we might have in contemplation. The most terrible lesson of history is that almost all the deeds which posterity condemns as wicked or foolish were regarded at the time as good and wise; if not absolutely, at least as the best and wisest course open in the circumstances.

It may be true, as Lord Acton[1] said, that power tends to corrupt, and that absolute power corrupts absolutely.[2] But the sufferer always seems to be unaware of the corruption which he has undergone. It would be difficult, if not impossible, to point to any historical figure, whether Pope or Sovereign, bishop or statesman, who has deliberately used his power in a way which he sincerely believed at the time to be morally wrong. If he has been driven to courses which he could hardly help admitting to be morally questionable, he has probably justified himself in his own eyes by reflecting that he has acted under pressure of circumstances for which he is not solely responsible, and by envisaging the solid benefits which his policy will confer upon the Church or the kingdom in a future which may be expected to prove not very remote.

Our main object in reading history should be to discern the growth and working of principles. By what principles were the men and women of former ages guided? From what sources were they derived? How far were they successful, and for what reasons?

---

[1] Sometime Professor of Modern History at Cambridge.
[2] *Historical Essays and Studies*, p. 504.

How far did they fail, and what were the causes of their failure? What fruit did they bear, whether good or evil?

For these purposes I think that the study of Church history is more profitable than the study of political or social history, if indeed it can be separated from them. It might be better to say that history has more to teach us when studied from the stand-point of religion than of any other.

In the first place, religion exhibits more continuity than any other interest to which men can apply themselves. The Church represents the most stable and enduring element in any society. It is, in fact, the only permanent one. It is less affected than anything else by the rise and fall of dynasties, or by changes in the form of civil government.

Secondly, the rulers of the Church have always known that they are bound to act in accordance with permanent principles. This makes it possible for them to take what are known as long views, as politicians seldom can.

I am not suggesting that politicians are as a whole more unprin-cipled or short-sighted than any other men. But they are, and must be, swayed to a very large extent by considerations of expediency. From time to time they are called to deal, more frequently than ecclesiastics, with crises which were not foreseen and probably could not have been averted. Whatever form these take, they always have one feature in common. They cannot be permanent, and probably will not last for very long. War is the commonest example of a crisis of this kind.

An instance of another kind arose in England a hundred years ago. An unusually bad harvest in 1845 had brought the country within measurable distance of real famine. The immediate and pressing problem before the Government was how to bring a very large quantity of foreign corn into the country as quickly and as cheaply as possible. To effect this it was necessary to repeal the Corn Laws, by which such imports were restricted. Sir Robert Peel did so. The expedient worked very well for a time. But it brought progressive calamity upon English agriculture, which at the beginning of this century culminated in almost complete ruin.

Two wars have taught us the vital importance of our own

agriculture. We have learned that we dare not neglect it, and are now trying to re-establish on a secure and lasting basis the fabric of agricultural prosperity which Peel overturned a century ago. But he can hardly be blamed for what he did.

If analogous instances of short-sightedness are not entirely absent from the history of the Church, they are less frequent and conspicuous there than in secular affairs.

The most important principle to be discerned in the history of the Church is the development of the Christian conscience, which is not yet complete. This runs through it all and gives it a unity and coherence unlike anything to be found elsewhere. Naturally the process has not been uniform or uninterrupted. There have been periods of moral stagnation and of moral decline. But it has gone on. And with it has marched, always keeping step, Liberty.

The Christian Church is the only institution which has ever believed wholeheartedly in liberty as a principle, or has even pretended to do so. It would be foolish to ignore the dangers which liberty brings in its train, because of the heavy tax which it places on the character of the individual. But for all that, Christian belief in it is invincible, because character can develop fully, and the human spirit bear its finest fruit, only in an atmosphere of liberty.

On any but Christian lips *Liberty* has never meant more than liberty for a small privileged class, at the expense of everybody else. This is comparatively easy to procure, if difficult to maintain indefinitely. It will be worth while to enlarge a little upon this by calling attention to the two most signal triumphs of the Christian conscience, up to the present time. They are so great and so complete that many people today accept them as a matter of course, knowing nothing of the process by which they were won.

The first is in relation to slavery: the second in relation to women.

Christianity was born into a world in which slavery was an immemorial, universal and unchallenged institution. It was regarded as the only possible foundation of civilized life; as credit in its varying forms (including the use of paper money) is today. Throughout the Roman empire the slave population out-numbered the free by at least two to one. Almost every relation in life was poisoned by it to some extent, and the ruling classes lived in dread of a slave rebellion. Nothing can be more terrible, because as a slave has nothing to lose he is desperate, and in that world was as well armed as the troops which could be employed to suppress him. No doubt there were some kindly and humane slave owners, such as the younger Pliny,[1] some of whose letters[2] in this connection are pleasant reading. But such were probably exceptional. And no personal kindness displayed by an individual could affect the institution as a whole. The following story will illustrate the effect of slavery upon the owners of slaves.

There was, a little before the beginning of our era, a wealthy knight at Rome named Vedius Pollio who used to fatten the fish for his table by throwing live slaves into their pond. On one occasion when the Emperor Augustus was dining with him a slave broke a cup. Pollio proposed to punish him in this way, but the emperor interfered and ordered the pond to be filled up. The story is told by Seneca twice,[3] and repeated by Tertullian[4] a century or so later. But Augustus does not seem to have questioned Pollio's right to put a slave to death for breaking a cup; nor apparently did the slave expect any lesser punishment. The unhappy man only asked that he might not be eaten alive. After the manner of many nouveaux riches Pollio had committed a social blunder by eating fish which had been fed on human flesh, and in sentencing a man to death in the presence of the emperor. No moral reproach attached to his conduct on either score.

Christianity never attacked slavery directly. But little by little the institution melted before Christian influence, like a snow-drift in spring. At first slaves were given some small rights, hardly exceeding those which our laws secure to domestic animals, so that they could no longer be termed "live tools". Then came varying degrees of serfdom, and finally complete emancipation.

[1] Governor of Bithynia during the reign of Trajan, A.D. 98–117.
[2] iv. 10, viii. 16.
[3] De Ira, iii. 40; De Clementia, i. 18.
[4] De Pallio.

But so convenient was slavery that it was maintained in the West Indies under our flag until 1829, and in the United States for a generation longer. As in these instances the slaves were negroes, a justification was found in Genesis 9. 25.

Slavery has always held its ground in heathen societies, unless European intervention has brought it to an end, and probably always will. It reappeared in our own day, in everything but name, in Russia and Germany as soon as the rulers of those States had repudiated Christianity. Its disappearance from the Christian world represents a moral and social change so immense that if the Christian conscience had nothing else to its credit it would still have to be recognized as a unique factor in the history of mankind.

The second triumph relates to the status of women.

In primitive societies a woman has always been regarded primarily as a possession, as much as a cow or a sheep. Her position is not very different in Moslem or heathen countries today.

In the greatest days of Athens and at a moment of heightened national consciousness, Pericles[1] had no more to say to the wives and daughters of his fellow citizens than not to be worse than nature had made them, and that the less they were heard of the better. Roman law never treated a woman as a *persona*. She had always to be under male guardianship; that of father, or husband or son, or other relative.

From the very beginning, Christianity gave women a new recognition and a higher status, by insisting that they must worship by the side of men. This was a complete breach with all heathen ways of thinking, and therefore St Paul had to caution women to be careful not to outrage public opinion more than they could help. As with slavery, little was said directly about the status of women. But it was recognized instinctively that the heathen estimate of women is incompatible with the Christian way of looking at things. As any society has become more Christian the position of women in it has risen steadily, and their influence for good has increased.

Here again the Christian conscience has brought about an

[1] Thucydides, ii. 45.

immense, if gradual and silent, revolution, the extent of which cannot be appreciated by people who know nothing of the conditions which obtained before the change had taken place.

Because Christianity and liberty have always gone hand in hand, tyrants of all kinds have always found the Church their most formidable enemy. Sometimes they have tried to destroy it outright. This policy has never been successful. The alternative is to try to control and corrupt it to serve political ends. This is the more hopeful enterprise, but most people who have taken it in hand have found the result disappointing.

The first systematic attempt at extermination was made by the emperor Diocletian at the beginning of the fourth century, because he found that the Church could not be fitted into his political system. Ever since its inception, which may be dated 31 B.C.,[1] the Roman Empire had become more and more despotic, and (it is only fair to add) more and more efficient. As constitutional government waned, the emperor became more and more important, because everything turned upon him. Soon he came to be regarded as more than human, if only after his death. Before the end of the first century of our era, full divine honours were paid to him during his lifetime, in the provinces, if not in Italy.

Diocletian, who came to the throne in the year 284, swept away the last pretence of constitutional rule and completed the fabric of despotism. The empire became a very highly organized totalitarian state, of which the basis was the person of the divine emperor. There was no other idea on which it could rest, and it embraced the entire civilized world. At this point, however, a difficulty arose. The Christian population refused absolutely to pay divine honours to any emperor alive or dead. Accordingly an attempt to destroy them was made, which had to be abandoned after eight years as a failure.[2] Christianity was accorded legal toleration for the first time in its history. But the empire was left, as it were, in the air. Some foundation for it had to be found, and a

---

[1] The battle of Actium was fought on 2 September, B.C. 31.

[2] Previous persecutions had been local, and for the most part set on foot by more or less accidental circumstances.

few years later Constantine adopted Christianity. He recognized that the old basis of the imperial power was gone for ever and its place could only be filled by the new institution which had proved too strong for it.[1]

For nearly fifteen hundred years Christianity as the basis of all government was never challenged. On this foundation the European civilization which we know was built up little by little. Liberty increased and became more secure.

Towards the close of the eighteenth century the doctrinaire atheists of the French Revolution repudiated Christian belief, and did their best to exterminate the Church as far as their power extended. As a symbol of their New Order they enthroned a common prostitute as Goddess of Reason on the high altar of the Church of Notre Dame de Paris. This emphasized their freedom from all moral and religious restraint. Robespierre's attempt to supplant Christianity by a cult of the Supreme Being was more serious and more respectable. But when, a few years later, Napoleon replaced their tyranny by his own, he found that the Church was not dead and that he dared not ignore it. He made terms with it, hoping no doubt to use it as an effective buttress of his power without allowing it to interfere with his political ambitions. His policy was not as successful as he had hoped.

In our own day, beginning in the year 1916, the rulers of Russia made a systematic attempt to extirpate Christianity from their territory. Less than thirty years later the patriarchate of Moscow has been re-established with the acquiescence, if no more, of their successors.

When Mussolini restored a shadow of temporal power to the Papacy he hoped, no doubt, to secure at least a measure of support for his ambitions from it. Indeed, he is reported to have said at the time that he had now made it certain that the Pope would always be "a good Italian". He was presumably incapable of understanding that the papal claims depend upon the supra-

---

[1] In justice it must be said that he appears to have undergone some sort of conversion at the battle of the Milvian Bridge, if his religious ideas remained cloudy.

national position of the Pope. If he were in reality a good Italian (or a good Frenchman or a good Englishman) from the political standpoint there would be very little reason why the Papacy should exist. Mussolini lived to see his tyranny go down in utter ruin, and after a period of captivity and exile met an ignominious death.

The German record is not dissimilar. Within Germany Hitler seems to have wavered between attempts to extirpate Christianity and to harness it to his chariot. It is still uncertain what measure of success rewarded either enterprise. Some effort was made to provide a new and quasi-religious basis for the State by the creation of a pagan cult. (Probably the authors were not familiar with the career of the Emperor Julian, 361–3.)[1] If Hitler did not claim divine honours for himself, some of his admirers, notably Bormann and Rosenberg, do not seem to have stopped far short of ascribing them to him.

In all the countries which the Germans overran they found an unexpected and formidable obstacle in the Christian conscience. That made the consolidation of their tyranny impossible, and persecution failed to break it down. If the full story of the last few years in Denmark, Norway, Holland, Belgium, France, Czechoslovakia, Poland and Greece is ever told, I believe that it will be a record of courage and endurance as heroic as anything to be found at any earlier period of Christian history.

The reason for all these persecutions was exactly the same as in the time of Diocletian. A would-be despot found that Christianity could not be fitted into his system of government.

What has been written above will illustrate the peculiar continuity of ecclesiastical history and the way in which, again and again, the Christian Church has shown itself capable of resisting tyranny successfully, when all other opposition seemed to be at an end.

There is, of course, another side which must not be ignored. There is the melancholy story of persecution directed by one set

---

[1] He tried to resuscitate paganism, and lived long enough to know that he had failed.

of Christians against another, though never without provoking protest.[1]

Moreover, again and again superstition and ignorance, and perhaps worst of all worldliness almost unalloyed, have brought discredit upon the Christian name.

More than once men have thought, not altogether without reason, that the day of the Church was over and it must speedily dissolve through its own internal corruption. But the event has always proved them mistaken. Revival has always come, usually in unexpected ways and from unforeseen sources. We cannot but admit that as an institution the Christian Church is unique. Its characteristics, especially its power of recovery when all seemed lost, are without parallel. It is altogether unaccountable and unintelligible, except upon its own theory of itself—namely, that in origin it is a divine institution, not a human invention, and that the springs of its indestructible life do not rise in this world. The most cogent criticism which can be directed against this theory is that if it were true the history of the Church ought to have been still more remarkable. But no one has yet succeeded in producing a convincing alternative.

[1] See Appendix A.

2

The First Sowing

IT would be an advantage if people in general would consult maps more than, as a rule, they appear to do. A good deal of history cannot really be understood without some knowledge of geography. The course of history has often been shaped by geographical features which are permanent. The story of our own country is a good illustration of this.

A glance at the map of the world will show that our position now is singularly advantageous. We are not far from the centre of the habitable regions of the globe. Beside this, our shores are never ice-bound. We are readily accessible by sea at any time of the year. The Thames discharges towards the European continent, which is not very far from its mouth. Unlike many tidal rivers, it has neither bar nor bore. London is as well placed to be the commercial centre of the world as was Alexandria, when the world meant the countries which surround the Mediterranean.

But our present central position is the outcome of the discovery of America. Prior to the sixteenth century, when the Atlantic Ocean was regarded as impassable because it had no further shore, we were on the outer edge of the civilized world, if not beyond it altogether. Our attempts to improve our position by securing permanent possessions in France once came very near to success, but ended in diasaster.

The first traveller from Mediterranean lands known to have visited our shores was Pytheas, who came from the Greek colony of Massilia (Marseilles) about the year 340 B.C. His object was probably to discover the sources of certain articles of export which came from beyond the seas into Gaul, and eventually down the Rhône to the Mediterranean.

The stories of the visits of Phœnicians to Cornwall in search of tin are to be received, with caution. The *Cassiterides* (Tin Islands) of which we hear cannot be the isles of Scilly, because there is no tin to be had there. They are probably to be identified with a group of islets off the Spanish Finisterre, which are said to be full of ancient tin workings.

It is sometimes said that traces of Phœnician blood are to be found in Cornwall today. But it is more probable that these "Phœnicians" are members of the dark-haired Mediterranean race (sometimes called Iberian) to which the Phœnicians and Greeks, amongst others, belonged. They were dispossessed by the Celtic-speaking peoples, who seem to have reached our shores during the sixth century before our era. It is not unlikely that traces of them may still survive in Cornwall, parts of Wales, and in the west of Scotland and Ireland.

After Pytheas' visit no one seems to have paid much attention to our island until the year 55 B.C.

From 58 to 51 Julius Cæsar was engaged in the subjugation of Gaul; roughly the modern France. Probably few men have done more to change the course of history than he. But for his campaigns it is not unlikely that the Gaulish tribes would have overrun Italy during the first century before our era, as the Gothic tribes did nearly five hundred years later. If this had happened there would have been no Roman empire. If there had been no Roman empire the history of a large part of Europe and of the Christian Church would have been very different.

Julius Cæsar found, as many others have done, that a career of conquest once started cannot be halted at will. It must be pursued until it reaches some virtually impassable natural obstacle, such as a range of high mountains, or a wide expanse of sea or desert. A river may form a convenient boundary for a province, but has usually proved inadequate as a frontier for an empire.

There could be no secure peace in Gaul so long as the island which lay off its northern shore, and was visible in part in fine weather, could offer an asylum to rebellious chiefs whence they could emerge as soon as his back was turned. Accordingly, on

2 September 55, he landed on the coast of what is now Kent. The tides which scour the Straits and the short, choppy seas of the shallow channel were a new experience.

This was not much more than a reconnaissance. Next year he returned with a larger force, and crossed the Thames somewhere in the neighbourhood of Chertsey. He did not go much farther north, and returned to Gaul. Circumstances never allowed him to make a third expedition.

The Romans must have been surprised by the extent of the island; as ultimately they were, in a sense, defeated by it. The largest islands they knew were Sicily and Sardinia, and they had no reason to suppose that Britain was larger. It is probable that the sight of the Thames gave Cæsar pause. It was obvious that a river of that size could not exist in a small island. He could not have suspected that the measurement of the country from south to north (the Solent to the Pentland Firth) is nearly double the longest stretch from east to west (the North Foreland to Land's End).

It was this northern extension which eventually proved too much for the Roman armies. It took them a very long way from their bases, and as the land became more mountainous it was easier to defend and harder to subdue. The Roman soldier of that day had much less advantage in the matter of arms and equipment over his less civilized opponent than has been enjoyed by white men in recent times over their opponents in Asia, Africa and America.

After Cæsar's departure the British question slumbered for nearly a century. But the Romans always knew that it would have to be faced again. A fresh attempt was made in the year A.D. 43 with very much larger forces than Cæsar had employed, and a permanent foothold in the south-eastern corner was secured. The work of conquest was carried on by a succession of very able soldiers, and by the year 85 had been extended to what is now the Scottish border. In that year Agricola went still further and fought a successful battle at the Graupian hill (*Mons Graupius*). The site has never been identified, but is probably somewhere in Perthshire. No Roman army ever penetrated so far north again.

He also despatched a fleet to ascertain whether Britain was really an island, or a peninsula jutting out from some vast mass to the north, as are Greece, Italy and Spain. The account of this adventure given by his son-in-law Tacitus is as follows:

> Thule was sighted in the distance. Their orders were to go no farther than that, and winter was approaching. Besides, the sea was sluggish, which made hard work for the rowers. They say that it could not even be raised by the winds.[1]

The last sentence is not easy to understand, and is not borne out by the experience of more recent navigators in those waters. (*Experto crede.*)

Thule was the traditional name in the Græco-Roman world for the most northerly spot on the globe. In this passage commentators have identified it with Iceland, Faroe or Shetland. A more probable conjecture is Fair Isle, which is about halfway between Orkney and Shetland. It is just visible on a clear day to anyone rounding the Orkney group of islands, and, as seen from the deck of a ship, there is nothing to suggest that there are any more islands beyond it.

The Romans found that they could not subdue the mountainous north of Scotland, or possibly decided that the attempt would cost more than it was worth, since the country could not be very productive. Agricola thought it would be advisable to conquer Ireland, in the interest of British peace, but the additional troops which would have been required could not be spared.

Accordingly a line of fortifications was drawn from the Forth to the Clyde to serve as a permanent frontier, but their hold upon the country immediately to the south, which they called Valentia, was never very secure. In the year 120 the Emperor Hadrian virtually abandoned it, and constructed, or at least began, what is known to-day as the Roman Wall along the seventy miles from the mouth of the Tyne[2] to a point on the Solway. This fortified strip—it was more than a wall—was virtually impregnable as long as a sufficient garrison could be maintained. Such

[1] Dispecta est Thule quia hactenus iussum, et hiems appetebat. Sed mare pigrum et grave remigantibus, perhibent ne ventis quidem attolli. *Agricola*, C. x.
[2] The *Wallsend* colliery preserves the memory.

remains of it as there are today are as impressive a monument as anything to be seen in our land. The turbulent and powerful Brigantes were blocked into the Yorkshire dales by a chain of forts, York being the key of the system, so that they could not join hands with the unconquered north, and Britain settled down to more than three centuries of peace and civilization. It was incorporated into the great political and social system which had its centre at Rome. York was the capital, for obvious military reasons; London was probably the largest city.[1]

There were occasional insurrections which were repressed with severity. Towards the close of the fourth century a Gaulish adventurer named Carausius induced the Roman fleet stationed at Gesoriacum (Boulogne) to mutiny, assumed the imperial title *Augustus*, and declared Britain an independent sovereign state. This first British empire lasted only from 287 to 293. Carausius was murdered by one of his officers, and soon afterwards Diocletian re-established his authority. With this exception the Roman peace was never seriously imperilled.

If we are accustomed to think of the empire as brutal and oppressive, the following brief extract from a fairly lengthy poem, written about the beginning of the fifth century, when the star of Rome was obviously waning, will show that it could inspire other sentiments beside fear and respect. It is addressed to the City:

> She alone has taken the conquered to her bosom
> and has cherished all mankind under one name.
> She has shown herself a mother, not a mistress.
> She has called those whom she has subjugated
> Citizens, and has linked the ends of the earth
> with a bond of love.[2]

---

[1] Roman London covered approximately the area of the modern City: about 324 acres, or half a square mile.

[2]   Haec est in gremium victos quae sola recepit.
    Humanumque genus communi nomine fovit.
    Matris non dominae ritu: civesque vocavit
    Quos domuit, nexuque pio longinqua revinxit.
        Claudian, *De Laudibus Stilichonis*, iii. 150-4.

(Stilicho was a successful general who was Consul in the year 400.)

This tribute is the more remarkable because the author was not a member of the ruling race. He was born at Alexandria, and is said to have begun life as a slave.

By this time the Empire was beginning to be hard pressed on its more vulnerable frontiers. The British garrison had to be reduced, and the last troops were withdrawn in 409. Britain then ceased to be a province of the empire. In the following year the Goths entered Rome, and it seemed to St Jerome in Palestine that the end of the world had come. Little more than a generation later the Saxon infiltration into our land had begun.

During the Roman occupation Christianity obtained a footing here. How or when it came about we do not know. The legends about Joseph of Arimathæa and Philip the Apostle, which arose during the later days of Glastonbury, have no foundation in history.

It may have been brought by soldiers, or by traders from Gaul. (The latter supposition is perhaps the more probable, because Mithraism, a form of sun worship which originated in Persia, seems to have been very popular in the army.) We cannot say to what extent it prevailed. Tertullian, writing in Africa about the year 180, could say that it had penetrated to parts of Britain which the Romans had never reached.[1] If this is true he must be referring to Ireland or to the north of Scotland. The statement may be no more than a rhetorical flourish. Some sixty years earlier Juvenal (who may have visited Britain) asserted: "We have advanced our arms beyond the shores of Ireland, and the Orkney Islands which we have taken recently."[2]

The first part of this statement cannot in the nature of things be true. As to the second part, there is a difference between sailing round a group of islands and taking them.

Tradition makes St Alban the first British martyr and represents him as a soldier, and as having suffered about the year 304. There is nothing inherently improbable in this story. What is known as the Great Persecution was inaugurated by Diocletian in the year

---

[1] Britannorum inaccessa Romanis loca. *Adv. Iudaeos*, 7.

[2] Arma quidem ultra Litora Juvernae promovimus, et modo-captas, *Orcadas*, iii. 159–61.

303. It was not very severe in our land, because Constantius, who was the Cæsar (a position roughly equivalent to what we should mean by Viceroy), obviously had no liking for it and did not do more than he could help. When he became Augustus, which meant that he had no superior, he seems to have let it drop. But if Alban were a soldier a refusal to offer incense to the genius of the emperor (the recognized test) might have been construed as mutinous. His execution would then have been a matter of military discipline more than of religious persecution.

The first certain fact is that in the year 314 three British bishops attended a council at Arles in southern France. Their names are given as Restitutus of London, Eborius of York and Adelfius of Colonia Londinensium, which probably stands for Lincoln (or alternatively Caerleon upon Usk). If these details cannot be accepted without caution their presence at the Council is not in dispute. In view of the length and hazards of the journey it may be thought unlikely that the entire episcopate went. But if there were other bishops in the land we know nothing of them. Colchester, St Albans, Norwich, Chester, Wroxeter, Gloucester, Southampton, Cirencester, Bath and Exeter (to give the towns their modern names) would be the sort of places most likely to have been chosen as See towns.

Christian symbols have been found in the mosaic pavements of some Roman houses,[1] and the site of what is generally considered to have been a church has been found at Calleva Atrebatum, afterwards known as Silchester, on land which now forms part of the Duke of Wellington's property at Strathfieldsaye in Hampshire. The whole area of the town was about 100 acres, and the sites of temples have been found there as well.

The church is very small. The main part seems to have been about 30 feet long by 10 feet broad. On either side there was a colonnade about 5 feet in width ending in two small transepts, which may have served the purpose of the modern vestry. At one end there is a semi-circular apse. A patch of mosaic of finer quality than the rest of the flooring near the chord of the apse

[1] All, I believe, in the south of England. At York and on the Wall only traces of pagan cults have been found, as far as I know.

may be presumed to mark the site of the altar. At the other end is a porch running the whole width of the building and about 7 feet deep. Part of this may have been used as a baptistery or for instructing candidates for baptism. The longitudinal axis of the building runs east and west.[1]

This church can hardly have been constructed before the year 311. Prior to that date Christianity was always illegal, if the law was seldom enforced strictly. Meetings in private houses for worship might be overlooked. A church in some out-of-the-way spot far from any Roman road (such as Glastonbury with its surrounding belt of marshes) could be ignored, if its existence were known. But to build a church within a walled town literally under the eye of authority would have been a piece of impudence hardly to be tolerated.

When churches could be built pagan temples were not fitted to serve as models, partly on account of their associations (although after the collapse of paganism in the fifth century some temples were used as churches), but chiefly because the design was not suitable. A temple was built for the honour of the god whom it housed, without any reference to the convenience of his worshippers. Congregational worship as understood by Christianity was no part of paganism. The religious festivals which took its place were held in the open air. The Jewish synagogues were planned for congregational use, but there again there were undesirable associations, and they were probably not at all common in western Europe; if indeed they existed. But there was one building which was to be found all over the empire in any town of any importance, and that was the basilica or Roman law court. The standard pattern was a rectangular oblong building with a semicircular apse at one end and a portico at the other. The roof was usually supported by two rows of pillars, so that the floor was divided into three passages, the middle one being the widest. The presiding magistrate sat in the apse with his clerks and officials behind him. In front of him, we may assume, there was a table of some kind for his law books and writing materials. A short

[1] See *The Romanization of Roman Britain*, by F. Haverfield, 4th edition, pp. 43 and 64.

distance beyond that there were some low railings (*cancelli*) within which the people whose cause was being heard were summoned. Suitors waiting for their turn, and members of the public who were interested, stood about in the "nave" and "aisles". The Romans understood that justice will be done better if it is done publicly, and their law courts were planned accordingly. It was intended that everyone present should be able to see and hear what was going on at one end. Here was an almost perfect model for a church, which could be copied without difficulty. For this reason it is not always easy to decide whether a building of which nothing but the floor remains was a church or a law court. Only if there are definitely Christian symbols to be found can the identification be beyond dispute.

In a church the presiding minister took the place of the magistrate; if he were the bishop, with other clergy to his right and left; and the movable table became a permanent altar. The tradition of this primitive arrangement has been preserved at Rome. When the Pope officiates in person at the high altar of St Peter's he faces the congregation across it.[1]

Glastonbury was the only sanctuary of the Church of Roman Britain which passed intact to Saxon hands. The date of its origin is unknown. The spot had been inhabited in pre-Christian, almost in prehistoric times, as the remains of two lake villages, one at Glastonbury itself and one a short distance away at Meare, attest. The water of the so-called "Chalice Well" possesses some of the chemical elements which are more pronounced in the more famous springs at Bath, less than thirty miles away. This may have attracted settlers in pre-Roman days. At some very early date— the third century is perhaps a reasonable conjecture and the second not an impossible one—a little church of clay and wattles was built upon an island in the marsh. It became known to subsequent generations as the Old Church (*vetusta ecclesia*) and by the time of St Patrick was famous and a resort of pilgrims. In the year 633 Paulinus (Bishop of York 625–33)[2] built a shelter of wood over it to preserve it from dissolution. So it stood for more than another

---

[1] At Norwich the bishop's throne is behind and above the high altar.
[2] Subsequently of Rochester.

five centuries, during which the monastery which had gathered round it became the most famous in England. Everything at Glastonbury perished in the fire of 29 May 1184. Nothing prior to that date is to be seen above ground now. No single fire in England can have destroyed more that was ancient, interesting and irreplaceable. The old church was rebuilt in stone on the old site, and pains were taken to ensure that the new structure should be exactly the same length as the original. When the visitor of today enters the ruins of St Mary's Chapel he knows that he stands on ground which was holy when our land was a province of the Roman empire. There is no other place in the British Isles of which this can be said with confidence.

It has been thought that the church of St Martin at Canterbury dates from Roman days. The truth appears to be that it is built of material quarried by Saxon hands from Roman buildings in the neighbourhood. Parts of the abbey church at St Albans were constructed in the same way at a much later date. The Saxons were not expert masons and most of their buildings were of wood. The stone church which Edwin, King of Northumbria, built at York in the year 627 was almost certainly of Roman material; of which there is still plenty to be found there.

Ethelbert, King of Kent, married a Frankish princess named Bertha who was a Christian. It is a tempting conjecture that he had St Martin's church built for her use before the arrival of St Augustine. Her influence may have contributed to the favourable reception of the missionaries from Rome. If the Roman occupation had lasted for another hundred years, or if the Saxon infiltration had not begun until the middle of the sixth century, it is possible that the Romano-British Church might have occupied the land effectively. It might then have been strong enough to survive the shock of the Saxons, and to have converted them piecemeal as they came.

It is impossible to say whether it is or is not a matter for regret that this did not happen. There is virtually nothing to be said about the subsequent history of the Church of Roman Britain. In the sixth century there was a Church in south Wales of which St David, who died probably about the year 601, is said to have

been archbishop, if he did not exercise any metropolitical jurisdiction. Also in West Wales or Damnonia (now Cornwall). But
whether either had existed continuously since Roman days it is
impossible to say. A little earlier Christianity had reached the
north of Ireland[1] and the south-west of Scotland.[2] But the outcome of this, as far as it concerns us directly, belongs to the next
stage of our Christian history, in which the British Church played
no part.[3]

[1] St Patrick.   [2] St Ninian.   [3] See Chapter 3, p. 37.

3

The Second Sowing

From the arrival of St Augustine to the death of Archbishop Theodore—597–690

THE Saxon infiltration seems to have begun before the middle of the fifth century. It continued steadily for more than a hundred years. The newcomers were not as the Romans had been, or as we are in India. They had come to find new and permanent homes, which meant that they must exterminate the native population as far as possible to make room for themselves. They were savages, bent on destruction. Before them the entire fabric of Romano-British civilization crumbled away, and such Christianity as there was went with it.

By the end of the sixth century the process was complete. The Saxons were in possession of the entire country except Wales, West Wales (Cornwall), and part of the region between the Dee and the Solway, known as Strathclyde.[1] Among their latest conquests were Aquæ Sulis (Bath) in the year 577 and Isca Dumnoniorum (Exeter) at about the same time. The latter was the western terminus of the great Roman road which ran south-west from Lincoln and is now known to us as the Fosse Way.

The Roman roads had been made for military purposes and kept as far as possible to high ground, as many of the prehistoric trackways had done. There were obvious reasons for avoiding marshes, and on the higher ground there would be less big timber to be cleared. The Saxons made little use of them, or of the sites of Roman towns. They entered England by the river mouths, and as far as the rivers were navigable their progress was rapid. Beyond

---

[1] This had apparently formed part of a Pictish kingdom, which had its head-quarters in the south-west of Scotland, perhaps not far from the modern Glasgow. It was not readily accessible to invaders from the east.

that point it was naturally slower, and the Britons had more chance of offering resistance.

If King Arthur was a historical personage, he was probably a Romano-British chieftain who made some stand in the south-western peninsula. It is known that early in the sixth century the Saxons received a check at a place called Badon Hill. It has never been identified, but may be presumed to be somewhere in Wiltshire or Dorset.

As the sixth century drew to a close it was clear that if England (the name had not yet come into use) was to be a Christian and civilized country a new start would have to be made. It is true that by this time there was a Church in Wales, and perhaps in West Wales. But nothing certain is known of this British Church prior to the episcopate of St David who probably died about the year 601. It can therefore hardly be a survival from Roman times. Probably it owed its origin to Irish missionaries.[1] It took no part in the conversion of the Saxons.

The Cornish language survived until the eighteenth century, and both the Bible and Prayer Book were translated into it. The last church in which they were used is pointed out not far from the Lizard. There must also have been for some considerable time a pocket of Britons, descendants of the Brigantes whom the Romans had never subdued thoroughly, existing in the Yorkshire dales. To this day the shepherds of Nidderdale use—or at any rate did use until very recently—the Welsh numerals from one to twenty when counting sheep. They have been considerably corrupted by oral transmission amongst people who have long ceased to use Welsh for any other purpose. But they are quite recognizable.

With these exceptions, of which Wales is the only considerable one, the repopulation of the land was complete, though no doubt in some parts some Welsh blood still runs in English veins. No other country in Western Europe has had a similar experience in historical times. When the Roman empire crumbled, and Italy, France and Spain came under the rule of barbarian invaders from the north, the population was not exterminated. Christianity

---

[1] E.g., St Piran, whose name is preserved in one or two places in Cornwall.

was not destroyed, and with it a considerable stratum of Latin civilization remained. The vernacular speech of those countries today is manifestly derived from Latin. Ours, equally manifestly, comes from another source. This fact alone is sufficient to illustrate the difference between the two processes.

The only parallel with the catastrophe of Britain is the destruction of Christianity and civilization in North Africa by the Vandals during the fifth century. Perhaps neither had struck root very deeply in the native population. Both were Roman, and could not survive the fall of the Roman power.

Everyone knows the story of Pope Gregory I (590–604) and the fair-haired boys from England exposed for sale in the slave market at Rome. Whether this is true or not, something directed his attention to our land, and he despatched a band of missionaries, headed by St Augustine. This is our first debt to the Papacy, if by no means the last.

He dismissed them formally from the church of St Andrew (now SS. Andrew and Gregory) on the Cœlian hill at Rome. A long flight of steps leads away from the door, and I have sat at the top of them trying to picture St Augustine and his company starting on their adventure. It was a hazardous one. For more than a century our island had been almost entirely cut off from the Continent. It had retired, as it were, into the northern mist. Beyond the fact that it existed hardly anything can have been known about it at Rome.

As the missionaries made their way across Gaul such information as they could gather was not encouraging. The Saxons were reported to be ferocious and inhospitable. Their language presented an almost insuperable difficulty. Anyone who attempted to convert them to Christianity was more likely to perish than to succeed. The Romans' hearts failed them, and they asked permission to return. But Gregory was inexorable, and in the spring of the year 597 they landed in Kent. They were favourably received by King Ethelbert, who was perhaps the most powerful ruler south of the Thames, and he was baptized on Whitsunday (1 June).

By this time monastic institutions were firmly established

throughout Western Europe. St Augustine and his companions were all monks; as was St Aidan. Christianity and monasticism reached our shores together, and this fact, beside increasing our general debt to monasteries, affected the history of our Church very deeply.

Many of our cathedrals were monastic—that is to say, were manned by monks instead of by secular[1] canons. This arrangement was peculiar to our country, and naturally when the monasteries were dissolved in the sixteenth century the cathedrals affected had to be reconstituted. They are therefore now said to be *Of the New Foundation*, as distinct from those which could retain their existing statutes and are therefore now described as *Of the Old Foundation*.[2]

On 16 November 597 Augustine was consecrated in Gaul as Archbishop of the English. The title is significant. There was as yet no English nation, and for many years to come the land would be divided into a number of separate, independent kingdoms. But the Archbishop could furnish a centre for the different tribes long before they had come to recognize any common sovereign, and the Church was a unifying force. English nationality is to a very large extent the creation of the Church. It grew round the Church in a way to which there is perhaps no parallel elsewhere.

In the year 601 Augustine met the British bishops, perhaps at Aust, on the southern shore of the Severn estuary, almost opposite the mouth of the Wye. Nothing came of the conference. Perhaps the Britons thought him proud and overbearing. He seems to have found them sulky and suspicious. The two Churches pursued their courses independently.

Meanwhile the Pope had drawn up a scheme for two provinces, each with twelve dioceses, the Archbishops being at Canterbury and York. But progress was not destined to be as swift and smooth as that. The northern province never contained more than four suffragan-sees, until the creation of the see of Ripon in 1836.

[1] *Secular* clergy are clergy living in the world (sæculum) as distinguished from *regular* clergy who have withdrawn from it to live by a monastic rule (regula).

[2] Instances of New Foundations are Canterbury, Winchester, Durham and Ely; of Old Foundations, York, Lincoln, St Paul's, Wells and Hereford.

The ideal of twelve was not realized until the see of Blackburn was formed in 1922.

Augustine died in 604. He was succeeded by Laurentius, who died in 619. Then followed Mellitus (619–24) and Justus (624–77).

On Justus' accession the time seemed to have come for a new step to be taken. Paulinus went north with the title of Bishop of York, and in 627 Edwin, King of Northumbria, was baptized. His dominions extended from the Humber to the Firth of Forth, where Edinburgh (Edwin's Town) preserves his name to this day. Saxon institutions were strongly monarchical, so that if a sovereign accepted baptism his subjects, great and small, followed suit almost as a matter of course. Necessarily such mass conversions did not go very deep. But the prospects opening before the Church in Northumbria were dazzling.

Six years later disaster came. Northumbria was attacked by Penda, King of Mercia, in alliance with Cadwallon, King of Gwynedd (North Wales). Penda was a heathen. Cadwallon was nominally a Christian, but hatred of Saxons was his dominant motive. A battle was fought at Heathfield, probably near Doncaster, on 12 October 633. The Northumbrians were defeated and Edwin was killed.

Bishop Paulinus fled with the widowed Queen Ethelburga, who had been a Kentish princess. To have remained would have meant death for him, and death or worse for her. Subsequently he became Bishop of Rochester, where he died on 10 October 644.

Edwin's nephew and heir, Oswald,[1] escaped. Next year he rallied his forces and defeated the Mercians and their allies at Heavenfield, near Hexham. His cousin Osric, prince of Deira

---

[1] He was a saint as well as a king. During his reign Northumbria became so pre-eminent that he was not far short of being king of England, long before the title was claimed by Edgar, King of Wessex. He was killed on 5 August 662, at Maserfield (probably near Oswestry), fighting against his old antagonist Penda. Penda cut off his head and placed it on a pole. It was rescued, taken to Lindisfarne and buried in St Aidan's grave. In 875, when the monks had to flee inland for fear of pirates, they placed it in St Cuthbert's coffin, where presumably it is still. The coffin is believed to be somewhere beneath the pavement of Durham Cathedral. For this reason St Cuthbert is sometimes represented in art carrying St Oswald's head.

(roughly the modern counties of York and Durham), and his brother Eanfrid, prince of Bernicia (roughly the modern counties of Northumberland and Berwick), who had apostatized, were both killed. Northumbria was once more united under a Christian sovereign. One man had stood his ground after the disaster of Heathfield—James the deacon, who continued to preach and baptize in the neighbourhood of Catterick on the river Swale. But the conversion of Northumbria had to be begun again.

Now a new factor comes into play, for the understanding of which we must go back more than two hundred years.

Towards the close of the Roman occupation, or shortly after it had ended, Christianity obtained a footing in Ireland, where the Romans had never landed, and in the south-west of Scotland, which they had never occupied effectively.

The conversion of Ireland is always associated with the name of St Patrick, if he were not actually the first man to break ground there. There is some uncertainty as to his date. Some scholars have placed him as early as the second century. But this seems to be impossible, unless we assume that there were two Romano-British apostles of Ireland of the same name, separated by some two centuries.

The Patrick (Patricius) who founded the see of Armagh in the year 444 and died in 461 must have been born about the year 400, or a little earlier. There seems to be no good reason for doubting the genuineness of his *Confession*, a copy of which is preserved in the *Book of Armagh* in the library of Trinity College, Dublin. From this it appears that he was kidnapped by Norse or Danish pirates, carried to Ireland and sold there as a slave. He tells us that his home was on the bank of a great western river, and it has been assumed that, since all the places especially associated with him (Slemish, Saul-patrick, Armagh and Down-patrick) are in the north-eastern corner of Ireland, the river must have been the Solway or the Clyde. But there is no reason why it should not have been the Severn, and there are certain facts which point to that conclusion:

  1. Patrick was a Christian of the third generation. His father was a deacon, and his grandfather (also a Christian) had been a

decurio—i.e., a town councillor. This implies a settled Christian and municipal life such as might well have existed in southern Britain during the second half of the fourth century, but is unlikely in the far north.

2. He appears to have known of Glastonbury and is believed to have visited it more than once, as did other Irish saints: notably St Patrick's friend and successor at Armagh, St Benignus,[1] St Brigit of Kildare, who died in 523. Indeed, so close was the connection between Glastonbury and Ireland that an islet near by in the marsh, where presumably Irish visitors found it convenient to stay, was called Beokery, which is said to mean *Little Ireland*. Possibly it is a corruption of Bach-Eire.

3. The fact that he was landed in the north of Ireland is really irrelevant. If his captors proposed to make their way home round the north of Scotland, what is more likely than that they should make use of the magnificent almost land-locked sheet of water, now known as Strangford Lough, in the County Down, for a rest and a refit, and to embark provisions and fresh water before attempting the most hazardous stage of their voyage? The present of a slave would be an obvious method of establishing friendly relations with the natives; or he might have been exchanged for some of the stores which they needed. We may therefore feel justified in claiming St Patrick for the west country and in placing his home in the neighbourhood of Avonmouth or Aust.

It would be out of place to give an account of his life here. It will be enough to say that he kindled a fire which never died out, and burned very brightly when darkness was spreading over England.

The beginnings of Christianity in Scotland are associated with the name of St Ninian, the Apostle of the Picts, who seems to have been a slightly older contemporary of St Patrick. He is said to have been a prince of Cumbria, an appanage of the larger Pictish kingdom of Strathclyde, which at one time extended as far southwards as the river Ribble. He may therefore have been well acquainted with the Pictish language.

---

[1] St Benignus appears to be the true dedication of one of the two parish churches at Glastonbury, now known as St Benedict.

Very little is known about the Picts. The Romans regarded them as a different race from the other inhabitants of what is now Scotland, if they classed all the northern tribes together as Caledonians. (It does not follow that this was what they called themselves.)

The word *Pictus* in Latin means *painted*. In the fourth century Claudian, who had probably met people who had seen them, thought it an apt description.[1] Possibly they practised some form of tattooing. Their headquarters seem to have been at Inverness, which suggests that they had reached Scotland by sea from the north-east. At the height of their power their kingdom extended across Scotland from north-east to south-west, and some distance into north-western England. Their last strongholds are said to have been in Galloway and in the island of Fetlar, which belongs to the Shetland group but lies some little distance to the east of the principal island. There is a story that they could distil a delicious and intoxicating drink from heather, the secret of which died with them. Possibly this calamity led to the manufacture of whisky. Some prehistoric earthworks and stone "raths" to be seen in Scotland today are attributed to them. Beehive dwellings (or store-rooms) to be seen in Orkney are known as Picts' houses.

St Ninian planted Christianity firmly amongst them, and since the Saxons did not penetrate to their territory it was never eradicated. This was destined to have a very important outcome in the sixth century. Ninian seems to have worked principally in Galloway, and he built a church at Whithern in Wigtonshire. As it was known as *Candida Casa* (the White House) it was presumably of stone. Subsequently a diocese of Whithern came into being, and for a time formed part of the province of York.

What purport to be the ruins of St Ninian's church are to be seen today. When I visited them some years ago I did not think that they looked older than the eighth century at earliest. The workmanship seemed to me to resemble that of the Seven

[1] *Nec falso nomine* (panegyric on the third consulship of the Emperor Honorius, v. 54). He is referring to the exploits of the emperor's grandfather Theodosius, which included a campaign in Britain.

Churches at Glendalough, Co. Wicklow; the site may, however, be the original one.

We must now return to Ireland, where our concern is with one man, St Columba.

He was born in Donegal about the year 521, and is said to have been of royal blood. He founded monasteries in the north of Ireland. He became involved in one of the tribal wars to which his countrymen have always been prone. It is unnecessary to go into details, which may be real or fictitious. The important point is that he was excommunicated by a synod for the part which he had taken in the battle of Cooldrevny in the year 561, and sentenced to leave Ireland. In 563 he departed with twelve companions and settled in the island which, under the name of Iona, was destined to become famous. He was received hospitably by the people of Dalriada, as that part of Scotland was then called, because they were Christians, thanks to St Ninian and his successors. Without their good offices it is hard to see how he and his companions could have escaped dying of starvation before they had passed a year in their new home.

The island is about three and a half miles long by one and a half broad. It is separated from the larger island of Mull, which in its turn is separated from the mainland by a very narrow strait, by about two miles of sea. The soil appears to be sandy and can only produce light crops. The original name seems to have been Hi or I. Some scribe made a Latinized adjective out of this and wrote *Ioua insula*. Some successor seems to have misread the first word as *Iona* (the letters *n* and *u* are easily confused, especially in manuscript) and took it to be a substantive, and the name of the island. So Iona it became.

There St Columba founded a monastery which soon became a great centre of religion and learning. It was the seat of a bishopric for a short time in the fifteenth century. The existing church, which was at one time ruinous, has been restored and brought into use by the Church of Scotland. I have visited it twice, but could not see anything which looked to me older than the fifteenth century. Not far from it are the remains of what may be presumed to have been the monastery. When I saw them they had not been excavated, and were so overgrown with vegetation that it was impossible to form any opinion about them. In recent times I believe that the Church of Scotland has established something of the nature of a monastic establishment there to prepare young men for its ministry. Nothing could be in closer keeping with the ancient tradition of the island.

By the beginning of the seventh century the fame of Iona stood so high that no less a personage than Edwin of Northumbria sent his nephew Oswald there to receive a Christian upbringing and education. As soon as Oswald had recovered his kingdom he appealed to Iona for Christian teachers. The first emissary, Corman by name, was unsuccessful. He returned home after a year and reported that the Northumbrians were unteachable. (It may be worth while to remember that twice at the beginning of our history people who had some superficial acquaintance with our forefathers declared that it was impossible to convert them to Christianity.)

Fortunately there was at Iona a greater man than Corman. Having heard what he had to say, Aidan offered to go in his place. He was consecrated as Bishop of Lindisfarne in 635, and travelled about Northumbria for sixteen years. When he died in 651 the Church was firmly re-established. It is impossible to give details of his life and work here. It will be enough to say that he seems to have been an exceptionally beautiful character. Bishop Lightfoot thought that he ought to be regarded as the Apostle of England rather than St Augustine.[1] Modern historians are disposed to question this view. He made his headquarters on the island of Lindisfarne, known ever since as Holy Island, some three miles off the coast of Northumberland, opposite the royal palace of Bamburgh. It may have been more of an island then than it is now. Today it can be reached on foot, except for about two hours on either side of high water.

In view of our debt to the Celtic and northern saints, it must be admitted that the Prayer Book has not done them justice. Patrick (17 March), Ninian (16 September), Columba (9 June), Aidan (31 August), Oswald (5 August), Hilda, Abbess of Whitby

[1] *Leaders in the Northern Church*, p. 9.

(17 November), and Cuthbert, Bishop of Lindisfarne (20 March), ought all to have had a place in our calendar. The calendar proposed in 1928 offered reparation.

By the middle of the seventh century paganism was not extinct in England. But the area of Saxon conquest had been covered by various missions: speaking roughly, the southern half from the Continent,[1] the northern from Iona via Lindisfarne.

This meant that there were two rather different types of Christianity. Which was to prevail?

The Celtic Church was loosely organized. In the regions in which it arose the basis of society was tribal rather than territorial. In recent times Ireland, Scotland and Wales have been divided into counties for purposes of administration. But the county does not mean as much there as it does in England. Saxon institutions soon became territorial. Our county boundaries have altered very little since before the Norman conquest. To us the county is the community and the foundation of our national life. At the present day an Englishman asked for details about himself would name his county or his town. A Highlander or an Irishman would be more likely to name his clan or sept.

From very early days, if not right from the beginning, the unit of the Church has always been the territorial diocese,[2] as was natural inasmuch as it was born into the highly organized, territorially planned, Roman empire. Each bishop's area of jurisdiction was defined as exactly as that of any civil administrator.

In the Celtic Church the bishop does not seem to have had any fixed area of jurisdiction. He lived in a monastery of which he was not the head, whence from time to time he went out to

[1] The south-east by Augustine and his successors; the south-west by Birinus, an Italian, first Bishop of Winchester. East Anglia, which was almost cut off by the vast watery waste of the fens, by Felix, a Burgundian, aided by Fursey, an Irishman. The kingdom of the South Saxons (Sussex), which was almost inaccessible except by sea, was not evangelized effectively until some thirty years later by Wilfrid, sometime Bishop of York.

[2] The word is Greek and means an *administrative area*. In the fourth century the empire consisted of twelve dioceses, each of which contained several provinces. The *diocese of the Britains* was one. I do not know when the Church borrowed the word and used it to mean the jurisdiction of a bishop. In ecclesiastical usage a province contains several dioceses.

discharge episcopal functions as need arose: much as judges go on circuit today.

I do not think that this unusual arrangement throws any light on the vexed question of the origin and development of episcopacy. I believe its *raison d'être* to have been economic. The regions in which it obtained were very sparsely populated, as parts of them are still. Much of the soil was barren, and the climate was not very favourable. The struggle for existence must have been hard. Almost every man must have had to wring his daily bread from the land by the daily labour of his hands. A priest attached to a church could be very largely, if not entirely, self-supporting. He could till his own piece of ground and harvest his own crops. Sometimes he might be able to reinforce his larder by catching fish or snaring birds or rabbits; and all this without interfering unduly with his sacred duties.

A bishop who necessarily travelled from place to place could not do this. Nor could he rely on living on the country through which he passed. He needed some base where he could be maintained by the labours of others, and where he could be furnished with provisions when he started on one of his journeys. Nothing but a monastery could provide this, and as he was bound to be absent from it frequently he could not be the head of the community. The arrangement was, however, an anomaly, born of a group of local conditions. It would not have been desirable had it established itself in the north of England. The Roman territorial system was obviously to be preferred. Subsequently this was adopted in Scotland and Ireland.

Beside the difference of practice there were two matters in dispute: one relating to the date on which Easter should be kept, the other to the form of the tonsure, which was the outward mark of a man in Holy Orders. The former is known as the Quartodeciman Controversy (from the Latin words *quartus decimus*, which mean *fourteenth*). Statements made about it are not always very clear, but the point at issue appears to have been as follows:

The Jewish year consisted of thirteen lunar months, instead of the twelve solar ones which the Greeks and Romans used.

(The names of our months are the Roman ones; the Greeks used a different set.) Accordingly, by the Jewish calendar the moon was always full on the fourteenth day of every month. The Passover was kept on the fourteenth day of Nisan, which would mean a day (not always the same day, as the two calendars did not keep step) in the Roman April. In view of the close connection, historical and mystical alike, between the Resurrection and the Passover, some people thought that Easter should be kept then, whatever the day of the week might be. Probably this was the original practice, in view of the fact that many of the earliest converts to Christianity were Jews. There was much to be said for it.

On the other hand, the *raison d'être* of the Christian Sunday is the Resurrection. Our only reason for regarding the first day of each week as holy is that upon it the Lord rose from the dead. Christians who knew little of the Jewish calendar, and had no special reason for respecting Jewish ceremonies, felt that it was almost absurd to keep Easter on any day but a Sunday. The Sunday nearest to the Passover (probably the next after it) would satisfy all the requirements of tradition, and be more suitable. Probably no one would wish to dispute this now.

Our present arrangement—the first Sunday after the full moon on or after the spring equinox—was a very ingenious and successful plan for ensuring that the whole Christian world should keep Easter on the same day. The spring equinox was a fixed point recognizable by everyone, whatever calendar he used. Nor could there be any mistake about the full moon, whatever the day and name of the month.

With regard to the second point. The Roman tonsure was effected by shaving a small circular patch on the crown of the head. The Celtic practice was to shave the whole front part of the head from ear to ear. The matter may seem to us entirely trivial. But in a world in which there were no newspapers, no political interests and very few books, and conditions were such that most people seldom moved far from their own immediate neighbourhood, local customs were not unlikely to become invested with more importance than they merited.

In 664 a conference was held at Whitby under the patronage

of Oswin and Eanflæd[1], the rulers of the two Northumbrian kingdoms, and the north decided to turn its back upon Iona and to adopt the usages of Rome. No one could foresee how far-reaching would be the effect of this decision. Bishop Lightfoot thought it upon the whole a mistake. I venture to disagree with this judgment. It was important that the Church should be united, and the south would never have adopted the Celtic usages. Beside this, had we turned our backs upon the Continent we could hardly have escaped intellectual and probably moral stagnation.

There are advantages in living upon an island, as we realized in 1588, 1801, 1914 and 1940. But there are also drawbacks. We are bound to be always in some danger of insularity, and great as was our debt to Iona it could never, as the years went on, have contributed as much to our spiritual inheritance as did Rome. An outstanding instance was destined to occur almost immediately. In 664 Frithonas,[2] the first Saxon to become Archbishop, died. His successor, Wigheard, held the see for less than a year, if indeed he ever occupied it effectively.[3] When he died there was no one in England really qualified to take his place. The bishops appealed to Pope Vitalian I, and he after much consultation despatched Theodore, a monk of Tarsus in Gilicia, of whom no one in England could have heard. This is our second great debt to the Papacy.

Theodore appears to have been over sixty years of age at the time of his appointment. It would be difficult to speak too highly of the courage and devotion of a man who at that age was willing to abandon the civilization which he had known to go to the end of the world, and to spend the rest of his life amongst a people who were at least semi-barbarous by his standards, of whose various languages he cannot have known one single word. Few bolder appointments can ever have been made, and fewer still can have justified themselves more completely.

---

[1] *Leaders in the Northern Church*, p. 50.
[2] He usually appears in printed lists under the Latin name which he adopted —*Deus dedit*, which means *God gave*.
[3] His name is omitted from most printed lists.

He held the primacy from 26 March 668 to 19 September 690—a tenure which has not been exceeded very often. He brought to the Church the organizing power which it needed and could not have supplied from its own resources. He left fourteen territorial dioceses, covering the whole area of the Saxon occupation:

1. Canterbury.
2. Rochester.
3. London (roughly, the modern counties of Middlesex, Hertford and Essex).
4. Dunwich (Suffolk).
5. Elmham (Norfolk).
6. Stow (Lincolnshire).
7. Winchester (from the edge of Kent to the river Parret in Somerset, and to the shore of the Severn estuary between the Parret and the Avon).
8. Worcester.
9. Hereford.
10. Leicester (the southern and eastern midlands).
11. Lichfield (the northern and western midlands, with the county of Flint).
12. York (roughly, Yorkshire and Lancashire).
13. Hexham (Durham and the southern part of Northumberland).
14. Lindisfarne (the northern part of Northumberland and the country between the Tweed and the Firth of Forth).

Cumberland and Westmorland, together with what is now the Furness district of Lancashire, still formed part of the Celtic or Pictish principality of Cumbria, so did not come within his purview.

It is doubtful whether Theodore can be considered to have made a beginning of the parochial system. It was certainly not completed as we know it until some time after the Norman conquest. It is not unusual to find Roman roads as the boundaries of parishes today.[1] This suggests that the boundary line was drawn when the road was still conspicuous and easily recogniz-

[1] I owe this piece of information to a lecture delivered by Professor E. Haverfield.

able. How long this would be after the departure of the Romans can only be a matter of guesswork. But I should think not much more than three or four centuries.

Our word *parish*, like many ecclesiastical terms, has come to us from the Greek through the Latin. The Greek original meant *provision* or *supply*. A *parochia* was therefore apparently the provision of a church with a priest to serve it. By a natural process it came to be applied to the area for which the priest was responsible (perhaps by people who did not understand its original significance), and so acquired the sense which we attach to the word today. The earliest appearance in Christian history, so far as I know, of what we understand by a parish now, is at Carthage in the middle of the third century.[1]

The formation of parishes in England was probably made considerably easier and more rapid than it might have been by the distinctive Saxon institution of tithe. From time immemorial, probably even before our ancestors had begun to cross the North Sea, the Saxon land-owner had been under an obligation to maintain a temple and a priest on his property. It was recognized that part of his duty to his dependents, by whose labour he was enriched, was to make provision for their spiritual welfare. For this purpose a tenth of the produce of the land was set apart. As paganism died out the Christian priest naturally took the place of his predecessor, and was maintained in the same way. The tithe-payer, who was an individual and the sole land-owner, continued to appoint him, only now the nomination could not take effect without the consent and co-operation of the bishop. Towards the close of the eighth century the right of the Church to the tithe was formally ratified by legislation. No new tax was imposed, but a widespread custom of long standing was recognized as beyond challenge, and made universal in perpetuity, which is one of the functions which legislation, especially in England, has always existed to discharge.[2]

[1] See *Cyprian: His Life, His Time, His Work*, by E. W. (Abp.) Benson, pp. 112-3.

[2] It may be worth while to point out that tithe was never a tax on land, but a form of property in land, as is evinced by the fact that the payer could always buy the owner out. It would be held by corporations (e.g., monasteries), or

Beside his administrative gifts Theodore brought to our shores a knowledge of Greek, which perhaps never quite died out.

It is not too much to say that he found a number of separate or at least loosely federated missions, and left a Church which extended from the Channel to the Firth of Forth and from the North Sea to the British frontier. It could not yet be termed the Church *of England*, for there was no England. But it was the Church of the English, and was destined to play a large part in the growth of their tribes into a nation.

With his death the Second Sowing of the Christian faith in our land may be considered to have come to an end.

after their disappearance by colleges. Some part was, however, always reserved for the man who served the church of the parish. After 1836 it was no longer paid in kind, but at a rate determined by the average price of wheat during the last seven years. It therefore fluctuated in amount, sometimes to the advantage of the payer, sometimes to that of the owner. Eventually in 1936 the Government compelled all owners to surrender their property in return for about three-quarters of its value in a new stock bearing interest at the rate of three per cent.

4

Growth

SOME eighty years ago Richard Church, Dean of St Paul's, preached a course of sermons entitled *The Gifts of Civilization*, which immediately became famous. I read them again last year, and thought that the passage of time had diminished their value very little if at all. In them he showed how as Christianity spread it came to different peoples at different stages in their development. It did not reduce them to one uniform pattern, nor did it seek to do so. On the contrary, it raised and developed the distinctive gifts of each, that each might make its own special contribution to the Church. These differences need not impair the unity of the Church Catholic any more than (say) county differences, activities and even rivalries impair the national unity of England today.

I have just used the word *Catholic*. We are familiar with it in our Creeds and in the prayer for *All Conditions of Men*. It will therefore be appropriate to say something here about its origin and meaning.

It has come to us through the Latin from the Greek, and is centuries older than Christianity. In many eyes the Christian world is divided into Catholics and Protestants, and opinion differs as to which of these two terms is the more appropriate description of the Church of England. That division is, however, of recent growth and does not help us to understand the original meaning of *Catholic*.

The Greeks used to speak of *Catholica* when they meant Universal Principles, which hold good anywhere, at any time, in any circumstances. The simplest examples are the fundamental truths of mathematics—e.g., that twice two is four, or, That any two sides of a triangle taken together are greater than the third side.

The word *Catholic* was applied to the Church originally to emphasize the fact that it is a diffused whole. However widely it may be distributed geographically it is, and must always be, regarded as One. This was a new idea. Christianity was born into a world which regarded it as a matter of course that every nation should have its own religion, as much as its own language, and that no nation could be directly concerned with any religion except its own.

When Ignatius, Bishop of Antioch, wrote, about the year 110, "Wherever Christ Jesus is there is the catholic Church,"[1] he meant, "There is an institution not peculiar to or restricted to any particular place."

When sects began to appear early in the second century, if not before, they all professed to be putting forward the true version of Christianity, as Christ had meant it to be. (By this time there were no personal disciples of the Lord left alive to speak with final and indisputable authority.) These sectaries were called *Heretics*, a Greek word meaning *Choosers*, because they had selected for themselves such elements of Christianity as they thought desirable, and had discarded the rest. Sometimes they extended their selection to the books of the New Testament, discarding freely anything in them which they disliked.

The Church's answer to them was, in effect: "Public opinion is against you. People who think as you do are only to be found in one place, or neighbourhood. The Universal Church, wherever it is found, is in agreement, and its teaching is not yours."

In this way *Catholic* being contrasted with *Heretical* acquired the sense of *Orthodox*.

About the middle of the fourth century circumstances, about which more will be said in a later chapter, combined to enhance the prestige of the see of Rome and to make it increasingly the

[1] *Smyrneans*, viii.

standard for the Christian world. (The see of Constantinople was never completely successful in securing the parity which it claimed.) It must not be forgotten that Christendom was then, and for many centuries to come, predominantly if not entirely the Mediterranean world.

It also befell in the fourth century that Constantine made the profession of Christianity first safe and then fashionable. The result was an influx into the Church of people whose grasp of Christian truth was not very firm and whose loyalty to Christian principles not very fervent. There was no longer any likelihood of being called upon to suffer for either. Inevitably they brought with them a large measure of their old pagan ways of thinking, which did not become any less pagan by being translated into the language of Christianity.

When Christianity came to Asia Minor, Egypt, Greece and Italy, it found an ancient and splendid civilization in possession. It found an art which it could not rival, a religion which presented many elements of real nobility, if with a curious admixture of what was childish and disgusting, and systems of law and philo-sophy which are by no means dead yet. It had to be grafted on to all these things, and therefore the substratum of paganism on which it had to be built remained very strong.

It has always been a struggle to keep the Church really Christian. This is not meant cynically. It does not relate to the personal conduct of individuals, but to the outlook of the Church as a whole. It is always difficult to maintain that at its true level. The Christian outlook is not something which we could ever have arrived at by ourselves. It has been given to us by Divine Revelation. It is as it is because at various times in the past God has acted in ways which men could never have imagined. Divorced from these acts Christianity really becomes preposterous; or at least much too good to be true.

The paganism of the Græco-Roman world into which the Church was born, and within which it lived, moved and had its being for at least the first five centuries of its history, represents the supreme achievement of what St Paul meant by "the natural man"—that is, of mankind untouched by the unique Christian

4

revelation. As such it must compel the admiration of everyone who knows anything about it. But just because it is a human invention it is easier of acceptance than what Christianity has to offer, especially in respect of its religious ideas. They are in many ways simpler than the Christian ones, and at first sight more obviously true. Therefore they continually tend to reassert themselves, perhaps more than half unconsciously, within the Church. Their power is naturally greatest in the regions where they had reached their highest development. They may be summarized briefly as follows:

1. Religion consists primarily of a series of transactions with God, each complete in itself, rather than in a continuous personal relationship. Their due performance is a matter of public duty more than of private conscience. This tends to lower, or at least does nothing to raise, the standard of conscience, and divorces religious practice from personal conduct. (In most forms of paganism the connection between them is very slight, if it can be said to exist.)

2. There is an immense number of subordinate divine, or semi-divine, personages who may be induced to influence God in some particular way in accordance with the wishes of the individual worshipper, if they are approached properly. Sometimes they may even be able to extend supernatural aid to him directly. If they were at one time inhabitants of this earth, supernatural power radiates from their mortal remains.

Pausanias' *Description of Greece*, which was written about A.D. 180, attests the enormous number of shrines of heroes, each with its own cult, to be found then on Greek soil. Possession of them was a matter of great importance, because the occupant could be relied on to prove himself a valuable ally in time of trouble. If he lay on the frontier he was a sure shield against invasion. If his bones were carried before an army he would lead his own people to victory.[1] Such shrines seem to have been less numerous on Italian soil.

---

[1] This was done at the battle of Salamis, 480 B.C., when the Greek fleet defeated a larger Persian one. The bones of certain heroes were brought from the island of Aegea and placed on the deck of the Greek admiral's ship.

Beliefs of this kind lower our whole conception of God.

3. By the use of magic, effects can be produced which stand in no relation to spiritual principles, or to the moral conduct of the operator.

This lowers our conception of the nature of the spiritual world, and of the laws by which it is governed. It is obvious that the Christian Sacraments may easily be degraded to the level of magical charms. The following story will show how far this might be carried even as early as the fourth century.

St Ambrose (Bishop of Milan 374–97) had a brother named Satyrus who once suffered shipwreck on the north coast of Africa. He would probably have been drowned had not one of his fellow passengers had with him a supply of consecrated Eucharistic bread, with which he had apparently provided himself in view of such a contingency. He gave some to Satyrus, who wrapped it in a napkin which he tied under his chin, and then cast himself boldly into the sea, and reached land in safety. The bishop recounts the episode with warm approval in the course of a funeral oration which he delivered over his brother some years later, and adds, "He did not try to get a loose plank from the ship to help to keep his head above water; since he had sought the weapons (*arma*) of faith alone. And so, thinking himself protected and upheld sufficiently by these, he did not feel the want of any other aid."[1] (It is worth noting that he does try to justify the proceeding on moral and religious grounds.)

It is unnecessary to dwell upon the tendency to reassert themselves within the Church which the ideas briefly summarized above have shown; nor upon the extent to which they have prevailed. At best they can only be termed sub-Christian.

The situation in England was entirely different. At the end of the sixth century our ancestors had not reached a level of civilization approaching that on which the dwellers in the Mediterranean lands had stood for a thousand years and more. Their paganism crumbled much more quickly, and they had very much less traditional intellectual equipment to carry over into their Christian life. But they had certain well-marked national charac-

[1] *De Excessu Fratris sui Satyri*, i. 43.

teristics,[1] chiefly a respect for law (regarded more as a body of traditional custom than as a logically complete theoretical system) and a respect for individual liberty. Both perhaps spring from one root: an unusually strong sense of personal moral responsibility. How this came to be I cannot pretend to say. But it is observable throughout the history of our race. It is the principle which runs through all our history, whether regarded from the political or from the religious standpoint, gives it coherence, and does more than anything else to make it intelligible. This must always be kept in mind.

National consciousness developed more rapidly in England than in the continental States, partly no doubt on account of our geographical isolation. As it grew our national characteristics became more pronounced. Our whole attitude became more distinctive, and had less and less in common with that of our continental neighbours. This difference was accentuated, with very far-reaching results, when the political ties with France which were formed in the year 1066 were severed in the fifteenth century.

This ingrained respect for law and for individual liberty (the two must never be divorced) may be regarded as the most precious part of our national inheritance, and as something to be preserved at all costs. Is it too much to say that it has enabled us to do more to uphold, extend and protect freedom than all the rest of the world put together, and that it is, now even more than at any previous time, the best contribution which we have to make to the common welfare of mankind?

More will be said in a later chapter about the part which it has played in shaping the Church of England.

The selection of the year 1189 as the end of the period of our Church's growth may be considered arbitrary. The same objection might be brought against any date which could be chosen. Epochs seldom if ever begin or end with statistical precision. Any exact year which may be assigned cannot really mean much

---

[1] The Empire was in essence supranational, and therefore did not foster the development of anything national.

more than that by this time changes which had been going on, perhaps almost unnoticed, have advanced so far that they cannot be ignored or overlooked.

Now, I think that the best way of forming a judgment as to the general characteristics of an epoch is to look at the buildings which were produced during it, and to take account of them as they are in themselves and of the purposes which they were designed to serve. A building is the only product of men's hands which can aspire to be both a work of art and a piece of practical utility. It must be designed to serve some definite purpose, and (within limits) must be appraised by the success with which it does so. But it can also be a thing of beauty, in fashioning which the creative genius of the artist can find expression. Its construction, if it is on any considerable scale, must always be a matter of difficulty, labour and expense. It is also, as a rule, intended to be permanent; or at least to outlive its makers. By looking at the buildings which have been left to us by former ages we can form some opinion as to what manner of men the makers were. We can see what they thought it worth while to attempt, and form some estimate of the measure of artistic and engineering skill which they had at their command.

I have chosen the year 1189 as marking the end of an epoch because it was during the decade 1180–90 that Romanesque building, generally known to us as Norman, began to be superseded by the style known to us as Gothic. It also happens to have been adopted for legal purposes by Edward I.[1]

The chief characteristic of the former is the round semicircular arch (a legacy to Western Europe from the Romans); of the latter, the pointed arch,[2] which the Romans never used.

Wells Cathedral is perhaps the earliest example of the new style to be seen in England, at any rate upon any considerable scale.

Gothic architecture really amounted to a revolution, and the effects were far-reaching.

[1] See Chapter 5, p. 77.
[2] The process by which it was developed can be seen in the presbytery at Durham. Also at Christ Church Priory in Hampshire.

It allowed buildings to be made loftier, because the height of a round arch can never be more than half its span, whereas the height of a pointed arch may equal, or even exceed, its span. Increased height meant more dignity and the admission of more light. The latter was a great benefit in such climates as ours and that of central and northern France, in which the sun is the friend to be welcomed instead of the enemy to be kept at bay, as on the shores of the Mediterranean.

What is known as the Gothic vault, an ingenious system of crossing stone ribs, made it possible to collect the weight and thrust of a stone roof[1] at certain points on the outer wall of the building. These could be strengthened to any extent by means of external buttresses. As the wall between each pair of buttresses had very little to carry it could be cut away freely and the windows increased in size. It is not difficult to find Gothic buildings the sides of which contain more square feet of glass than of stone. The Lady Chapel of Wells Cathedral is an example.

As the area of wall space diminished it offered less field for decoration. Fresco painting (which the dampness of our climate does not suit) and mosaic work (almost an Italian monopoly) became inapplicable. The window became the unit of decoration, and the new art of glass-painting was born. The translucence of the glass enables the painter to achieve a depth and richness of colour impossible on an opaque background. This art reached its zenith in northern France and in England during the thirteenth and fourteenth centuries. Outstanding examples of it can be seen at York and Wells, to make no mention of many other churches. This change in the methods of construction and decoration may fairly be considered to mark a new epoch in the life of the Church.

A few years after Theodore's death the fourteen dioceses which he had left became sixteen. A bishopric was established at Sherborne, for the western half of the unwieldy diocese of Winchester, and another at Selsey for the South Saxons. Two centuries later the diocese of Sherborne was divided by Edward

---

[1] To be preferred to a wooden one as lessening the danger of fire. This was demonstrated at Norwich Cathedral during the war of 1939–45.

the Elder, son of Alfred, and new sees were established at
Ramsbury, which had belonged to Winchester, Crediton and
Wells. The see of Wells was moved to Bath in 1090, but was
restored to Wells about the middle of the next century, when a
joint system of election by the chapters of the two churches
was established. Finally, in 1244 Bishop Roger[1] of Salisbury made
Wells his permanent residence, taking the title of *Bath and Wells*,
which has continued to the present day. Probably the situation
of Bath at the extreme eastern end of the diocese made it incon-
venient, and relations between the bishop and the monks of the
priory church (known today as *Bath Abbey*)[2] may not always have
been easy. The church at Bath is still a sort of secondary cathedral,
though it has neither dean nor canons.

(The South Saxon see of Selsey was moved to Chichester,
a little further inland, in 1070.)

The eighth century was a notable period in the history of our
race and Church, as it saw our first contribution to European
civilization. We began to produce men of learning and also
(especially in Northumbria) men skilful in the art of illuminating
manuscripts. This seems to have been the only art in which the
Saxons attained a really high degree of proficiency. Little of their
architecture has survived, probably because it was for the most
part of wood. Stone churches are to be seen at Bradford-on-Avon
in Wiltshire, at Deerhurst in Gloucestershire, and Worth in
Sussex, but they are all small, and it is not unfair to call their
workmanship rude. The finest examples of Saxon masonry are
the tower of Barnack and the chancel arch at Wittering
and at Brixworth, all in Northamptonshire. The churches of
St Benet's, Cambridge and St Michael's, Oxford, built during the
eleventh century, retain towers. The church at Bradford has
been attributed to St Aldhelm, but the existing building is not
as old as that. It was lost sight of for many years, having been
closely surrounded by other buildings, and was used as a ware-
house. It was rediscovered in modern times (it is said, by someone

---

[1] See *Somerset Historical Essays*, by J. Armitage Robinson, pp. 54–72, 1921.

[2] An *abbey* is a new foundation. A *priory* is a colony planted by an abbey. The
head is a Prior, and was always subject to the Abbot of the mother house.

who happened to catch sight of it from the top of the tower of the parish church) and restored to its legitimate use.

(There is a wooden church at Greenstead, in Essex, which probably dates from the first half of the eleventh century. Some incongruous additions in brick-work have been made to it in modern times.)

In the year 732 the see of York attained the metropolitical dignity contemplated by Pope Gregory I. This was probably due to the greatness of the kingdom of Northumbria more than to any recollection of the Pope's far-reaching plan. The King of Northumbria could not brook that the bishop of his capital should be subordinate to any ecclesiastical authority except the Pope himself. For a similar reason there was one Archbishop of Lichfield (Hygebeorht, 787–99) when the kingdom of Mercia was at its zenith.

In the middle of the eighth century it might have been difficult to predict whether the king of Wessex or of Northumbria or of Mercia would eventually become king of England. The balance was tilted in favour of Wessex when it came to include London and Kent. That gave it direct access to the Continent from a number of ports, and control of all the shortest and most convenient routes. Northumbria was too far away, and Mercia had no access to the sea except the coast of Lincolnshire, which does not possess a really good natural harbour. Boston, near the north-western corner of the Wash, is the best, but was not to be compared with the estuary of the Thames, or even with the lesser harbours to be found on the coasts of Kent, Sussex, Hampshire and Dorset.

Each kingdom has left its mark upon our history.

The royal family derives its descent from the rulers of Wessex.

The see of York has retained its metropolitical dignity, and displays in its arms the royal crown of Northumbria in place of the *pallium* (a white or ermine scarf shaped like the letter Y) which is the usual mark of an archiepiscopal see. When communication between the north and south of England was almost destroyed by the Danish invasions, the Archbishop of York became in effect the temporal as well as the spiritual head of all that lay between the Humber and the Tweed. Had the country been larger, and had the Danish intervention lasted longer, he might have become an independent sovereign ruling an ecclesiastical principality, such as came into being at some places on the Continent.[1] So late as 1745 Archbishop Herring was commissioned by the Crown to raise forces to resist the Jacobite invasion should it come that way.

The Mercian language seems to have prevailed. The midland counties have much less dialect than the north, the west or the east, which suggests that their speech is the ancestor of what may be called now standard English.

Mention must now be made of four outstanding figures. Two belong to Northumbria and two to Wessex.

1. Ealdhelm (Aldhelm), Abbot of Malmesbury, became first Bishop of Sherborne in the year 705. He was the first Englishman who knew Greek and Latin, and the first to write poetry in English. The story goes that he used to seat himself on the bridge across the river at Sherborne and sing, accompanying himself on the harp, in order to attract the attention of the passers-by. If this is true he may be regarded as the father of the type of missionary work which is carried on from time to time in our own day on the sands at such places as Blackpool and Weston-super-Mare. He died on 25 May 709 at Doulting, about eight miles to the east of Wells, where a spring which bears his name is still to be seen. The exact date of his birth appears to be unknown, but as few people in that world passed, or even reached, the age of seventy, it may be placed conjecturally somewhere between the years 630 and 640.

2. Bede (673–735) was a monk, and spent his whole life at

---

[1] Until the year 1836 the Bishop of Durham exercised sovereign rights in the county of Durham. But that was on behalf of the Crown. It was to the interest of the Crown to have a powerful viceroy in the path of possible invasion from Scotland, and the bishop was to be preferred to any secular noble; if only because he could not found a dynasty. The Bishop of Ely had similar powers in the Isle of Ely, probably because the surrounding fenland had made it so difficult of access that it was easier for the Crown to act through a man who had his permanent home there.

Jarrow-on-Tyne. He had a good knowledge of Greek and Latin, and some acquaintance with Hebrew. He was also interested in natural science and arithmetic, so may be considered to have taken virtually all the knowledge then available as his province. He was a prolific writer, his principal works being his *Ecclesiastical History of the English People*, a series of *Lives* of the Abbots of Wearmouth and Jarrow, and a biography of St Cuthbert. He is virtually our only source of information about Saxon England down to his time. He died on 27 May, just as he had finished dictating the last sentences of an English translation of St John's Gospel. This was the first version of any part of the Bible in the vernacular of any part of our country.

By tradition the adjective *Venerable* is always applied to him. It is not very happy, as to us it suggests a man unusually far advanced in years, or an archdeacon. When Bede was styled *Venerabilis*, as he appears to have been very soon after his death, the word really signified *Worthy of Respect*. *Admirable* would represent it better than any other English word today. *Respectable* does not carry sufficient weight

3. *Boniface* (680–755) is sometimes styled the Apostle of Germany. He was brought up in a monastery at Crediton, but as his real name appears to have been Winfrith he may have been born at the village of that name near the coast of Dorset. He was the first Englishman to become a missionary in the modern sense —that is, to leave his native land in order to preach the Gospel to heathen who had never heard it. He worked with great success, being encouraged and supported in every way possible by the Papacy, and became Archbishop of Mainz. He and all his companions were murdered by the Frisians, who inhabited the coastal region between the mouths of the Elbe and the Rhine. Their name is preserved in the Frisian Islands and in Friesland, the most north-easterly province of Holland. He is the first *English* martyr (St Alban was a Briton, if he were a native of our country), and is commemorated on 5 June.

4. *Alcuin* (about 735–805) was brought up in the schools of York, and St Peter's school there claims him as its founder. He soon became distinguished for his learning and spent a large

part of his time at the Court of Charles the Great, which was one of the principal strongholds of Christian civilization in Western Europe. He was the first English scholar to acquire what we should call a European reputation, which means that his attainments were recognized outside his own country. Opinion differs as to whether he was a monk or a secular clerk. Before his death the Viking raids on England had begun.

The ninth century was a dark age for Western Europe, and not least for England. The ruins of the Roman empire had crumbled into rubble. The attempt to revive it made by Charles the Great (who was crowned as emperor by Pope Leo III in St Peter's on Christmas Day 800) did not come to very much. This may have been due to the feebleness of his successors. (If four sovereigns are known as "The Bald", "The Fat", "The Stammerer", and "The Simple", it may be inferred that their royal line was not conspicuous for its moral or intellectual qualities.)

It is hardly too much to say that the very existence of Christendom was imperilled. First there was the threat from the southeast. The Moslems had overrun the whole of North Africa. Sicily, Greece, the Balkan peninsula and Spain were in their hands. The eastern empire, shrunk to a fraction of its former extent, was almost in the position of a blockaded island.

In the previous century the conquerors of Spain had once penetrated to central France. The victory gained by Charles Martel at the battle of Tours[1] may be considered to have saved England as well as France. The invaders were flung back beyond the Pyrenees. But as they had crossed them once it was possible that they might do so again.

And now a new danger, in which we were more closely concerned, appeared from the north. Scandinavian seafarers (*Northmen*, *Norsemen* and ultimately *Normans*) began to descend on our shores. Invaders from Norway occupied Shetland and Orkney (which remained an appanage of the Norwegian Crown until the fifteenth century) and part of the mainland of Scotland. Such names as Thurso and Wick record their presence: as, doubtless,

[1] October 732. The battle is said to have lasted for a week.

the fact that the most northerly county is still called by a name which signifies *The Southern Land*. They pushed southwards via the Hebrides as far as the Isle of Man, where the map reveals a curious mixture of Gaelic (Manx), and Norse names. The *Sodor* in the double title of the see[1] stands for *Sudrey-oer*, which means *The Southern Isles*. These were the Hebrides, which formed part of the jurisdiction of the see, as distinct from the *North Isles*,[2] which meant Orkney and Shetland. The see remained in the ecclesiastical province of Trondhjem for a considerable period after the Norwegian kings had ceased to exercise authority in the island. It is said that in the twelfth century three bishops-elect in succession were drowned while trying to reach Trondhjem for consecration, whereupon the fourth, John by name, betook himself to York about the year 1151. The election seems to have belonged to the monks of Furness (in Lancashire). In 1219 one of John's successors repaired to Dublin. The see was incorporated formally in the province of York by Act of Parliament in 1542.

England suffered little from the Norwegians. Our invaders were Danes. They were horsemen, which the Saxons were not, and could therefore move with a speed which bewildered and terrified their opponents, as Attila's Huns on their Tartar ponies had done four centuries earlier. To make matters worse, another Danish horde established itself on our flank in the south-east of Ireland. Their kingdom of Waterford was not brought to an end until the year 1014, when Brian Boroimhe (who was killed) gained a complete victory over them at Clontarf, now a suburb of Dublin, on Christmas Day. It is said that Odin himself came to lead his followers, but the sanctity of the day made his aid ineffective. When the battle had gone irrevocably against the Danes he was seen, as darkness fell, riding towards the sea on his horse Sleipnir, which having eight legs was twice as fleet and enduring as any four-legged rival. This seems to have been

---

[1] The first bishop (Roolwer) whose name is known appears to have lived about the middle of the eleventh century.

[2] This description was in use until very recent times, if it has been dropped now. At the beginning of the present century I sailed for Shetland from the port of Leith in a ship whose destination was announced as *Aberdeen and the North Isles*.

the last appearance of a pagan divinity on European soil which history records.

The outstanding Englishman of the ninth century was King Alfred. He was born probably in 848, and died probably in 901. Exact dating at this period is difficult, because the copies of the *Anglo-Saxon Chronicle* which exist are not always in agreement. Possibly the scribes did not all begin the year on the same day.[1]

Little by little, Alfred was forced back until nothing of his kingdom remained to him except a few hundred acres in Somerset protected by almost impenetrable marshes. There he rallied his forces, and the place has ever since been known as Athelney, which means *The Island of the Nobles*. Thence he sallied out and defeated the Danes at the battle of Ethandune in May 878. The site has never been identified, but a strong case in favour of Butleigh on the Polden Hills, some four miles to the south of Glastonbury, was put forward by a contributor to *Notes and Queries for Somerset and Dorset* in June 1934. The name may, however, be considered to point to Edington,[2] some ten miles farther west.

A few days later the remnant of the Danish army capitulated. The king Guthrum or Guthram (either spelling appears to be permissible) consented to receive baptism, and his adherents followed suit. A treaty was signed at Wedmore, some seven miles to the west of Wells, by which the Danes undertook to withdraw to the north of the Thames, which meant that they would leave Wessex alone. English Christianity, and with it English nationality, were saved.

When Alfred regained his ancestral kingdom it was enveloped in thick darkness. Many lamps of religion and learning had been extinguished, and those that remained were very dim. The Danes were heathen destroyers, as the Saxons had been, and the monasteries in particular, on which almost everything depended, had suffered very heavily. It is unlikely that the Danes regarded them with special hostility, but they were easy to find and worth

[1] See *The Times of St Dunstan*, by J. Armitage Robinson (Ford Lectures, 1923).
[2] Not to be confused with a place of the same name in Wiltshire, which some modern writers have taken to be the scene of the battle.

plundering, and their occupants were unlikely to be able to offer much resistance. It would, however, be an exaggeration to say that monastic life in England was entirely destroyed. Glastonbury, for example, does not appear to have been ravaged, though it had sunk to a very low ebb. In his heroic and not unfruitful efforts to revive religion and learning (the ignorance of the clergy was one great obstacle) Alfred got help both from Mercia and Wales. When he died, England was well on the way to recovery, if much still remained to be done.[1]

If it is true that great men are to some extent the product of their circumstances, which furnish them with opportunities, it is at least equally true that all great movements need great men to lead them. Six names may be mentioned as having brought about the wonderful revival of England during the tenth century. Three belong to kings, Edward the Elder, son of Alfred, who reigned from 901 to 924; Athelstan, son of Edward, who reigned from 924 to 940; and Edgar, son of his brother Edmund, who reigned from 959-975. The other three are those of ecclesiastics— Dunstan, eventually Archbishop of Canterbury, 960–88; Ethel- wold, Bishop of Winchester, 963–84; and Oswald, who succeeded Dunstan in the see of Worcester in 961. In 972 he became Arch- bishop of York, and held the two sees together until his death in 992.

Of these six Athelstan and Dunstan are unquestionably the greatest. Edward the Elder was primarily a soldier, and too much occupied with strengthening his hold upon his inheritance to be able to do much for religion or learning. Mention has been made above of the three new bishoprics which he founded in Wessex. He also began to build a new church at Winchester. This seems soon to have fallen on evil days, and drastic reforms were carried out in the next generation by Ethelwold, whose name suggests that he was of noble birth.

Athelstan came to a more secure inheritance, which he increased. He was crowned as King of Wessex and Mercia at Kingston on 4 September. In 927 he established his authority

---

[1] The Danish kingdom of East Anglia seems to have come to an end in 902. The Scandinavian kingdom of York lasted until 954.

over York, and in 934 invaded Scotland and added Cumbria to England in perpetuity. In 937 he defeated a combination headed by Anlaf Guthfrithson (a Dane from Dublin), Constantine, King of Scots, and Owen, King of Strathclyde. The site of the battle has never been identified, but is probably in Northumbria. After this he styled himself *basileus*[1] (sovereign) of all Britain. If his claim were not universally recognized, he ruled a wider dominion than any man of his race had done before. He also added West Wales to England, and established a bishopric at St Germans in Cornwall. The see was joined to that of Crediton in 1027, and when Crediton was moved to Exeter in 1050 ceased to have an independent existence.

But he was more than a successful soldier. His gifts to the Church were many, and he was especially generous to the Abbey of Malmesbury in Wiltshire, where he is buried. He also founded the Abbey of Muchelney in Somerset. He is perhaps the only sovereign who was an assiduous collector of relics of all kinds.

His court was a brilliant centre of culture, and established many links with the more advanced civilization across the Channel. It was visited, apparently more than once, by Hywel the Good, who was perhaps entitled to style himself King of Wales.[2] What concerns us more closely is that it was at that court that the young Dunstan, whose uncle Athelm (or Æthelhelm)[3] had been the first Bishop of Wells, came to the king's notice.

Dunstan was born at Baltonsborough, some three miles to the south-east of Glastonbury, about the year 910, and was educated at the abbey. As a child he may well have heard of Alfred's heroic stand and decisive victory from men who had played some part therein. It is impossible to give details of his career here. It will

[1] The word is Greek, and was probably understood to signify a higher rank than the more familiar Latin *rex*. *Imperator*, which has given us the word "emperor", originally meant no more than Commander-in-Chief of an army in the field. It acquired the meaning we attach to it because the Roman "emperor" was in fact commander-in-chief of all the forces of the State.

[2] A little more than fifty years ago I saw an inn in an out-of-the-way valley in Merioneth which displayed his name, with a pictorial accompaniment, as its sign. It did not occur to me to try to find out whether this was a piece of anti-quarianism or a genuine survival of tradition.

[3] Archbishop of Canterbury 914–23.

be enough to say that in 945 (possibly a year or two earlier) King Edmund made him Abbot of Glastonbury. The story goes that the king's mind had been poisoned against him maliciously, and the bestowal of the abbey was an act of reparation for injustice done, and a thank-offering for a narrow escape from death when during a stag-hunt he had ridden too close to the edge of the cliffs which overhang the famous gorge of Cheddar.

Dunstan introduced the Benedictine rule at Glastonbury, and did so much to raise the standard of the house that he may almost be regarded as its second founder. In 957 he became Bishop of Worcester, in 959 he was translated to London, and in 960 to Canterbury, where he remained until his death on 19 May 988. During his tenure of the primacy he might almost be termed Prime Minister. When on 11 May 973 he crowned Edgar as the recognized King of all England the final fruits of Alfred's work were garnered. Then and there England became a nation, even if national consciousness were not to reach its full development for nearly four hundred years.

Unlike some ecclesiastics who have played a large part in the affairs of state, Dunstan seems to have kept himself singularly unspotted from the world. He was beyond question a saint as well as a scholar and a statesman. From the day of his death he was an object of popular veneration, until he was to some extent over-shadowed by Thomas Becket, who had crowned his life's work by a martyr's death.

The legend that Dunstan was once visited by the devil, and put him to flight by pinching his nose with a pair of hot tongs, seems to have arisen from the fact that his interest in mechanical arts and antiquarian lore during his earlier days at Glastonbury led him to be suspected of magical practices. A representation of the scene may be seen in a small scrap of glass in a window in the south transept of Wells Cathedral.

Perhaps the wonderful recovery of England during the earlier part of the tenth century was a little too rapid. Perhaps it depended too much on a small number of exceptional men who left no successors who approached their stature. Be that as it may, it was followed by a period of decline.

The Danes, who had never quite lost their footing in the country, became more active and aggressive. In 1016 Canute, son of Sweyn Forkbeard, was recognized as king of all England. For twenty years he ruled over a Viking empire, of which Norway and England were the principal components. He died in 1036 at the age of about forty. Had he lived twenty years longer, or had his successors been more competent, it is just possible that his empire might have lasted. Had it done so, our history and that of a large part of Europe would have been very different. But under the conditions of the time it would have been very difficult for any colossus to have remained astride of the North Sea in perpetuity. Certainly it would not have been to our interest. Both the Church and the nation stood to benefit more by having their faces turned towards France and the Mediterranean than by having Norway and the Baltic as their horizon.

The Saxon line was restored when Edward (the Confessor) was crowned on 3 April 1043. He reigned as acknowledged king of an independent England until his death on 5 January 1066. In all the practical affairs of life he was as incompetent as any man could be. But no English sovereign has impressed himself more deeply upon his subjects. He was felt to be not altogether of this world. He was credited with having worked miracles during his lifetime, and was recognized as a saint as soon as he was in his grave. The abbey church on Thorney island does not seem to have been of special importance until he rebuilt it.[1] It owes its unique prestige primarily to the fact that he is buried there.

Within a few feet of St Edward's shrine every king of England since has been crowned with St Edward's crown. William I had obvious reasons for inaugurating the practice. (The original crown was lost when all the regalia were stolen[2] from the chapel of the Pyx in the cloister of Westminster, in or about the year 1322, when Edward II was campaigning in Scotland.)

[1] The work was begun about 1042 and completed in 1065, only a few days before his death.

[2] The thief is said to have been named Roger de Pudlicote. He was taken, and is said to have been flayed alive and his skin nailed to the chapel door. Minute strips of it are still to be seen. Very little of the booty was recovered. The monks of Westminster were suspected of some measure of complicity.

St Edward is the original patron saint of England, and although the superstructure of his shrine has been destroyed, no sacrilegious hands have ever disturbed his bones. (Perhaps St Cuthbert is the only other English saint of whom this can be said, and the exact position of his coffin is a secret.)

Henry III, the greatest builder and patron of the arts who has ever occupied the throne of England, thought that no setting could be too splendid for St Edward's shrine. He did not hesitate to pull down the Confessor's church and to begin the structure which we see today. In respect of architectural magnificence and historical associations it ranks with any church in the world.

The story of the Norman conquest is too well known to be worth re-telling here. It brought an infusion of new blood and energy, of which Saxon England stood in need. Its most important outcome was that it made us a part of the European continent. For almost exactly four hundred years (for nearly five hundred if we count the "bridge-head" of Calais, which remained in our hands until the days of Mary Tudor) we had possessions in France; sometimes very extensive ones. Henry II ruled the entire western half of France from the Straits of Dover to the Pyrenees. We therefore became part of the continental system, of which the Papacy was the hub, instead of being very loosely attached to it as we had been before. It would be difficult to exaggerate the effect which this change of political status had upon the English Church and State.

Visible evidence of Norman energy and skill is furnished by the great buildings, churches and castles, which arose under this rule. Saxon masons could not create anything comparable. There was also a complete reorganization of the Church under Lanfranc.

A number of sees were moved to more important centres of population. The South Saxon see of Selsey went to Chichester, a few miles further inland. The Mercian (originally West Saxon) see of Dorchester-on-Thames was moved to Lincoln. The see of Sherborne, in which that of Ramsbury had been merged, was transferred to Salisbury.[1] Wells went to Bath, to return in the thirteenth century after an uneasy partnership, which now survives

---

[1] To Old Sarum, a few miles from its present site.

in titular form only. The growing importance of Norwich made it obviously a better centre than Elmham or Thetford.

Finally, in 1109 a new see was placed at Ely, where Etheldreda, wife of Sebert, king of the East Saxons, had founded an abbey in the seventh century, and twenty-four years later the extension of the episcopate was completed by the creation of a bishopric of Carlisle. After this the number of dioceses remained unaltered until the reign of Henry VIII.

The mention of Ely, where an existing monastic church was raised to cathedral rank, makes it appropriate to say something about the fusion of monastery and cathedral, which was, I believe, peculiar to England. It is probably due to the fact that in the sixth century Christianity and monasticism reached our shores together. We never knew a Church in which monasteries were not an important feature. In France, Spain and Italy they appeared as additions to a well-established system. Whatever the precise reason, it came about that of the seventeen cathedrals which existed in England prior to the Reformation eight[1] were staffed by colleges of monks (Carlisle by Augustinian canons regular) instead of secular canons. At this distance of time it is not easy to judge whether the arrangement worked well or not. On the good side, it probably promoted a higher standard of life and better discipline. On the bad, it is not unlikely to have given additional occasions for friction between the chapter and the bishop. When the monasteries were dissolved these cathedrals had to be provided with a new constitution to take the place of the old monastic rule by which they had been governed. They are therefore known today as *Of the New Foundation*.[1] The others[2] which went on unchanged are *Of the Old Foundation*. To any one familiar with cathedrals the difference between the two types is still apparent in many ways.

The secular chapters (i.e., the canons of the non-monastic cathedrals) were organized more elaborately on the French model.

---

[1] Durham, Norwich, Ely, Canterbury, Rochester, Winchester, Worcester, Carlisle.

[2] York, Lincoln, St Paul's, Chichester, Salisbury, Wells, Exeter, Hereford, Lichfield.

Lincoln and Salisbury, to some extent, set the standard. The arrangements of the Saxon chapters were probably much less formal, but little is known of their detail. I believe that the only Saxon statutes which exist are those of Beverley[1] in the East Riding of Yorkshire. I have never seen them, so can say nothing about them.

Besides the development of the cathedral system, religious houses both for men and for women multiplied rapidly. The parochial system was also brought nearer to the form in which we have inherited it. In short, the organizing power of the Normans made itself felt throughout the Church from top to bottom, to our great advantage. It was something which Saxon England could never have supplied for itself. The two Archbishops of Canterbury immediately after the Conquest, Lanfranc (1070–89) and Anselm (1093–1109), both Italians by birth, may be considered to rank with any Primates we have ever had.

As the administration of the Church and the State became more efficient, and enlarged its scope, the danger of some collision between the two powers increased. It can never be very remote, especially when both are in vigorous health and under the direction of able and conscientious chiefs. It came with violence between Henry II and Thomas Becket, who was Archbishop of Canterbury 1162–70. It would take too long to give the full history of the dispute here. It will be enough to say that it related to clerical immunities. There was more to be said for them in that world than may be immediately apparent today. In a rough society, which had not advanced very far beyond semi-barbarism, there was a real value in the existence of a class of persons who were entitled to exceptional consideration on *moral* grounds. It showed that there is something beside force which deserves respect. The advance of civilization and the stability of any society depend upon the extent to which that is generally recognized. But the people to whom the immunities are extended must not be too many, and the moral basis of their claim must be irrefragable. In other words, the system must be

[1] A collegiate church, which perhaps served as a sort of secondary cathedral for the vast diocese of York, as did Ripon and Southwell.

kept within somewhat narrow limits, otherwise it will become mischievous and defeat its own ends.

Henry II had inherited a kingdom in a state of anarchy, and he devoted his great abilities and tireless energy to the restoration of a coherent system of justice. Most people know that the system of travelling judges which continues in the "circuits" of today originated with him. The first step towards the restoration of order after a period of anarchy is to ensure that criminals do not escape their deserts. In his attempts to give effect to this principle the king found himself thwarted by the privileges of the "clergy". Whatever charge might be brought against them, they could be tried only in the bishops' courts, which might degrade them from their office and pass sentence of excommunication, but, as was right, could only impose *moral* penalties. The efficacy of a moral penalty must depend almost entirely upon the moral level of the person upon whom it is imposed.

Unfortunately the "clergy" by this time included all persons in "minor orders", whose position corresponded with that of vergers, sextons, cleaners and similar officials employed in connection with the Church. They were very numerous, and undoubtedly a number of men of bad character got themselves admitted to these orders for the sake of the life-long immunity which went with them. Of course, some "criminous clerks" were of higher rank. On the king's side it was argued that a clerk who had been formally degraded might be regarded as a layman and brought before a civil court. The archbishop would not consent to this, on the ground that a man could not be tried and punished twice for the same offence. In principle this was unassailable, but it ignored the fact that in the eyes of men of really bad character the punishment which the bishop's court could inflict was negligible. It would have helped matters had the archbishop agreed that "clergy" should not include any one below the rank of sub-deacon. This would have been at least a partial solution of the difficulty. But it does not seem to have occurred to anyone.

On the one hand, the king found his efforts to do justice and restore order thwarted by the fact that many notorious evil-doers were outside his jurisdiction. On the other, the archbishop felt bound to uphold all the privileges of the Church; which, as is usual in England, custom had transformed into rights.

The dispute was exacerbated by the personal character of the two leaders. Both were able and energetic; both (especially the king) were men of fiery temper.

Everybody knows the lamentable outcome. When the king was in France he let fall a hasty expression which some of those who heard it construed as at least a hint to make away with the archbishop. Four men, Reginald Fitz-Urse, William de Tracy, Hugh de Morville and Richard the Breton, determined to act upon it. After they had started upon this errand suspicion was aroused, and a messenger was sent after them to charge them to attempt nothing against the archbishop's person. He arrived too late. At about 5 o'clock on 29 December 1170 Becket was brutally murdered in Canterbury Cathedral.

All moral considerations apart, it is hardly possible to conceive a more foolish act. The public conscience was shocked, and the explosion of feeling which resulted was so violent that it came near to costing the king his throne. Henry could only right himself by doing penance publicly at the martyr's shrine. Becket became immensely popular and was canonized, though taken as a whole his character does not bear comparison with that of either Dunstan or Anselm. Nearly two centuries later his shrine was the magnet which drew Chaucer's pilgrims to Canterbury, and thereby enriched our literature permanently with the *Canterbury Tales*. Several churches still bear his name. It was removed from the Calendar by order of King Henry VIII, who did not wish to preserve the memory of an archbishop who had proved himself stronger than a king.

5

Flower and Fruit

From the accession of Richard I to the death of Edward I—1189–1307

D URING the thirteenth century medieval Christendom was at its zenith.

As an epoch the "century" may be considered to extend from 1189 to 1307, as far as England is concerned.

The former date is the year of the accession of Richard I, and the day of his coronation (3 September) was fixed during the reign of Edward I as the limit of legal memory. It was ruled then, and the ruling still holds good, that no documentary evidence need be produced in support of any claim which could be shown to have been recognized at that date.

Besides this, by the year 1189 Gothic architecture had made its appearance, if its magnificent possibilities were hardly suspected. It was a natural outcome of the older Romanesque (Norman), and was probably adopted originally for its engineering advantages.

But, apart from them, it afforded scope for architectural and artistic achievement far beyond anything previously possible. It may be questioned whether the spirit of man has ever found nobler expression than in the Gothic architecture of the thirteenth century.

About the same time came a great development of heraldry. This *Noble Science*, as it came to be called, is a prominent feature of the medieval world, and certainly added a great deal to its colour and general picturesqueness. It has never died out in England, though after the beginning of the sixteenth century, when it became almost entirely decorative, it sank to a low ebb.

It probably reached its nadir about the beginning of the nineteenth century. Since then there has been some recovery. It is difficult for us to imagine any kind of pageant to which it does not make some contribution, and its disappearance from seals and inn signs would be a matter for regret.

Its remarkable development during the period under consideration was due to the invention of the closed helm.[1] This type of helmet gave the wearer greatly increased protection. But as it concealed his features, it made him unrecognizable by friend or foe. It was necessary to devise some method by which he could be identified in a moment with complete certainty in the heat of battle. A heraldic device displayed on his shield, or on a linen surcoat worn over his armour, served the purpose perfectly. The designing of these "coats" became a very elaborate process which called for wide knowledge and a high degree of technical skill, and in due course developed its own terminology. It belonged to a good herald to recognize any coat wherever he saw it. In this, as in most of the arts and amenities of life, France set the standard.

This period was perhaps the least insular in our history. England was part of the continental system, of which the Papacy was the hub, to an extent not easy for us to appreciate now. An Englishman in France, the Low Countries, western Germany, Switzerland or Italy found himself much less of a stranger in a strange land than he does today. Wherever he went he found a common culture, with a common religious and philosophical background and, to a much larger extent than today, a common language. If he went to Spain, which was perhaps less likely, his experience would be similar, provided that he did not enter the Moorish kingdom of Granada in the south of the peninsula. When universities became prominent scholars passed freely from one to another to listen to the most famous masters. There was no linguistic difficulty as there is now, because all lectures were delivered in Latin, with which everyone capable of benefiting by them was familiar. The disappearance of Latin as the common tongue of

[1] See *Arms and Blazonry of the Colleges of Oxford*, Barnard and Sheppard, Oxford University Press, 1929.

all educated people is perhaps as severe a blow as European civilization has ever received. If it could be revived, that would probably do more to establish peace and security than any number of
treaties and conferences. A United States of Europe would not
be a remote possibility.

In 1307 Edward I died. By this time the Papacy had fallen from
its high estate,[1] and its seat had been transferred to Avignon by
Clement V. Monastic institutions had obviously passed their
prime. We had owed a very great deal to them. While the conversion of the heathen Saxons was in progress they were the
spear-heads of the missionary advance. Later they were the chief,
if not the only, strongholds of religion and learning in a very dark
world. But by the beginning of the fourteenth century it was
becoming apparent that there was not very much left for them
to do, at any rate on the old lines. They would have to find some
new justification for their existence if they were to continue in
anything approaching the numbers they had reached. When the
sceptre passed from the strong grasp of Edward I to the feebler
hands of Edward II an epoch in English history really did come
to an end.

If we attempt to assess an epoch as a whole, what is to be our
real criterion? For my own part, I think the best of which it was
capable. I think that that gives a truer picture than the worst,
or even the general average. For all real progress, especially
perhaps in England, has always been the work of a few outstanding
characters. The divine purpose which gives coherence and meaning to history is worked out through selected individuals. From
time to time men appear who are conspicuous in their generation,
and in many respects in advance of it. Their work shapes the
course of events. They embody new ideas which are gradually
absorbed, to some extent, by the majority of their fellows, but do
not as a rule bear their full fruit until the next generation or
even later. And from this standpoint I should venture to criticize
Dr J. H. Moorman's learned and valuable book.[2] He calls

---

[1] See Chapter 6, "The Papal Power."
[2] *English Church Life in the Thirteenth Century*, Cambridge University Press,
1945.

attention to the enormous number of clerics of various kinds, perhaps nearly one in fifty of the entire population. In such an army it was inevitable that many should be men of little education, and some of less than reputable character. He dwells upon the lamentable state of affairs revealed by the records of episcopal Visitations. But such inquiries naturally record only what the visitor found amiss. Sometimes this amounts to no more than small imperfections or deficiencies in the furniture and fittings of the church in question, such as are to be found almost anywhere today. There can be very few churches, indeed, in which an observant eye can detect no room for any improvement or addition. The resources available have also to be taken into account. Besides this, anyone familiar with such records knows that *omnia bene* (*all well*) is not an uncommon entry after the name of a parish. Even if parochial life as a whole was at a low ebb there is another aspect of the picture. Politically, intellectually and artistically the achievements of the thirteenth century were of great and lasting value.

It will be convenient to take the political aspect first, for that set the stage.

Richard I reigned for ten years, of which barely six months were spent in England. His personal interest in his English dominions seems to have been limited to the amount of money which he could extract from them for military adventures elsewhere. It was fitting that he should be buried at Fontevrault, as his father had been, rather than anywhere in England. But as he embodied in a very conspicuous degree the qualities which were admired most at that time—a noble presence and extraordinary prowess in battle, to which his courage and physical strength contributed about equally—he probably enhanced our prestige as a nation in the eyes of the world at large.

In November 1197 he demanded a supply of men from the episcopal estates for service against the King of France. Some of the bishops were disposed to concede it. But the Bishop of Lincoln (Hugh of Grenoble[1]) was inflexible. He did not dispute the obliga-

---

[1] Sometimes called *of Avalion*, a place in Burgundy. He was canonized, and his day is 17 November.

tion of the Church to provide money for the king's wars wherever they might be waged. But he would not admit that it was bound to find men for service outside the kingdom. He was supported by the Bishop of Salisbury (Herbert Poore). When the news reached the king he was furiously angry and ordered all the possessions of both sees to be confiscated. His commands were executed against the Bishop of Salisbury, but the character of the Bishop of Lincoln stood so high that the royal officials dared not sequestrate his lands. Subsequently he went to France and met the king face to face. He must have known that he ran a considerable risk. But Richard respected courage when he saw it, and a reconciliation was effected. The incident is worth recording as an illustration of the way in which an outstanding bishop could restrain a sovereign who tried to exceed his legitimate rights, and so help to strengthen the respect for law and liberty which has been the foundation of our national life.

It is unnecessary to dwell upon the details of the reign of King John. His lamentable record of misgovernment, which led to his humiliation at the hands of the Pope, and the part which Stephen Langton (Archbishop of Canterbury 1207–28) played in compelling him to grant the Great Charter on 15 June 1215, are matters of common knowledge.

But mention should be made of two other events which occurred during this period to which perhaps sufficient attention is not always directed. Both were destined to produce lasting results of great importance. First, the loss of Normandy in 1204, and secondly, the emergence (it would not be quite true to say the beginning) of the Universities of Oxford and Cambridge.

1. The loss of Normandy was, of course, a severe blow to the prestige of the Crown and to John personally, as his unsuccessful attempts to recover the duchy showed. No doubt it was also largely responsible for his chronic condition of financial embarrassment. But in the long run it was to the advantage of England. Since 1066, England and Normandy had formed a single State. England was the more extensive, and potentially the richer, if not yet actually. And *King* is a higher title than *Duke*. But the fact remained that the Duke of Normandy had added England to his

patrimony, and the centre of gravity remained on the southern side of the Channel. If there were any conflict between English and Norman interests, ours would have to give way. This state of affairs could hardly have been permanent. After 1204 we became a sovereign State again. Our other French territories were beyond question appanages of the Crown of England. They enriched it and enhanced its dignity, but could never infringe its supremacy. The foundations upon which Edward I was to build his massive polity three-quarters of a century later became more stable and secure through John's loss. The Channel Islands are the only fragment of the Norman duchy which has remained in our hands. I believe that French map-makers term them *The Norman Archipelago*.

2. The question is sometimes asked, Why were the original English universities (until the nineteenth century was well on its way, the only ones) founded at two unimportant provincial towns? As with many questions, no direct answer is possible within the assumptions of the questioner, because his difficulty does not really arise. They never were "founded" as modern universities are. The real question is, How did the Schools of Oxford and Cambridge become so much better than any to be found elsewhere that people resorted to them from far and wide, and their certificates of proficiency (degrees) commanded more than local respect? A number of factors combined to bring this about: the geographical ones were probably the most important.

To us the natural division of England is between North and South, corresponding very closely with the provinces of Canterbury and York. But the division of medieval England was between East and West. The North did not really count. So much of the land was barren that it could only support a very sparse population, until the development of industries which lived by coal and iron; which really means until near the beginning of the nineteenth century. Besides this, until the union of the Crowns in 1603 border warfare made life "beyond Trent" too dangerous and unsettled to admit the growth of a great centre of learning. Cromwell is said to have contemplated universities at York and Manchester, but if he entertained the idea seriously nothing came of it. Perhaps the time for northern universities was hardly ripe, even in the middle of the seventeenth century.

If a line is drawn from the mouth of the Humber to the mouth of the Mersey, the region to the south of it is the England that mattered during the twelfth and thirteenth centuries and for long afterwards. And for this England Oxford is as convenient a centre as could be found. It is also at the head of our greatest water-way[1]—another very important point, when rivers were used for passenger traffic as well as for the transport of goods to a much larger extent than they are today. The same river which made Oxford easily accessible to scholars also allowed the importation of food for them. In the medieval world few towns could stand any sudden and considerable increase of population without the risk of serious scarcity, if not of downright famine.

Cambridge was convenient for the region for which Oxford was not; chiefly the (then) wealthy and populous counties of Norfolk and Suffolk. Besides this, the Great North Road, which probably represents a prehistoric trackway from what is now the Border to London, passes within about fifteen miles of it at Alconbury in Huntingdonshire. It was, therefore, more accessible than Oxford for any people who might wish to come from the north. (This has been a permanent factor in the life of the university, and is probably responsible to some extent for the curiously persistent difference between Cambridge and Oxford.)

Cambridge is upon the edge of the Fen, which meant that it was within easy reach of corn-land as fertile as any in England, and of unlimited supplies of fish and wild-fowl, so that the supply of food was abundant and easy to increase. It is also not unlikely that the great religious houses, such as Crowland, Ely, Burgh (Peterborough, as it is called today), Thorney and Ramsey, to name some of the best known, would from time to time send some of their inmates there for convalescence. Life in the Fen must have been hard, especially for men who had been born and brought up in more genial climates, and the ague, which did not disappear until the middle of the last century, must have been

---

[1] The Thames can hardly be considered a navigable river above Oxford. Probably it was even less so then than now.

a scourge. The schools are said to have come into being as follows.

> In the year 1109 Joffrid, Abbot of Crowland, successor of Ingulfus, sent to his manor of Cottenham,[1] near Cambridge, Gislebert, his fellow monk and professor of divinity, and three other monks who had followed him into England.[2] From Cottenham they daily repaired to Cambridge. There they hired a public barn, made open profession of their sciences, and in a little time drew a number of scholars together. In less than two years' time their numbers increased so much from the country as well as from the town that there was never a house, barn or church big enough to hold them all. Upon which they dispersed themselves in different parts of the town, imitating the University of Orleans. Three of them taught grammar, logic and rhetoric.[3] Gislebert preached on Sundays and holy days.[4]

If this is not absolutely exact, it is probably not far from the truth. Oxford is sometimes said to have owed its origin to a number of scholars who were expelled from Paris in 1167. But it is not easy to see why they should have gone there unless there had been schools of some sort already in existence.

What is certain is that soon after the year 1200 Innocent III, who was an indefatigable letter writer, began addressing the masters and scholars of Paris, and shortly afterwards those of Oxford and Cambridge, as *universitas vestra*, which meant that he did not regard them as a fortuitous association, but as a body corporate, capable of acting as one man. This implies that they had been in existence for some time, and that their reputation was well established.

This seems to be the origin of the meaning which attaches now to the word "university". *Universitas* can be applied to any body of men who can be considered to have a corporate existence—e.g., the dean and canons of a cathedral. It does not necessarily imply a seat of learning or place of education.

---

[1] About five miles to the north of Cambridge. In modern times it gave its name to a cheese little inferior to its more famous counterpart the Stilton, which is produced in Huntingdonshire.

[2] From Orleans.   [3] This course was known as the *Trivium*.

[4] *On the Origin of Universities*, p. 92, by Henry Malden, London, 1835, He is quoting from Peter of Blois in Camden's *Britannia*: appendix to *Ingulfus*.

The collegiate system, which, if not peculiar to Oxford and Cambridge, has developed more extensively there than anywhere else, came later. The oldest college in Oxford is University, which is believed to have been founded about the year 1250. The oldest at Cambridge, St Peter's, commonly known as Peterhouse, was founded in 1284 by Hugh of Balsham (a village near Cambridge), who was Bishop of Ely from 1257 to 1286.

Colleges were originally charitable foundations. They were intended to provide the undergraduates, many of whom were hardly more than children, with decent accommodation, where they would be under some sort of supervision and be protected from the rapacity of the townspeople. Possibly Bishop Hugh knew by experience what lodgings in the town of Cambridge were like.

These foundations were endowed, if not lavishly enough to enable them to admit scholars entirely free, sufficiently to lessen the cost of a university education, and so to make it more widely available. The fact that colleges continued to be founded in both universities at intervals during the next three centuries attests the success of the original experiment. It would, in fact, be difficult to point to any institutions which have contributed more to the welfare of Church and State in England.

When Henry III came to the throne in 1216 he was only nine years old. Nine days later he was crowned in the abbey church of Gloucester, which was not then of cathedral rank, by the papal legate Cardinal Gualo in the presence of the bishops of Winchester,[1] Worcester,[2] Lichfield and Coventry[3] and Bath,[4] who were conveniently near at hand. This somewhat hole-and-corner proceeding may have been prompted by an honest desire to secure the succession, though since Henry was indisputably the lawful heir it is not easy to see on what grounds his title could have been impugned by anybody. On the other hand, it may have been an attempt on the part of the Papacy to establish the principle that the Crown of England is in the Pope's gift. No attention seems to have been paid to the ceremony, and on

[1] Peter des Roches.   [2] Silvester of Evesham.
[3] William Cornhill.   [4] Jocelin of Wells.

Whitsunday 1220 the king was crowned properly by the Arch-bishop of Canterbury[1] at Westminster.

As a ruler Henry III was not successful. He was supported in his misgovernment by the Papacy, which lost ground in England thereby. It would be out of place here to dwell upon this aspect of his reign. It will be enough to say that the nobles were even-tually stirred to open rebellion and that the Church was upon their side. They gained a complete victory at the battle of Lewes on 14 May 1264, and the principle that the law is above the ruler was vindicated. Next year the patriotic party (as it may fairly be termed) was defeated at Evesham, and its great leader the Earl Simon (de Montfort) was killed. But the young Prince Edward, who commanded the royalist army, was a wiser man than his father. He did not abuse his victory, and the principles for which Earl Simon had fought and died were accepted as the foundation of the monarchy, and with it of the national life. To this the Church had made a notable contribution.

Henry's failure as a ruler concerns us less than his patronage of the arts. This was magnificent, and contributed largely to his chronic condition of financial embarrassment, which in its turn drove him to attempt oppressive and illegal methods of raising funds. He seems to have been one of the people who really have no sense of money, and never stop to consider how they propose to pay for the gratification of their desires.[2] His reign was there-fore one of great building, and the architects and masons got opportunities of showing what they could do with the new Gothic style. Almost every cathedral church received some notable additions to its fabric during this period. At Wells, to give one instance, the west front was completed[3] and adorned with its wealth of superb statuary. The cathedral church of Salisbury is the only one which was begun and completed, with the excep-tion of the spire, during this period, approximately between the years 1220 and 1270. There the Gothic style which we know

---

[1] Stephen Langton.

[2] George IV, especially when he was Regent, seems to have been another. He also was a patron of the arts.

[3] In 1239.

as Early English can be seen at its very best. It combines austerity and restraint with delicacy and grace in a way which recalls the best Greek poetry. It is not unreasonable to regard Salisbury Cathedral, as viewed from without, as the most beautiful work of man to be seen in this country. Many great buildings—e.g., the cathedrals of Durham and Lincoln, Windsor Castle and Arundel Castle,[1] owe something to a natural site. But the very site of Salisbury is the work of men's hands. When the see was removed from old Sarum the marshy ground beside the river Avon had to be drained to provide a place for the new church. Subsequently it was turfed and planted with trees. As a work of art Salisbury Cathedral is comparable with the Parthenon.[2] Both are artistic triumphs which are as they are by virtue of their perfect proportions and beauty of line. Both outstanding examples of purity of design. But the builders of the church added to their artistic equipment an inspiration of which the builders of the Parthenon knew nothing. It is perhaps true to say that it was not until the thirteenth century that the two streams of the classical and the Christian tradition were really joined. If Dante embodies both more completely than anyone else, Robert Grosseteste (Bishop of Lincoln 1235–53), whom Bishop Lightfoot once described as "possibly the greatest academic personage of all time",[3] does not lag far behind. Latterly they have tended to diverge more and more widely, and it would be hard to say which has lost most by the separation.

It is sometimes said that the architects of the great medieval churches are unknown. This is not really true. In most instances most of the names are discoverable, if not all.[4]

The "Decorated" style, which began to supersede the Early English about the year 1300, is extraordinarily rich, and has its own beauty. The Lady Chapel at Wells, the roof of which is

[1] The present castle is modern and is seen to the best advantage from a distance.

[2] The temple of Athene on the Acropolis at Athens, built in the fifth century before our era.

[3] *Historical Essays*, p. 167.

[4] See (e.g.), the report of the Royal Commission on Historical Monuments, vol. i, Introduction, pp. 5 and 6.

architecturally a *tour-de-force*, is a notable example of it. By increasing the size of the windows it gave the glass-painter more scope than he had had before. But I do not think that it can be counted an advance upon its predecessors. It seems somehow to be less spontaneous and more self-conscious. *Luxuriant* is the epithet which is suggested by its window traceries and carvings, and where luxuriance is found, decay is probably never very far off. The two styles may be compared with the schools of Pheidias and Praxiteles in the fifth and fourth centuries before our era, and opinion may perhaps differ as to their merits. In each case it may be true to say that if the later school possessed a higher degree of technical skill and a more complete mastery over their material, the earlier reveals a loftier and purer inspiration.

The most notable event in the reign of Henry III was the coming of the friars, who appeared at Oxford in the year 1224. They were the last great irruption of foreign influence[1] which we received. The words *monk* and *friar* are sometimes used as if they were interchangeable, so it is important to distinguish clearly between them. A monk was (and is) a resident member of a settled community. His duties lie there, and as a rule he has little occasion to leave the precincts of his house for any purpose. His position is not unlike that of a resident Fellow of any college in Oxford or Cambridge. The resemblance was closer a century ago, when all resident Fellows were unmarried and many of them seldom spent a night outside the college, than it is today. A friar was an itinerant preacher, whose work lay principally amongst the poor of the towns, many of whom lived in a state of squalor and overcrowding such as was bound to be a hotbed of disease. Many of the parochial clergy seem to have neglected this part of their ministry. The friars set themselves to fill the gap, and it would be difficult to praise their work too highly. They may be

---

[1] The Huguenots, who came to England in 1685 after the revocation of the Edict of Nantes by Louis XIV, were a valuable economic asset. But they were hardly sufficiently numerous to affect our national life, and they confined themselves for the most part to London and the neighbourhood. Mention should perhaps be made of the French émigrés during the revolution. They and the clergy who accompanied them, together with the Irish immigrants of the nineteenth century are the basis of the Roman Catholic Church in England today.

compared with the emissaries of the Salvation Army today, except that they were all male. The word is an Anglicized form of the French *frères*, which means *brothers*, and was applied to them because their own description of themselves was *fratres minores* (*lesser brethren*). The names *Blackfriars*, *Whitefriars*, *Crutched Friars* and (probably) *The Minories* still record their presence in London.

The original friars are known as Franciscans, because they were instituted by St Francis of Assisi, who was born about the year 1182 and died in 1226. Any account of his singularly beautiful life would be out of place here. Other orders, Carmelites, Augustinians and Dominicans, followed in due course, and members of all of them made their way to England. The fact that the first Franciscans[1] went straight to Oxford shows that its reputation stood high on the Continent, and their presence raised it to an extraordinary pinnacle. For even during the lifetime of their founder a change had come over them, which was not a matter for regret. They had come to include men of learning. The popular evangelists were producing men of the highest intellectual distinction. Three at least of the most eminent must be mentioned here.[2]

1. Alexander of Hales, who died about the year 1245, was known as *Doctor Irrefragabilis* (Who could not be confuted).

2. Roger Bacon, who was born about 1214 and died in 1294, was known as *Doctor Mirabilis* (The wonderful). He is the father of the experimental method upon which the whole study of every form of natural science depends. Few men can have affected the course of civilization more. If it is true to say that he made the discovery of the atomic bomb possible, it is only fair to add that he could not have foreseen how far his disciples would travel down the road which he had marked out for them. Naturally he was suspected of practising "unlawful arts" and was unable to publish anything until he was expressly invited to do so by Pope Clement IV (1265–8). The fact that the invitation was

---

[1] Robert Grosseteste was their first rector.
[2] For a fuller account of them see Bishop Lightfoot's *Historical Essays*, pp. 166-81.

extended shows that the Pope must have possessed a more liberal outlook intellectually than was customary, and a very high degree of moral courage. No other authority could have taken the responsibility, had it wished to do so. As soon as Bacon had got his opportunity he produced three large books in the course of eighteen months. As a feat of industry it is difficult to imagine that this achievement has ever been surpassed.

3. Duns Scotus was born probably about the year 1265 and died about 1305.[1] His nationality is uncertain, but as by this time *Scotus* had ceased to mean Irish and had acquired modern significance, it is reasonable to conjecture that he came from across the Border. If so, his first name may point to the little town of Duns, which is now the capital of Berwickshire, as his native place. He was known as the *Doctor Subtilis* (The Subtle).

A fourth name should perhaps be added to the list: that of William of Ockham. But as he seems to have been born about the year 1280, and to have died about the year 1349, he really belongs to a later period.

These men are the principal English representatives of the Schoolmen, of whom the greatest is perhaps St Thomas Aquinas[2]. The Schoolmen were the leading theologians and philosophers of their day, and did a great deal towards moulding the thought of the medieval Church. Of late years a considerable amount of attention has been directed to them in the Roman Church, and to a lesser extent in the Church of England. It is difficult to assess the value of their work as a whole. As an example of clear and acute thinking and of logical reasoning it would not be easy to find anything which can be ranked above it. As a mental gymnastic, the writings of the Schoolmen are undoubtedly a profitable study.

The real value of their conclusions is, however, another matter. Their horizon was necessarily narrow. They knew little history, and their only contact with the philosophy of ancient Greece was through the medium of translations of Aristotle. At best he only represents half of what the Greek thinkers have to teach us. Their

---

[1] Both these dates seem to be uncertain.
[2] Born 1227, died 1274.

attitude towards Scripture was entirely "uncritical"—that is to say, they knew nothing of the dates at which any of the books which it contains were written, or of the background of their authors. Besides this, they worked within the axiom *constat quod ipsa ecclesia non errat* (it is acknowledged that the Church[1] itself does not make mistakes), and for them *ipsa ecclesia* meant that part of the Church which acknowledges the unlimited supremacy of the Bishop of Rome, and is recognized by him. This principle meant that any belief or practice which had established itself in the Church and had received the sanction of the Papacy was not really open to adverse criticism. However strange it might appear, it must be capable of complete theoretical justification. This attitude, which was destined to lead to very undesirable results,[2] is disavowed expressly by the Church of England in Articles XIX (*Of the Church*), XX (*Of the Authority of the Church*), XXI (*Of the Authority of General Councils*) and XXII (*Of Purgatory*).

The Schoolmen have been likened to men who, being desirous to construct a great city, found that the area of land available for their purpose was rigidly limited. Because they could not expand superficially, they were compelled to raise their buildings to fantastic and disproportionate heights. This task they discharged with amazing skill. This comparison seems to me to be neither inapt nor unjust. I have never seen the towering structures on Manhattan island, and must therefore speak of them with reserve. But I imagine that while they must command admiration as triumphs of engineering skill, they can hardly be regarded as architecture. They are the product of a particular set of local conditions, and it is unlikely that anyone would want to reproduce them anywhere else. No town-planner of today would take them as his model.

Mention has been made above of Stephen Langton and Robert Grosseteste. A third outstanding ecclesiastic during the reign of Henry III is Edmund Rich, who was Archbishop of Canterbury from 1234 to 1240. Within a week of his consecration he remonstrated in very plain terms with the young king on his misgovern-

---

[1] As distinct from any part of it, which might fall into error temporarily.
[2] See Chapter 7, "Indulgences and Dispensations."

ment; apparently with some effect, at any rate for a time. Three
years later he protested solemnly against the admission of the
Cardinal Otho into the kingdom without the knowledge and
consent of the bishops and nobles. The cardinal had been despatched by Pope Gregory IX, ostensibly to carry out various
reforms in the Church, in accordance with decisions which had
been reached at the fourth Lateran Council in the year 1215.
Some of them may have been needed. The real objects of his
mission were, however, financial. The Archbishop's attempts to
resist his demands proved ineffectual, and he retired to Pontigny,
where he died after a few months. He was canonized a few years
after his death as St Edmund of Abingdon, being the first graduate
of the University of Oxford, and the last Archbishop of Canterbury, to receive the distinction. The fifteenth-century chantry
chapel on the south side of the nave of Wells Cathedral has been
said to be dedicated to him. I think it more probable that the
St Edmund in question is the East Anglian king who was done to
death by the Danes in the year 870, because the sculptures on the
east side of the north porch of the church represent scenes from
the story of his martyrdom. His name appears in the Prayer Book
under date 20 November. The later St Edmund is not included
in our calendar.

When Edward I ascended the throne in 1272 he came to reign
over a nation united as it had not been for more than two
centuries. By the last quarter of the thirteenth century the
Norman and Saxon elements had coalesced. No doubt there
were families who took pride in the purity of their descent from
either stock, as there may be now. But, whatever their line, they
were now English first and Saxon or Norman afterwards. By this
time, too, the friars had ceased to be foreigners. The great
majority of them, at any rate, were English born.

Besides this, the constitutional question had been settled, at
any rate for a time. The king must govern in accordance with
known laws, which must be made with the consent of the leaders
in the Church and State and could not be set aside at will. This
situation was entirely congenial to Edward I. One of the tasks
which he set himself was to base the national life on a coherent

legal system which should amount to more than codified custom
and common sense. In this he was largely successful. His two best-
known statutes, *Quia emptores* and *De donis conditionalibus*, are
still the foundation of our law of real property.

The Crown still had important possessions in France, which it
is not unlikely he hoped to extend. But he saw that engagements
or commitments on the Continent might become a source of
danger unless our flank and rear were secure. His first act was the
conquest of Wales. This was completed in 1283. The last armed
resistance on the part of the Welsh was in the mountainous region
of which Snowdon is the centre, and the castles which Edward
built in that district show how firm was the hold which he laid
upon the land. Conway and Carnarvon are the two most notable.
The Principality was annexed to the Crown of England in perpetuity, and has furnished the title borne by the heir-apparent to
the English throne ever since.

Three years later the affairs of Scotland acquired a sudden
prominence.

In 1296 Alexander III, who had married Margaret, a sister of
Edward, died. He left no descendants except a grand-daughter,
also named Margaret, whose father was Eric Magnusson, King of
Norway. Edward proposed that she should marry his eldest son.
This would have brought about the permanent union of the two
Crowns, and would have been in the best interest of both countries. Three hundred years of border warfare would have been
avoided, and Scotland would have escaped the fearful carnage of
Flodden,[1] which is perhaps not quite forgotten yet in the border
country. On our side, we might have avoided the civil war
and the sixty years of Jacobite intrigue which came to an end at
Culloden. But the little princess, who was not ten years old, died
on her way from Norway to Scotland. After this disaster a number
of claimants to the Scottish throne appeared, of whom three
deserved to be taken seriously. Edward asserted his right to
decide the question, relying perhaps partly on the claim made

---

[1] 9 September 1513. For a graphic if imaginative picture of what that battle
meant to Scotland, see "Edinburgh after Flodden" in Aytoun's *Lays of the
Scottish Cavaliers.*

by Athelstan in the tenth century, but probably more on his superior strength, and eventually appointed John Balliol, Lord of Galloway and grandson of the eldest daughter of David, Earl of Huntingdon, a brother of William the Lion. On 26 December 1292 Balliol did homage to Edward for his kingdom, thereby acknowledging the English sovereign as his overlord. The arrangement was an uneasy one, and was hardly concluded before the Scots began to resent it. They formed a treaty with France, which as a vassal kingdom they had no power to do.

In 1296 Edward was compelled to invade the country. He gained a complete victory at Dunbar, and removed from Scone the stone on which the Scottish kings were wont to be crowned. The kings of England have been crowned upon it ever since, and I believe that it has never left Westminster Abbey except during the war of 1939–45, when it was removed for safety to a secret place; known now to have been the crypt of Gloucester Cathedral. On 2 July Balliol made an irrevocable resignation of his crown to Edward, and the union of the kingdoms appeared to be an accomplished fact. It was, however, never very secure. Edward's difficulties were much the same as those with which the Romans had met a thousand years before. The defeat of Edward II, who was an entirely unworthy successor to his father, at Bannockburn on 24 June 1314 brought it to an end.

I have called your attention to this episode because it was not a mere act of aggression on the part of Edward I. It was a piece of real statesmanship. He realized, what must be apparent to anyone who looks at the map, that nature has ordained that Great Britain at least shall be a political unit. That does not mean that racial and local characteristics ought to be ignored, or that they need disappear, but that every part of the island must recognize that it cannot look for any future except in the closest and fullest partnership with the rest. Probably the southern Irish will find that the same inexorable law applies to all the British Isles.

Edward I was in advance of his age, and therefore he just failed. He died at Burgh-on-Sands, near Carlisle, in 1307, as he was about to invade Scotland for the second time. Almost his last act was to pass the Statute of Carlisle, which forbade alien priories (daughter houses of continental abbeys) to pay the customary tribute to their mother houses, as that tended to drain the country of the gold and silver which he required for his wars. He was buried in the Confessors' chapel at Westminster, and his very plain tomb bears the words *Scotorum Malleus* (Hammer of the Scots), and *Pactum serva* (Keep troth), which is perhaps a later addition.

The most notable ecclesiastic of the reign was John Peckham, who was Archbishop of Canterbury from 1279 to 1292. He made great efforts to carry out some of the reforms which had been recommended by the fourth Lateran Council, chiefly in relation to pluralities (the holding of a number of benefices by one man) and non-residence. But he found himself unable to accomplish very much. The thirteenth century was a period of great brilliance and of solid achievement. But as time went on two ominous factors began to make themselves felt more and more. Both were economic. The first was the increasing financial demands of the Papacy, of which more will be said in a subsequent chapter; the second, the practice of appointing bishops and other ecclesiastics to offices of State. This meant that the revenues of the Church were used to save those of the Exchequer and that bishoprics and other offices in the Church were filled by men who were intended to devote most of their time and energy to purely secular affairs. If no one saw whereunto these things would grow, the harm which they were doing could not be ignored.

Besides this, the universities were beginning to provide new centres of learning and education, which might prove to be a serious challenge to the almost immemorial supremacy of the monasteries.

As the year 1300 approached it was clear that the stage was being set for far-reaching changes. They were precipitated with startling suddenness when in 1303 the partisans of Philip IV of France laid violent hands on the person of Boniface VIII at Anagni. This was a blow to the prestige of the Papacy from which it never really recovered, and the entire fabric of medieval Christendom was shaken.

6

The papal power, from the accession of Gregory VII to the death of Boniface VIII—1073–1303

IT is impossible to understand the medieval Church without reference to the Papacy. That was the hub round which the religious and political system of medieval Europe revolved. It will therefore be appropriate at this point to attempt a brief sketch of the growth of the papal power.

It is not a matter of historical interest only. It is an immediate and pressing question today. For every point at issue between the Church of England and the Church of Rome leads ultimately to this fundamental question, What is the position of the Bishop of Rome in the Church?

No one can deny that he is the first of all bishops. Primate of Christendom, if we like so to say. It is impossible to consider translating him to any other see. Even an Archbishop of Canterbury can, or could, be translated. That has happened at least twice in the past. Robert Kilwardby, who became archbishop in 1273, was translated five years later to the cardinal-bishopric[1] of Porto; and in the next century Simon Langham, who had become archbishop in 1366, resigned his see in 1368 on being created a cardinal, and six years later was appointed cardinal-bishop of Palestrina.

Everyone would be ready to concede to the Bishop of Rome the kind of primacy in the whole Church which the Archbishop of Canterbury has today in the Anglican Communion. But the Roman Catholic claim goes far beyond that. It declares that the Pope is the absolute head of the whole Church, and the only

[1] See note on *The Sacred College* at the end of this chapter.

source of all spiritual authority and jurisdiction. He is the Vicar
of Christ on earth, so that to impugn his authority in any way is to
impugn the authority of our Lord himself. From this it follows
that any doctrine or practice which has received papal sanction is
outside the sphere of discussion. The only Christian course in
relation to the Pope is absolute, unquestioning submission. This
tremendous claim is based primarily on two well-known passages
in the Gospel:

1. "And I say also unto thee, That thou art Peter, and upon
this rock I will build my church; and the gates of hell shall not
prevail against it. And I will give unto thee the keys of the kingdom of heaven: and whatsoever thou shalt bind on earth shall be
bound in heaven: and whatsoever thou shalt loose on earth shall
be loosed in heaven" (Matt. 16. 18–19).

2. "Feed my lambs . . . feed my sheep . . feed my sheep"
(John 21. 15–17).

Here, it is said, we have a direct commission, given by our
Lord himself to St Peter and to his successors for all time, who
are the Bishops of Rome. He and they are divinely ordained to be
the supreme and only head of the Church on earth for as long as
this world shall last. But this interpretation of the words is
certainly not beyond question even in relation to the apostle.
St Paul saw no reason why he should not oppose him when he
believed him to be mistaken (Gal. 2. 11–16), and in Acts 15
St James presides over a meeting before which St Peter appears,
and pronounces the decision which has been reached. Besides
this, no one can pretend that the Gospel contains any reference
to any successors of St Peter, nor any hint as to the place where
they would be found.

It would certainly be convenient, in many respects, and up to
a point perhaps highly desirable (according to our ideas), if our
Lord had given some definite constitution of this kind to his
Church. If he had appointed one supreme visible head for all
time, divinely equipped to deal rightly with every question which
could arise, many difficulties and much confusion might have
been avoided. My own criticism of that theory is primarily that it
is a little too convenient. I believe that God has taught us that he

does not work in that kind of way. He does not create institutions, but reveals principles; and we have then to frame the institutions which we think best to secure their preservation and promote their effectiveness, according to our ability. But once an institution of any kind has established itself, it is seldom difficult for those who find it most convenient to adduce some text of Scripture which can be pressed into its service, and used to drape it with the inviolable mantle of direct, divine sanction.[1] The Papacy was, and is, a tremendous fact. It is, to say the least, one of the greatest institutions which the world has ever seen.

But to say that does not amount to conceding all that it claims for itself. If it is possible to show that the papal power waxed gradually, and that a number of intelligible factors of various kinds contributed to its growth, then we can envisage it as something which is to be judged by its fruits, and may hope to arrive at a conception of its origin and nature which we may fairly regard as more trustworthy than any which depends upon a questionable interpretation of a few passages of the New Testament isolated from their context.

Regarded as a religious society, without reference to the facts which brought it into being, the Christian Church is unique. From its earliest days it aimed at becoming world-wide, and yet at remaining essentially one. Both these ideas are inherent in its nature, but both were new to the world into which Christianity was born. Pagan religion was national, or racial, and local. A pagan saw no more reason for trying to persuade a member of another race to change his native religion than for trying to persuade him to substitute another language for his native tongue. Divinities were many, and different rites were proper to different shrines, which were also many, even when the Being to whom the worship was offered was nominally the same. A missionary religion which aimed at unlimited conversions whilst preserving its identity unimpaired and recognizable was an undreamed-of phenomenon. If Judaism must be regarded as a partial exception to this statement, it was always primarily racial, and was not particularly anxious to make converts. Proselytes could be

[1] This was true even of negro slavery.

admitted, but they were not very numerous and could never rank with the true seed of Abraham. What are known as the mystery-religions were semi-private cults which went on side by side with the official religion approved by the State, whatever form it took. On the whole, public opinion was against them, chiefly because they were secret, and in all probability they never numbered many adherents outside Greece, Asia Minor and Egypt.

In its early days Christianity spread rapidly, and by the end of the second century had come near to covering the Roman empire—that is to say, there were places in almost all parts of the empire where some Christians were to be found, if they were not more than a tiny minority of the whole population. Therefore local differences, due to race, circumstances and so forth, were bound to creep into the worship of these little scattered Churches. It was impossible to exclude them altogether, and it would have been undesirable to try. But it was very important that they should not be carried too far, as might easily be done through inadvertence and ignorance of the ways of other Christian communities. Accordingly the need was soon felt for something of the nature of a universal referee: not an autocratic head, but someone who could be consulted in any difficulty and trusted to give good advice. (On a smaller scale the relation of a bishop to the parishes in his diocese is similar. One very important function of the episcopate is to preserve the unity of the Church.)

If anything resembling a universal referee is to exist he must satisfy certain conditions, which may be enumerated briefly as follows.

1. He must be readily accessible to those who may wish to consult him personally. This condition works both ways, as it means that he can keep himself better informed than would be possible if he lived in some remote spot to which few visitors were likely to penetrate. He must have more than local knowledge and a more than local outlook.

2. Since his qualification cannot be purely personal, because that would involve looking for a new referee at comparatively short intervals, he must occupy some position of recognized importance. This will in itself command respect and lend weight

to his utterances, and the more important the position the more likely is a man of more than ordinary capacity to be found in occupation of it. In other words, for the purposes of the Church he must be bishop of some outstanding see.

When the Christian world meant the Mediterranean world, as it did for the first six hundred years of the Church's existence, a glance at the map will show that there were only four places where these conditions could be satisfied. First Rome, secondly Alexandria, thirdly Antioch, fourthly Carthage. In the fourth century a fifth must be added in Constantinople, the new city on the Bosphorus which Constantine built to take the place of Rome as the capital of the empire and called by his own name. It was consecrated solemnly as a Christian as well as an imperial city in the year 330.

It will be worth while to say a little about each of these places in turn.

Rome was the capital of the world. In pagan eyes a supernatural *aura* hung about the imperial city, and this reverence found expression in the cult of *dea Roma* (the goddess Rome), and in the payment of divine honours to the emperor, who was the embodiment of all the power and glory of the city. At first these were not rendered until after his death, but after A.D. 81 they became customary during his lifetime, in the provinces, if not in Italy, or at Rome itself. Christians could make no terms with these practices, but they cannot have been insensible to the splendour and greatness of Rome.[1] Besides, there was for them the immense additional interest and prestige derived from the connexion of the Roman Church with St Peter and St Paul. If St Peter's presence at Rome is traditional only, there is no adequate reason for disputing the tradition, even if he were never Bishop of Rome, as we should understand the phrase. It is more than probable that both apostles are buried at Rome, whether the position of their graves is known or not. From the very beginning a Bishop of Rome was bound to be an exceptionally important personage in the Church.

The situation of Rome was perfect as long as the Roman

---

[1] E.g., "I must also see Rome" (Acts 19. 11).

territory did not extend beyond Italy. For the capital of a Mediterranean empire it was not quite so good. Foreign visitors who came by land could enter Italy only at its northern extremity, and then had to make a journey of some seven days at least down the peninsula to reach the capital. If they came by sea there was no good harbour within a hundred miles on either coast. Ostia, at the mouth of the Tiber, could never take anything much larger than a fishing boat, and the river is too rapid to be navigable. The ship in which St Paul made the last stage of his journey was probably a corn ship whose cargo was intended for the capital. It must have been of considerable size, and it put in at Puteoli (near the modern Naples), a hundred miles or thereabouts to the south. These considerations, which were also important strategically, are probably responsible, at any rate in part, for Constantine's decision to move the seat of government from Rome to the entrance to the Black Sea, in the fourth century. Mediolanum, the modern Milan, then became the administrative capital of the West, because it was on the great Via Aemilia, which ran from east to west and crossed the northern plains of Italy, almost skirting the foothills of the Alps. Politically Rome became a provincial town.

Alexandria had no great history. If there was a fishing village at the Canopic mouth of the Nile there was nothing more until, in or about the year 332 B.C., Alexander the Great came that way and perceived the possibilities of the site. The city which he founded and called by his own name was an immediate success. It became the capital of the Greek kingdom of Egypt, and Egypt was the chief granary of the Mediterranean world. The Nile gave it direct and easy communication with regions far to the southward, and its harbour enabled it to become the commercial clearing-house of three continents. In population it stood second only to Rome, and it was also a famous seat of learning. Tradition ascribed the foundation of its church to St Mark, a statement which is not inconceivable, if it does not admit of proof. The bishop of such a city was necessarily an outstanding figure.

The history of Carthage is different. It began as a Phœnician colony. In the ninth century before our era, a hundred years before the traditional date of the foundation of Rome, Phœnician seamen, feeling their way cautiously westwards along the forbidding and dangerous southern shore of the Mediterranean, came upon a good natural harbour at the north-eastern corner of what we call Tunisia, immediately to the west of the Cape Bon peninsula, where the German forces capitulated on 12 May 1943.

As has happened more than once in our own history, the trading port became the capital of an empire, which at one time stretched from Cyrenaica to the Straits of Gibraltar, and included the islands of Sicily and Sardinia and a large part of Spain. The name of the city of Cartagena, which the Romans knew as *New Carthage*, records its Phœnician origin. Three wars were fought between Rome and Carthage for the mastery of the western Mediterranean. We know enough of the Phœnicians and their ways to have good reason to be thankful that the Romans were finally victorious. In the year 146 B.C. Carthage was taken and destroyed. For about a century it lay derelict, but the harbour was too good to be abandoned,[1] and a little before the beginning of our era the name was perpetuated by a Roman colony upon the old site. This became the capital of Roman Africa (which meant what we know as Tunisia today) and by the second century was one of the most important places in the empire. No one knows how or when Christianity came to Roman Africa, but by the year 180 Carthage was the headquarters of a flourishing Church, which produced a succession of great writers, culminating in St Augustine (354–428). Africa was the first place in which Latin was used for Christian purposes. Until after the middle of the second century the language of the Church was Greek, even at Rome.

Antioch had been selected as a capital by the Greek (Seleucid) kings of Syria and the territories adjoining. They spent a great deal on making it magnificent, but it was always a somewhat artificial creation for political purposes, as Washington, Ottawa, Canberra and perhaps Madrid are today. It had a harbour, but

---

[1] It appears to be out of use now, possibly because it is too shallow for modern ships. But it seems to have been important as late as the fourteenth century, as Chaucer says of his Shipman, "There was none such from Hull unto Carthage" (*Canterbury Tales*, Prologue, 406).

its position at the extreme eastern end of the Mediterranean was too remote, and it was not very readily accessible by land. Much of its hinterland was mountainous and barren. Its prominence in the earliest days of Christianity made the see an exceptionally honourable one, and in later days it was a seat of Christian learning, if not quite the equal of Alexandria. Early in the second century it produced a very famous martyr in St Ignatius, whose letters written on his way to Rome to be thrown to the wild beasts in the amphitheatre are of exceptional interest and importance. But, despite its prestige, the see of Antioch never counted for as much as those of Rome, Alexandria or Carthage. By the middle of the third century each of these three was recognized as pre-eminent. Such titles as Metropolitan, Patriarch, Primate and Archbishop had not yet come into use, but the bishops of Rome, Alexandria and Carthage are by that time exercising what might be called primatial functions over considerable areas. If the title *Pope*[1] might be applied equally to any of them, the Bishop of Alexandria might perhaps have been considered to have the strongest claim to it.

In the fourth century a new Christian centre appeared when Constantine built the city upon the Bosphorus which bears his name, and made it his capital. There had been an old Greek trading port called Byzantium on the site for many centuries. It had been destroyed in A.D. 196 by the Emperor Severus, as a punishment for having supported an unsuccessful rival claimant to the throne. But, as with Carthage, the site was too valuable to be thrown away. Perhaps there is no place in the world better fitted by nature to be a supranational capital; certainly none when the world meant the Mediterranean countries. From its superb harbour there was direct access to the Mediterranean in one direction and the Black Sea in the other. On the northern shore

---

[1] *Pope* (*Papa*) is really the equivalent of *Daddy*. It appears first in the writings of Tertullian (*De Pudicitia*, xiii). He applied it almost comtemptuously to Callistus of Rome (219–23), whose pretensions seemed to him excessive. In the next century it became a respectful form of address to bishops in general. Ennodius of Pavia seems to be the first person to use it distinctively of the Bishop of Rome, early in the sixth century. It is the title usually given to any parish priest in the Eastern Church today.

of the Black Sea lay the fertile plains of southern Russia, which were then as now one of the great granaries of Europe, and the rivers which flow across them were the highways by which Byzantine Christianity and civilization were in due course brought to the Tartar tribes of the interior. Nearer at hand there was access to the mouth of the Danube, which has always been the great thoroughfare of central Europe. Besides all this, at the Bosphorus Europe and Asia meet. Any city planted there must necessarily be of the first rank. The see of Constantinople was barely fifty years old when it was formally given precedence next after that of Rome, "because Constantinople is New Rome."[1] To this day the Bishop takes the title of Œcumenical Patriarch, which means *Patriarch of the whole world*. His claims are really as far-reaching as those of the Pope of Rome, though they are not based on any title to divine or even apostolic authority. They have been pressed by similar methods and have met with about the same measure of success and failure.

About the year 350, or a little later, Ausonius of Burdigala (Bordeaux) wrote a set of verses which he called *A List of Famous Cities* (*Ordo Nobilium Urbium*). Inevitably he begins with Rome, to which, however, he assigns only a single rather perfunctory line. Constantinople comes next, as the imperial capital, but Carthage is bracketed with it. Antioch and Alexandria follow, also bracketed together. Ausonius was nominally a Christian, though he calls Rome "Home of gods" (*Divum domus*), but he was not writing from the Christian standpoint. His interest in the cities (sixteen in all) which he commemorates is determined by their natural amenities, their wealth, their beauty and their history. But it is worth noting that the five outstanding Christian bishoprics were at the five places which head his list.

If the primacy of Rome could hardly be challenged seriously, even by Alexandria, during the second and third centuries, soon after the beginning of the fourth the course of events, ecclesiastical and political, enhanced the pre-eminence of the see to a remarkable extent.

About the year 311 a dispute broke out concerning the Person

[1] By Canon III of the first Council of Constantinople in the year 381.

of Christ, which extended afterwards to the Person of the Holy
Spirit. It is known as *Arianism*, because it originated with a man
named Arius, who was one of the clergy of Alexandria. It would
be out of place to go into details here. It will be enough to say that
Arius' opinions destroyed the doctrines of the Incarnation and
the Trinity alike, whether his adherents realized this or not.
Arianism spread rapidly, partly because it appeared to be simpler
than the orthodox Christian teaching (as indeed it was), and therefore commended itself to the common sense of the plain man,
which, while invaluable in the jury-box, is, beyond a certain
point which is soon reached, an extremely untrustworthy guide.
Councils and synods were held in the hope of bringing the dispute
to an end, but did not meet with much success. The two best
known are those of Nicæa (near the modern Turkish capital of
Ankhara) in 325 and Constantinople (381–3), which between
them gave us the "Nicene" creed which we use today. The West
was much less troubled than the East, partly perhaps because
Greek was now little used west of the Adriatic, and Latin does
not lend itself so readily to theological discussions of this kind.
As the weary business dragged on men began to look more and
more to the great apostolic see of the West, whose occupant was
more likely than anyone else to be able to bring it to an end,
because he had his head far enough out of the smoke to see how
the battle was going, and had not committed himself to either
side. But no exceptional rights or powers were attributed to
him until the year 347, when the Council of Sardica, which was
predominantly Western, gave Julius I the right to hear appeals
from any bishop who had been condemned for his opinions
elsewhere. This was a wise provision, because local synods might
be "packed" or terrorized, either by ecclesiastical or civil
authority, and the issues at stake were too important to be left
entirely in local hands. It strengthened the hands of the Pope,
as he may now be called, enormously, and he used his position
well. One very important aspect of the resolution passed by the
Council is, however, often overlooked. It is quite clear that the
members did not consider that he had any such right, whether
by long custom or in virtue of his see, still less as a direct gift

from our Lord through St Peter. To offer to anyone a right which he already possesses would cover the donors with ridicule, and possibly evoke a sharp reply from the recipient. What would be the position of any ecclesiastical assemblage in the province of Canterbury today if it solemnly declared that the archbishop is entitled to hear an appeal against any decision which it, or any similar body elsewhere, might reach?

Eventually in the year 451 the Council of Chalcedon[1] was thankful to receive a letter from Pope Leo I containing a phrase (*Two natures in one Person*) which everyone was prepared to accept, to bring the matter to an end. The formula still stands, and has proved workable, if by no means free from difficulty.

After Constantine created his new capital no emperor ever lived permanently in Rome again. Many never saw it. This meant that the bishop was the most important personage in the city.

Shortly before the Council of Chalcedon was held the Vandals overran North Africa. Roman civilization was swept away, and Christianity went with it. The see of Carthage was destroyed, and the only possible rival to the Pope in the West disappeared.

In the year 476 the western empire fell, and Odovakar the Herulian made himself King of Italy. This left the Pope as the most important figure, as well as the largest land-owner and richest man, in the whole peninsula. In the course of the next century Italy was recovered for the empire by a campaign not unlike that of 1943–4, and an exarch (imperial governor) was placed at Ravenna. But as he represented the jurisdiction of the Greek emperor at Constantinople he was always unpopular and of little account in Italy. Almost inevitably the Papacy became more and more the focus of Italian national feeling.

Gregory I (590–604), who probably deserves the title *Great* as well as anyone upon whom history has bestowed it, came to the throne at a time of great distress. Rome was stricken with famine and pestilence, and hard pressed by the Lombard armies. He rose to the occasion in a way which it would be difficult to praise too highly, and made the Papacy the avowed and indisputable centre for whatever of spirit or energy was left in Italy.

[1] On the Asiatic shore of the Bosphorus.

Even Gibbon is constrained to admit that he "might justly be styled the Father of his country."[1] To his outstanding capacity as a national leader he added the wisdom, charity and missionary zeal which become a bishop, and the great tradition which he established was maintained by his successors during the next century.[2]

Before the seventh century had run its course the Mohammedan invasions had destroyed the apostolic sees of Antioch and Jerusalem, and had reduced Alexandria to a shadow. Three of Ausonius' five greatest cities were lost to the Church, and the position of Constantinople was none too secure. It was besieged twice, once by Persians, and from 668 to 675 by the Moslems. Nearly eight hundred years were to pass before the final catastrophe, but it is not too much to say that during the whole of that period the eastern empire was more or less in the position of a beleaguered fortress, for which there was little hope of relief.

The Emperor Leo III, who reigned from 718 to 741, recognized that he would have to fight Islam with the sword of the Spirit as well as with the arm of the flesh, and to that end set himself to reform the Church. He is commonly known as the *Isaurian*[3]; whether that description of his origin is correct or not, he was not a Greek by birth, and appears to have been what we should call a Puritan. In his eyes the lavish use of statuary in churches had made Christianity at least semi-idolatrous in practice, and there-fore no match for the pure and virile monotheism of Islam, which no doubt appealed strongly to a man of his temperament. A better case can be made out for the use of images as aids to worship than the Jews were prepared to admit.[4] But experience shows that what is intended to symbolize a divine reality is always in danger of being confused with the reality which it represents, at best imperfectly. Accordingly Leo decided that the churches must be cleansed from such things, and the word *iconoclast*

[1] *Decline and Fall*, vol. v, p. 38.

[2] For our direct debt to him and his successors see Chapter 3, p. 38.

[3] From the mountainous country lying to the north-west of the Adriatic Sea whence he was believed to have sprung.

[4] E.g., Ps. 115.

(*breaker of images*) was applied to him in consequence. Naturally he provoked a storm of resistance, and was compelled to act with an extreme degree of violence. Where he could exert his own immediate authority he was eventually fairly successful. To this day the Eastern Churches eschew sculpture and make use of sacred pictures (*icons*) instead. In the West it was otherwise. Perhaps the abuse—for it cannot be denied that there was real abuse—was less flagrant and the Moslem peril was certainly less imminent. The Pope headed the resistance. The exarch at Ravenna was besieged in his palace and barely escaped with his life. The emperor was defeated, and Gregory II (726–31) found himself undisputed master of Rome.

His successors strengthened their position by an alliance with the Frankish kingdom, which was now rising into prominence, and when the western empire was restored (if not in much more than name) Leo III placed the imperial crown on the head of Charles the Great in St Peter's on Christmas Day in the year 800. This ceremony may be compared with the coronation of our sovereign. The first bishop of the Church to which the new ruler belongs recognizes solemnly a right which does not derive from him, and consecrates the lawful holder for the duties of his great office.

But Charles's successors were weak and Leo's were strong. Seventy-five years later Charles the Bald received his crown from the hands of John VIII, not as his right but as a papal gift. In the interval Leo IV (847–53) had fortified what has been called the Leonine City in consequence ever since. This is virtually identical with the Vatican City of today. It is roughly a triangle, on the western side of the Tiber, which at that particular point runs from north to south, containing a little more than a hundred acres. The ground rises from the river sufficiently to be counted as a hill in Rome, and this eminence was called *Mons Vaticanus*. The origin of the name seems to be unknown. At the end of the first century it was covered with vineyards whose wine was not of the best quality.[1] Probably the fact that it was not already occupied by buildings had led to its selection at a later period as a site

---

[1] Martial, vi. 92.

for the basilica of St Peter and a papal residence adjoining the church.

About the year 850 some important documents saw the light. the first is called the *Donation of Constantine* and purports to be a deed of gift, by which the emperor when he quitted Rome for good made the city over to the Pope (Sylvester) and his successors for ever. The other is a group of papers known as the *Decretals*. These purport to be a collection of letters and decrees of early Councils exalting the episcopal office, but subjecting all bishops everywhere immediately and absolutely to the Pope.[1] The authority of Isidore, who had been Bishop of Seville rather more than two hundred years before, was claimed for them. All these are forgeries, and no one takes them seriously now. But they proved extremely useful, as they enabled Nicholas I (858–67) to establish what may be called an absolute monarchy over the clergy.

In considering the moral aspect of this proceeding we must look at it from the standpoint of the ninth century and not from our own. The people who produced the *Donation* and *Decretals* knew perfectly well that they were not what they professed to be. But by this time the bishop of Rome had acquired a unique and very powerful position. No one knew anything of the steps by which it had been reached, nor of the various factors which had contributed to make it possible. So great a *fait accompli* must, it seemed, have received some high and irrefragable legal sanction, as otherwise it could never have come into existence. If the documents which must have existed could not be found now, it was advisable to reconstruct them to put the papal power, as it then stood, upon a secure legal foundation and guarantee its permanence. It is, after all, only fair to say that a large part of legal practice does consist in the recognition and codifying of existing customs, however such customs may have originated. In the middle of the ninth century the whole position of Christendom was precarious,[2] and religion and civilization were both at a

---

[1] In the Roman Church today this has been carried so far that every bishop has to apply to the Pope for a "renewal of faculties" every three years.

[2] See Chapter 4, pp. 65 ff.

low ebb within it. A strong central government, which indeed could hardly be too strong, was certainly in the interest of the Church: it might not be too much to say essential if the Church were not to decay beyond hope of recovery. The Papacy did in fact provide such a government, and there was no possible substitute for it. It followed therefore that anything which could promote the strength and stability of the Papacy was to be welcomed. The obvious method, and the one which would commend itself most to the general ideas of the time, was to provide the definite legal basis, of which all record had unfortunately disappeared. Unfortunately, however, experience has shown repeatedly that there is at least a large measure of truth in Lord Acton's *dictum*, "Power tends to corrupt, and absolute power corrupts absolutely."[1]

The next great step forward was taken by Gregory VII (1073–85). By this time the dark age was passing. The general position of Christendom was much more secure. A new civilization was taking shape in Western Europe, which, if it could hardly be said to be built upon the ruins of the Roman empire, was able to make some use of Roman materials.

Gregory declared that the temporal power (as being ultimately of the devil) must always and everywhere be entirely subordinate to the spiritual. The Pope ranked far above any temporal ruler, and had the right at any time to absolve the subjects of a wicked prince from their allegiance. His purpose was lofty, inasmuch as he aimed at securing that all authority of every kind should be exercised strictly in accordance with Christian principles. But he inaugurated a struggle for *political* supremacy between ecclesiastical and civil authority which has never done any good to either, and is not quite at an end in Europe yet.

He was an ardent reformer, but the abuses which he attacked proved too much even for his strength, energy and courage. On his death-bed he is said to have exclaimed, "I have loved righteousness and hated iniquity[2]—and therefore I die in exile." If he did, it was not far from the truth.

---

[1] *Historical Essays and Studies*, p. 504.   [2] Cf. Ps. 45. 7.

During the next century his great claims were to a very large extent realized by his successors. They were brought to fruition by Innocent III (1198–1216), who is probably to be regarded as one of the most remarkable men and the most eminent lawyer who has ever occupied a throne anywhere. He dictated successfully to England, France and Germany, and his letters show that he bestowed an almost incredible amount of attention upon minutiæ of various kinds. In them he appears as virtually director-general of the affairs of Europe. His position was further strengthened by the rise of the mendicant friars. They were immediately and directly under him, and thus amounted to a papal militia, which went everywhere and commanded the respect and admiration which it deserved.[1] Innocent founded the States of the Church—that is to say, he transformed the lands belonging to the see of Rome into an independent Principality.

No doubt he felt that he needed a secure territorial basis, partly to ensure that he would always be able to feed Rome, and perhaps ultimately with the idea of freeing the whole Italian peninsula from foreign domination and uniting it[2] under himself. The immediate effect was to turn the Pope into an Italian prince, who did not differ conspicuously from his secular compeers. He possessed certain advantages over them in that he enjoyed a unique moral prestige, and was not dependent upon his principality for the whole of his revenue. Besides, he was in the nature of things never youthful and inexperienced, and was probably always better informed about foreign affairs generally than anyone else in Europe.[3] In diplomacy he was likely to be more than a match for any opponent. He was also never averse from disguising the real character of his projects by claiming the highest moral sanction for them. Inevitably the Papacy became more and more secularized as time went on.

[1] See Chapter 5, pp. 88 ff.
[2] This was not achieved until 20 September 1870, when Victor Emmanuel led his troops into Rome, in spite of all the Pope could do to keep him out. Seventy-five years have seen the end of the House of Savoy, and have left room for doubt whether United Italy has been of sufficient benefit, either to the Italians or to the world at large, to justify the continuance of the experiment.
[3] This is probably still true.

A sovereign prince has to meet expenses beyond those which ordinarily fall upon a large land-owner. Innocent IV (1243–54) put the finances of the Church upon a sound business footing, at the cost of lowering the moral prestige of the Papacy. At the Council of Lyons in 1250 Robert Grosseteste, Bishop of Lincoln, preached a sermon before the Pope in which he attacked the abuses to which the financial demands of the Papacy gave rise. He did not attack the authority of the Pope—in his eyes that was sacred and unassailable—but what was done on his behalf and in his name. If abuses are manifestly flagrant and continue unchecked it is almost certain that a time will come when the whole nature of the authority under whose ægis they flourish and abound will be called in question.

Papal claims were carried to their zenith by Boniface VIII (1294–1303), who applied to himself the words of Jeremiah 1. 10: See, I have this day set thee over the nations and over the kingdoms, to pluck up and to break down, and to destroy and to overthrow; to build, and to plant. (They appear also in the Bull of Pius V excommunicating Elizabeth in 1570.)

In the year 1296 he published a bull (*clericis laicos*) forbidding any taxation of the clergy without his consent. This was an attempt, perhaps the most promising which has yet been made, to render war impossible. No Government can make war without borrowing money, and in that world the clergy were almost the only people who had it to lend, and personal service in the field was not required of them. He was thwarted by Edward I in England, who made the clergy understand that if they would not contribute to the needs of the State they could not claim the protection of its laws; and by Philip IV in France, who forbade the export of gold and silver from his dominions, which meant the disappearance of a large part of the papal revenue. In both countries the clergy sided with their sovereign, and Edward at any rate had the nation with him.

In the year 1300 Boniface held the customary papal Jubilee. The best general description of this ceremony is to say that for a year the Papacy does all in its power to make Rome spiritually attractive. Exceptional opportunities of seeing relics are afforded,

and indulgences are distributed with more than customary pro-
fusion. The most eloquent preachers and the most experienced
confessors who can be found officiate in the churches in many
languages. A papal Jubilee is comparable with the Conventions
which are held from time to time in the Church of England today.
A number of people are brought together with a view to deepen-
ing their spiritual life by means of religious exercises. The
difference is that a Convention is local, and does not as a rule last
for much more than a week. A papal Jubilee is world-wide and
continues for a year. If its spiritual value is impossible to assess,
its effect upon the papal treasury is not open to question.
Originally it was held once in a century, then at intervals of
thirty-three years, and finally once every twenty-five years. This
is the practice today.

In 1300 Rome was crowded with pilgrims and the Pope was
greeted with immense enthusiasm wherever he appeared. Boniface
seems to have exaggerated the real value of such demonstrations,
and to have assumed that his position was impregnable. In the
early autumn of 1303 partisans of Philip IV of France seized his
person at Anagni. No injury was done to him, and he recovered
his liberty after three or four days, but he died very soon afterwards, on 12 October—really, it would seem, from shock. The
prestige of the Papacy was shattered, and the entire medieval
system of which it was the centre received a mortal wound, if it
would be too much to say that it was destroyed. The humiliation
of the Emperor Henry IV at Canossa by Gregory VII had been
reversed.

Clement V (1305–14) removed the Papacy to Avignon. This
was Neapolitan territory,[1] but dangerously near the French
frontier. Clement, who was a native of Aquitaine, probably
thought he would be safer from molestation there than anywhere
in Italy, but if it would be too much to say that the Papacy became
an appanage of the French Crown, it was obvious that a Pope at
Avignon was almost bound to become a tool in the hand of the
French king. This naturally stiffened English resistance to his
claims.

[1] Strictly, a papal fief belonging to the kingdom of Naples.

The chronic financial embarrassment of the see was also increased. A new palace had to be built, upon a magnificent scale, and naturally pilgrims of all kinds were fewer than they had been at Rome, where there was more to see. The situation was found to be intolerable, and in the year 1378 Urban VI returned to Rome. The moral prestige of the Papacy no longer stood very high, and it was now lowered still further by what is known as the *Great Schism*. For some forty years Europe was scandalized by the spectacle of two, sometimes even three, rivals for the chair of St Peter and the position of Vicar of Christ on earth, who did not hesitate to press their claims with every weapon of which they could lay hold. Eventually Martin V (1417–31) was recognized as sole Pope.

During the first half of the fifteenth century two important Councils were held, the first at Constance from 1414 to 1418, and the second at Basel, which met intermittently from 1433 to 1449, though its principal activities were over by 1437.

The first object of the Council of Constance was to end the Great Schism (which it did); the second to "reform the Church in head and members", which meant the Pope and the Court (*Curia*) of Rome. Beyond condemning Hus as a dangerous heretic it did not attempt to deal with anything beyond the administrative machinery of the Church, which meant the financial demands of the Papacy and its ever-increasing interference with things in general. The Council of Basel was even less successful. One of its proposals was that the clergy should be permitted to marry. The situation was complicated by the presence of Greeks, who solicited the help of the Papacy against the Turks. The Pope's terms were unconditional surrender, and they were not prepared to pay the price. Both Councils failed, for much the same reasons that the League of Nations failed in our own day. National and sectional rivalries and jealousies made themselves increasingly felt, and there was no authority capable of commanding the respect of the delegates. The most tangible result was that the Papacy emerged from the conflict stronger than it had gone in. Before the middle of the fifteenth century it was clear that reforms, by common consent long overdue, would not be effected by any general Council, and would probably have to be brought about in spite of the Pope.

As the century wore on the Papacy did not escape the general moral degradation of the time. Pius II (1458–64) was a humanist, and hardly pretended to be anything more. The Renaissance in Italy was much more pagan than in England or, I think, in France, partly no doubt because the greatness of the pagan past is much more in evidence there. In our country the only really impressive monuments of Roman civilization to be seen outside museums are the baths at Bath and the wall in Northumberland, and the number of people who ever see either (especially the wall) is small. Of monuments of Greek civilization there are none. Of Alexander VI (1492–1503) Creighton observed that if he has gone down to posterity as a monster of exceptional infamy it is because, unlike the majority of his contemporaries, he did not add hypocrisy to his other vices.[1] Leo X (1510–21) appears to have been an unabashed pagan, and is credited with having said, "Let us enjoy the Papacy, since God has given it to us." When he ascended the throne his position seemed to be entirely secure. But seven years later Luther attacked the system of indulgences with very far-reaching results.[2]

I cannot sum up the general picture which I have been trying to sketch of the Papacy from the time of Gregory the Great to the beginning of the Reformation better than by borrowing the words with which Macaulay closes his famous essay on Bacon. In intellectual stature Bacon may be considered to rank with any Englishman who has ever lived. Newton is perhaps almost the only figure who can even be placed beside him. As a philosopher and a lawyer he is supreme. As a judge he took bribes and tortured prisoners, being, I believe, the last man on our Bench who did. (In the first sentence of the quotation I have substituted the word *religion* for *philosophy* to make it applicable to the Pope.)

"Had his civil aims continued to be moderate he would have been not only the Moses but the Joshua of religion. He would have fulfilled a large part of his own magnificent predictions.

[1] *History of the Papacy*, vol. v, p. 50.
[2] See Chapter 7, p. 131.

He would have led his followers not only to the verge, but into the heart of the Promised Land. Mankind would then have been able to esteem their illustrious benefactor. We should not then be compelled to regard his character with mingled aversion and gratitude . . . and we should conclude our survey with feelings very different from those with which we now turn away from the chequered spectacle of so much glory and so much shame.''

NOTE

THE SACRED COLLEGE

Nominally the College of Cardinals contains seventy members —six cardinal-bishops, fifty cardinal-priests and fourteen cardinal-deacons. In practice the tale of priests is very seldom complete. The cardinal-bishoprics are, in order of precedence, Ostia, Porto, Sabina, Palestrina (the ancient Præneste), Frascati (the ancient Tusculum) and Albano.

These are all small places in the immediate neighbourhood of Rome, and are not in themselves of any importance now. Originally, no doubt, the bishops of them acted as an advisory Council to the Pope, and therefore, as the organization of the Papacy became more elaborate, the sees acquired a special distinction.

At the present day they are almost always held by Italians, as the occupants necessarily live in or near Rome. The last of the Stuart princes, Henry, sometimes called the Cardinal York, who lived until 1809, was bishop of Ostia at the time of his death. The bishop of Ostia ranks next after the Pope in the Roman Church, and crowns him in St Peter's.

Most of the cardinal-priests are archbishops or bishops elsewhere, and therefore only visit Rome occasionally. Each takes a title from a church in Rome, where he displays his arms. In theory the cardinal-priests are the parish clergy of Rome, and only certain churches, presumably all very ancient foundations, can furnish a title. The common practice of speaking of a bishop who is also a cardinal as a cardinal-bishop is therefore inaccurate. The full style and title of such personages is: ''His Eminence

A.B., Bishop or Archbishop of *C.*, Cardinal Priest of the Holy Roman Church by the title of *D.*"

He can be referred to as "Cardinal", followed by his surname.

Early in the year 1946 Pius XII created thirty-two cardinal-priests, thereby bringing the college up to full strength; it was said, for the first time for more than a century. Probably there had been few if any creations during the years of war. One of the new cardinals died very soon afterwards.

The fourteen cardinal-deacons discharge various functions at Rome, probably for the most part in connection with Papal charities, and the temporalities of the Church generally. They must therefore as a rule be Italians, but Reginald Pole, who was an Englishman, was a cardinal-deacon when he became Archbishop of Canterbury in 1556.

It is interesting to note that, according to Eusebius,[1] there were in the Church at Rome in the middle of the third century, besides the bishop, forty-six priests, seven deacons, seven sub-deacons, forty-two acolytes, fifty-two exorcists, and fifty-two readers and doorkeepers. This looks as if there were about fifty churches. The number of deacons and sub-deacons was probably determined by the fourteen "regions" into which the Emperor Augustus had divided the city shortly before the beginning of the Christian era for purposes of police and general administration much as the city of London has been divided into "wards", since when the memory of man runneth not to the contrary. An area which had been found convenient for civil purposes would serve equally well as an administrative unit for the charity and welfare work of the Church, especially as its boundaries would be clearly defined and well known.

[1] *Historical Ecclesiastica*, v. 43. Written a little before the middle of the fourth century.

7

Parasitic Growths—2

*Indulgences and Dispensations—From the accession of John VIII
to the death of Clement VI—872–1352*

IN the previous chapter an attempt has been made to sketch
briefly the rise of the see of Rome. Naturally Rome was
always one of the most important Christian centres. As time went
on a number of factors, some geographical, some historical,
some political and some theological, combined to enhance its
prestige and extend its influence, until as the Papacy it became
the hub of Western Europe. Its only possible rival after about the
year 700[1] was Constantinople, sometimes termed *New Rome*.
But, partly because it was new, the imperial capital on the
Bosphorus could never in popular imagination rank with the
older capital on the Tiber, which could trace its Christian origins
to apostles, and show the graves of innumerable martyrs.

During the great days of the Papacy (roughly from the end of
the eleventh to the beginning of the fourteenth century) and for
two centuries afterwards the Pope was even more than the most
august occupant of any throne. Sovereigns are as a rule perforce
remote from the great majority of their subjects, and the more
extensive their dominions the more remote do they become.
But in the medieval world it was almost impossible for anyone
to lose sight of the Pope for a moment. His power and authority
touched the daily lives of almost all his subjects, whatever their
rank or station, directly and continually, as no other could. This

[1] See above, Chapter 6, p. 104. Alexandria had been captured by the
Mohammedans on 17 October 641.

close and extensive contact, quite unlike any relationship which any secular ruler could have with his subjects, was brought about by two far-reaching systems of ecclesiastical jurisdiction, Indulgences and Dispensations.

It is impossible to understand the working of the medieval Church without some knowledge of the theory and practice of these two systems. The Reformation, whether in Germany or England, can hardly be considered without reference to them. Speaking generally, both originated in the best intentions, and were developed with remarkable ingenuity until they reached an almost unbelievable degree of completeness. For centuries they were the principal buttresses of the Papal power and a very important source of Papal revenue. Eventually the abuses to which they had given rise became so enormous that an explosion took place which shook the Papal throne and wrenched a large part of Europe from its sway.

The system of indulgences was probably the more widespread of the two, and led to more, and more flagrant abuses. It will therefore be convenient to consider it first. The story is a long one, and so intricate that it would be rash for anyone to say positively that he really understands it all. Roughly, it is a record of the outrunning of theory by practice, and then, when return appeared to be impossible, or at any rate too difficult and dangerous to attempt, of the adjustment of theory to suit the demands of existing practice. From this point of view alone the system is worth studying, because it conveys a warning which no part of the Church can ever afford to neglect. It shows what may happen, what is indeed bound to happen, if the clergy do not really understand the principles of the Church, and rely on their natural kindness of heart to guide them through the difficulties and perplexities which arise in the course of pastoral work.

The word *Indulgence* suggests to us something morally questionable, if not worse. It is something of which we may describe ourselves as "guilty" and for which we feel that some sort of apology is due. But this is only a meaning which we have read into it, perhaps in consequence of the abuses of the medieval system. The word is Latin, and it very rarely happens that the real significance of any Latin word is expressed accurately by the meaning which we attach now to the English word which looks and sounds most like it.

Indulgentia was a technical legal term in the Roman world, and meant simply "Remission of taxation". Throughout the empire the provincial towns paid an annual tax, proportionate to their wealth, to what we should call the Imperial Exchequer. In that world it was known as the *fiscus* and regarded as the emperor's privy purse. From this source all imperial expenses such as the maintenance of the army and so forth were met. The money was spent at the sole discretion of the emperor. No one could ask to see the accounts or question any outlay. It was his income which he used to discharge his duties as *Imperator*, which meant originally commander-in-chief of the armed forces of the State. If a town had suffered some exceptional calamity, such as earthquake (by no means an uncommon experience in Asia Minor or Greece), or fire, or flood, or pestilence, the emperor would remit the tribute due, either in whole or in part, for such period as he thought fit. This remission was an *Indulgentia*. It was perfectly legitimate, as it was granted by the competent authority who alone lost by it, and was intended to promote economic recovery after a disaster for which no one could be held responsible. It was an exceptional measure, to deal with exceptional circumstances, and as such no fault could be found with it from any point of view. Everyone must have been familiar with the word, and have known exactly what it meant when the Church took it into use. The only difference lay in the application, because the Church was not concerned with economic catastrophes but with moral ones. From its very earliest days the Church found that it had to deal with sin. Promises made at Baptism were not always kept. The high hopes with which new members had been received into the Christian community were sometimes disappointed. All this was inevitable, if unforeseen. The first six chapters of 1 Corinthians illustrate the situations which arose from time to time amongst the Christians of the first generation. In attempting to deal with sin the Church had to grope its own way and develop its own technique. There was no help or guidance to be had from the pagan world in which it was set. One of the respects in which Christianity stands in the sharpest contrast with all other forms of religion is in its conception of sin. At the very beginning the difference may not have been realized fully. But as time went on its depth and width became increasingly apparent. In pagan religion the sense of sin is always inadequate and sometimes scarcely exists; chiefly because there is no adequate sense of the Holiness of God. The Greek word for sin (*hamartia*) means no more than *a bad shot*. To have missed the target indicates some lack of skill and judgment—the eye may not be clear or the hand may be unsteady. But there is nothing moral about failures of this kind, and it may be possible to rectify them with little difficulty. To have missed with one shot does not make it more likely to miss with the next; in fact, rather the reverse, because the experience gained by the first failure can be turned to good account at the second attempt. As long as sin is thought of in this kind of way, some form of ceremonial purification will be sufficient to wipe out any wrongdoing and its consequences for good and all.

The Roman conscience was, perhaps, better than the Greek, but fell short of the lowest standard in which Christianity could acquiesce. It did not recognize, any more than the Greek, that after moral failure there is necessarily what may be called moral leeway (to borrow a convenient metaphor) to be made up. Not only must the actual failure be repaired, as far as possible, but the offender must recognize that he is on a lower level morally than he was before. His will has been weakened by his own act, so that recovery is likely to be slow and difficult. This is an outcome of sin which must be faced. Otherwise the sinner will go from bad to worse until his moral degradation is almost complete. The last fifteen verses of the first chapter of Romans show how far this process had gone in the world into which Christianity was born. We know enough from other sources to say that the sombre picture which St Paul draws is not too dark.

It is probably impossible for us to understand the demoralizing effect of slavery, which was an immemorial and almost universal institution, upon the whole of pagan society from top to bottom.

In the long run the owners probably suffered most,[1] even if the assumption of Roman law that a slave could not be expected to speak the truth except under torture was justified.

Accordingly the Church very soon found the need of some form of penitential discipline, which had to serve two purposes. First, to vindicate the moral standard of the Christian community as a whole, by showing that certain acts, in which pagan society saw little or no harm, could not be ignored or condoned. Secondly, to promote the moral education of the offender by impressing him with a sense of the enormity of his conduct, and at the same time to strengthen his will to enable him to recover the ground which he had lost, and to stand firm in the future. All this had to be worked out gradually and experimentally. So far as I know the first appearance of a fairly complete articulated system is at Carthage soon after the middle of the third century.

In the year 250 a sharp persecution was inaugurated by the Emperor Decius. It lasted for some eight years, though after the year 253 its severity was relaxed. Perhaps the Church of Carthage had grown too rapidly, so that its roots had insufficient deepness of earth. Though there were a number of martyrdoms there was a very widespread collapse. As soon as circumstances allowed the bishop (Cyprian) to take action the Christian community was found to consist of two classes, the Steadfast (*Stantes*) and the Fallen (*Lapsi*). The latter were divided into three grades, first the Surrenderers (*Traditores*), who had given up copies of the Bible, or of other Christian books, for destruction. The usual course of a Roman persecution was to begin by demanding the surrender of sacred literature, which was necessarily regarded as treasonable. This was generally accompanied by the imprisonment (or removal to some lonely island) of one or two leaders. It was hoped that the obnoxious religion would then disintegrate quietly, so that no further steps need be taken against it. The policy was to avoid bloodshed as long as possible, and to proceed to it only when milder measures had proved unsuccessful. (Probably much the same might be said of most persecutions. Once bloodshed has begun it cannot be stopped. It has to increase, until all hope

[1] See above, Chapter 1, p. 19.

of its success has to be abandoned and the whole business dropped.)

The guilt of the *Traditores* was the least. Next came the Certificated (*Libellatici*). These were people who had procured certificates to say that they had satisfied the demands of the Government by paying divine honours to the statue of the emperor,[1] although in fact they had not done so. These were probably obtained through the good offices of some of the minor clerks employed in the prætor's office. If they could be produced on demand no one was likely to be too inquisitive about their provenance, and of course no repetition of the act need be required. It is to be remembered that it is one thing for someone at headquarters to order persecution, and quite another thing for those who actually have to carry the order out; and the process becomes additionally distasteful if the victims are the neighbours, friends and relations of the persecutors. Add to this the general tendency of government officials all the world over not to take more trouble than they need, and it becomes obvious that in times of persecution ways of escape which did not involve downright apostasy might be found by those who were not ashamed to take advantage of them. The purchase of *libelli* was probably as safe and easy as any.

Last came the Offerers of Incense (*Thurificati*), who had performed that act, which was understood to mean that they recognized the emperor as a divine being.

All these were excommunicated for a period proportionate to the gravity of their offence, the bishop (or perhaps the bishop-in-council) being the judge. There is no suggestion that this was a new departure. We are therefore entitled to infer that at Carthage at any rate, and if at Carthage presumably elsewhere, there was established by the middle of the third century a recognized system of penance for offences against the faith and order of the Church.

The issue was complicated at Carthage by the action of the *Confessors*. These were people who had stood their ground

---

[1] To speak more accurately, "To the *genius* of the emperor," of which his statue was the symbol.

valiantly, and had suffered, though not unto death. They had been imprisoned (in itself a much more severe penalty than it has become today) and perhaps tortured as well. They had also had to pay fines, which may have amounted to deprivation of everything which they could be proved to possess. Naturally they were highly extolled for their conduct, and the admiration which they received seems to have turned their heads. They took to issuing, on their own authority, Certificates of Reconciliation (*Libelli Pacis*), by which they cancelled, or at any rate shortened, the sentences which had been passed, and restored the offenders to Communion, and any other privileges which they might have forfeited, without more ado. This seems to be the first appearance of an idea of which more will be said later, that the intrinsic merits of one person may be so far in excess of his own requirements that they, or part of them, may be used for the benefit of someone else; as a sum of money may be transferred from a bank account which is in credit to one which is overdrawn.[1]

Now there are necessarily two aspects to every piece of wrongdoing. From one point of view, it is a breach of some law, whether of the Church or of the State. As such it calls for some penalty proportionate to its gravity, which has to be paid immediately. Once paid, the offender is restored to any position which he may have forfeited in the community, and no more need be said about the matter.

From another point of view, it is a sin against God, the penalty for which will have to be paid elsewhere. Ecclesiastical or civil authority can remit any temporal penalty which it can impose, but cannot forgive sin. That rests with God. We believe that true repentance will always be met by divine forgiveness. But the genuineness of the repentance professed in any instance can be known only to God. Confession and the performance of some penance, which could not be enforced, may be accepted by the Church as a mark of true repentance, but in the nature of things the evidence can never be quite conclusive. Absolution given in the Church's name puts away the offence and restores the penitent

---

1 For a full account of the persecution and its aftermath see *Cyprian*, by E. W. (Abp) Benson, pp. 60–79 (Macmillan, 1897).

to Communion. But it does not *per se* obliterate sin. Only divine forgiveness, granted to true repentance, can do that. Absolution pronounced on behalf of the Church is therefore only conditional. Whether the conditions needed to make it the expression of something ultimate have been fulfilled or not can be known only to the Author of all forgiveness.

It therefore follows that as the Church built up its penitential system, without which the Christian moral standard could not be upheld, the drawing of the distinction between the two aspects of wrongdoing became increasingly important. The danger of confusion between them can never be remote. It increased as the Roman Empire crumbled and the Dark Ages drew on. The clergy who represented what survived of the old régime had to deal with the new lords of the soil, who were intellectually and morally half-savage children, as best they could. Many of them were no doubt almost illiterate. Almost inevitably it came to be assumed that the performance of penance was an atonement for sin, and that remission of penance in whole or in part expunged moral guilt and all its consequences.

In Article XXII, *Of Purgatory*, our Prayer Book makes mention of *Pardons* (i.e., Indulgences) immediately after it has spoken of ''The Romish Doctrine concerning Purgatory'', which reminds us that the two were (and are still) intimately associated. Any discussion of the doctrine of Purgatory would be out of place here. As a matter of history it seems to have appeared first on African soil.[1] It received a great impetus at the end of the sixth century from Gregory the Great.[2] He had very definite visions of the souls of the departed (amongst them that of the Emperor Trajan, who had reigned from A.D. 98 to 117) in fiery pits. It is not, I think, unreasonable to regard these visions as no more than the feverish dreams to which the circumstances in which the Pope was situated were not unlikely to give rise.[3] The doctrine gained general acceptance during the Dark and Middle Ages, but

[1] Tertullian, *De Anima*, c. 58. Perhaps in the *Passion of S. Perpetua*, c. vii and viii. Clement of Alexandria, *Stromateis*, Bk. VI, c. vi, § 46, S. Augustine, *Encheiridion ad Laurentium*, c. lxix, and *De Civitate Dei*, Bk. XXI, c. xiii.

[2] *Dialogues*, IV, c. xxxix.   [3] See above, Chapter 6, pp. 106-7.

was not finally ratified by a judgment of the Church until the Council of Florence in 1439. The pains of Purgatory were, as the word implies, remedial and purifying, and are therefore not to be confused with those of hell. From the latter there could be no escape. But it came to be believed that Indulgences could at least shorten the former, which almost everyone was bound to experience for some period of time before he could be fit to enjoy the Beatific Vision. This belief enhanced their value enormously, and strengthened the authority of the Church.

If the system did not originate with the Crusades, they certainly stimulated its development. Pope John VIII had declared in 882 that all who died fighting for the Church against the heathen received life eternal (Islam made a similar promise to its followers who fell in battle against Christians), and that he gave them absolution as much as he had power to do. This reservation was entirely proper, but it is not surprising that most people thought that in the mouth of the Pope it meant nothing. It was assumed that absolution given by him must be complete and final, and a degree of authority which he had been careful to disavow was ascribed to him. The Council of Clermont in 1095 seems to have had fewer qualms.

The commutation of personal penance for a payment of money, to be devoted to some pious or charitable purpose, seems to have begun in the seventh century. In itself the practice is not open to any objection. It rests upon the same principle as "the option of a fine", which has a place in the legal system of every civilized country. Small breaches of the law which cannot be ignored altogether, but obviously do not deserve more than a few days' imprisonment, can be dealt with satisfactorily by the imposition of a fine; but the practice must be kept within bounds. The foundations of justice would be destroyed if any offence, however grave, could be disposed of in this way.

An Indulgence was, and is, a concrete thing. It is a piece of paper on which certain words have been written. It might be compared roughly to a ticket of admission to some place otherwise inaccessible, as it confers upon the holder some privilege which he could not enjoy without it.

Anything which is received in exchange for a payment of money may be considered to have been bought and sold. As the idea that Indulgences were not restricted to penance in this life, but extended to the pains of Purgatory, gained ground, so did the idea that it is possible to buy not only exemption from penance but pardon for sin. It would have been extraordinarily difficult to prevent the growth of this belief. It is not clear how much attempt was made. Once established, it would necessarily be almost impossible to dislodge. It presented itself as something eminently satisfactory to all parties. The purchaser felt that he was getting good value for his money. The authority of the Church, which the vendor represented, was enhanced, and a very abundant source of revenue had been discovered.

When theology revived in the thirteenth century, the School-men found themselves confronted with a very difficult situation. A system by which the Church professed to forgive sin was firmly established, and no one knew how it had grown up. To a theologian it must appear, *prima facie* at any rate, incapable of justification. But on the scholastic premise to which reference has been made in Chapter 6[1] there must be some complete justification to be found. St Thomas Aquinas, to quote a single instance, wrote:[2] "Everybody admits that Indulgences are of some real force, because it would be impious to say that the Church does anything to no purpose." A theory was found in the doctrine of "Works of Supererogation," which is condemned by our Prayer Book in Article XIV. The word *supererogare* means originally *to make an additional payment*. It is used in the Latin Bible (the Vulgate) in Luke 10. 35, where the Good Samaritan, having made what he thought ought to be adequate provision for the wounded traveller, promises to refund any further expense to which the innkeeper may be put, next time he passes that way.[3]

The Schoolmen began by drawing a clear distinction between the "Precepts" and "Counsels" of the New Testament, developing the line adopted from time to time by St Paul (e.g., in 1 Corin-

[1] P. 109.
[2] *Summa*, Supplement to Pt. III, q. xxv, Art. 1, Conclusion.
[3] "Whatsoever thou spendest more."

thians 7). The former must be observed by all to secure eternal life; the observance of the latter is desirable but not essential. An obvious illustration lay ready to hand. The Church regarded celibacy as the highest form of Christian life. But it was impossible to say that the married state is sinful, though heretical sects had done so from time to time. If married couples who led godly lives could be held to have done well enough to win eternal life, it followed that those who had added to the common-place virtues the crown of celibacy must be considered to have done more than was necessary. They had accumulated a balance of merit which they did not need and could not use. This was not to be left idle, but could be employed by the Pope at his discretion. The medieval mind saw no difficulty in thinking of a spiritual matter in the terms of a commercial transaction. To us the theory appears monstrous, but so was the system which it sought to justify. It is extremely ingenious, and it is not easy to see anything which could have taken its place. No one as yet was prepared to say that the practice of indulgences had outrun any conceivable theory and must be reformed drastically, or abolished outright.

Accordingly Boniface VIII could feel that he was on fairly firm ground when at the Jubilee of 1300 he offered the fullest possible pardon (*plenissimam veniam*) for their sins to all who for fifteen days, during the Holy Year of Jubilee, should visit the churches of St Peter and St Paul at Rome. (The practice of attaching an indulgence to a particular church so that it would be received automatically by all visitors has been traced back to the closing years of the eleventh century by Dr H. C. Lea.)

Eventually Clement VI, who probably found himself very hard-pressed for money at Avignon, set out the theory of the "Treasure of the Church" divinely entrusted to the successors of St Peter, in the bull *Unigenitus* (*The Only-begotten*). The system was then complete. Its theological foundation was irrefragable; as an adjunct to the papal power it had proved itself invaluable.

Indulgences could be procured for others, even after their death, to an almost unlimited extent.[1]

By the middle of the fourteenth century the Pardoner was a

[1] See *Life* of Bishop Creighton, vol. ii, p. 87.

familiar figure on the roads. Chaucer describes one in the Prologue to the *Canterbury Tales* as having a wallet "Bret-full (Brimfull in modern speech) of pardons come from Rome all hot," besides a number of sham relics of all kinds, by the sale of which he did very well. Chaucer's portrait is simply of a cheerful hawker who could make himself pleasant company, and was probably not much more dishonest than wandering hucksters are apt to be.

The penitential system of the Church, which aimed at upholding moral standards and at rebuilding character after some moral failure, had come to mean that pardon for sin could be bought and the pains of Purgatory abbreviated, if not abolished altogether. This meant that it was defeating its own ends and debasing all moral standards.

Indulgences were sometimes used to induce people to contribute to charity or to works of public utility. In the registers of the diocese of Ely, I have noticed a considerable number in connection with "burnings". Houses in the Fen were presumably almost always made of wood and thatched with reed, and surrounded by reed-beds. The average rainfall is less than in most parts of England, and there are still places where at certain times of year to drop an unextinguished match might devastate acres. Fires must have been common, and the man who had had his house burnt over his head was ruined. For bishops to grant an indulgence to anyone who would subscribe to his relief was the easiest way of setting him up again, and gave the contributors some return for their money, besides the consciousness of having done a charitable deed. This was less objectionable than the activities of Chaucer's Pardoner.

In the registers of the diocese of Bath and Wells I have not noticed any "burnings"; probably most houses were of stone. But there are several mentions of repairs to bridges and causeways. Considerable tracts of the county of Somerset are often waterlogged today, and the flooding was probably much more extensive in the fourteenth and fifteenth centuries.

One object, which one would think was unusual, is the support of a hermit who had established himself in the forest of Selwood. It would be interesting to know what form contributions took, as money would be of little use to him unless he quitted his hermitage, and how generous was the response elicited.

In the register of Thomas Beckington, Bishop, 1443–65, it is usually stated that indulgences for such purposes are to be granted to "contrite and confessed" persons only. That shows that he did try to uphold some moral standard by refusing to grant them without some evidence of repentance. He seems to have been a very careful bishop in more respects than one. For example, he tried to raise the intellectual standard of the clergy by the institution of what are called now Examining Chaplains.

On a buttress on the west front of Wells Cathedral, near the entrance to the north aisle of the nave, there is an inscription which, though considerably defaced, can be read as follows: "Pray for the soul of John of Pitney and you will have thirteen days of pardon."[1] The date is about 1430, and the person referred to is presumably buried near the foot of the buttress. To grant an indulgence for thirteen days in return for a prayer is no doubt better than selling it for cash. But it is unlikely to deepen the recipient's sense of sin.

(It is interesting to note that the inscription is in French. As it is designed to catch the eye of the passer-by it must be assumed that anyone who could read would be familiar with that language, which reminds us how close the ties between England and the Continent had been for nearly four centuries.)[2]

The explosion came in 1517. Julius II (1503–13) had pulled down the old basilica erected by Constantine and begun to build the vast structure which occupies its site today. The work was continued by Leo X (1513–21). The cost was enormous. All Western Europe was laid under contribution, and papal collectors went everywhere in search of funds. One of them was a very eloquent Dominican friar named Tetzel, who passed through southern Germany on a preaching tour. His mission was connected with Albert of Brandenburg's payment for his bishopric and his debt to the Fuggers. He was immensely successful, and there appeared to be a great religious revival. Crowds flocked to

[1] S.R.S., vols. 49 and 50.   See Chapter 10.
[2] See Chapter 9.

listen to his sermons, and it is said that he was almost over-whelmed by the number of confessions he had to hear. He was amply supplied with indulgences, which were to be had for money. His own view of what he was doing might have been stated more or less as follows, without unnecessary reference to Bishop Albert's private finances.

"I have been the instrument by which your hearts have been touched. You have confessed your sins, which have been many and grievous. You have pledged yourselves to lead a new life. Now if, as a proof of your contrition, you will contribute to the great and glorious work now going forward at Rome, the building of the most magnificent church in Christendom to house the tomb of the Prince of the Apostles, which is most dear to the heart of the Holy Father, he will of his goodness bestow upon you here and now the spiritual benefits for which you would otherwise have had to go to Rome."

If the real character and scope of these benefits had not been universally misunderstood, little fault could be found with Tetzel's offer. But Luther said roundly that he was selling pardons for sin. Whatever Tetzel's own view of the matter may have been there is no doubt that that was what the people who dealt with him believed.

On 31 October Luther nailed his famous ninety-five theses to the door of the castle church at Wittenberg (the usual way of publishing such things) and the Reformation had begun. Whether he realised it or not at the moment, this was very different from the attacks which had been made by Bishop Grosseteste in the thirteenth century, or by the Councils of Basel and Constance in the fifteenth. They had been concerned with administrative abuses only, of which the Pope himself might be ignorant. They had been directed primarily against the *curia*—i.e., the bureau-cracy which had its centre at the Vatican—not against the Papacy. Luther struck at the Papacy itself. Its power to forgive sins was the very heart of the system. If that could be challenged, the whole institution was shaken if not shattered.

The system of indulgences had developed gradually through some twelve centuries. A penitential system of some kind was (and is) absolutely necessary. Each step was taken with the best intentions, and satisfied some popular demand at the moment. When learning and civilization were at a very low ebb it got completely out of hand. When they revived, there was no turning back, and the keenest intellects in Europe set themselves to provide it with a solid theological foundation. They succeeded only too well, and any uneasiness which might have been felt about it was allayed. It flourished immensely, until Luther denounced it as a monstrous and indefensible abuse, and took the conscience of a large part of Europe with him.

His personal history and character lie outside the scope of these lectures. It will be enough to say that he exhibited in a very marked degree most of the qualities, good and bad alike, which the world now recognizes as characteristic of his nation.

When the Papacy found that Luther could not be ignored it said that the questions which he had raised could not be discussed. He was threatened with imprisonment or worse, unless he withdrew all his theses. This was a mistake in policy. It aroused resentment in Germany, which raised Luther to the rank of a national figure, and made his position unassailable by any form of violence. He is still a national hero in the eyes of many Germans, if not of all.

It is sometimes said that indulgences could be acquired prospectively, which would make them equivalent to licences *for* sin. For my own part I doubt this, and shall continue to do so until someone produces one which bears upon its face the words *vel committendis* ("or to be committed") in addition to the usual *Pro peccatis commissis* ("For sins committed").

Dispensations are less intricate, both in theory and practice, than indulgences, but their effect upon the Church was at least as great. They too grew out of an essential function of the Church —namely, the necessity of furnishing men with guidance in their daily lives. They too became a buttress of the papal power, and an important source of revenue. Little by little they too led to a state of affairs which the conscience of a large part of Europe could tolerate no longer. In Germany the Reformation was precipitated (to borrow a metaphor from the vocabulary of chemistry) by indulgences, in England by dispensations. In neither case were they the real cause, any more than the murder of the Austrian Archduke Francis Ferdinand and his wife at Serajevo on 28 June 1914 was the cause of the war which broke out five weeks later, and involved the greater part of Europe (to say nothing of the British Dominions and the United States) before it was brought to an end.

The Latin word *dispensatio* means *management* or *administration*, usually with the idea of money somewhere in the background. *Dispensator* is a common word for *steward*—i.e., someone authorized to administer some kind of property of which he is not the owner.

From the very beginning Christianity offered men a way of life as well as a way of worship. The *Way* was, as we know, the earliest title given to Christianity.[1] This characteristic of the new religion must have caught pagan attention at least as much as any other. To us religion and conduct are inseparable, but in the pagan world it was not so. People who wanted moral and ethical guidance did not resort to the priest and the temple, but to the philosopher and the lecture room. And the philosopher was not unlikely to be suspected of atheism, sometimes not without reason. The epistles of the New Testament (most of which, be it remembered, are the earliest Christian writings which we possess) throw light on the kind of problems which confronted Christians living in a pagan society. Some were ethical rather than strictly moral, inasmuch as they were concerned with social customs more than with the moral law. In dealing with them St Paul was at pains to make clear that he was not legislating, but offering advice. He believed it to be good advice, but did not pretend that it was or could be more.

In the year 313 Christianity received full legal toleration from the State, which meant that the Church could come, as it were, into the open. Councils could be held freely on any scale at any place, and could make any decisions they might reach widely known. Previously if they could be held at all the whole business

---

[1] E.g., Acts 9. 2.

had to be kept as quiet as possible. The Government was as a rule prepared to overlook the doings of this new and mysterious religion. But Christians on their part had to do all they could to make such complaisance decently possible. They did not want to attract the attention of authority more than could be helped, because if they did authority might feel compelled to enforce the law against them; which it was not particularly anxious to do. In the new atmosphere which prevailed after the failure and abandonment of the persecution inaugurated by Diocletian, Councils could be held as openly as religious conferences or ecclesiastical assemblies are in England today, and the conclusions reached were public property.

Most Councils, if not all, were summoned primarily to deal with doctrinal disputes, but naturally usually extended their survey to include some ecclesiastical and ethical matters as well. For instance, the Council of Elvira, which was held in Spain very early in the fourth century, passed one canon directing that while Christians must remove all idols from their houses as far as possible, some may be allowed to remain if their pagan slaves are likely to become obstreperous,[1] and another to the effect that Christians who are put to death for breaking idols are not to be counted as martyrs, because the practice is not commanded by the Gospel, and was not followed by the apostles.[2] (The second of these suggests a date before 313.)

The conclusions reached by early Councils were always embodied in what were called *canons*, never *laws*. The difference may seem to be merely verbal, but it is in fact very wide and important. The fact that the distinction came to be ignored subsequently was responsible for a vast amount of mischief.

The word *canon* is Greek and meant originally a straight rod or bar of any kind. Hence it came to mean a measuring rod, and so a standard by which anything could be tested. In this connection *regulation* is the nearest English equivalent. There is a quite fundamental difference between laws and regulations. A law is rigid, and of universal application within the area covered by the authority of the maker. It is intended to be enforced, and

[1] XLI.   [2] LX.

therefore its standard can never be very high. It represents the minimum below which public opinion will not allow the conduct of any individual to fall. If it is too detailed it will prove impossible to enforce, and if its enforcement is not supported by public opinion it will be disregarded with impunity until it becomes ridiculous. Also it concerns a man in relation to his fellows. It is impossible to legislate for what concerns the private conscience of an individual only.

A regulation is elastic and is passed with reference to some particular set of circumstances only. It sets a standard at which to aim, for people to apply for themselves in private life, as well as in public relationships. The early Councils (except perhaps that of Nicæa) were local. They were dealing with known circumstances, and envisaged only contingencies which could be foreseen.

After the fall of the Roman empire in the West, the part of Europe which it had covered entered upon a long period of political instability. The Church acquired an immense social influence, chiefly because it was the only thing which appeared to offer any solid background for life; partly, perhaps, because most of the clergy were much better educated than anybody else. Accordingly the Church became more and more the educator of society. There was nothing else which could take its place. It threw itself into the task with exemplary zeal, and set itself the highest standard of thoroughness. Little by little a vast body of advice (for the most part very good indeed) was built up which aimed at providing for every contingency which could possibly arise in the life of any Christian between the cradle and the grave. Inevitably anyone who is trying to educate half-savage people will find himself almost compelled to give numerous and explicit directions. But if direction is carried beyond a certain point the system ceases to be educative. The individual cannot grow to his proper stature unless he is left with a measure of moral and intellectual responsibility, which means, with a measure of freedom. This means in its turn that the probability that he will sometimes go wrong must be taken into account.

If the system of direction was over-minute, it became much worse when what was really a body of advice was codified and

9

treated as a system of law, and an attempt made to administer it as such. This came about when what were originally local systems framed with an immediate eye to particular needs were treated as a whole, and as something to be administered from Rome.

The beginning of this, or at least an early instance, is to be seen in the questions which St Augustine submitted to Gregory I. The Pope's answers were quite admirable, but since he knew nothing about conditions in Britain except what Augustine's messengers could tell him, it was obvious that they could not be more than advice, such as might be given today by an Archbishop of Canterbury to a bishop overseas who had consulted him.

During the sixth century the Emperor Justinian at Constantinople had carried through a vast codification of the whole system of Roman jurisprudence. It is possible that this had some effect upon the Church. If the empire had supplied itself with a complete code of law, it might seem natural that the Church should follow suit, and as the power and importance of the Bishop of Rome increased steadily it was inevitable that the administration of such a system must be in his hands. Be this as it may, the process was carried forward and was consolidated in the twelfth century. Bishop Creighton has described this as "the most important fact in the history of the medieval Church".[1]

This vast *corpus* was known as the *Canon Law*, a phrase which is almost a contradiction in terms. It was very imposing, but proved quite impossible to administer. It failed to recognize the inherent limitations of law, because instead of furnishing a framework within which such arrangements can be made as may be found necessary from time to time, it tried to provide a formula to cover every possible contingency. (It is worth while to remember that whenever our Lord was pressed for a definite ruling on a point of conduct He always refused to give one. He referred His questioners to some permanent principle which it was for them to apply to their difficulty.[2] Most people know, however, that it is easier to obey a rule than to apply a principle, and therefore prefer the former course.)

[1] *The Church and the Nation*, p. 191.
[2] See Matt. 22. 15-40; Mark 10. 25-37; 12. 13-35.

The canon law could only be made to work by authorizing breaches of its provisions—in other words, by the continual granting of dispensations. Of course, a dispensation could not touch the moral law. It could not sanction (say) murder or adultery. It dealt only with ecclesiastical rules, such as fasting. The medieval mind saw no objection to this arrangement. Abstractions appealed to it strongly, so that the theoretical completeness of a system was regarded as much more important than the way in which it worked in practice.

The whole matter is of such importance and is so little understood that an illustration from the constitution of our Church at the present day will not be out of place.

There are in the provinces of Canterbury and York forty-three cathedral churches. Each is governed by a separate set of statutes, to which an Order in Council has given the force of law. As institutions all cathedral churches have something in common, but they differ very widely, more widely perhaps than is always recognized, in their antecedents and local circumstances, as in the work which they can attempt. All cathedral statutes are similar in some respects, but no two sets are identical. If an attempt to impose uniform statutes upon every English cathedral church were made, the result would be something very voluminous which never could be observed in its entirety anywhere. Yet England is quite a small and homogeneous part of the Church. An attempt to put every cathedral church in Europe upon a uniform legal basis would lead to complete chaos. Each would have to go its own way, whatever the law said. Cathedral statutes as they are now have been drawn up with due regard to the limitations of law, which professional lawyers generally understand better than amateur ones. That is to say, they do not attempt to prescribe every detail. They provide a framework within which those who have to administer them from day to day are bound to keep, and give the administrators (the dean and chapter) power to make by-laws as need arises. A by-law may not contradict any statute. It deals with some point which the letter of the law does not cover in the spirit of the system. It can always be revoked if it proves to be unnecessary or mischievous.

If the medieval Church had worked in this kind of way its history would have been very different. As it was, it built up an immense system which could only be made to work by being broken perpetually, and therefore became more and more unintelligible and chaotic as time went on. The law, as it was in theory, and the exceptions which were permitted in practice, furnished sufficient material for the study of a lifetime. To be known as "a good canonist" meant having a foot planted firmly on the ladder of ecclesiastical promotion. Such a system was bound to place a very heavy tax upon the person with whom it rested to authorize or to forbid the law to be broken. It demanded almost superhuman wisdom and a very high degree of integrity on the part of the Pope. If his impartiality could ever be questioned the foundations of the entire system would be shaken.

The marriage laws provided the most fruitful field for the exercise of the dispensing power of the Papacy. It was here that the second storm arose which shook the Papal throne in the sixteenth century. The details will be considered in a later chapter.

It will be sufficient for the moment to speak generally. The Church held that marriage is indissoluble, so that there was no such thing as divorce, as we understand the word today. But there were a number of grounds on which a marriage could be annulled; not dissolved, because there was nothing to dissolve, but declared never to have been a marriage at all. Annulment might take place after a man and woman had lived together for years in all good faith, honestly believing themselves to be united in lawful wedlock. They might suddenly discover that they had really been living in sin, and that any children which had been born to them were illegitimate.

One ground of annulment, and perhaps the commonest, was that the parties had been related too closely before marriage, or in the language of the time had married "within the prohibited degrees". Degrees of relationship were reckoned by counting the steps up to the common ancestor and down again. Thus a brother and sister were related in the second degree, uncle and niece in the third, first cousins in the fourth, and so on.

At one time the Church tried to prohibit marriages within the seventh degree—that is to say, between people who had a great-grandfather in common. But this was found to be impossible, and dispensations had to be granted for marriages between what we should call "second cousins", occasionally perhaps for first. Besides the degrees of consanguinity, degrees of affinity, in which there was no blood relationship whatever, were also reckoned as impediments, which only a dispensation could remove. This was sometimes carried to lengths which can only be called absurd. For instance, if a man and woman were godparents to the same child their descendants were considered to stand in the same relationship to each other as they would if the godparents had been man and wife. The upshot was that in a small and fairly stationary society it was not very easy for people to find anyone whom they could marry with safety, especially if they were of noble, or still more of royal, blood. If at some subsequent time either partner got tired of the other it was usually not very difficult to unearth some impediment which had been over-looked or ignored and to bring the marriage to an end by declar-ing that it had never taken place. It is not easy to imagine a system better calculated to destroy the sanctity of marriage, which it had been framed to uphold.

Opinions differ as to how far canon law, which really meant papal law, was ever operative in England. William Lyndwood (Bishop of St David's, 1442–6), who was born about 1375 and died in 1446, tried to answer the question by compiling what is known as the *Provinciale*, which is a summary of the constitutions approved by successive synods in the province of Canterbury from the time of Stephen Langton (Archbishop 1207–28) to Henry Chichele (Archbishop 1414–43). But this work, which ranks as a high authority on canon law in England, takes no account of the province of York. Whatever force canon law ever had did not survive the statement of fact made in Article XXXVII, *The Bishop of Rome hath no jurisdiction in this realm of England*, except as regards such parts of it as had been incorporated in our statute law, and derive their authority from the Crown and Parliament. After the Reformation an attempt was made to produce some simplified and workable equivalent under the title *Reformatio Legum Ecclesiasticarum* (Reformation of the Laws Ecclesiastical), but it was never carried through. A set of canons limited in its range was produced in 1603. An attempt to revise them and bring them to date is in progress now (1948). Some people today profess to regret the desuetude of pre-Reformation canon law, and to desire its revival in our Church. It is permissible to wonder how far they really understand what they are talking about.

Papal dispensations were naturally most in evidence and most important where royal marriages were concerned, and it was in this connection that they began to be regarded with suspicion. The fourteenth and fifteenth centuries saw a development of national consciousness in the several States of Western Europe. This meant that the affairs of royal houses became less purely dynastic than they had been. They were matters of national concern. The Pope had become an Italian prince, and men began to wonder whether in his decisions in such cases he regarded the interests of the individuals and nations directly concerned, or whether the paramount consideration was the political interest of the Papacy itself.

The medieval Church fell because it was too kind, and because it tried to be more omniscient than it is given to human beings to be. Animated by the best intentions, it sought to help the penitent upon his way, and ended with a system calculated to destroy all sense of sin. To employ a convenient metaphor, it substituted for the steep ascent of heaven a gently undulating path which led the pilgrim back to the point from which he had started. It sought to direct all human life to an extent which would have been intolerable had it not proved impossible. It ended with a system which could not be observed, and therefore brought the whole idea of law into contempt. Both temptations, to be too kind and to attempt to be too wise, will always exist. To yield to them will always lead to much the same result.

8

Change and Decay

From the death of Edward II to the accession of Henry IV—1307–99

WHEN Edward I died on 7 July 1307 the medieval period may be considered to have come to an end. The prestige of the Papacy had been badly shaken, if not destroyed outright, and its removal to Avignon by Clement V did nothing to repair the loss. England awoke to national consciousness, and the development of national feeling was as inimical to the medieval system as it had been to the Roman empire. A supranational system can be politically strong only if the sense of nationality amongst the various peoples who live under it is weak. If its authority is spiritual, it must depend upon the prestige of its head, which means that the administration must be morally beyond reproach, or at least upon a very high level. The activities of the papal tax-gatherers, which increased steadily as the fourteenth century[1] wore on, did not conduce to this end.

Little need be said of the reign of Edward II. His misgovernment stung the Scots into revolt, and his feebleness led to his defeat at Bannockburn on 14 June 1322. By that battle Scotland recovered a precarious independence, at the cost of nearly three centuries more of border warfare, grinding poverty and almost complete separation from the main stream of European civilization. It must rest with those who had to pay the price to say whether it was excessive or not.

During this period the delicate austerity of the architectural style known to us as *Early English* was superseded by the style which we call *Decorated*. In France it is termed *Flamboyant*, which is perhaps a better description. It is extraordinarily rich, and

---

[1] See Chapter 7, p. 120.

represents a triumph of design and technical skill. The eastern part of the Quire of Wells Cathedral, and the Lady Chapel beyond, are outstanding examples. The Chapter House at Southwell is another. No one can dispute their beauty, but it is obvious that in any but first-rate hands the richness of decorated architecture would soon become affected and intolerable. To me, at least, it always suggests the luxuriance of tropical vegetation from which the odour of decay is never remote. It is one expression of the increase of sentimentality in religion which becomes discernible at this time. Another is the portrayal of the Figure on the Cross. He becomes the tortured, dying and (it is not too much to say) defeated Jesus, with whom we are familiar. The change may be due in part to the influence of St Bernard of Clairvaux (1101–53), who fastened attention upon the Sacred Humanity as a protest against devotion to the Virgin Mary and a cult of relics which he thought was in danger of becoming excessive. His whole outlook was affected very deeply by his meditations upon the Sacred Wounds, and his immense influence made itself felt in art. The physical aspect of the Passion was emphasized and the instruments (the scourge, the crown of thorns, the nails, etc.) begin to appear. The tortured Figure is in keeping with this, and appealed to people who were naturally disposed, as most Europeans seem to be, to think pictorially rather than symbolically, a habit which in modern times has been fostered by the development of photography. But if it can be regarded as true to life in the sense that it depicts what might have been seen by an eye-witness, it misses the truth which the older symbolism expressed. The majestic Figure crowned and robed of earlier art reveals a better understanding of the meaning of the Crucifixion. When Venantius Fortunatus (Bishop of Poitiers in the seventh century) wrote the famous hymn *Vexilla Regis prodeunt*[1] he was on a higher religious level than the designer of the central light of the east window of Wells Cathedral nearly seven hundred years later.

Sentiment has a real part to play in religion, because it is a

---

[1] "The royal banners forward go," No. 96 in *Hymns A. and M.*, No. 94 in the *English Hymnal*.

real part of us. But it always needs to be kept in check. The Christian revelation is fundamentally austere, and if too much concession is made to the emotions in art and worship the appeal to conscience is weakened, and that means that all moral standards are lowered. The process may be so gradual that it may be almost imperceptible, until it has gone so far that recovery has become difficult. The general lowering of moral standards which eventually brought about the decline and fall of the medieval Church may be considered to have begun early in the fourteenth century.

When Edward III came to the throne on 25 January 1327 he did not attempt the reconquest of Scotland. His interests and ambitions lay on the other side of the English Channel, where there was a prize better worth the winning. He contented himself with compelling the Scots to return the regalia which had been lost at Bannockburn, and knew that he had nothing more to fear than an occasional raid.

In the autumn of 1346 David Bruce attempted an invasion, probably at French instigation with a view to counterbalancing the disastrous defeat of Crecy on 26 August; but he got no farther than Nevill's Cross near Durham. On 12 October his army was dispersed by Henry Percy, whom Edward had left in charge of the Border, and he was taken prisoner. He was kept in England for the next eleven years, while his subjects were collecting the 100,000 marks required for his ransom.

In January 1340, Edward III assumed the title *King of France*, thereby inaugurating the great adventure which was destined to last for approximately a hundred years. Its course was chequered, but for a moment, at the accession of Henry VI, it seemed to have achieved complete and final success. Irreparable disaster then overtook it very swiftly. It is idle to speculate on what the course of history would have been had Henry been able to transmit the crown of France to his successors in more than name.

It is impossible to deny that the war was an act of nationalist aggression on our part, and as such difficult to justify. It is commonly observable that when boys and girls first become conscious of the fact that they are no longer children, but men and women, they pass through a period of unpleasant self-assertion. As a rule they outgrow it before much serious harm has been done. This seems to hold good of nations as of individuals. When a nation first becomes fully conscious of the fact that it is a nation, and may look forward to a more ambitious future than it had contemplated in its earlier days, it is always liable to employ its newly discovered power in acts of aggression against its nearest neighbours. It usually attempts to find some moral basis for these; which is more convincing in its own eyes than in those of anyone else. In accordance with the general tradition of his time Edward's basis was primarily legal.

Philip III of France, who reigned from 1270 to 1285, had two sons—Philip, who reigned from 1285 to 1314, and Charles, Count of Valois.

Philip IV had three sons, who reigned in succession as Louis X (1314–16), Philip V (1316–22) and Charles IV (1322–8), and one daughter, Isabella. None of the sons had any male issue, so that after the death of Charles IV the son of the Count of Valois became King as Philip VI. He reigned from 1328 to 1350, and his son John II was taken prisoner at Poitiers on 19 September 1356.

Isabella, daughter of Philip IV, had married Edward II, therefore if the laws of France had been as the laws of England Edward III would have had a better title to the throne of France than the descendants of the Count of Valois, or at least as good a one. But everyone knows that they were not. The crown of France cannot be worn by, or pass through, a woman and therefore Edward's claim to it was invalid. It was at most not more than a pretext which could be used to impart an appearance of legality and justice to what was really nothing but a piece of aggression. However, as has been pointed out by many writers, four successive generations of Englishmen would never have been induced to fight in a purely dynastic quarrel, especially if they had reason to think that their leader was in the wrong. They must have felt that the cause was in some sense their own, which meant that they looked upon it as a national enterprise.

An indication of the new temper which had developed in

England may be seen in the formal adoption of St George as our patron saint, in place of the gentle St Edward (*The Confessor*).

St George is one of the saints (St Giles is another) who for some reason became exceedingly popular, though it is hardly possible to produce a single certain fact about them. Calvin went so far as to doubt whether St George can be regarded as a historical personage, but it is not easy to see how he could have acquired the title of the Great Martyr, by which he is known in the Eastern Church, if he were a purely allegorical figure. Tradition associates him with Cappadocia, on the southern shore of the Black Sea, and it may be presumed that he was martyred during the Great Persecution (303–13), which is known to have been especially severe in that region. His introduction to Western Europe seems to have come through the Crusades. By that time he had become a symbol of military prowess in the cause of righteousness, and he was believed to have appeared to the Christian armies more than once. In the year 1222 a Council held at Oxford ordered the observance of his day in England. In the year 1415 Archbishop Chichele raised it to a feast of the first rank and put it on a level with Christmas Day. In the first Prayer Book of Edward VI it appears a "red letter day" with its special Epistle and Gospel. It was discarded by the second, though retained in the Calendar as a "black letter day". In modern times a "Royal Society of St George" has come into being with a view to promoting the observance of his day (23 April). It is not clear whether this represents more than an attempt to exploit religion in the interests of patriotism.

In 1348 Edward III founded the Chapel of St George in Windsor Castle, which soon afterwards became the headquarters of the Most Noble Order of the Garter. The chapel which we see today was built by Edward IV rather more than a century later. The formal adoption of St George as the patron saint of England dates from 1349. It is said that in that year Edward III invoked him, in conjunction with St Edward, during a battle in the neighbourhood of Calais. The victory which ensued attested the power of the soldier-saint, and established him as the appropriate patron for a nation which was committed to a great and arduous military enterprise. His banner, a red cross on a white field, is still the flag of England, and as such is flown by an admiral. The flag of the United Kingdom (known colloquially as the "Union Jack") has been formed by superimposing the white saltire of St Andrew and the red saltire of St Patrick upon the banner of St George. War is necessarily always horrible, but we may perhaps see in the fact that we fight under the sacred symbol of our Redemption an acknowledgment that even in battle the moral restrictions which Christianity imposes do not cease to exist.

It would be out of place here to attempt to trace the course of the war in detail. It will be enough to say that it was not as smooth and easy as the brilliant victories which marked its earliest stages may have led the king to expect. Its most enduring outcome was that for nearly six hundred years France and England regarded themselves as natural and hereditary enemies (an attitude of mind which the interlude of the alliance against Russia in the middle of the nineteenth century did little to alter) instead of as natural allies, as the geographical situation of the two countries has obviously ordained them to be. As the war dragged on it placed an increasing strain upon our national resources, which was aggravated by the Black Death.

This pestilence, which appears to have been what is known today as bubonic plague, is probably the worst calamity which has befallen us in all our history. It appeared first in Dorset in the summer of 1348, and is said to have come in a bale of cloth brought from the Continent by a pedlar. It spread with appalling rapidity and the medical knowledge of the time could do nothing to check it. Hardly anyone who caught it recovered. It seems fairly certain that in about sixteen months something like one-third of the population of England and Wales was carried off. It was at its worst in the eastern counties, where the loss may have amounted to nearly one-half. Norfolk and Suffolk never quite regained their position as the most populous and wealthy part of the country—the Lancashire and West Riding of the time. No complete statistics are available, the only figures on which estimates can be based are the institutions to benefices. From them it appears that almost exactly half the beneficed clergy in the county of Somerset died between October 1348 and April 1349.[1] In Cambridgeshire and farther to the east, where lists of former incumbents are displayed in churches, it is quite common to find that the parish had two incumbents during these deadly months, and sometimes more. From which it may be inferred that the parochial clergy did their duty, and died like men amongst their people. I know of one place in Norfolk[2] where the survivors of two ravaged villages joined forces, and the abandoned site is marked now by a few green mounds. No doubt there are many others. Possibly taking the country as a whole it may not be an exaggeration to say that nearly half the entire population perished. Apparently the plague never reached Scotland. Perhaps the population to the south of the Border was too scanty for it ever to take hold, and the intercourse between the two countries too occasional to transmit infection. After the end of 1349 it abated, though it did not disappear entirely for some years. A moderate amount of plague of some kind was nothing unusual in those days. It has been estimated that by 1377 the population of England had been diminished by about two-fifths.

The economic life of the country was dislocated. Much of the land, which constituted a much larger proportion of the entire national wealth then than it does now, went out of cultivation for lack of hands to till it. The surviving labourers felt themselves in a position to demand higher wages, and refusal to grant these led to discontent, and eventually to violence. More than a century elapsed before the loss of population was made good. Probably in the long run the Church suffered more than anything else. Reference has been made to the very high death rate amongst the parochial clergy. Probably the mortality in the monasteries was little less, and the result was that the standard required for admission to the priesthood or to a religious house, which was none too high before, had to be lowered so that the necessary minimum at any rate of the vacancies might be filled. When a

---

[1] *The Black Death in Somerset*, by E. H. Bates Harbin, *Somerset Archæological Society*, lxiii. ii. 91–103, 110. I owe this reference to the Reverend C. Woodforde, Rector of Steeple Morden.

[2] Holm-Hale near Swaffham.

standard has been lowered it is always difficult to raise it again. Perhaps the religious houses were affected most adversely. People did not necessarily expect a great deal of their parish priest, provided that he performed his duties in the matter of services reasonably well. But monastic institutions, especially upon a large scale, can justify themselves only by maintaining a really high standard of life.

Despite all this devastation at home the war went on in France. Probably Edward thought it could be made profitable and that St George might enable him to recoup himself, at any rate in part, for his losses by means of French plunder. In 1360, however, he was compelled to call a halt, and the treaty of Bretigny left him possession of the wide and wealthy lands of Poitou and Aquitaine. This was something considerable, if a long way short of the Crown of France. When public activities could be resumed, and church building became possible, a new style of architecture appeared. It is known as *Perpendicular* and is a development of the Decorated style which preceded it. It has never been practised outside this country. The earliest example is at Gloucester, and seems to have been virtually completed before the full force of the Black Death had been felt.[1] But it does not seem to have been adopted generally until the last quarter of the fourteenth century. It is rectilinear, and if it would be too much to say that it reveals a decline in artistic taste and architectural skill, it cannot be regarded as an advance. The most characteristic feature is the window, which reaches an immense size. The stonework is treated as no more than a frame to hold as much glass as possible, and does not add to the beauty of the design as does the earlier Decorated tracery.

The size of the window made it necessary to insert two long shafts of stone work rising from the side to support the wide arch at the top. They divide the window into three sections of approximately equal size. They are quite unmistakable and are the easiest feature of the style to recognize. Very often there is a heavy stone bar, called a transom, running horizontally across the window about halfway up. Perhaps the east window in Wells

[1] Between the years 1337 and 1350.

Cathedral, which may be dated about 1330 and is therefore a little earlier than any of the work at Gloucester, may be considered to mark the transition from the older to the newer style. It is unquestionably Decorated. But, on account of its unusual width (seven lights instead of the customary five), there are two vertical shafts running from the bottom to the top exactly as in a Perpendicular window. The upper part of the south-western tower at Wells is a genuine example of Perpendicular. It may be dated about 1390, as it was built by means of a legacy from Bishop Harewell, who died in 1386. The upper part of the north-western tower is about forty years later, as it was built by means of a legacy from Bishop Bubwith, who died in 1424. It is interesting to compare the two, and to note how the style developed and became more ornate.

Virtually all the churches built in England from about the year 1400 down to the Reformation are in the Perpendicular style. There are many fine examples, especially in the counties of Norfolk, Suffolk, Gloucester and Somerset. But the finest of all are not parochial foundations. They are the chapels of Eton College and King's College, Cambridge, both begun in the reign of Henry VI[1] (although the latter, owing to the ruin which came upon the House of Lancaster, was not completed until after the beginning of the sixteenth century); St George's Chapel, Windsor, which was built by Edward IV;[2] and the Chapel of Henry VII[3] at the east end of Westminster Abbey, which was completed by his son. These two buildings are sometimes described as "Tudor Gothic." The Priory Church of SS. Peter and Paul, colloquially known as *Bath Abbey*, is parochial now. It was rebuilt by Bishop King (1495–1503) for monastic use and is spacious. The height of the vault and the arrangement of flying buttresses which support it show that the architect was a good engineer. But it is quite obviously the product of a dying system.[4]

I have had the good fortune to be familiar with many fine examples of Perpendicular architecture, including the four royal chapels mentioned above, since I was a boy. But despite its

[1] 1422–71.
[2] 1461–83.
[3] 1485–1509.
[4] See Chapter 8.

magnificence there is to me something self-conscious and self-assertive about it, as if the architect were determined that everyone should recognize the splendour and costliness of his offering to God. For this reason it is not in the first rank either religiously or artistically. If the word "decadent" would be too strong, it is a departure from earlier standards, not for the better.

After the Reformation English church architects received no fresh inspiration, except for the Palladian interlude, which we owe almost entirely to the outstanding genius of one man,[1] until the building of Liverpool Cathedral during the present century.

The most important figure in the Church during this period is John Wiclif.[2] In fact, he might be considered to rank with any ecclesiastic whom we have ever produced. His reputation stood very high during his lifetime, and the influence exerted by his writings after his death was immense and not restricted to England. A full biography of him by Dr H. B. Workman has been published recently.

He was born at Hipswell, a little village in the north of Yorkshire near Catterick, not before the year 1329 and not long afterwards. By some means he got himself to Oxford. He may have entered Balliol Hall (as it was then called), but seems to have removed himself to Merton College, where his name appears amongst the Fellows in the year 1356. In 1361 he was appointed Master of Balliol, but not long afterwards the college presented him to the benefice of Fillingham in Lincolnshire, which he subsequently exchanged for that of Ludgershall in Buckinghamshire. In 1374 he was presented by the king to the rectory of Lutterworth in the county of Leicester, where he remained until his death in 1381. Most of his principal books were written there. If he never resided permanently at Oxford for any considerable period he visited it often enough to be a well-known figure there, and his lectures attracted a great deal of attention. So much in fact that cautious parents and abbots sent their sons and young monks to Cambridge to avoid contamin-

[1] See Chapter 13, pp. 267–8.
[2] The account of him which follows is taken chiefly from Bishop Creighton's "John Wiclif" in *Historical Essays and Reviews*.

ation. The Oxford Movement of the nineteenth century may
have had a similar effect in some circles. Unless there has been a
confusion between him and a John Wytcleve or Whitecliffe he
was appointed Warden of Canterbury Hall, which had recently
been founded by Archbishop Islip, in the year 1365. The appointment was contested on the ground that the Warden ought by
the statutes to be a regular (i.e., a monk), and after a considerable
amount of litigation the decision was given against Wiclif.

He was primarily a moralist, and attacked abuses whenever
and wherever he saw them with outspoken courage and strong
common sense. With regard to those directly connected with the
papal administration, he said little more than Robert Grosseteste
had said a century before. They had certainly not diminished in
the interval.

Wiclif also attacked the regular clergy, monks and friars. The
latter at any rate had deteriorated very much since their early
days, and many of them had ceased to be even reputable characters.
Most serious, perhaps, of all, he inveighed against the doctrine of
Transubstantiation.[1]

When he denounced the wealth and worldliness of the clergy,
especially of the bishops, he had obviously a good case and took
the greater part of the nation with him. The practice of appointing bishops to the great offices of State, to which reference has
been made in Chapter 5, had gone much further and was
undoubtedly proving mischievous. It meant that most of the
bishops were primarily politicians, and could be relied upon to
behave as such, especially in times of difficulty or danger. It was
beginning to be resented by the nation generally, on the grounds
that it made the Church too powerful. Without wishing to
defend the practice, it may be worth while to point out that it
was extremely economical for the taxpayer. The great servants
of the State must be provided with incomes sufficient to enable
them to do their work and uphold a fitting dignity. If the revenues

[1] It would be out of place to embark on any discussion of the doctrine here.
It will be enough to say that it arose as an attempt to check grossly materialistic
views of the Eucharist by stating the doctrine of the Real Presence in the terms
of the best modern thought. It was not successful chiefly because the philosophy
on which it depended was unintelligible to the ordinary man.

of the Church had not been used to support them, which meant appointing them to bishoprics or other wealthy benefices, the money would have had to be raised by new direct taxation. The king could not have found it on his own. This aspect of the matter does not seem to have struck Wiclif or any of his supporters.

I have said that he was primarily a moralist. He also possessed a powerful and subtle intellect and his thought was at bottom academic. Oxford had given him the training of a schoolman. It sometimes happens that a great academic figure does not realize what effect his utterances, especially on economic and social questions, may have upon people who do not share his moral and intellectual background. Thus, when Wiclif said that the clergy ought not to hold any property, but should be content to live on charity from day to day, he was enunciating a principle for which there is certainly something to be said, although it does not appear that he ever tried to order his own life in accordance with it. But a possible deduction, that to rob the clergy by refusing to pay tithe, or by more violent methods, is a righteous act is more open to question. If he would not have drawn it himself, some of those who heard him might have considered it self-evident. Again, when he said[1] that because all authority is of God it must be exercised in accordance with the will of God, no fault can be found with him. But when he went on to say that any authority not so exercised must be disobeyed, and that the individual is competent to decide for himself whether it is being so exercised in any instance, he was really preaching anarchy, or at any rate something which might easily lead to anarchy. Naturally teaching of this kind, apart from his religious opinions, provoked a measure of alarm and hostility. At the present day, if it was generally understood that Oxford had given its blessing to Communism and that an extreme form of it was being taught there to enthusiastic if immature audiences, there would probably be a good deal of uneasiness throughout the country. A question might be asked in Parliament, and voices would probably be heard calling upon the Government of the day to put a stop to it. In

[1] In *De Civili Dominio*, which may be translated *Of the Authority of the State*.

1377 Wiclif was brought to trial in the Chapel of Lambeth Palace before Archbishop Sudbury, partly in consequence of strong pressure from the Pope. The archbishop dismissed him with a caution to be a little more careful with his tongue and pen in future, and he retired to his rectory, where he lived unmolested until the day of his death.

Some writers hold that the archbishop's decision was due to fear of the populace of London, who were in sympathy with much of what they believed Wiclif's teaching to be. There is, however, no reason to refuse him the credit of having acted with courage and good sense. Whatever some people (including the Pope) might think, one great Englishman saw no reason for trying to silence another. Wiclif was deeply interested in the relations between the temporal and the spiritual power; or, as we might put it, between the Church and the State. That has been a matter of difficulty ever since the early part of the fourth century, and it is unlikely that any permanent and final adjustment will ever be reached anywhere. There are three obvious theories upon which it is possible to act.

1. That the Church must be entirely subject to the State.
2. That the State must be entirely subject to the Church.
3. That there ought not to be any relationship of any kind between them.

It is not easy to say off-hand which is the worst. The adoption of the first means that the Church becomes an instrument in the hands of the State for inculcating as much of Christian morality as seems likely to make the business of government easier. There are few things which politicians have more ground for fearing than the Christian conscience, because when it passes beyond a rudimentary stage it is always liable to become as it were a handful of grit in the wheels of the machine which they wish to keep running smoothly. A State which thinks it is entitled to control the Church in its own interest will soon become hostile to religious toleration.

The adoption of the second means, ultimately, the secularization of the Church, at least in all its higher offices. This has been the policy of the Papacy since the days of Gregory VII, and the story is plain for all to read. So far as it succeeds it is at the price of turning the Church into a State, and into an unlimited autocracy, which is almost the worst possible form of State.

The third course is really impracticable if the Church possesses any endowments of any kind, or even any buildings for its corporate purposes. As soon as property is involved the State will claim the right to see that it is not being used in such a way as to constitute a breach of trust. That amount of contact between the two there must be. To say that, with that exception, each should ignore the existence of the other means that the State as such has no religious or moral basis, and is therefore exempt from the restrictions which religion and morality impose on conduct. We have seen the outcome of this doctrine in Russia, Germany and Italy, since the present century began.

It is a matter of common knowledge that Wiclif held pronounced views on the authority of Scripture and the competence of the individual to interpret it for himself. He contributed largely to an English translation which bears his name and was extremely popular.[1]

It would not be true to sum him up as no more than a Protestant hero who suffered persecution at the hands of a corrupt and worldly episcopate. He was a very great Englishman morally and intellectually. He had no quarrel with the system of the Church, only with the abuses which had established themselves within it. By attacking them he undoubtedly gave an impulse to some of the many forces which were destined in due course to bring the Reformation about. It is doubtful whether his teaching can be considered to have been in any degree responsible for the dreadful events of the summer of 1381.[2]

Another indication of spiritual decline may be seen in the development of chantries. These began during the thirteenth century, or possibly a little earlier. A chantry is a mass said or sung for the benefit of a particular person, living or dead; usually

---

[1] See *The Bible in its Ancient and English Versions*, ed. H. W. Leeth Robinson (Clarendon Press, 1940).

[2] See p. 159.

the latter. For this purpose special chapels were built, and endowments provided for priests to officiate in them. It is a mistake, if not an uncommon one, to refer to the chapel itself as a *chantry*.

Not much fault can be found with the desire to secure perpetual intercession whether for the dead or the living. But the practice is open to two obvious criticisms. First, if the centre of the act of intercession is a mass, that means that the Eucharist is being celebrated for the exclusive benefit of some particular person or family and is therefore no longer thought of as an offering of the whole Church to the Father of all mankind. Secondly, it placed the well-to-do, who could afford to build and endow the chapels, in a position of spiritual advantage as compared with those who could not. As time went on and the doctrine of Purgatory developed the idea arose that each mass said for the soul of the deceased founder of the chantry shortened the period of his suffering.[1] Therefore, each became a definite transaction with God, comparable with the paying off of an accumulated debt in a series of instalments. This transactional view of the nature of religion is one of the legacies from paganism which the Church has inherited, and perhaps the worst of all. Besides this, the chantry priests were inevitably idle—as, their mass said, they had no other duties—and not always men of very reputable character.[2] The system developed further during the fifteenth century, and the reformers were unquestionably right in regarding it as an abuse which must be brought to an end.

The *Canterbury Tales* appear to have been published about the year 1390, and the prologue gives a very vivid and interesting sketch of what may be called a cross-section of English society. We are concerned with the ecclesiastical personages only.

The Prioress[3] appears as an attractive lady of fashion. It is not implied that her life was not virtuous, but it may be doubted whether her vocation for the cloister was very strong. Nothing is said about the nun and the three priests who attended on her.

[1] See *Article* XXXI, paragraph 2.
[2] One of the good traits in Chaucer's poor parson of a town is that he did not try to get himself a chantry (509–12).   [3] 118–64.

The monk,[1] who may or may not have got permission to take part in the expedition from his superior, is represented as a genial personage addicted to open-air life and sport. He did not try to conceal his opinion (which Chaucer himself shared) that the rules of his Order were obsolete, and that the observance of them would make more useful occupations impossible. He is, in fact, a country gentleman who enjoys life. He has not withdrawn from the world in any sense.

The friar[2] is described as "a wanton and a merry." He made a good living out of his calling by taking money in lieu of penance, and was a familiar figure in the tavern of every town. If it would be too much to call him a bad character, he was unlikely to command much respect either for his person or his calling.

To set against these, there is first the Clerk of Oxenford.[3] He is a scholar with a real love of learning and a profound contempt for money and luxury. The staple of his studies was Aristotle, probably in Latin translations, perhaps from the Arabic, and the account of him ends:

> Sounding in moral virtue was his speech
> And gladly would he learn and gladly teach.

Beside him, there is the really beautiful portrait of the "poor Parson of a town" and of his brother the ploughman. The account of the former is too long to reproduce in full here, but the last five lines may be quoted:

> A better priest I trow that nowhere none is
> He waited after no pomp or reverence,
> Ne maked him no spiced conscience
> But Christe's lore and his apostles twelve
> He taught, but first he followed it himself.[4]

The other characters in the Prologue may be for the most part types, noted by a man who should perhaps be classed with Shakespeare and Dickens, amongst the most observant Englishmen who have ever lived, but it is difficult not to think that these

---

[1] 165–207.   [2] 208–71.
[3] 287–310.   [4] 479–530.

two are drawn from life. They are men whom Chaucer really knew. The parochial clergy are always the backbone of the Church, and the state of religion throughout the country as a whole depends primarily upon them. If there was even a sprinkling of parish priests of this kind, then the Church was not entirely demoralized, however corrupt and worldly the dignitaries may have become.

During the last few years of his reign Edward III deteriorated rapidly. When he died on 21 June 1377 he was virtually imbecile. It was a great misfortune for England that his son Edward (the Black Prince) died before him, so that he was succeeded by his grandson Richard, a boy of ten. The new king came to the throne at a time of difficulty and danger. We had met with disaster in France, and had lost almost all our possessions there. The effects of the Black Death were still felt and discontent was increasing steadily amongst the peasants. Under the system which had been in force at any rate since the Norman Conquest there were on every manor a number of villeins. A villein was not a slave, inasmuch as he had real and important, if limited, rights. He could not be turned out of his house or dispossessed of his holding of land. His "rent" was paid by so many days' labour each year upon his lord's demesne. But he was not entirely free, as he could not leave the manor without his lord's permission. His lord could transfer him to another manor, where his position would be unaltered either for better or for worse, and he could not refuse to go. As his work was intermittent other labourers had to be hired for tasks which had to be performed regularly every day, such as milking the cows and looking after the herds of swine to see that they did not stray too far. These labourers could make a free contract with their employer, and while they had not the security of the villein they could take themselves off when and as they pleased. Thus on every manor there were two classes of labourers working side by side. From about the beginning of the fourteenth century the villeins seem to have begun to regard the position of the free labourer as preferable to their own. Englishmen have always tended to put personal freedom above anything else, and this characteristic may have been intensified

by the heightened sense of national consciousness to which
reference has been made above. The battles of Creçy and Poiters
may also have contributed. They were the first great triumphs of
the long bow (which no other nation ever really learned to use)
over the armoured horseman.[1] For some two centuries he had
been the decisive factor in battle, so that the fate of kingdoms had
depended upon him. If that were no longer true, it meant that
the old order of things was passing very quickly. Besides this,
the armoured horseman belonged to and represented the upper
classes. But the hands which held the long bow, and aimed its
deadly arrows, were those of peasants. Prowess in war was
esteemed above all other qualities. If the English peasant had
proved himself more than a match for the proudest chivalry of
France, not unnaturally his opinion of himself went up, and he was
still less likely to be content with his old status when he went
home. The astonishing completeness of the victory at Poitiers
was made more remarkable by the fact that the French army
outnumbered the English considerably. Pope Innocent VI had
done all in his power on behalf of the French cause, and a rather
profane quatrain appeared scribbled on walls at Vienne, where he
was living, and elsewhere. It may be translated as follows: "Now
is the Pope become French and Jesus become English; now shall
we see who will do most, the Pope or Jesus." (Knighton's
Chronicle, ii. 93, cited by G. G. Coulton A Medieval Garner,
pp. 4 and 6. I am indebted to the kindness of Canon Smyth for
this reference.)

The Black Death introduced an economic factor into the social
situation. Prices went up, because much land went out of cultivation, and as labour was very scarce men who were free to make
their own terms could secure higher wages and had no difficulty
in finding employment anywhere. The reduction in the total
number of labourers available naturally made the lord more
anxious than ever to retain all his villeins who had survived, while
to the villein the prospect of escape by flight to begin a new life as
a free labourer elsewhere became more and more attractive, even

---

[1] The Earl of Surrey's victory over James IV of Scotland at Flodden on
9 September 1513 was the last.

if it meant loss of house and land. The grounds of his discontent were, however, primarily social.

In 1350 an attempt was made to regulate wages and prices by the means of the Statute of Labourers. Its terms and failure do not concern us directly now. It might, however, be studied with advantage by anyone who is tempted to confuse social with economic grievances, or to imagine that the grim facts of economics are malleable and that legislation can shape them at will to suit the interest of one class, whether high or low.

The situation was made still more difficult by the return of the remnants of our defeated armies from France. It is a matter of common experience that ex-soldiers are not always easy to fit into the framework of civil society.

Besides all these factors, the great Schism in the Papacy[1] broke out in 1378, and weakened respect for authority generally throughout the whole of Western Europe.

Accordingly, when Richard II came to the throne the materials for an explosion had all been collected. It was really only a question of how and when the magazine would be fired.

The story of the peasants' rising, associated with the name of Wat Tyler, need not be recounted at length. For a few days during the month of June, 1381, it looked as if England was to experience a very bloody revolution. The insurgents gained possession of London, and something like a reign of terror ensued. On the 14th the Tower was stormed and Archbishop Sudbury, who had taken refuge there, was dragged out and murdered in the presence of a howling mob on Tower Hill. His head was subsequently displayed on London Bridge. His unpopularity was due primarily to the fact that as Chancellor he had enforced the detested poll tax, as it was his duty to do. The fact that he was archbishop did not deter his assailants. The extent to which moral standards had become debased is illustrated by the fact that the murder produced no outburst of popular feeling such as that which had (literally) brought Henry II to his knees at the tomb of Becket some two hundred years before.

The story of the famous meeting between the two sides at

[1] See Chapter 6, pp. 114 ff.

Smithfield on the following day is well known. Wat Tyler was struck down, probably by the hand of the Lord Mayor, and for a moment it looked as if there would be a pitched battle. The king rose to the occasion in a way worthy of his parentage. At the risk of his life he rode towards the insurgents and declared himself their leader. His courage, youth and good looks carried the day. The promises of redress were, however, not all kept, and the smouldering embers of rebellion were stamped out with much severity. Roughly the entire country to the east of a line drawn from Hull to Bristol, to which Somerset, Dorset, Devon and Cornwall must be added, had been affected.[1] It was long before the memory of the terrible year died out, and its effect may be seen in the severity of the measures directed against heretics in the next century.[2]

The brilliant promise with which the reign had opened was not fulfilled. In twenty years Richard had degenerated into an arbitrary autocrat, and on 30 September 1399 he was deposed by Parliament and his cousin Henry, Duke of Hereford, son of John of Gaunt, Duke of Lancaster, was placed upon the throne. He was not the direct heir, as his father had been the third son of Edward III, and a daughter of Lionel, Duke of Clarence, Edward's second son, was still living. But he was near enough to the throne to serve. By this revolution the monarchy became a new thing. It was established that the sovereign is not above the law, and that the crown is, within limits, at the disposition of Parliament. It might be said that ever since that day the King of England reigns by hereditary title, but governs with the consent of Parliament. Charles I and James II were unable to understand or unwilling to admit this.

The intimacy of the relation between Crown and people which was established in 1399 is one reason why our monarchy has outlived many others. The older conception is summed up in the words which Shakespeare put into the mouth of Richard II:[3]

---

[1] See *England in the Age of Wycliffe*, by G. M. Trevelyan, map opposite p. 254.

[2] See Chapter 9.   [3] Act III, Scene ii.

Not all the water in the rough rude sea
Can wash the balm from an anointed King;
The breath of worldly men cannot depose
The deputy elected by the Lord.
For every man that Bolingbroke hath pressed
To lift shrewd steel against our golden crown,
God for his Richard hath in heavenly pay
A glorious angel: then if angels fight,
Weak men must fall, for heaven still guards the right.

The attempt of Charles I and James II to revive it was perhaps prompted by an uneasy suspicion that England was not inclined to accord them as much respect as they considered to be their due. It brought ruin upon their house and did grievous injury to the Church.[1]

Richard died at some time before 14 February 1400. The exact date and the circumstances in which he met his end are not known. In Shakespeare's time it was believed that he was murdered and that Henry was not an accessory before the fact,[2] if he did not regret the *fait accompli*.

The best feature of the period taken as a whole is the increase of collegiate foundations at Oxford and Cambridge. Four new ones were established at Oxford (Exeter, 1314; Oriel, 1326; Queen's, 1340; and New College, 1379) and five at Cambridge (Clare, 1326; Pembroke, 1347; Gonville and Caius, 1348; Trinity Hall, 1350; and Corpus Christi, 1352). A century or so earlier some new monasteries might have appeared.

The influence of the colleges upon the life of the nation for centuries has been enormous, possibly far in excess of anything contemplated by their founders, whose primary purpose was to reduce the cost of a university education and to increase the amenities of university life.[3] Today the Colleges have become the principal strongholds of religious toleration and intellectual freedom to be found anywhere in the country, if not the only ones remaining.

It may be fair to say that they took up the kind of work which the monasteries were showing themselves less and less capable of doing, and have carried it on over a wider field ever since.

[1] See Chapters 12 & 13, pp. 247 & 275. [2] Act V, Scenes v and vi.
[3] See Chapter 5, p. 85.

9

The Leaves Fall—1

From the Accession of Henry IV to the end of the French Adventure—1399–1453

DURING the fifteenth century the forces which led to the
Reformation in the sixteenth gathered strength steadily.
During the fourteenth century the medieval system in which
Europe had been educated was obviously dying, if indeed it were
not already dead. But it is probably true to say that down to the
year 1450 or thereabouts the decline of the Church might have
been arrested. If the Councils of Constance[1] (1414–18) and Basel
(1433–7 and intermittently until 1439) had succeeded in carrying
out some real reforms, they might have left the Church in a better
position to meet the flood of new knowledge with which it was
soon to be confronted. Then doctrinal and administrative changes
might have been carried out gradually, as they became necessary,
and the violent eruptions of the sixteenth century might have
been averted. The Reformation, whether in England or Scotland
or upon the Continent, would have presented fewer regrettable
features had it not been staved off too long.

It is true that the former Council did bring the Great Schism[2]
to an end, and that the latter suspended Eugenius IV in 1438 and
deposed him in the following year. But all this merely made the
Papacy as an institution stronger than before and established
more firmly the vast bureaucracy of which it was the centre.

Naturally the Papacy became more and more averse from any
criticism and more and more hostile to anything which might
interfere with the smooth working of the vast and complicated
machine through which it acted, and upon which it depended for

[1] See Chapter 6, p. 114.　　　　　　　[2] See Chapter 6, p. 114.

its revenues. The Church became such a triumph of organization that the purpose for which it exists was in danger of being obscured. When men began to question the truth of some of its premises, and to ask whether the system was concerned with any interests but its own (which were now primarily those of an Italian principality), it had no answer to give which could command their intellectual and moral assent.

Henry IV had been placed upon the throne by Parliament, and the monarchy had become a new thing. But, in spite of the close relation between Crown and people which had been established, he did not find his seat very secure. Richard II had his partisans, more perhaps after he was dead than during the closing years of his life, and there was a serious rebellion in Wales, which for a time met with a very considerable measure of success. Besides this, the great house of Percy was a source of trouble in the north. Richard le Scrope, Archbishop of York, was executed on 8 June 1405 for the support he had given to a rebellious movement headed by the Earl of Northumberland. Archbishop Arundel was anxious to prevent the execution, but arrived on the scene too late. This act increased the unpopularity which Henry had already incurred by his extravagance, but did not really shake his throne. If a king, especially one whose right to reign was not beyond question, could put an archbishop to death with impunity, respect for the Church had obviously sunk to a low ebb. The Papacy was not in a position to act, as it could have done two hundred years earlier. These domestic distractions made it impossible for Henry to pursue the war in France, and the French king was unable to take any action against him for similar reasons.

Wiclif's influence had not ended with his death. Besides his writings, his followers continued for nearly fifty years. His "poor priests" almost became an Order resembling the friars of the thirteenth century: almost, but not quite, because they had no rule of their own, no distinctive habit and no particular head-quarters. Probably they were not unlike the itinerant Methodist evangelists of the eighteenth century. Their principal strength sppears to have been in the south-western part of the country.

They were known as Lollards, but the derivation and meaning of the title are uncertain. Traditionally it is said to have come from the Latin *lolium*, which means *tares*, because they were as weeds in the fruitful field of the Church, and the word is, in fact, applied to them in a Papal communication. More probably it is connected with a late Latin verb which has given us the first syllable of the word *lullaby*. On this theory the title means the *Chanters* or, perhaps, the *Crooners*, and was presumably given to them because they sang hymns of some kind. From the days of the Donatists[1] in North Africa, at least, if not from a still earlier period, many people have found hymn singing a valuable vehicle for the propagation of their religious opinions.

William Courtenay, who was Bishop of London 1370–81 and Archbishop of Canterbury 1381–96, does not seem to have taken them very seriously, but his successor, Thomas Arundel,[2] was less lenient. In 1401 the statute *De heretico comburendo* (*On the burning of a heretic*) was passed by Parliament, and a man named William Sawtre suffered almost immediately.[3] In 1406 a petition was presented to Parliament calling for more extensive and vigorous action. Finally, in the year 1414, when under the leadership of Sir John Oldcastle[4] they attempted something not unlike a revolution, a more severe Act was passed to enable the secular power to put them down. After that they declined steadily. They seem to have disappeared completely by the middle of the century. It is not easy to determine now how dangerous they really were. They were credited with subversive activities, principally perhaps because no one knew exactly what their aims were. The dreadful events of the summer of 1381 had not been forgotten. The country was in a disturbed and unsettled state, so we cannot wonder if Parliament was nervous and not inclined to take risks. The Lollards were certainly a nuisance, and might become a danger if they were not checked in good time. They seem to have held ultra-socialistic, if not communistic, views on the subject

[1] During the fourth and fifth centuries.

[2] He was deposed by Richard II for political reasons and translated to the see of St Andrews. Henry IV restored him to Canterbury in 1399 and he held the see until 1414.

[3] See Appendix A, *Persecution*.   [4] He was burned in 1417.

of property, and to have been disposed to put the conscience of the individual above the law to an extent which might make government impossible. So far, if no farther, their claim to be disciples and heirs of Wiclif was perhaps justifiable. But they never produced anyone approaching him in intellectual or moral stature. They might have stirred up a political and social revolution, but could never have brought about a religious reformation. Wiclif's only real heirs were in Bohemia, and the story of them is outside the scope of these lectures.

On 20 March 1413, Henry IV, whose health had been failing for some months, was taken ill in Westminster Abbey, apparently with what would now be called a cerebral hæmorrhage. He was carried into the great parlour of the abbot's house, which communicated directly with the Church and has always been known as *Jerusalem*,[1] or the *Jerusalem Chamber*, and placed on a couch in front of the fireplace. He regained consciousness and asked where he was. When he was told "In Jerusalem," he said that he knew that his end had come. Many years earlier a hermit had told him that he would die in Jerusalem. Naturally Henry had assumed that he meant the Holy City and had intended to go thither on a pilgrimage, as soon as the state of the kingdom should allow, to expiate any guilt which he had incurred by his seizure of the throne. He died a few minutes afterwards.

When Henry V came to the throne England as a whole had recovered from the effects of the Black Death and the French war was prosecuted vigorously. The campaign which culminated at Agincourt on 25 October 1415 was so brilliant that whoever was responsible for the strategy, whether the young king himself or his uncle John, Duke of Bedford, must be considered to rank with any soldier whom we have ever produced. The battle, which was one more triumph for the long-bowman over the armoured knight, gave him the whole of Normandy. In the speech which Shakespeare put into his mouth on the eve, there is a notable acknowledgment of the wrong Henry IV had done which must reflect the general opinion of the Elizabethan age

[1] It is one of the few rooms in the Deanery House which escaped destruction in 1941.

Not to-day, O Lord,
O not to-day, think not upon the fault
My father made in compassing the Crown;
I Richard's body have interred new;
And on it have bestow'd more contrite tears
Than from it issued forced drops of blood:
Five hundred poor I have in yearly pay,
Who twice a day their wither'd hands hold up
Toward heaven, to pardon blood; and I have built
Two Chantries, where the sad and solemn priests
Sing still for Richard's soul.
                                        (*Henry V*, Act IV, Scene 1.)

On his return to England the king went in state to St Paul's to return thanks. A special hymn was written for the occasion beginning,

Our King has gone through Normandy

with the refrain

Deo Gratias Anglia redde pro victorio[1]

at the end of each verse. The music is said to be one of the earliest English compositions known.

From the secure base of Normandy he extended his power to the banks of the Loire, and concluded an alliance with Flanders on the south-east to Burgundy on the east. Since we already had Guienne (the country round about Bordeaux which we had held for centuries) he was now master of more than half France. By the Treaty of Troyes in May 1420 he was recognized as heir and regent of the realm of France, and in the following month he consolidated his position by marrying Katharine of Valois, daughter of King Charles VI of France. The long struggle was over. Our success was all but complete and promised to be permanent.

Naturally England was proud of the achievement. But there seems to have been a certain amount of misgiving in some quarters. It was all to the good that the Crown of England should have important possessions in France. But was it altogether desirable that the same man should be king of both countries? If two king-

[1] *England, give thanks to God for victory.*

doms between which there is a wide disparity in respect of size, population, and wealth are united, it is almost inevitable that the smaller should become not much more than an appanage of the larger, especially if the latter is more advantageously placed geographically. How would England fare if it were governed from Paris by a sovereign whose visits to London would probably become brief and infrequent?

It is impossible to say what would have happened had Henry V lived a little longer. He died of an attack of pleurisy on 31 August 1422, just before completing his thirty-fifth year. The saddle which he is believed to have used at Agincourt is still to be seen on the crossbeam of his chantry-chapel in Westminster Abbey, where his body lies.

There is one memorial—or, to speak more accurately, out-come—of these years of victory still to be seen, if the majority of those who pass it today do not recognize it for what it is. At the beginning of the fifteenth century Thomas, fifth Lord de la Warr, was in Holy Orders, and became rector of the parish church of Manchester. As a peer he was duly summoned to Parliament, but as a priest could not render personal service in the wars. In the ninth year of King Henry V, which means a date between 21 March 1421 and 20 March 1422, he obtained a licence to make the church collegiate. He established a warden and a number of priests to offer perpetual intercession for the good estate of the king and their founder in this world, and for their repose and welfare in the next. His new foundation was dedicated in the name of St Mary, St Denys[1] and St George. It is reasonable to suppose that this amounted to what is known in legal phraseology as a *cy-près*. Lord de la Warr intended to give the king the best help in his power, in lieu of the service from which he was debarred by his calling. The foundation survived the Reformation, if its original function lapsed, and in 1847 the church became the cathedral of the new diocese of Manchester. The dean and canons are the modern representatives of Thomas de la Warr's College of Priests, and the church is still in name collegiate as well as cathedral. Except for the Derby chapel,

[1] Patron saint of France.

which was built about the year 1520, and a nineteenth-century porch, the fabric remained as he left it until our own time. It was damaged very severely during the recent war. When it has been repaired the dedication which attests its origin will be equally appropriate and the building will be a link between the campaign of 1414–15 and that of 1944–45, much of which was fought over the same ground, if not against the same enemy.

Henry VI was not quite nine months old when his father died. A few weeks later (11 November 1422) he was proclaimed King of France. He is the only man who ever wore the crowns of both countries. It is interesting to speculate as to the course of European history for the last five hundred years had he been able to transmit them to his successors. (The title *King of France* was not abandoned by the sovereigns of England, and the French lilies did not disappear from the royal arms until the year 1801.) The war was prosecuted vigorously by his great-uncle, the Duke of Bedford, and the victory at Vermeuil over a combined French and Scottish force on 16 August 1427 placed Maine in our hands. Next year the Duke moved against Orleans. That was the last bastion of French resistance. If that had fallen the whole of the south-eastern part of the country, which had naturally held out longest, as it was farthest from the shores of England, must have capitulated. But in two years a complete change came over the scene. By 1431 it was obvious that our cause in France was lost, though we kept a few troops there for more than twenty years. The last battle, an unsuccessful attempt to recover Guienne, was not until 1453. That left us with nothing but Calais, which was more a token than anything else. A century later it was destined to show that a naval base may be very difficult to defend against attack from the rear unless its garrison has plenty of room in which to manœuvre on the landward side.

The story of the Maid of Orleans is too well known to need retelling here. It is unnecessary to consider the genuineness of her "Voices". The sober truth may be stated briefly as follows. We awoke to full national consciousness before France[1] and attacked her in the pride of our newly recognized strength. Our prolonged

[1] See Chapter 8, p. 143 ff.

assault hammered France into a nation. Joan of Arc provided the symbol and focus needed. As soon as French national conscious-ness came to life it was much too strong for us. She was taken and burned as a witch at Rouen on 30 May, 1431, and on 17 December of the same year Henry was crowned King of France in Paris. But nothing could quench the fire which she had kindled. Probably, in fact, her death helped to fan it. It may be worth while to say in passing that Mr Shaw's play *St Joan* does not seem to me to deserve the acclamations with which it was greeted when it was published. A professional cynic is not really well-fitted to deal with a story in which sincere religion and equally sincere patriotism are the dominant factors, and more than dramatic imagination is needed for a real understanding (assuming such a thing to be possible) of the outlook and system of the medieval Church.

Ten years later we were—whether for good or bad, and there is something to be said on both sides—an island kingdom as we had not been since the Norman conquest, and the Crown was poorer and weaker than at any time for nearly four hundred years.

Some real good, however, came to England out of our French losses, which may be considered to have more than balanced them by now. They made it possible for Henry VI to found his two great colleges at Eton and Cambridge which have now served the Church and the Commonwealth for more than five hundred years. More will be said of them later in this chapter.

The king and the Maid of Orleans have both been formally canonized[1] in our own time by the Roman Church. No one need grudge either the honour. Yet it may be argued that no two people did more than St Henry and St Joan to make the Reformation

---

[1] Henry was unofficially canonized in England, as other people have been, very soon after his death in 1471, if not before. His figure appears among the saints in Yorkshire and East Anglia, and a hymn invoking his protection exists in a manuscript at Corpus Christi College, Oxford. (It has been printed by Sir Stephen Gaselee in his *Anthology of Mediæval Latin*, who puts its date at about 1480.) It is used now in his college at Eton, and was known there fifty years ago. But whether it was handed down by continuous tradition or brought to light by some nineteenth-century antiquary I cannot say.

possible. Her flaming patriotism and his unsoldierly character between them ended our career as a continental power. Therefore we sat more loosely to the Papacy, which could do less than before to advance or impede any interests of ours, and in the next century felt ourselves sufficiently outside the continental system to be able to defy the public opinion of Europe.

Two years after our final defeat in France a brawl between two parties of discharged soldiers in the streets of St Albans led to the outbreak of what are known as the Wars of the Roses. This struggle, which lasted for thirty years, was hardly a civil war in the ordinary sense, as no political, social, religious or economic principle was at stake. It has been described by Professor Trevelyan as a faction fight with the Crown of England as the prize. It was virtually a family feud between the two great houses of Lancaster and York, and this aspect of the affair is emphasized by the fact that their badges, red for Lancaster and white for York, have given the struggle its name. Once it had broken out, Henry VI, who was now almost imbecile, could do nothing to stop it. England as a whole does not seem to have been deeply interested, and was perhaps less disturbed than might have been expected.

The Eton College register for the years 1441–1698 has recently been published,[1] and it shows that during the years 1455[2]–85 222 boys were admitted to the college. A considerable proportion, perhaps rather more than one-third of the number, came from within a radius of fifty miles. The rest were drawn from every county in England except Northumberland.[3] Their social range seems to have been almost equally extensive. There are none of definitely noble birth, but the parents of some were well-to-do gentry. Others were London tradesmen, and the college carpenter and a doorkeeper at Windsor each sent a boy. It is interesting to note how many parents in various walks of life were willing to send their sons a considerable distance to secure a better education than anything to be had nearer home; also that small boys

[1] Edited by Sir Wasey Sterry.
[2] The outbreak of the Wars of the Roses.
[3] Unless *Durham*, which is fairly frequent, means the diocese of Durham, which then included the county of Northumberland.

could apparently travel safely despite the war. One wonders how long it took to reach Eton from Yorkshire or Norfolk or Cornwall, and exactly how the children made the journey. There are no Welsh boys: possibly they would not have understood English sufficiently to benefit by going to school in England. It is also to be noted that during the same period Edward IV could find the money to rebuild the Chapel of St George in Windsor Castle on a magnificent scale.

If the nation as a whole stood aloof, the war took a heavy toll of the nobility and gentry. Almost every noble family was related in some degree to one or other of the protagonists, and therefore naturally took part. Any of them would welcome the prospect of a kinsman on the throne, who would, as in duty bound, reward the services of those who had helped to put him there. The gentry naturally supported their overlords. For such the battles were bloody, if the total number of men engaged was small, as they tended to resolve themselves into hand-to-hand duels which could hardly end except by the death of one combatant, if not of both.

When Henry VII ascended the throne he found that he had to govern an impoverished and disordered kingdom with and through new men. The old governing class had been reduced considerably.

It was during this period that artillery came into use. At Agincourt the archer had once more asserted his supremacy over the armoured knight. But after this it was found that a man and a horse could just carry, at any rate for a time, armour so thick that no arrow could pierce it. The problem arose again, how to prevent these ironclads from making the charge which, if it were pressed home, would scatter everything before it and decide the day. Probably it could not be repeated, but a second would not be necessary. The cannon, or bombard[1] as it was sometimes called, gave the answer. Possibly it often proved as dangerous to those who were concerned with discharging it as to those against whom it was pointed. But no doubt it frightened the horses and so parried the blow which would have been deadly could it have been delivered with all its weight.

[1] A corporal in the Artillery is still called a bombardier.

John Gunthorpe, who was Dean of Wells 1472–98, ornamented his house very lavishly with carvings of this new weapon. There are said to be one hundred of them, but I have never been able to find more than ninety-eight. His name was a fortunate coincidence, as the family appears to have come from the village of Gunthorpe in Nottinghamshire.[1]

The long struggle ended on 22 August 1485, when Henry Tudor defeated and killed Richard III on the field of Bosworth and inaugurated a new dynasty. His chief title to the throne was *de facto* power. He was at the head of a victorious army. He had just killed a king whose character had not been such as to evoke any fervent loyalty to his person, and there was no one left to dispute his claim.[2] So far as family went his only title was derived from three marriages. His grandfather, a respectable if undistinguished Welsh gentleman named Owen Tudor, had married Katharine of Valois, widow of Henry V. They had a son, Edmund, who was created Earl of Richmond as a recognition of his mother's rank. He married Margaret Plantagenet, only daughter of John Duke of Beaufort, and a great-great-grand-daughter (through John of Gaunt) of Edward III. Their son Henry married Elizabeth Plantagenet, daughter of Edward IV. England was so weary of the struggle that his succession to the throne was generally welcomed. So great was the anxiety to secure peace that the Pope was persuaded to declare that if Elizabeth died without children and Henry married again, his son by his second wife, whoever she might be, was to be the lawful heir to the throne of England. Such being their antecedents, the Tudors never had any illusion about themselves. They knew nothing about the *Divine Right of Kings* with which the Stuarts (whose only title to the English throne was their descent from Henry VII) brought ruin upon themselves, and did almost immeasurable harm to England and the Church.

Henry VII was not a very attractive character. But he had one quality indispensable to success as a ruler. He could face fact

[1] There is another Gunthorpe in Northamptonshire and a third in Norfolk.
[2] Of course, pretenders appeared after a time, but no one took them very seriously.

and see them as they are. Compared with the realm which Henry VI had inherited, the kingdom which he had was of little worth. He set himself to rebuild it, first by restoring its shattered finances. For that he had to turn to the middle classes of the towns, who had made money while their betters were destroying each other. Naturally he was counted avaricious, but his policy in this respect was what was needed. His only extravagance was the magnificent chapel which he planned for his burial at the eastern end of Westminster Abbey. No one can regret that, and perhaps that too was part of his policy and was intended to be a visible memorial of his royal dignity to all generations. It was completed by his son. Part of the dowry of Katharine of Aragon had been a window of Flemish manufacture in which she appears with Arthur. It had been intended for the chapel in Westminster Abbey. (Naturally Henry VIII did not care for it and it is now in St Margaret's Church). His reign was also marked by a considerable increase of diplomatic activity by which he aimed at recovering some of the prestige which had been lost by our final failure in France. The marriage between Arthur, Prince of Wales, and Katharine of Aragon, upon which much that was unexpected was destined to turn, was probably planned for the same reason. He was too clear-sighted to imagine that we could have any future upon the continent of Europe, but if it is impossible to say whether he saw far enough to guess that we might have a greater future elsewhere, he seems to have been the first person to perceive the possibilities of Southampton and Portsmouth.

During the second half of the fifteenth century three things happened which were destined to affect the history and civilization of Europe very deeply.

First, the Revival of Learning, commonly called the *Renaissance*. It is impossible to date the beginning of this exactly, or to say what brought it about. Quite suddenly, it seems, men awoke to the interest and importance of Græco-Roman civilization. No doubt the capture of Constantinople by the Turks on 29 May 1453 stimulated the movement, because many of the survivors fled westward, bringing their own knowledge of Greek and their Greek books with them. The final fall of Constantinople was a shattering event. It had been an imperial capital for more than eleven centuries. For nearly ten of them it had been the most civilized city in Europe and for more than seven had kept Islam at bay. The emperor was the heir of all the Cæsars, and we ought never to forget that he held the eastern gate of Europe against the Mohammedan invader until the petty and half-barbarous kingdoms of the west were strong enough to resist him themselves. When Spain had been overrun and the crescent had appeared for a moment in France[1], all Christian civilization was imperilled. It is not easy to see how it could have stood had other Mohammedan armies been able to cross the Bosphorus, where lies the main highway from Asia into Europe.

It is probable that the knowledge of Greek which Theodore of Tarsus must have brought in the seventh century had never quite died out in England. When Dr M. R. James was Provost of Eton College he found at the College of Arms what he identified as part of a Greek dictionary made by or for Robert Grosseteste, Bishop of Lincoln in the thirteenth century. In or about the year 1325 there was a "professor" of Greek, Hebrew and Syriac established at Oxford.[2] But the circle of people who took part in such studies was small. Certainly the knowledge of Greek became diffused much more widely during the second half of the fifteenth century than it had ever been before. Men realized that there had been a brilliant civilization, the remains of which were worth studying, which the Church had done nothing to create. It is difficult for us now to appreciate the almost overwhelming effect of this discovery. The nations of Western Europe had owed everything to the Church. It had brought them out of barbarism step by step. It was the only educator they had ever had, and the sole source, at least as they believed, of all the civilization which they had ever known. It commanded all the knowledge to which man could ever hope to attain. Now, if their debt to the Church

[1] The Saracens were defeated by Charles Martel and driven back across the Pyrenees at the battle of Tours in October, 732.

[2] A receipt from the rural dean of Oakham to the abbot and convent of Westminster for a payment towards his stipend was found in the muniment room at Westminster Abbey in or about the year 1903. It was printed in the *Athenæum*. I happened to be present when the discovery was made.

still stood, it could not be disputed that there were other sources of knowledge with which it had had nothing to do. The Church could no longer profess to be omniscient; possibly its title to infallibility might prove to be no better founded. Questions which could not have been asked before might well arise now and would have to be answered. When the New Testament could be read in the language in which it was written it might appear that the Church which for a thousand years had relied upon a Latin translation had not always interpreted it aright.

Secondly, the invention of printing. This appears to have originated in Germany about the year 1460. Our connection with it begins about twenty years later, when Caxton set up the first printing press in England under the patronage of Edward IV. The effect of the new invention was immediate and enormous. First, the monastic scribe became obsolete. If he continued to practise his art (as in fact he did) for another generation his old importance was gone and the position of the monasteries as possible centres of learning was weakened still further. Secondly, it became possible for the first time in the history of the world to produce a number of copies of a book all exactly alike in every particular, and to do this with a rapidity of which no one had ever dreamed. Of course, the ease and rapidity of production made each copy much cheaper than it could have been before. Without the printer the new learning would have spread much more slowly, which might have meant that its effect would have been less disturbing.

While full credit is due to the printer for his contribution to the spread of learning, we must not forget his humble ally the paper-maker, without whom the volume of his achievement must have been much less. Except for stone, metal and clay tablets, which do not lend themselves readily to literary composition on a large scale and are not very portable, the ancient world possessed two types of writing material. First, papyrus, and secondly, parchment. Papyrus is made from a reed which grows in the Nile and apparently nowhere else. Attempts were made to cultivate it in Sicily, but did not meet with sufficient success to be of any commercial value. A few clumps can be seen in the river Anapur at the present day. The word has come to us from the Greek, and was probably the attempt of Alexandrian tongues to reproduce the native name for the plant. It is tempting to think that it has given us our word *paper*. Papyrus made excellent writing material, but the supply was limited and the Egyptians, who held the monopoly, could charge what price they pleased.

Parchment is animal-skin. The word is said to be derived from Pergamum, a city in Asia Minor, where it was first manufactured some time during the second century before our era. The story goes that a library which was being formed there under the patronage of a wealthy and enlightened sovereign provoked the jealousy of the scholars of Alexandria. They could not tolerate the idea that there should be any rival to their library anywhere, and thought that the best way of securing their supremacy was to make it impossible for the scholars of Pergamum to get anything on which to write their books. Parchment was the answer to this very mean attack. It can be made of the skin of almost any animal, but the best is calf (vellum). Good vellum is perhaps the best writing material which exists, besides being the pleasantest to see and handle. Parchment is more durable than any form of paper but is, unfortunately, always expensive. An animal of some kind has to be killed, to start with, and although the makers became very skilful at splitting the hides so as to get two or more sheets out of a single skin, the amount of writing material which one calf could be made to yield was not very great. However rapidly it might be possible to print, there could not be a very large number of copies of any book as long as the supply of material on which to print was scanty and expensive.[1] Something was needed which could be produced easily almost anywhere, so that there could be no monopoly, and in almost unlimited quantities and therefore sold cheaply.

The Chinese are said to have discovered how to make paper out of flax, hemp, or rags by the second century of our era. By the fifth the art had reached Baghdad, whence it spread gradually through-

---

[1] The abbreviations and contractions in which mediæval MSS abound were probably employed more with the object of economizing in the use of material than of saving the scribe time and labour.

out Western Asia. In the seventh century the Moslems made use of paper for the purpose of religious propaganda. This led Christendom to regard it with suspicion, if not as an invention of the devil outright, because it was a new and very powerful weapon in the hands of the infidels. It is said to have been introduced into Europe via Spain about the middle of the twelfth century, but the manufacture spread alowly. For the first ten years or rather more Caxton had to get his supplies from Holland. None was made in England until about the year 1495.

Thirdly, the maritime discoveries. Everybody knows that Christopher Columbus, a native of Genoa, "discovered America" in the autumn of 1492. In fact he landed upon one of the small islands which abound in the Caribbean Sea.[1] If he ever saw the American continent, he never set foot upon it, and to the end of his life believed that the islands which he had reached were off the east coast of China. Still, he had shown that the Atlantic could be crossed. The western ocean had a further shore which was inhabited by human beings, and was not the abode of the dead, as had been supposed since the days of Homer at least. For more than half a century before Columbus sailed Portuguese navigators had been creeping down the west coast of Africa. Finally, after a voyage of nearly eleven months (July 1497–May 1498), Vasco da Gama rounded the southern point of the African continent and eventually reached Calicut on the south-western coast of India. His achievement was really fully equal to that of Columbus, if less spectacular. Both voyages were undertaken with the same purpose—namely, to find a way by sea to India, China, and what were called "The Spice Islands", because the overland route was barred by the fiercely hostile Mohammedan power which dominated the eastern end of the Mediterranean and the whole of western Asia. Da Gama's voyage was therefore completely successful. He found what he had set out to find. Columbus's voyage was a failure, though he never knew it. It was not until the year 1513 that the Pacific Ocean was seen by the Spanish explorer Balboa and it dawned upon Europe that the American continent really was a new world. During the years

[1] Probably Watling Island, one of the most easterly of the Bahamas.

1519–22 Magellan circumnavigated the globe, thereby revolutionizing all preconceived ideas as to the shape and extent of the world.

It is impossible to say how soon Englishmen began to realize what a change in our position the discovery of America had made. Hitherto we had been on the outskirts of civilization and almost on the edge of the world. Now we were approximately at the centre of the habitable globe. That was an indisputable fact, if the effect which it was to have upon our fortunes during the next four hundred years could not be imagined. These astounding geographical discoveries were crowded into no more than thirty years. Many people who had heard of Columbus's departure, and perhaps prophesied that the voyage could only end in disaster, must have lived to hear of the triumphant return of the *Vittoria*, Magellan's ship with her handful of survivors.

Here again were wonders which had been outside the horizon of the Church. Not only had the world had a brilliant past to which the Church had contributed nothing, but there were vast seas and lands and many races of men of which it did not know. If there were bounds to its knowledge there must be limits to its sovereignty over the minds and consciences of men.

Such in brief outline was the world, pregnant with new knowledge of every kind, the outcome of which no one could attempt to foresee, any more than its extent could be predicted, when Henry VIII occupied the throne of England.

Everyone knows that the reign of Henry VIII was an epoch in the history of the Church. But the real facts which underlay the changes which took place are often misunderstood, and sometimes misrepresented deliberately for controversial purposes. It will therefore be worth while to recount them carefully here, and to remember at every stage that the king's personal conduct is a matter of less importance than the general state of affairs which made it possible for him to behave as he did. For that he was in no way responsible. The outline of the story is as follows:[1]

---

[1] I have borrowed freely from Creighton's essay "The Abolition of the Roman Jurisdiction" published in *The Church and Nation*.

On 14 November 1501 Arthur, Prince of Wales, who had celebrated his fifteenth birthday on 19 September, married Katharine, daughter of Ferdinand of Aragon and Isabella of Castile. By this time Spain had become a united kingdom and the Moors had been expelled, after more than seven centuries.

The marriage between Arthur and Katharine had been under consideration for some time and must be regarded as primarily a diplomatic success on our part. If the heir to the throne of England married the daughter of the King of Spain our prestige would be enhanced. (Probably the abortive scheme for the Spanish marriage of Charles I was prompted by similar considerations.) Arthur died on 2 April 1502, aged fifteen years, six months and thirteen days. The marriage had lasted for a little less than five months and his health had never been robust. Had the union ever been a marriage in the full sense? Katharine's dowry was to have been paid in three instalments, of which the first only had been received when her husband died. Her father requested that it should be repaid to him, but this course did not commend itself to Henry VII. Eventually it was agreed that she should marry his second son, Henry, who was now heir to the throne, as soon as he had completed his fourteenth year, which would be on 28 June 1505. By this arrangement Henry VII would keep the money and presumably get the remaining two-thirds in due course and Katharine would be Queen of England after all.

The treaty for the marriage was concluded at Richmond on 23 June 1503, and both sovereigns agreed to do all in their power to procure the dispensation which would be required. At the moment the Pope was Alexander VI, a Borgia and a Spaniard, upon whose goodwill Ferdinand no doubt thought he could rely. But Alexander died during the following August and his successor, Pius III, reigned for less than a month. He was followed by Julius II, who reigned from 1503 to 1512. Julius obviously felt that a dispensation for a man to marry his brother's widow needed careful consideration. In July 1504 he wrote a letter to Henry VII in which he spoke of issuing it a little later. But Isabella was now dying and was very anxious to see her daughter settled in life.

Before long the Bull appeared.[1] It was ante-dated 26 December 1503, perhaps to suggest that the Pope had not really felt much hesitation about it. On 27 June 1505 the young prince, then on the eve of his fourteenth birthday, protested that the marriage had been arranged without his consent, and refused to ratify what had been done for him in his minority. This was really his father's answer to Ferdinand's continual refusal to pay the rest of Katharine's dowry. Eventually it proved effective. The matter rested there for almost exactly four years. On 11 June 1509 the marriage took place, Henry VII having died on 21 April. It was the outcome of a long series of tortuous negotiations and was widely regarded as dubious, to say no more, on moral and legal grounds alike from the very beginning. Pope Julius II came out of the business better than anyone else, assuming that his hesitation was really due to moral scruples, and that he was not merely holding out for a higher fee. (He was committed to very heavy expenditure in connection with the building of the vast basilica of St Peter at Rome.) It is impossible to say what the real feelings of either bride or bridgroom may have been. When Henry VIII came to the throne he was not quite eighteen. Nature had endowed him lavishly for the part he had to play, and in all respects save one his affairs prospered exceedingly. With the aid of Wolsey the power and prestige of England increased steadily. In 1513 there was a successful expedition against France which ended with the capture of Tournai. A Scottish invasion met with complete disaster at the hands of the Earl of Surrey at Flodden Field in Northumberland on 9 September 1513, and James IV, Henry's brother-in-law, was killed. The wonderful chapel which Henry VII had begun at Westminster was completed, and with the exception of the top part of the western towers, which was added during the eighteenth century, the Abbey became much as we see it today.

In 1520 the King of Spain, who had now become Emperor and was by far the richest and most powerful sovereign in Europe, actually came to England to visit his uncle by marriage, and he

---

[1] The signed statement of Ferdinand that the marriage with Arthur had been fully consummated, which had been denied in England, was qualified by the word *forsan* (perhaps).

had hardly left our shores before Henry crossed to France on a visit of reconciliation with Francis I, and made a most magnificent appearance. There could be no question about it. England was once again a first-class power. Next year Henry's personal prestige was enhanced still further by the receipt from Pope Leo X of the title *Fidei Defensor* (*Defender of the Faith*), which has been borne by his successors ever since, in recognition of a book which he had written in defence of the seven sacraments against the views of Martin Luther.

But all this success was overshadowed by one increasing cloud. He had no son. There had been a daughter born in 1518, and I believe several other still-born children. Probably modern medical knowledge could have accounted for this, and perhaps have prevented its recurrence, but we cannot wonder if Henry came to regard it as a mark of divine displeasure. After eighteen years of married life the position might almost be termed desperate. It was imperative that he should have a male heir, and Katharine could not give him one. He had seen Anne Boleyn and wished to marry her, and so the question of the validity of his marriage arose.

The word "divorce" was freely used at the time and is often employed in connection with this case today. In fact it is inaccurate. There was no such thing as divorce in that world, as the word is understood now. Once a marriage had been validly contracted nothing but death could bring it to an end. But a marriage might be annulled—that is to say, declared never to have been a marriage at all, because, for some just cause which was unknown or ignored at the time, it ought never to have taken place. Henry's union with Katharine had always, as we have seen, been regarded as dubious. He instituted an inquiry as to whether it had ever been, or could have been, a marriage at all. If we cannot condone his conduct entirely, we must remember that his motives were not wholly selfish or merely sensual. His religious scruples were perfectly genuine. Moreover, his dynasty, with which the welfare of England was linked, had to be taken into account. To understand his outlook we must also consider his family history.

1. His father, Henry of Richmond, had married his mother,

Elizabeth of York, at his accession. A dispensation had been necessary as they were related in the fourth degree: in modern phraseology, they were first cousins. Everybody wanted the marriage to take place to end the war and settle the succession to the Crown. Innocent VIII not only gave the dispensation required, but assigned the crown to the descendants of Henry VII if Elizabeth should die childless and he should marry again. This award met with general approval.

2. His sister Mary had been the third wife of Louis XII of France. Louis' first wife had been Jeanne of France, and for the marriage a dispensation had been required, as not only were they related in the fourth degree, but the bride's father had been godfather to the husband. As the law then stood this put the two young people spiritually in the relationship of brother and sister. After Louis came to the throne an opportunity of securing the great duchy of Brittany for the Crown of France presented itself. Accordingly he got his existing marriage annulled, on the strength of evidence supplied by himself, and married Anne, the heiress of Brittany, the widow of his former wife's brother. After her death he married Mary of England.

3. After his death she married Charles Brandon, Duke of Suffolk. He was already married by dispensation within the prohibited degrees. He pleaded that this dispensation was null, as he had been contracted previously to another lady, and carried his point.

4. Henry's other sister, Margaret, had married James IV of Scotland, also by dispensation, as they were related in the fourth degree. After his death in 1513 she married the Earl of Angus. She grew tired of him and in 1527 got the marriage annulled, by a sentence which Wolsey described at the time as "shameless".

In a world in which such things could happen the standard of domestic morality amongst royal or semi-royal personages could not be expected to be very high. But what are we to say of the supreme authority on all moral questions, the source and interpreter of all Law, who had made them possible? Is it wonderful if a man who had grown up in such an atmosphere should consider that the law could be manipulated to any extent, provided that

the interests involved were sufficiently important? Any condemnation of the conduct of Henry VIII must apply equally to the
system of the Church as it had come to be. The suggestion that
the case was a struggle between a lustful sovereign who was
determined to have his own way, and a Pope who was doing his
best to uphold the moral law, is remote from the truth.

By 1530 it had become clear that the Pope was not likely to do
as Henry wished, and steps were taken to ascertain the opinions
of the universities of England, France, and Italy. The idea is believed
to have originated with Thomas Cranmer. The step was significant, because it meant that a new intellectual authority had
established itself in Europe. The universities had been waxing in
importance for more than three hundred years, while the monasteries had waned, and now their reputation stood so high that
the Papacy need no longer be regarded as the sole and final arbiter
in any dispute in which the law ecclesiastical was concerned.

The universities of Oxford, Cambridge, Paris, Orleans, Angers,
Bourges, Toulouse, Bologna, and Padua took the view that the
dispensing power of the Papacy was limited. It could deal freely
with ecclesiastical regulations, but could not override the moral
law. If Henry could bring pressure upon Oxford and Cambridge,
the other universities were beyond his reach. It would not have
been worth while to consult one in the emperor's dominions.

Thomas Cranmer became Archbishop of Canterbury on
30 March 1533. On 23 May his court declared that as Katharine
had really been Arthur's wife, no dispensation to marry his
brother could be valid and that her union with Henry was therefore null and void. The judgement bore hardly upon her and her
daughter,[1] but for my own part I have always thought that
Cranmer and the universities were right.

Clement VII had not spoken definitely. Probably he hesitated
until he had decided whether he had more to fear from Henry or
the emperor. The latter naturally sided with his aunt, and both
ends of the Italian peninsula were in his hands. He had one
viceroy at Milan and another at Naples. On 11 July 1533 the Pope,

---

[1] Adequate provision for them was made at Kimbolton in Huntingdonshire.
Katharine died in 1536 and was buried in what is now Peterborough Cathedral.

to whom the audacity of Cranmer's judgment had probably come as a complete surprise, declared that the dispensation granted by Julius II was valid, and that the marriage must therefore stand. Even if he had been a free agent he might well have thought that to revise a decision of one of his predecessors might shake the entire fabric of the papal power. Probably he had no suspicion of the course which England would take. Sixteen years before Luther had challenged the system of Indulgences. Now Henry had challenged the system of Dispensations. Both attacks were very different from anything which the Papacy had had to face before. It was not now a question of administrative abuses, which are in a sense superficial, and betoken failure in practice more than defect in theory. Now the very foundations of the papal power were threatened.

Two questions had been raised. First, What is the nature and extent of the Papal power in relation to sin? Secondly, What is its relation to the law? Once raised, they could not be shelved, and together they provided the impetus which brought about the Reformation.

Perhaps the best feature of the period under review is the interest taken in education. The foundation of colleges in Oxford and Cambridge, which the Black Death had interrupted, was resumed and went on steadily.

At Oxford	At Cambridge
Lincoln, 1427	King's, 1441[1]
All Souls', 1437	Queens', 1448[2]
Magdalen, 1458	St Catherine's, 1473
Brazenose, 1509	Jesus, 1496
Corpus Christi, 1516	Christ's, 1505
Christ Church, 1532	St John's, 1511

Archbishop Chichele made use of a number of "alien priories" —that is to say, colonies from the religious houses in France planted in England—for his foundation of All Souls, as did Henry VI a few years later for his foundations at Eton and

[1] To which must be added the sister foundation of Eton College, 1440.
[2] Refounded 1465.

Cambridge. So long as England and all the northern part of France were united under one crown, there was no objection to these institutions. After the loss of our French possessions they could not be allowed to continue as they were, and it was not considered worth while to staff them with English inmates. Colleges were a better way of using the money.

A little later John Alcock, Bishop of Ely, suppressed the nunnery of St Radegund to found Jesus College, Cambridge, making use of the conventual buildings as far as they were suitable.

A generation later Wolsey suppressed twenty-nine small religious houses to provide for the great foundation which he called *Cardinal College*. After his fall it was refounded as Christ Church, but its coat-of-arms still attests its origin. These facts are worth noting as showing that many people thought that the day of religious houses was nearly done before Henry VIII laid hands upon them. Had they been, taken as a whole, popular and flourishing institutions, he could not have dealt with them as he did.

The system of Chantries[1] also developed considerably, largely at the instance of the Trade Guilds of the towns. When they were collegiate—that is to say, when a number of priests were attached to a single church—they sometimes had some definite educational work assigned to them. A conspicuous instance of such an arrangement was Jesus College, Rotherham, founded by Thomas, known alternatively as *Scott* or *Rotherham*, who was Archbishop of York from 1480 to 1500. He had become Bishop of Lincoln in 1468, and as he was admitted a scholar of King's College, Cambridge, in 1443, must be the first member of the foundation who rose to distinction. It is doubtful, having regard to dates, whether he can ever have been a scholar of Eton in more than name. But it is a tempting conjecture that his college at Rotherham was an attempt to provide an Eton for the north. It is a matter for regret that the foundation soon came to an end. All Souls' College, Oxford, is probably the nearest approach to a collegiate chantry which exists in England today. Probably no other pre-Reformation foundation has changed less.

[1] See Chapter 10.

10

The Leaves Fall—2

From the beginning of the Wars of the Roses to the Act of Supremacy—1455-1534

IN the preceding chapter an attempt has been made to sketch the general background, political, intellectual and social, of English life during the period 1400–1533. Each of those terminal years may be termed revolutionary. After a beginning of exceptional brilliance Richard II had proved himself increasingly incompetent and unworthy to rule. Eventually he was deposed[1] and Henry IV reigned in his stead. The monarchy went on, as everyone wished that it should. But it assumed a somewhat different aspect and a new relation between Crown and people was inaugurated.

In 1533 Archbishop Cranmer annulled the marriage between Henry VIII and Katharine of Aragon, without waiting for the judgement of the Papacy. Despite the great services which it had rendered in the past, the impartiality of the Papacy as the supreme legal authority could no longer be trusted. There were other courts of appeal in which more confidence could be placed.[2] Of course, this meant a violent ecclesiastical upheaval, and the Pope could not be expected to acquiesce in such flouting of his authority without at least a vigorous protest. The Church went on, as everyone intended. But it assumed a somewhat different aspect, and whether for good or ill was linked still more closely with our national life.

We have now to consider briefly how the Church fared between these two momentous happenings.

During the first half of the fifteenth century (approximately) the most important events were the Lollard movement[3] and the

---

[1] On 30 September 1399.   [2] See Chapter 8, p. 160.   [3] See Chapter 9.

Councils of Constance and Basel.[1] Enough has been said already about these. It may be added that when the Great Schism[2] had been brought to an end and Martin V was recognized as sole Pope he made a great effort to secure the repeal of the Statutes of Provisors and Præmunire. The former of these had been passed in 1351, and enacted that if the Pope presented, or attempted to present, to any benefice in England the right lapsed automatically to the Crown, and the *provisors*, as the papal agents were termed, were to be imprisoned until they had formally renounced their claim. It was modelled on the Statute of Carlisle, which had been passed in 1307 and forbade "alien priories" in England to make payments to their mother houses in France or elsewhere. It was reinforced two years later by the Statute of Præmunire, which forbade appeals to be carried to any authority outside the realm. This made it impossible for provisors to shelter themselves behind papal bulls. Both statutes were naturally resented by the Pope, as they diminished his power in England and affected his revenue adversely. But Parliament remained obdurate, though Archbishop Chichele wept in the House of Lords. As the fifteenth century wears on two facts force themselves upon our notice. First, the power of the Crown over the Church increases steadily. More and more bishoprics are used to provide salaries for the great officers of State, which meant that their occupants were politicians first and bishops afterwards. They were appointed for their proved political capacity, and their political activities were the first claim upon their time and energy. Thus the Church became increasingly secularized in its general outlook, and if the development was detected it does not appear to have been resented. But it meant a general lowering of moral and religious standards. Secondly, the domination of the Canon Law became complete.[3] The first step to preferment was to be known as a good lawyer. Archdeacons, for example, hardly professed to be anything else. As the whole system became more complex it became less intelligible and more difficult to administer. The cardinal mistake was that the difference between standards at which to aim and laws which must be enforced was ignored. It is always easier to comply with a rule than to apply a principle, and therefore the majority of people will always prefer the former alternative, and a Church dominated by lawyers is likely to be more than ready to give them their desire. Thanks to the system of dispensations[1] an exception to any particular rule could always be made in any particular instance, and this convenient arrangement, which was in fact almost necessary, brought an ever-increasing supply of grist to the legal mill.

Now, I think that the best way in which I can attempt to draw a general picture of the Church as it was immediately before the Reformation is to take the registers of seven successive bishops of Bath and Wells, which cover the period 1443–1532. They have all been printed,[2] so are readily accessible. The extent of the diocese was almost exactly as it is today—namely, the county of Somerset. It covered more ground than Canterbury or Rochester or London or Chichester, but much less than Lincoln or York or Winchester. It was a manageable area, and may be regarded as a fairly representative diocese.

Episcopal registers are perhaps less interesting reading than the records of episcopal Visitations, but historically of more value to anyone who wants to form a picture of the Church as a whole. Visitations only record what the visitor has found amiss. Sometimes, of course, these are very serious matters which call for correction, but very often the visitor's strictures relate only to small imperfections in the fabric or furniture of a church, such as might be noted by an observant eye almost anywhere at any time. The reader may easily overlook how often the only comment made upon a parish is *omnia bene* (all well).

The register is a bald record of all the bishop's acts, whether performed by him in person or by some accredited agent on his behalf, which were of legal or quasi-legal force. Thus they recount ordinations (but not baptisms or confirmations), Visitations, appointments, institutions to benefices and injunctions to clergy. They show how the business of the diocese went on day by day. They were not intended for publication, nor to express the author's opinions, but merely to record what was done. This

---

[1] See Chapter 7.   [2] By the *Somerset Record Society.*

makes them a more trustworthy guide to history than the literature of the same period can ever be. Literature may illustrate history, but can never do much more, because we do not know what sources of information were at the author's disposal, or how far he dealt with them impartially. Naturally he makes some use of his imagination, but at this distance of time it is impossible to say exactly how much. Allowance must also be made for personal bias, not to say prejudice. It is possible to combine a very wide knowledge of medieval literature with very little knowledge or real understanding of medieval history. Now to take the seven registers to which I have referred in order:

1. THOMAS BEKYNTON (1443–65)

The exact date of his birth is unknown, but it must have been about the year 1390; probably a little after rather than before. He became a scholar of Winchester in 1403–4, and is perhaps the first member of that foundation to rise to distinction. He proceeded to New College, Oxford, in 1406 and became a Fellow in 1408. He was born at Bekynton (now usually spelt Beckington), near Frome, in the county of Somerset. His father is said to have been a weaver. As he had no hereditary surname his origin was certainly humble. He remained at Oxford until 1420, and took the degree of Doctor of Civil Law.[1] He held various posts, one of them being the archdeaconry of Buckingham, to which he was appointed in 1424. He must have attracted attention to himself in some way, as in 1432 he was appointed one of three commissioners to negotiate a treaty of peace with the Dauphin. By that time the position of our affairs in France was almost hopeless, and the commissioners' instructions must have been to make the best they could of a very bad business. The fact that Bekynton was despatched on such an errand shows that he must have been regarded as a clear-headed and resourceful person whom it would be difficult to browbeat. He must have acquitted himself creditably, as in 1438 he was appointed as king's secretary. In that capacity he was very active in the matter of the two colleges which Henry VI was planning. Indeed, it is tempting to think that

[1] As contrasted with Canon Law.

the project may have originated with him. He knew what William of Wykeham's twin foundations had done for him and thought two more such would be the best service which the king could render to the Church and nation. He was consecrated as Bishop of Bath and Wells in the parish church of Eton on 13 October 1443, being the feast of St Edward,[1] the original patron saint of England. He celebrated his first mass as a bishop in the unfinished college chapel some two hundred yards away *under an awning*. It might have been rash to attempt to hold a service as lengthy as a consecration in a building which had no permanent roof, at that time of year. He is a good example of what may be called the civil servant bishop, a type which had now become common. He had earned his promotion by useful public service, and the general picture which we gather from his register is of an upright, industrious and munificent man. He supplied the city of Wells with the water which still runs down the gutters of the High Street from the springs in his garden, and built the covered passage across the roadway on the north side of the cathedral to connect the dining hall of the Vicars Choral[2] with the church. It is known today as the Chain Gate. He made persistent efforts to raise the intellectual standard of the clergy, and at institutions on more than one occasion is found insisting that the presentee must devote himself to improving his knowledge and under-standing of the Scriptures under some tutor approved by the bishop. In one instance he stipulated that the man must resign his benefice if, at the end of three years, he had not made satis-factory progress in his studies.

From the year 1459 he had a regular service of examining chaplains. During his episcopate, which lasted for a little more than twenty-one years,[3] a total of 1,876 persons was ordained in the diocese, 423 acolytes, 429 sub-deacons, 515 deacons and 509 priests. Some of these were monks and some fellows of colleges at Oxford or Cambridge. But the great majority were for

[1] The day of the translation of his body to its present resting-place in Westminster Abbey.

[2] The men of the choir, who formed an almost independent corporation which survived until 1936. By that time it had outlived its usefulness.

[3] He died on 14 January 1465.

parochial or chantry work in the diocese. The average number of deacons and priests ordained annually is between forty-five and fifty, the total population being probably barely one-tenth of what it is today. The last five years of his episcopate show a remarkable increase, for which there is no very obvious reason, the annual average being sixty-five. Certainly there does not seem to have been any lack of candidates for Holy Orders during the fifteenth century. Bekynton often officiated in person at ordinations. When he was away from home his place was taken by James Blakedon, who was bishop of Achonry in the province of Tuam from 1442 to 1452. In 1453 Blakedon was translated to the see of Bangor, which apparently took up more of his time and energy, as his name soon disappears from the register. After 1459 there was a regular suffragan in place of an informal assistant, named John Valens. He was an Augustinian canon and took the title of Tenos,[1] which was used subsequently by Thomas Cornish.

Soon after the beginning of Bekynton's episcopate a dispute arose in connection with the deanery of Wells. The story is worth repeating at length.[2] There was a certain John de la Bere who is said to have been of good family, but of indifferent character and almost entirely ignorant of Latin. He must, however, have possessed some ability, and he had ingratiated himself with Henry VI sufficiently to become a royal almoner and to obtain canonries at Salisbury and at Wells. This did not, however, satisfy his ambition. For some reason of which we know nothing he stood high in the favour of Eugenius IV. In 1443 the Pope granted him a bull sanctioning his appointment to various posts as soon as they should become vacant. The most important of these was the deanery of Wells, and the bull purported to set aside any statute or privilege of the church of Wells which might prevent the nomination from taking effect. This was a "provision" of the most scandalous type and entirely illegal. On 25 March 1446 John Forest, the dean, died. He had held the office since 1425, so was probably an old man, as old age was counted then. Possibly his

[1] A small island in the eastern Mediterranean belonging to the Turkish Empire.
[2] See introduction to vol. ii of the Register, pp. xliv–vii.

death had been anticipated sooner. Four days later the king wrote to Bekynton reminding him that he had promised to get the deanery for de la Bere as soon as it should become vacant. We do not know whether any such promise was really given. No doubt the king had mentioned the matter at some time and may have read into a polite and diplomatic reply from the bishop more than it was intended to convey. On 1 April the canons received licence to proceed with the election, and they met for the purpose on 8 April. The king's wish had no doubt been made known to them, whether directly or through Bekynton, and could hardly be ignored. They must also have known de la Bere, at any rate by repute. Accordingly they postponed the election until 22 August next. The Pope acted promptly, and on a date in May the Prior of Southwark with two others was commissioned to pronounce sentence of excommunication on everyone who had attended the meeting of 8 April. (This would have made it impossible for them to exercise any function until it had been removed.) The canons seem to have paid no attention to this, if it ever reached their ears. On 30 May de la Bere obtained a royal pardon for having got a papal provision contrary to the statute of 1351, and on 16 July letters patent were issued in his favour (whatever his other characteristics he must have been a plausible person). The five canons residentiary of Wells had lodged a protest with the king, claiming the right of free election, apparently during the month of June. This was referred to the Lords of the Council, who happened to be the Archbishop of Canterbury, who was also Chancellor of England, the Bishops of Salisbury and Bath and Wells, and William de la Pole, Marquess of Suffolk. They delivered a gracious message from the king, which they must have inspired, if they did not dictate it, granting the canons their desire. On 22 August, the day which they had fixed in April for their next meeting, they elected Nicholas Carent, son of a Somerset land-owner. De la Bere still persisted, and on 1 November a peremptory order was issued directing Carent to vacate the deanery, and the sub-dean and chapter to accept the Pope's nominee on pain of suspension, excommunication, deprivation and interdict. (Interdict would have meant that Divine Service could not be performed in the cathedral by anyone.) Possibly these bulls were never published in England. If they were, no notice was taken of them.

In March 1447, when Bekynton was charged by the Pope with having disregarded the original provision of de la Bere, he replied that no bull to that effect had come to his notice. It is difficult to accept this statement as entirely truthful. But if it had never been sent to him officially (it may have been issued before he became a bishop) his legal conscience might justify him in saying what he did. He must have heard of it, but hearsay is not evidence.

By this time de la Bere is said to have spent the large sum of 1,430 marks, which may have been as much as he could afford, or as much as he thought the place was worth. The problem before him now was how to get out of the business without having to admit complete defeat. A happy solution was found when he agreed to accept the arbitration of the queen. We do not know whether it was his own idea or not. The result was a foregone conclusion, as Carent was her secretary, but he could accept it without ruining his own prestige.

Nicholas V had become Pope in March 1447 and he accepted the queen's decision in the July following. He had had nothing to do with the issue of the original bull and could therefore as a gentleman defer out of courtesy to the wishes of a queen without compromising his dignity as Pope. It was the only way out of what had become a very awkward situation. But when in September he provided de la Bere to the bishopric of St Davids he "saved his face" by describing him as "Dean of Wells."

The story is not an edifying one. But it is a good illustration of what papal interference had come to mean, and of the corruption and intrigue rampant in the Church. Some people today cavil at our present system of Crown appointments, without perhaps much understanding of the theory on which it rests or much consideration of what other methods are possible. The system of today is not perfect; no system ever has been or can be. But it does, at least, preclude anything like this.[1]

It is also worth noting how little respect the Papacy commanded

[1] See Appendix E.

at this time. Eugenius IV brought all his heaviest artillery to bear, and was completely defeated. (It is only fair to add that he was to some extent under a cloud, as he had been deposed by the Council of Basel in 1439 and a substitute, Felix V, appointed in his stead. The sentence was never effective.)

The canons of Wells came out of the business best. They stood their ground with dignity and firmness. Credit is also due to the Lords of the Council, who were not prepared to see the law of England set aside by anybody.

Other points of interest in Bekynton's register are as follows:

Exchange of benefices and awards of a pension to a retired incumbent on the income of the benefice, occur from time to time. Both practices may be undesirable, but they did not originate during the nineteenth century as is sometimes supposed. Stephen Coye is invested as a hermit on 20 June 1445[1] with the following formula:

> In the name of the Fadre, of the Sonne and of the
> Holy Goost Amen. I Stephen Coye, single man
> not wedded, in youre presence reverend fadre in Gode.
> Thomas Bisshoppe of Bath and
> Wells make this profession. I promitte and
> avowe to God and to oure Lady Saint
> Marie and all the seynctes of hevene the full
> purpos of perpetuell chastitee after the rywle
> of Seyncte Poule[2] the heremite And in witness
> hereof I subscribe me here with myne awen hande.

A month later we come upon a grant, to be valid for a year, of forty days' indulgence to all contrite persons who shall give him alms and charity for the repair of the common way or public street leading directly from the bridge called Bowbrigge by Bristol to the town of Dandrey (sic), which is dangerous to travellers, and an order to all rectors, vicars and chaplains to receive the said Stephen when he comes to their neighbourhood to ask for alms and to expound the matter diligently to their congregations.

[1] There is a similar investiture of Robert Nayler (who could not write) on 7 June 1460.   [2] An Egyptian of the third century.

It would be interesting to know whether the combination of hermit and road-mender was common. Similar grants are found to all who will contribute to the repair of a bridge and various causeways in Bath.[1] The insertion of *contrite* or *contrite and confessed* shows that an attempt was made to keep these transactions on a high moral level. If the recipients of these indulgences understood that a subscription to a work of general public utility was accepted in place of some personal penance for some mild offence little fault could be found with the system. But if they thought that they were buying remission of guilt, and thereby shortening their time in purgatory, it was demoralizing in the extreme.[2]

Permission is granted to a chantry chaplain who had contracted leprosy to retire to the chapel or hermitage of Langley in the forest of Selwood, "withdrawing himself utterly from the society of men" for as long as the malady lasts. It would be interesting to know how he was expected to keep himself alive, and whether recovery from leprosy was considered to be possible.[3]

A marriage is annulled because the woman by "lifting from the sacred font" a natural son of the man who had subsequently become her husband had entered into such a bond of spiritual relationship with him that they are forbidden by the decrees of the Fathers to enter into the contract of matrimony. The marriage had taken place in Wales and the impediment, now confessed, had been concealed at the time.[4] Possibly the Welsh clergy were less careful than the English ones. It is difficult not to think that one or both of the parties must have wished to bring the marriage to an end, and to defend any system of law which allowed such an impediment.

The peril in which Europe had been placed by the fall of Constantinople is reflected by two orders issued during the year 1454, that special prayers be offered for the expulsion and utter removal of the power of the Saracens.[5]

In 1456 there is a dispensation to William Bussell, monk and prior of Athelney, to eat flesh on the days on which he performs divine offices. The reason is that the number of monks is now so

---

[1] 629, 648, 735. [2] See Chapter 7. [3] 362.
[4] 373. [5] 861, 911.

small that the prior has to perform divine offices most weeks in the year, so that he needs a more generous diet than the institutes of his Order allow if his health is not to break down.[1]

That the waters of Bath were in regular use appears from a report which has reached the ears of the bishop that although visitors of both sexes are in the habit of wearing decent bathing dresses (the men drawers[2] and the women smocks[3]), the citizens of Bath, by what they declare to be an established custom, are in the habit of stripping them naked.[4] This is to be stopped under penalty of the greater excommunication. It seems odd that the citizens of Bath should have acted in a manner not calculated to attract visitors to the city, especially as the value of the garments they took from the bathers must have been small.

The manumission of a bondsman of the bishop's manor at Cheddar with all his chattels and offspring is recorded on 24 September 1462.[5]

Lastly, on 27 May 1464 the bishop appoints Robert Hunt, a canon of Wells, and Thomas Overey to investigate the truth of reports which have reached him as to the healing properties of St John's spring, which issues within the bounds and limits of the parish church of Wembdon.[6]

Since Bekynton died during the January following, it is possible that this report never reached him. Apparently the spring itself was not a new one, but its medicinal qualities had only just been discovered. There is still a well known as the Holy Well in a garden of a house in Wembdon, occupied in 1947 by Mr E. H. Bond, Vicar's Warden. People still ask for water from it, which is believed to be good for the eyes. It is said to be very pure, but does not apparently possess any medicinal properties.

2. ROBERT STILLINGTON (1466–91)

He was a native of Acaster, near York, and apparently of gentle blood. The exact date of his birth does not appear to be known, but 1410 cannot be very far out. In some way he came into contact with Bekynton, who seems to have thought well of him, as in

[1] 980. [2] Femoralia. [3] Subunculae.
[4] 441. [5] 1455. [6] 1582.

1445 he appointed him his chancellor. A canonry at Wells, the vicarage of Congresbury, though he was only in deacon's orders, the prebendal stall of St Decuman's, and the archdeaconry of Taunton followed in quick succession; the last in 1450. He made his first appearance in politics in October 1448, when, possibly by Bekynton's advice, he was one of six commissioners empowered to treat with the Burgundian ambassadors concerning a violation of the truce between the two countries. This experience seems to have convinced him that politics were his *metier* and in 1460 he was appointed Keeper of the Privy Seal. The last carried a salary of £365 per annum, and as he held a prebend of St Stephen's, Westminster, and in addition the deanery of the free chapel of St Martin-le-Grand, he was now a rich man. He advanced money to the king, who before the year was out owed him £600. On 16 March 1466 he was consecrated as Bishop of Bath and Wells, and in the following year became Chancellor of England. His tenure of this office may not have been quite continuous, but no other Chancellor was appointed until 1473.

In 1472 he was sent on a mission to Brittany with a view to securing the extradition of Henry of Richmond, the Lancastrian claimant to the throne. He was unsuccessful, but naturally Henry never forgot it. In 1478 he incurred the displeasure of Edward IV, perhaps in connection with the treason of the Duke of Clarence. He was committed to the Tower and is said to have had to pay a large sum to secure his freedom. However, he was present at the funeral of Edward IV in 1483, and as Bishop of Bath and Wells walked beside Richard III at his coronation.[1] He is said to have found favour with Richard III by declaring the marriage between Edward IV and Elizabeth Woodville null, by reason of some pre-contract of which he professed to have personal knowledge. He drew the Bill declaring all the issue illegitimate, and then proposed that Elizabeth, the elder daughter of Edward IV, should marry a son of his own.[2]

[1] The origin of the privilege seems to be that at the coronation of Richard I, Reginald Fitz Jocelyn, who had been consecrated as Bishop of Bath and Wells on 23 June 1174, happened to be at that time the senior bishop in the province of Canterbury. [2] In 1486 she married Henry VII.

His career was ended on the field of Bosworth on 22 August 1485. Next day the new King of England, France and Lord of Ireland issued a warrant for his arrest. He took refuge at York and obtained pardon in view of his "grete age, long infirmitie and feebleness". All the same, he lived for nearly six years, and retained sufficient energy to get into trouble once more, in the spring of 1487; perhaps in connection with the abortive rising of Lambert Simnel. This time he took refuge at Oxford, whence he was removed to Windsor, apparently to the relief of his hosts. He was kept there, virtually a prisoner, until his death, which took place in May 1491. But during those years he was to be heard of at least twice at the manor of Dogmersfield, near Basingstoke, which formed part of the property of the see. Perhaps he was allowed to go there because it was within easy reach of Windsor, and yet far enough from both Westminster and Wells to prevent him from making trouble at either.

There is not much which can be said on his behalf. He appears as an ambitious and shifty politician, who unfortunately for himself espoused the Yorkist cause. Perhaps one of the least mischievous things he did was to build a large additional Lady Chapel at Wells projecting from the eastern limb of the cloister, where he was buried. The chapel disappeared in the sixteenth century. The foundations can be traced today, but the site of his tomb has not been identified.

The general trend of events during this period was to elaborate the machinery of government, which increased the power and added to the expenses of the Crown. An illustration of this process is the formation of a Council of Wales in 1478. Hitherto the maintenance of order on the Welsh marches had been an undefined responsibility of the Bishops of Hereford and Worcester. Now a new government department was instituted. Henry VII intended that the Prince of Wales should hold his Court regularly, and Arthur did so once at Ludlow early in the year 1502.[1]

---

[1] I believe that the last Lord President of Wales was Henry, third Marquess of Worcester and first Duke of Beaufort, who retired into private life at the accession of William III. The office appears to have lapsed then. The Duke of Beaufort is still hereditary keeper of Raglan Castle.

Naturally Stillington's register does not contain much of interest. He was constantly absent, so the routine business was in the hands of officials of various kinds. No doubt they were competent, and it all went smoothly enough. During the twenty-five years of his episcopate one hundred and twenty-five general ordinations were held, but he did not officiate personally at any of them. From 1466 to 1479 they were taken by John Valens, Bishop of Tenos, Bekynton's suffragan, who was also vicar of St Cuthbert's, the parish church of Wells; from 1479 to 1481 by John Wadman, Bishop of Ross, in the north of Scotland; and from 1481 to 1486 by Thomas Barrett, Bishop of Annaghdown in the province of Tuam. He was also rector of Banwell in Somerset, so perhaps never had any intention of returning permanently to his see. Some of the first bishoprics were probably only titular and the diocese could not have supported a resident bishop. He appears to have visited it once in the course of the year 1484. Finally, from 1486 onwards, ordinations were taken by Thomas Cornish, Bishop of Tenos, who served the diocese[1] until his death in 1513. It is probable that Stillington never saw any of the candidates for Holy Orders in his diocese and knew nothing about them.

A curious feature of his register is the number of disputes about the ownership of advowsons (the right of presentation to benefices). Possibly this reflects the heavy toll taken of the landed classes by the War of the Roses.

The following points are of sufficient interest to be mentioned.

In 1468 a subsidy was levied on all clergy, including all chaplains of chantries[2] with more than 100 shillings a year. There were 187 of these in the diocese.[3]

Forty days' indulgence to all ''contrite and confessed persons'' who within the next seven years contribute towards the repair of the bridge at Langport.[4] Forty days seems to be the standard period in such cases.

Other grants of indulgences, chiefly for the repair of churches, are found in 590, 603, 665. This method of raising money for

---

[1] From 1489 to 1508 the diocese of Exeter as well.
[2] See Chapter 9.   [3] 118.   [4] 518.

public purposes of one kind or another seems to have become increasingly popular as time went on, and may therefore be assumed to have proved successful.

In 1473 the abbot of Glastonbury presented John Gunthorpe, who had become Dean of Wells in 1472, to the chapel of Ditcheat, near Wells. The bishop dealt with the matter personally "in the low chamber of his inn without the Bar of the New Temple, London, in the parish of St Clement," and objected on the ground that the presentee already held two incompatible benefices— namely, the deanery of Wells and the archdeaconry of Essex. Gunthorpe, however, produced "apostolic letters sealed with lead with silken strings red and blue after the manner of the Roman Court" authorizing him to hold a third benefice. At the sight of these Stillington gave way.

The whole business was rather a farce, as Gunthorpe had been presented to Ditcheat as far back as 1466, and duly instituted while the see was vacant.[1]

In 1487 the bishop received a letter dated 2 April from the Bishop of London (Thomas Kemp) reciting an ordinance of John Morton, Archbishop of Canterbury, and endorsed by Convocation, to the effect that all clergy are to wear their proper distinctive dress so that they cannot be taken for laymen. Offenders are to be punished by the sequestration of the fruits of their benefices, if beneficed, and by suspension if unbeneficed.[2]

It does not appear how far this was effective.

An English summary of the bull of Innocent VIII in favour of Henry VII and his Queen is included amongst the entries for the year 1490.[3]

3. RICHARD FOX (1492–4)

Little is known about his early life. He was born probably about the year 1447, and seems to have decided to follow a political career under the auspices of Henry, Duke of Richmond. After the battle of Bosworth the king made him his private secretary, and his foot was planted firmly on the ladder of prefer- ment. In 1487 he became Bishop of Exeter and Keeper of the

[1] 572 and N.   [2] 862.   [3] 971. See Chapter 9.

Privy Seal. Five years later he was translated to the see of Bath and Wells, and immediately appointed Richard Nikke, canon of Wells, rector of Chedzoy (in Somerset) and archdeacon of Exeter, as his vicar-general. There is no evidence that he ever set foot in the diocese. The nine ordinations held during his short episcopate were all conducted by Thomas Cornish. In 1494 he was translated to the see of Durham, and in 1501 to that of Winchester, which he retained until his death, which took place on 14 September 1528. He was, therefore, not very far wrong when he said some years earlier that he thought he might have to see the end of monastic institutions. Towards the end of his life he is said to have been blind, but when the archbishop pressed him to resign he replied that he could still distinguish between right and wrong.

In the course of his career he achieved two notable diplomatic successes. In 1489 he negotiated a treaty with Scotland, and in 1503, after four years' hard bargaining, concluded the arrangements for the marriage between James IV of Scotland and the Princess Margaret, daughter of Henry VII, which was destined, a hundred years later, to place a Stuart on the throne of England in the person of James VI, and unite the Crowns. It was as Bishop of Winchester that he founded at Taunton the school which bears his name. The see had a very valuable estate there.

Naturally his register contains little of interest, but there is a manumission of various bondsmen belonging to the manors of Cheddar and Wookey, and of their issue present or future under date 20 May 1493.[1] Conditions and arrangements with which the last few years have made us increasingly familiar appear in the following decree[2] under date 6 August 1494.

The vicar-general recites that there has been some controversy between Thomas Goldenege, priest, vicar of Chewton-under-Mendype, and the inhabitants of the hamlets of Palton and Faryngdon, who complain of the withdrawal of two chaplains from their chapels. The vicar-general has ascertained by inquiry that the fruits of these chapels received by the vicar do not exceed 8 marks a year and are insufficient

[1] 1107. 1154.

for the maintenance of more than one chaplain, especially as the vicar has to pay 5 marks a year to the service of our Lady in the cathedral church of Wells. We therefore, sitting judicially in the chapel of our Lady by the Cloister,[1] decree that the two chapels situate very near together shall be served by one chaplain who shall minister in turn alternately.

It is interesting to note that apparently a chaplain could live on eight marks per annum.

4. OLIVER KING (1495–1503)

He was admitted a scholar of Eton in 1445 and proceeded to King's College, Cambridge, in 1449. He must therefore have been born about the year 1435, and is the first Etonian who rose to distinction. Like his two immediate predecessors, he was primarily a politician, and naturally supported the House of Lancaster. He became secretary to Prince Edward, son of Henry VI, which provoked the displeasure of Edward IV. Subsequently the king relented; perhaps he thought the young Lancastrian too able to be neglected, and he made him his first secretary for the French tongue in 1476. In 1480 he received a benefice at Calais, where he never resided, and a canonry at Windsor which he retained to the day of his death. He was also promoted to be the king's principal secretary. Richard III sent him to the Tower. The kaleidoscopic changes in the fortunes of the two great houses meant that the pathway of the aspiring politician between the years 1460 and 1485 was beset by pitfalls of this kind. However, Henry VII brought him out again, and thenceforward the tide of his fortunes ran strong and smooth. He became a canon of Wells in 1488 and Archdeacon of Taunton in 1492. He was installed by proxy on each occasion, and received a papal dispensation in relation to any duties which might be considered to belong to either office. In 1492 he was appointed Bishop of Exeter by the Pope, almost certainly at the king's request. It is doubtful whether he ever visited his bishopric. In 1496 he was translated to the see of Bath and Wells, and although he was enthroned by proxy he resided in the diocese from time to

[1] Stillington's building, see above, p. 198.

time. But all ordinations were left to Thomas Cornish, who held twenty-two between September 1497 and June 1503. He is remembered chiefly for his restoration, which amounted to a rebuilding, of the priory church of SS. Peter and Paul in Bath, commonly called Bath Abbey. He is said to have been moved to undertake the task by a dream of angels, whose figures are to be seen on the west front of the church, and a voice which proclaimed, "Let an olive establish the Crown, let a King restore the Church." It is the last piece of church building upon a large scale to be undertaken before the Reformation, and anyone who looks at it will see that it represents something from which the life was ebbing fast.[1]

It is to be feared that there must have been some arrangement between him and Henry VII which does little credit to either before he was appointed to the see, as he appears to have pledged himself to allow various posts in the diocese—prebends, archdeaconries and so forth—to be filled by the king with the diplomatic agents of which he found himself to be in ever-increasing need. How else, for example, can we account for the appointment of Francis, Archbishop of Besançon,[2] a prince of the Holy Roman Empire, to the archdeaconry of Wells in the year 1500?

Again, since 1493 the precentorship of the cathedral had been held by William Warham, who resigned it when he became Bishop of London in 1502. He had never resided, with the result that the house had become ruinous and the services of the church had been neglected. King wrote pointing out that a resident precentor was necessary, and laying claim to the right of making the appointment on the ground of his compliance with the king's wishes in relation to the archdeaconries of Wells and Taunton and the prebend of Yatton. He had, however, to pay £40 before he could appoint Thomas Cornish.[3]

Again, on 25 June 1498 John Gunthorpe, who had been dean since 1472, died. The bishop nominated William Cosyn, Archdeacon of Bath, a young man[4] in deacon's orders, who was the

---

[1] See Chapter 8.   [2] Sometimes misread as *Byzantium*.
[3] *Somerset Record Society*, vol. 57, p. 81.
[4] He had been admitted to King's College, Cambridge, in 1487.

son of his sister. Apparently he felt that his action needed some justification, as he wrote to Sir Reginald Bray, at that time a power behind the throne, "And for the Deanery I compounded with his grace as ye know wel."[1] The implications of this remark are certainly sinister, if the exact meaning is not entirely clear. It is not easy to see why the king should have had any particular interest in Cosyn's appointment. On the whole it looks as if the bishop had paid the king for the right of nomination, perhaps heavily, and therefore felt entitled to choose his nephew.

In October 1498 Cosyn was admitted a member of the cathedral body (which he was not necessarily, as Archdeacon of Bath) and given the prebend of Ilton. The formal election was held in the Chapter House on Christmas Day. The dean-elect was somewhere at hand and gave his consent "a little before dusk". A show of reluctance, or at least period for reflection, was expected before the acceptance of any important ecclesiastical office. On 10 April 1499 the new dean was ordained priest at Chartres, being described as a "Deacon of the diocese of London." It is not clear what he was doing there. Five days later the election, which had been held more than three months previously, was confirmed in the Lady Chapel of the Cathedral Church of Bath,[2] and the bishop's order for his installation was read in the Chapter House at Wells on 23 June. Two years, however, were to elapse before the new dean came into residence.

Oliver King's episcopate was a little less than eight years (6 November 1495–29 August 1503), so his register is not a long one. The following details may be recorded.

On 29 January 1497–8 a chapel in honour of the Assumption of our Lady and of St Katharine at the north end of the Vicars' Close[3] was dedicated and consecrated by Thomas, Bishop of Tenos, on behalf of the bishop of the diocese.[4]

---

[1] S.R.S., vol. 56, pp. xiv–xvi.

[2] The Priory Church was regarded as a secondary cathedral, as to a limited extent it still is. The churches of Ripon, Beverley and Southwell occupied a similar position in the diocese of York.

[3] The name given to the houses built for the most part during the fourteenth century for the vicars choral (Choir-men) of the cathedral.

[4] 62.

From time to time disputes as to the ownership of advowsons appear, similar to those in Stillington's register.[1]

There are also several abjurations of heresy, in relation to the Sacrament of the Altar, the worshipping of images and the value of pilgrimages. These may indicate the way in which the wind was beginning to blow.

There is the usual offer of forty days' indulgence to all penitent and confessed persons who shall contribute towards the building of two bridges in the parish of Lamport (*sic*, presumably Langport).

On 23 August 1499 the bishop, being at Bath, issued a commission to the vicar of Milverton to examine witnesses against John Strange of the parish of Porlocke, who when felling timber in a wood on Monday in Rogationtide is said to have seen blood flowing in the cutting of a loaf (*incisione panis*).

This is a curious story. It is not clear whether John Strange was suspected of witchcraft, or whether he was professing to have seen a miracle. If *panis* really means *loaf* in this connection (and it is not easy to see what else it can mean) the reference must be to some bread which he had taken into the wood with him for his midday meal. It is a pity that we do not know the outcome of the inquiry.[2]

Katharine Love of Wells is ordered by way of penance to lead the procession in the church of St Cuthbert's, Wells, on Sunday, 15 September 1499, in a shift, with bare head and skins and carrying one candle extinguished and one lighted, and to leave the town the following Tuesday, and not to remain within seven miles of it under pain of the greater excommunication. Her offence had been witchcraft, the medium employed being "droppings of holy candles". The exact method followed is, however, not described.[3] Probably it was what is known as invultuation, in which a wax figure of the person to be injured is made into which pins are inserted.

On 31 May 1499 Sir Roger Leyson, rector of Burnett (near Bristol), is deprived of his benefice for being absent from his church for more than two years without leave, and for having disregarded a citation to reappear within six weeks.[4]

<hr />

[1] 209. [2] 215. [3] 241. [4] 249.

On 29 April 1503 orders were sent to the archdeacon and dean of Wells to cause all rectors, vicars and chaplains with cure to make processions on Monday, Wednesday and Friday with prayers, for the peace of the Church, for the bishop of the diocese, for the welfare of the realm of England, and the increase of the fruits of the earth.[1] There is one record of the manumission of a bondsman, belonging to the manor of Compton Bishop.[2]

When Oliver King was Bishop of Exeter he had made arrangements to be buried in the Chapel of St George, Windsor, of which he had been a canon. Later he changed his mind, and wished to be buried in the Quire of his great church at Bath. Probably this was considered impossible, as the church was not finished at the time of his death. There is no record of his burial at Wells, nor at Windsor, where the Chantry Chapel which he had prepared for himself is still to be seen. His nephew and executor Cosyn refers to the expense to which he had been put in connexion with the funeral, but it is impossible to say where the interment took place.

5. Hadrian di Corneto or de Castello (1504–18)

He was a cardinal priest of the Roman Church by the title of St Chrisogonus,[3] who had been appointed Bishop of Hereford in 1507, and held the see until 1518. Such appointments, of which there were four in succession at Worcester covering the years 1497–1534, and one at Salisbury 1524–34, were purely diplomatic. It was thought that our interests at Rome could be served better by an Italian than by an Englishman, and no one saw any reason why the income of an English bishopric should not be used to pay him. The system of administering a diocese by delegation, through vicars-general and other officials, with bishops suffragan to discharge functions for which episcopal Orders were essential, had been brought to such a pitch of perfection that it really did not matter who the bishop was, or whether the people of the diocese from which he took his title and derived his income ever saw him or not.

[1] 486–7. Easter Sunday in that year fell on 16 April.   [2] 338.
[3] See note on the *Sacred College* appended to Chapter 6.

Hadrian was certainly in London from time to time, and may have paid an occasional visit to his diocese. But his real work was understood to be at Rome. In 1506 he made over all his ecclesiastical patronage in England to the king. He could not be expected to take much interest in it, or to possess the knowledge of people and places which was requisite. It was, however, probably at his suggestion that an Italian named Polydore Vergil,[1] who appears to have been a relation of his own, was appointed to the archdeaconry of Wells, which he held for more than forty years. He was installed in person, but does not seem to have spent much time at Wells afterwards. He wrote a history of his adopted country, which had some vogue, and is believed to have lost the only list of the sculptured figures on the west front of Wells Cathedral. The identification of many of them has been a matter of guesswork ever since. Naturally the register contains little but a bald record of necessary business transacted.

On 12 January 1506 Thomas Cleragh, who had become Bishop of Killala[2] in the province of Tuam, was instituted by proxy to the church of Chedzoy,[3] perhaps with some idea that he might serve as an assistant bishop.

On 19 December in the same year Thomas Cornish was formally commissioned as bishop-suffragan.

On 8 July 1507 the presentation of Sir John Golafer as chaplain, by the prior and convent of Bruton to the vicarage of Milton Clevedon, was annulled by the vicar-general in the cathedral church on the ground that he was an unsuitable person. No details are given.

From two cases of sheep stealing[4] it appears that the average price of a sheep was about 1s. 8d. Both offenders got off with a sentence of imprisonment (the length of which is not stated), which must be regarded as lenient. One of them served his "in a prison of the bishop called le Cowhowse in the palace at Wells." The place of incarceration of the other is not mentioned.

[1] See "The Italian Bishops of Worcester," by M. Creighton, in *Historical Essays and Reviews*.
[2] *Aladensis*. He seems to have retained the see until 1508.
[3] 679. [4] 917, 1085. In 1947 it was about 40.

On 8 June 1512 Thomas Chard, titular bishop of Solubria, was called to the vicarage of Wellington.[1] This may mean that Thomas Cornish's health was beginning to fail, and it was thought desirable to have an assistant bishop at hand. He died during the following year at some date between 15 April and 7 July. His long service to the diocese was recognized by burial in the cathedral church on 30 September 1513. Thomas Wulff, titular bishop of Lacerdæmon, was commissioned as bishop suffragan. By the year 1511 Hadrian's reputation had risen so high in political circles that he was regarded as a possible successor to Pope Julius II. Leo X was, however, elected in 1513. Soon afterwards Hadrian fell out of favour with Wolsey and the king, for reasons which are not clear.[2] Eventually in 1517 Henry sequestrated the revenues of the see, and the bishop's titular connection with it came to an end on 3 August. Leo X seems to have thought it judicious to accept the *fait accompli* without protest, but salved his dignity by declaring in the November following that the cardinal was deserving of deprivation not only for the reasons adduced by the King of England, but also for his many crimes; which appear to have been left unspecified. Final sentence was pronounced on him on 5 July 1518 and he died in obscurity.

6. THOMAS WOLSEY (sometimes spelt *Wulcy*) (1518–23)

He received the see *in commendam*, which means with permission to hold it together with another. He had been Archbishop of York since 1514, and there was no pretence that Bath and Wells would be more than a useful addition to his income. He needed money to represent England worthily, and the building of his vast palace at Hampton Court must have cost several fortunes. He resigned in 1523 to accept the see of Durham, which was probably still more lucrative. That was at least in his own province, and contiguous to the diocese of York.   His career is so much a matter of common knowledge that the details need not be given here.

His direct connection with the diocese of Bath and Wells began and ended with the appointment of vicars-general with very wide

[1] 977.   [2] See *Introduction* to his register, p. xx.

powers, and the routine business went on as smoothly as it had done when Hadrian was at Rome. I believe that in the park at Auckland Castle a clump of rushes of an uncommon kind is still to be found. They are said to be strongly scented, and Bishop Lightfoot thought it possible that they had been planted originally with a view to carpeting the great hall in preparation for a visit from Wolsey. If such a visit was ever contemplated there appears to be no evidence that it was paid.

Wolsey held the see of Winchester *in commendam* with York for a short time after he had relinquished Durham, to say nothing of abbacies and other posts. Probably he is to be regarded as the most enormous pluralist who ever lived.

7. JOHN CLERKE (1523–41)

He too was primarily a diplomatist, and was "provided" to the see by a papal bull dated 26 March 1523, apparently under pressure from England. He held the see until 1541, so saw the end of the old order and the beginning of the new. Unfortunately the last nine years of his register are missing, but a certain amount of information is available from a book of memoranda kept by Walter Cretyng, his vicar-general. During the earlier part of his episcopate he was seldom in the diocese: during the later he was usually to be found either at Wells or in his manors at Banwell or Chew Magna.

Two entries in the register are of sufficient interest to be worth recording:

1. *September* 1526. A dispensation, through the vicar-general to the master and convent of St John's Hospital, Bridgwater, "with regard to the services held in their Church by night when both young and old have suffered severely from cold,"[1] allowing the early mass to be at 6 a.m. instead of 5 a.m. from 1 October to 1 April. It is difficult to imagine that this kindly concession can have made much difference. Nothing seems to be known as to the methods of warming churches at this time. If nothing was done the buildings and their contents must have suffered from

[1] 262.

damp, at least as much as worshippers must have suffered from cold.

2. *17 and 19 September* 1532. Instruction of the prior of Christ Church, Canterbury, for "offering of prayers daily in Cathedral collegiate and parochial churches for the good estate of the English Church and of King Henry VIII, and the prosperity of his realm of England, and of the universal Church, and of those fighting against the tyranny of the Turks; on Fridays in cities, boroughs and important places, and on Wednesdays Fridays elsewhere."[1]

The archiepiscopal see was vacant at the moment by the death of William Warham on 22 August. It is perhaps remarkable that, in the circumstances, the issuing of instructions of this kind did not devolve automatically upon the Bishop of London as dean of the province of Canterbury. The reference to the Turks reminds us that they were still a formidable menace, especially since the fall of Constantinople had opened the eastern gates of Europe to them. Vienna had been threatened seriously by them only three years earlier.

Elections to the headship of religious houses needed episcopal confirmation, and in this way there is some information to be gleaned as to the numbers of the monastic population on the eve of its disappearance.

(a) 4 *October* 1523. Taunton Priory. Twelve electors, all in priest's orders.

(b) 16 *February* 1524. Glastonbury. All the brethren were present—viz., forty-four priests, one deacon and one subdeacon.

(c) 22 *December* 1524. Hospital of St John, Bridgwater. Eight present.

(d) 23 *June* 1525. Barlinch Priory. Eight priests, one deacon.

(e) 23 *June* 1525. Bath Priory. Nineteen present, including one proxy. One mortally ill and one in parts beyond the sea.

(f) 30 *August* 1525. Worspringe Priory. Five present.

It looks as if the inmates of these six houses numbered about ninety, or a little more. Glastonbury accounted for just about

[1] 417.

half, and Glastonbury and Bath together for more than two-thirds. It seems to have become difficult to get new recruits, which suggests that people were becoming more and more doubtful of the usefulness of monastic institutions.

This brief sketch will be sufficient to show the steady deterioration which the registers reveal after the death of Bekynton. No one who reads them in full can help being struck by that. No doubt the registers of any other diocese during the period 1465–1530 would tell a similar story. Externally the Church is as strong and splendid as it has ever been, and all the diocesan business is skilfully organized. But it is a business and not much more. The Church as a whole had become completely secularized. The higher offices were filled by politicians and lawyers, whose moral standards were no better than those of anyone else, if no worse. Things may have been better at the bottom. No doubt there were humble parish priests, more numerous perhaps than we may be tempted to suspect, who did their duty diligently by the light which they had, and lay people who made an honest attempt to live up to the best they knew. But taken as a whole the Church had, to borrow the phraseology of St Paul,[1] become conformed to this world so thoroughly as to be virtually indistinguishable from it. Nothing short of a transformation, to be brought about by the renewing of its mind, could provide a remedy.

Besides this, worship had, as it were, lost its way in a tropical jungle of ceremonial. The tractates *Concerning the Service of the Church* and *Of Ceremonies* prefixed to the *Book of Common Prayer* reveal something of the confusion which prevailed. Further information can be gathered from a manuscript in the possession of the Dean and Chapter of Wells.[2] It was written by William Cosyn, whose appointment as dean in 1499 has been mentioned earlier in this chapter. It appears to have been intended as a handbook to guide him in the arrangement of the services of the cathedral. The Calendar contains a list of 221 festivals of one kind and

[1] Romans 12. 2.
[2] Transcribed and edited by Dom A. Watkin of Downside, published by the Somerset Record Society in 1941 in *A Wells Cathedral Miscellany*.

another, each of which had to be marked by the colour of the vestments worn, at least. Blue, white, red, green and saffron are mentioned. Anyone who is familiar with the church now must wonder where the very large stock of vestments, etc., which must have been required was kept. The undercroft below the Chapter House seems to be the only place possible, and if the climate was then as it is now it must have been very difficult to prevent them from being damaged by damp there. The Consue-tudinary (*i.e.*, the record of the particular ceremonial prescribed for each occasion) is unfortunately not quite complete. The English translation occupies between fifty and sixty pages. Divine Service has been brought to such a pitch of elaboration that the amount of attention required to get all the details right must have been so large that the performers cannot have had very much to spare for the end to which it is directed. If public worship were to be intelligible, edifying, and educative it is obvious that a very drastic simplification had long been overdue. But to alter the type of service with which people are familiar is never a very easy undertaking. No doubt the arrangements in force in most parish churches were not quite so elaborate. But what went on in the cathedral would naturally have been regarded as a standard for the diocese.

11

Second Spring

From the Act of Supremacy to the death of Queen Elizabeth—1534–1603

S O much has been written about the Reformation that it is
unnecessary to attempt to re-tell the story in detail here. It
is almost impossible for anyone, or at any rate for any Englishman,
to write of it without bias, because he must regard it, taken as a
whole, either as a real reformation which was sorely needed, or
as a disaster which might have been averted, and is even now
perhaps not quite beyond repair. I can only touch upon a few
salient features and try to assess it as a historical process. Its
theological and liturgical aspects are outside the scope of these
lectures.

It is impossible that an upheaval on so vast a scale should not
present some regrettable features which no one can wish to
condone now. Some mistakes were made with the best intentions, and the motives which prompted some of the things which
were done were certainly not of the best kind. The period produced its martyrs, from both sides, whose constancy and courage
deserve our admiration. They all believed that they were dying
for some fundamental religious principle, and if we feel bound to
question their judgement that does not detract from their
sincerity. The executions which took place during the reigns of
Henry VIII, Mary, and Elizabeth were not, however, really very
many: it would be fair to say (as in most persecutions[1]), not more
than could be helped. They must be judged from the standpoint
of the sixteenth century, not from our own. It was a rough age
and human life was accounted cheap. Many of the punishments
habitually imposed then by the Civil Courts as part of the routine

[1] See Appendix A, *Persecution.*

administration of justice are in our eyes barbarous and excessive. Besides this, circumstances were such that certain religious opinions might be fairly regarded as treasonable on the score of their political implications, and in that world no sovereign felt himself sufficiently secure to tolerate the open expression of treasonable opinion. After 1533 anyone who thought that papal authority was beyond question was almost compelled to consider that Henry had forfeited his throne by his conduct, and could not doubt that any heir which might be born to him whilst Katharine was still alive was illegitimate. During Mary's reign anyone who disputed papal authority was bound to regard her as illegitimate, and therefore disqualified from being queen. During Elizabeth's reign anyone who accepted the papal authority was bound to regard her as illegitimate and (after 1571) heretical into the bargain: an opinion which naturally commanded the unqualified assent of the King of Spain. It is difficult to find much fault with Henry or either of his daughters, if from time to time they availed themselves of the protection which the law provided against such attacks on their thrones or persons.

The first decisive step was the passing of the Act of Supremacy in 1534. Like many enactments of many legislative authorities before and since, this did little more than furnish an unassailable legal basis for a state of things which was already established in practice. Since the middle of the fourteenth century the power of the Crown over the Church had increased steadily. By the beginning of the sixteenth it was complete in everything but name. The shadowy papal control was really very little more than an expensive nuisance which might just as well be brought to an end. England was now strong enough, important enough and sufficiently isolated to manage its own affairs without foreign interference.

The Act declared the king to be "on earth Supreme Head of the Church of England", and by an Order in Council under date 15 January 1535 these words were added to his title. Not un-naturally some people thought them shocking but they were never intended to mean more than the words used in the Bidding Prayer at the present day, where the sovereign is termed "over all persons and in all causes, as well ecclesiastical as civil within these his dominions supreme." No reasonable exception can be taken to this. To prevent misunderstanding, which was perhaps wilful in some circles, the word *Governor* was substituted by Elizabeth for *Head*. The change was merely verbal. Five years earlier the power of granting such "licences, dispensations, compositions, faculties, delegacies, receipts, instruments or other writings as had been accustomed to be had at the see of Rome or by authority thereof"[1] was transferred to the Archbishop of Canterbury acting personally or by commissary or deputy, which meant that papal authority in any effective form had really ceased in England.

In due course the taxes customarily paid to the Pope by clergy were transferred to the Crown. This made no practical difference to the payers, who found themselves required to subsidise their own sovereign instead of an Italian prince.[2] The complete independence of England as a sovereign state (in the language of the day, *an Impire* [*sic*]) had now been asserted beyond any possibility of doubt. But it had still to be made secure. Henry's next step was to proceed against the monasteries. Briefly, it is impossible to deny that the need for drastic changes in the system was imperative, or that what was done was done in the worst way possible. For nearly three hundred years the religious houses had been declining steadily. Many of them were heavily, and as it would seem perennially, in debt. This was probably due to ambitious programmes of building and to general mismanagement more than to luxurious living. Even by the end of the thirteenth century the financial difficulties of many houses were so great that if Edward I had not banished the Jews, to whom in most instances the debts were owing, many of them might have come to an abrupt end some two hundred years before they did. By the middle of the fourteenth century even Glastonbury, one of the most famous of all, was burdened with debt, and relief was given

---

[1] 21 Henry VIII, c. 25.

[2] These payments were relinquished by Queen Anne that the money might be used for the benefit of the clergy generally. This formed the nucleus of what is known today as Queen Anne's Bounty.

by the "appropriation" of churches.[1] This meant that income intended for the benefit of a parish was diverted to another purpose, and the incumbent was left to manage as best he could on a fraction of what he ought to have had This tended seriously to weaken the whole parochial system, and naturally made the beneficiaries unpopular. By the year 1530 the following question might fairly be asked of the religious houses; and could, indeed, hardly be evaded:

1. Are they centres of missionary zeal, as they had been in their earliest days?

2. Are they centres of learning and education, as they had been in the second phase of their greatness?

3. Are they setting a markedly higher standard of life, religiously and morally, than is to be found elsewhere? This was, after all, the *raison d'être* of all monastic institutions of every kind, and their principal justification.

Speaking generally, the answer to all these questions was bound to be *No*, if in relation to the third some qualification is necessary so far as the Carthusians were concerned. A fourth question then became inescapable—Is there any reason why they should continue to exist? And the answer was bound to be *None*, at any rate on anything approaching the existing scale.[2] Henry VIII did not attack a flourishing and respected system. If he had, he would probably have failed. He gave the final thrust to something which had long been tottering, and sent it all down in ruins. Besides all this, the monasteries were strongholds of papal sentiment and bastions of the papal power. Many of them (all those belonging to the Cistercian order) were *exempt*, which meant that they were independent of the bishop of the diocese in which they were, and acknowledged no superior except the Pope, who was conveniently distant. This tended to bring the whole government of the Church into confusion. Obviously the monastic system as a whole could never adapt itself as it was to the new state of things and was unlikely to welcome far-reaching reform. Many of the houses were bound to disappear. But it would be idle to pretend that much

---

[1] Chartulary *passim*.
[2] For some further remarks see Appendix C (*The Monasteries*).

cruel wrong was not done. Apart from all other considerations, the economic life of the countryside was seriously dislocated by the sudden disappearance of the genial, hospitable and charitable country gentlemen who had ruled so many of its acres (perhaps nearly one-fourth of the whole) for so long. The story of the execution of Richard Whiting, the last abbot of Glastonbury, which it would take too long to retell here, is one of the worst. It is difficult not to believe that some of the religious houses might have been preserved as centres of learning and education. The University of Leeds might, for example, have been anticipated by nearly four centuries if use had been made in this way of the Cistercian house of Kirkstall, which lay on the outskirts of the town. Besides this, there are always men and women who have a real vocation for the monastic life. They may never be very many, but they always exist and have a real contribution to make to the religious life of a Church and a nation. They ought to have an opportunity to make full proof of their highly specialized ministry. The successful revival of religious communities, both of men and women, in the Church of England since the middle of the nineteenth century is proof of this.

Seeing that much is sometimes made by writers, whose controversial zeal may outrun their historical knowledge, of the desperate straits to which dispossessed monks were reduced, it may be worth while to mention that £8,000, the equivalent of £80,000 at least today, was paid by way of compensation to the abbot of Muchelney in Somerset.[1] That may not have represented the full value of the property, but was certainly not negligible. It probably compares favourably with the composition which the tithe owners of England were compelled to accept in the year 1936, when the Government laid hands upon their immemorial property. There is no obvious reason why the abbot of Muchelney should have been treated with exceptional generosity.

At the least the libraries might all have been preserved and kept together. They could have been housed in the episcopal palaces, the libraries belonging to the cathedral chapters, and in the

[1] See an article which appeared in *Notes and Queries for Somerset and Dorset*, vol. xxiv, p. 120, in September 1944.

colleges of Oxford and Cambridge. It is impossible to estimate how much that was beautiful, precious and irreplaceable was wantonly destroyed during the years 1536–41 (approximately).

Six great monastic churches (Bristol, Chester, Gloucester, Oxford,[1] Peterborough and Westminster)[2] became the cathedral churches of new bishoprics which were endowed out of monastic funds. Others passed to parochial use. Hexham, Selby, Pershore, Romsey, Sherborne and Tewkesbury are well-known examples. But the majority were dismantled (the lead with which they were roofed was valuable and could be used elsewhere) and left to become the ruins with which we are familiar today. Some colleges at Oxford and Cambridge were enriched with some monastic property. But a great deal found its way into private pockets.

To understand Henry's general attitude towards the Church we must look at what he did in relation to the episcopate. Without endorsing an interpretation of the words *Apostolic Succession* which has become popular, but involves assuming more than we know to be true, we can say that since the end of the second century at latest (unless there is an exception to be found at Alexandria) episcopacy has been regarded universally as the core of the Church's system and as the guarantee of its continuity. All religious reformers whose ideas have been revolutionary and have wished to break as completely as possible with the past have always decided that there shall be no bishops in their new systems. However widely they may differ in other respects they have agreed in that. That is true of Luther, Calvin, Zwingli and Knox in the sixteenth century, and of our own nonconformists at later periods. There can be no question that they have been right. Anyone who wishes to part company with the Church in which he was brought up, and to substitute a new religious society for it, is bound to recognize that he must get rid of episcopacy, whatever else he may retain. Henry VIII acted in exactly the opposite way. His deliberate policy was to strengthen the English episcopate and make it more efficient. He raised the number of

[1] The Oxford bishopric had its original seat at Oseney. It was transferred to its present home in 1545.

[2] Thomas Thirlby, first Bishop of Westminster, was translated to the see of Norwich in 1550 when the bishopric came to an end.

English dioceses from seventeen, the figure at which it had stood since the formation of Carlisle in 1133, to twenty-three, thereby reducing some of the most unwieldy to more manageable dimensions. After him no new diocese was created until the see of Ripon was formed in 1836. But he did not stop there. The dioceses were still large and the bishops were still bound to be out of them from time to time, if only to attend the House of Lords. He therefore drew up a scheme for the provision of twenty-four bishops suffragan. In place of wandering friars in episcopal orders whose titular bishoprics had no real existence, supplemented occasionally by displaced Irish or Scottish prelates, he provided every diocesan bishop with a permanent assistant, who was to take his title from some place in the diocese which he served. This put the whole business upon a secure and intelligible footing. He meant England to have some forty-five bishops all told, permanently at work, a number which was in fact never reached until about the beginning of the present century. The scheme was not entirely successful, probably because of the difficulty, which is still acute, of providing support for bishops suffragan without diverting funds from some other purpose for which they were intended. Twelve of his suffragan sees were never occupied. In all there were some fifteen or sixteen consecrations in seventy years. With the death of John Sterne, rector of Witham and bishop suffragan of Colchester in the diocese of London in 1607, the system came to an end.[1] It was revived in 1870, when bishops of Dover and Nottingham were consecrated to assist the two Primates. Until near the beginning of the present century, bishops suffragan could take their titles only from the places specified in the Act of 1536. Now any place in the diocese can serve.

This immense scheme would never have been framed by a mere iconoclast. But it is exactly what might be expected of a very able man who understood and valued the system of the Church. He found that that system had been brought into almost complete confusion by two intrusions. First, the exorbitant

[1] The York *Books of Acts* show that the Bishop of Sodor and Man sometimes acted for the Archbishop of York during the seventeenth and eighteenth centuries. But this was merely a private arrangement.

claims of the Pope. Secondly, the monasteries. By these the whole machine had been, as it were, thrown out of gear. When he had cleared them away he determined to repair the damage which they had done by strengthening what he saw to be the real system of the Church. An episcopate freed from foreign interference exercising undisputed authority and sufficiently numerous to be really effective was his greatest legacy to his kingdom. It was not his fault that his scheme never came into full operation. Had it done so the history of the Church in the seventeenth, eighteenth and nineteenth centuries might have been very different.

The last important act of his life, which ended on 28 January 1547, was to sign the foundation charter of Trinity College, Cambridge (which celebrated its four-hundredth anniversary during the summer of 1947 in the presence of the king and queen and the two princesses). If he had never done anything else worth remembering, England, not to say the whole world of learning, would owe him a real debt for that.

His complete pedigree from Adam is to be seen in the library of his college today. Brutus of Troy is one of the important links in the chain of descent.

He was a masterful man and did not brook opposition easily. But he reigned for nearly forty years, a period which has been exceeded only by Henry III, Edward III, Elizabeth, George III and Victoria, and died in his own bed in one of his own palaces. Kings who habitually outrage the feelings of their subjects, and endeavour to dragoon them into acquiescence, do not fare as well as that—at any rate in England. The careers of Richard II, Richard III, Charles I and James II are sufficient proof. Henry VIII could not have done as he did had he not, speaking generally, carried the nation with him.

Little need be said of the next two reigns, except that fortunately they did not last very long. Together they cover a little less than twelve years (January 1547–November 1558), which is approximately the duration of the Commonwealth almost exactly a hundred years later; neither period was sufficient for much irreparable mischief to be done. Both may be regarded as no more than dismal interludes. Edward VI was not ten years old when he came to the throne and died before he had reached his sixteenth birthday. He was helpless in the hands of a group of unprincipled and rapacious nobles, and a shameless plundering of parish churches went on. Had he lived a little longer, and been able to assert himself, it is possible that the influence of continental reformers might have become paramount, and the Church of England might have been remodelled in accordance with their ideas.

When Mary emerged, after twenty years, from the dishonoured seclusion to which she had been relegated at the age of seventeen, she naturally knew nothing of the people over whom she was to reign, or of the world in which she had now to play an important part. By blood she was half Spanish, and her marriage a year after her accession to the King of Naples and Jerusalem, who was heir to the Spanish throne, widened the gulf in thought and feeling between her and her subjects. She believed that she could "put the clock back" and restore the England of her childhood, much as the Bourbons believed that France, as it had been before the Revolution, could be restored after the final fall of Napoleon. At first the omens were favourable, and the queen was determined to be as tolerant as she could. But Wyatt's rebellion in 1554 came sufficiently near success to be alarming, and strengthened the hands of those of her advisers who thought she had been too lenient. Yet a number of the rebels were pardoned. But as the violence of the opponents of her policy increased (and often expressed itself in shockingly profane ways),[1] so inevitably did persecution. The most famous martyrs were Bishops Ridley and Latimer, and Archbishop Cranmer. They were burned for heresy, after every effort to induce them to adjure their opinions had been made, at Oxford, where the Martyrs' Memorial commemorates them today: the two former on 16 October 1555; Cranmer on 21 March 1556. Because he was Archbishop of Canterbury it was

[1] E.g., on Easter Sunday, 14 April 1555, the celebrant at St Margaret's, Westminster, was attacked at the altar by a man named William Flower, who wounded him in the head. The assailant said that he had been "compelled by the Spirit" to make the protest against idolatry. He had got up early for the purpose on Christmas Day, but his heart had failed him. Possibly the darkness and cold had contributed something. Now he professed to be ready "to die for the Lord".

thought necessary to make him undergo a ceremony of degradation which we should regard as almost ludicrous, before he could
be executed. They all died like men. Mary could hardly have been
expected to spare Cranmer. Nothing could have made her see
that there was any right or justice in the sentence which he had
passed upon her mother, or that the real villains of the piece had
been Henry VII and her mother's parents.

An attempt to revive some monasteries came to very little. It
was recognized that they could be of little use now. The new
Archbishop, Cardinal Pole, who died on 17 November 1556,
having survived Mary by some twelve hours, probably knew that
their joint policy had failed, if the Queen herself never did. The
England of a generation ago could never be brought to life again.

History has hardly been just to the memory of Mary Tudor.
She was probably the best morally of all her line, as well as the
most amiable. It was her ill-fortune that in her reign, as in
Elizabeth's, heretical opinions were almost necessarily treasonable as well. When all is said and done the victims of the persecutions to which she felt herself driven were not very many, and
some of them, judged by the standards of the day, deserved what
they got. Fate placed her in a position of great difficulty which she
was quite unfitted to fill, and the advisers upon whom she relied,
especially Pope Paul IV, could read the signs of the times no
better than she.

One act of hers ought not to be forgotten, if only for the light
which it throws upon her character when she was not driven by
the exigencies of public policy. She completed the chapel of her
father's college at Cambridge; this being perhaps the only important piece of church building during her reign. This shows filial
piety of a very high order. Henry VIII had brought unspeakable
shame and humiliation upon her and her mother. He had defied
an authority which she regarded as divine and had destroyed
much which she revered as sacred. He had died under sentence
of excommunication: but for all that, he was her father, and she
would not leave his noble foundation incomplete. Anyone who
knows Cambridge will remember that above the east window of
the chapel over-hanging Trinity Street are carved the words

Domus mea domus orationis vocalitur (My house shall be called the house of prayer), and many a passer-by must have wondered (as I have often done) why they have been placed there.

Professor Trevelyan, the former Master, seems to have found the explanation in his little *History* of the college. As soon as the chapel was finished Mary was anxious that masses should be said for the repose of her father's soul. The Pope would not allow this because Henry had died in heresy and excommunicate. But if public corporate prayer for the dead king was impossible, he might be prayed for privately. The text which she had carved in the most conspicuous position which could be found on the outside of the building may well have been intended to suggest this. It was as far as she dared go, and no exception could be taken to it, by the Pope or by anybody else. Some, at least, might understand her intention and honour her wish. It was the best she could do for her father.

When Elizabeth came to the throne she had three great advantages over her half-sister. First, she had been born seventeen years later; secondly, she was only twenty-five at the time of her accession, whereas Mary had been thirty-seven, and thirdly, since her mother had been English, she was as entirely English by descent and upbringing as any sovereign we have ever had. Incidentally, the loss of Calais meant that she had taken her seat upon an entirely English throne, which no ruler of England had done since St Edward. She was therefore well equipped by circumstances as well as by natural ability to grasp the real facts of the very difficult situation in which she had to play her part.

Whatever her private feelings may have been (and there is no reason to suppose that she had any leaning towards Roman Catholicism), it was clear that Mary's policy could not be continued. Elizabeth had got to move very cautiously in some other direction. She soon left little room for doubt as to what it would be. It so happened that the episcopate was very seriously depleted in the autumn of 1558. There had been an unusual number of deaths, and the bishops who had been appointed by Mary would not recognize Elizabeth's legitimacy and were therefore compelled to retire into private life.[1] If she had wished to replace the Church of England by a "presbyterian" society of some kind it would only have been necessary to hold her hand for a few years. Nature would have effected the change for her with the least possible disturbance. The policy which she adopted was the exact opposite of this. She took particular pains to secure a Primate as soon as possible, that the other vacant sees might be filled in due course. Her choice fell on Matthew Parker, Dean of Lincoln, formerly Master of Corpus Christi College, Cambridge, who was consecrated in the chapel of Lambeth Palace on 17 December 1559, thirteen months after her accession. It was plain that whatever religious changes might be made, they would all be within the historic framework of the Church.

Four bishops officiated, as is the custom if there is not an archbishop available. The principal consecrator was William Barlow, who had been Bishop of St David's 1536–48 and of Bath and Wells 1548–54. He had been deprived by Mary, but in 1559 was translated by Elizabeth to the see of Chichester. He was assisted by Miles Coverdale, who had been consecrated as Bishop of Exeter in 1551, but deprived by Mary two years later, and by two bishops suffragan, John Hodgkin and John Salisbury, who had been consecrated more than twenty years before with the titles of Bedford and Thetford.

Controversialists have made efforts to set this consecration aside. They have first asserted that it never took place, and that all that was done was a ribald performance in a tavern which no one concerned took seriously. When this position could not be defended any longer they have then said that Barlow had never been consecrated. This is patently absurd, in view of the fact that he occupied two sees in succession for a total period of eighteen years, and that his status was never impugned until several years after his death, when there was an obvious motive for doing so.[2] The question was raised again at the end of the nineteenth century,

[1] Kitchin of Llandaff and Stanley of Sodor and Man are exceptions. They conformed and retained their sees until their death in 1566 and 1570 respectively.

[2] The official record of his consecration is not to be found now. There is evidence that the registers were carelessly kept at the time, so that little weight attaches to the fact.

when the Papacy found itself confronted with the necessity of finding some theoretical justification for the existence of a hierarchy of Roman Catholic bishops in England. Anglican Orders were then dismissed as of no effect because in 1559 (and for some years previously) the English Ordinal did not (as it does not today) contain some phrases and ceremonies which had established themselves from time to time (in some instances not before the middle of the fifteenth century) in the Roman books. This contention was disposed of effectively by the Archbishops of England in the year 1897.[1]

For the first few years of Elizabeth's reign our relations with the Papacy remained undefined. A reconciliation was certainly not out of the question and was desirable for political as well as religious reasons. Besides the healing of a lamentable breach in the unity of the Church, the queen's position would have been much more secure if her occupation of the throne had been formally approved by the Papacy.

The breach with Rome was not complete until 1570. On 25 June in that year Pius V, who had succeeded Pius IV in 1566, published the Bull *Regnans in Excelsis* (He who reigns on high). He was a Neapolitan and preferred vigorous action (possibly stimulated by Spanish pressure) to the lengthy intrigues of diplomacy. By the Bull he declared Elizabeth to be a heretic and as such deposed her from her throne. It is just worth noting that he did not declare the Church of England to be heretical, but rather implied that in his opinion it was not. The sentence carried with it the corollary that any "Catholic" prince who liked to add England to his dominions was at liberty to do so. England remained unmoved by this outburst, but it had the effect of linking the Church very closely with the cause of national independence, more closely perhaps than was altogether desirable, and this tie was destined to last for some twenty-five years.

Philip II of Spain was the only sovereign in a position to take advantage of the papal offer, and his case was strengthened by the fact that he considered that he had a valid title to the English throne in right of Mary Tudor, his wife. He necessarily regarded

[1] See Chapter 16.

Elizabeth as illegitimate as well as heretical. It is not clear how far the King of France would have welcomed his success. The only immediate outcome of the Bull was to make all Roman Catholics at least potential traitors. There were, inevitably, some executions, carried out with the barbarities which the law ordained. The sufferers showed admirable constancy, as they had done during the previous reign, when they were drawn from the other side, but it must be emphasized that they suffered for their political, not for their religious opinions. Elizabeth and her advisers had no animus against Roman Catholic opinions when they did not march hand in hand with treasonable ones. Meanwhile Roman Catholic agents began to enter the country from abroad and to become active. In our world they might have been termed "fifth columnists", as their object was to dispose men's minds favourably towards the queen's enemies. Many of them were Jesuits, members of the new Order which had been founded in 1540 by St Ignatius Loyola.[1] It had taken a very prominent part in the remarkable movement known as the *Counter-Reformation*, by means of which the Papacy had recovered large tracts of Europe, notably Poland, which it appeared to have lost for ever. England appeared to offer a promising field for further triumphs. It was impossible to ignore the Jesuit emissaries; they were too outspoken and too dangerous. They had to be hunted down and brought to the gallows when they were caught. The best known of them is Edmund Campion, who was executed on 1 December 1581. As in the previous reign, the list of executions lengthened as time went on. But it is true to say of Elizabeth's government no less than of Mary's that it did not persecute more than could be helped. The number of executions and the character of the victims are, however, less important historically than the development of the factors which had combined to make these terrible scenes not only possible but almost inevitable.

Philip probably expected that England would fall into his hand like a ripe plum. When he found that it would not, his preparations for the plucking were lengthy and elaborate. They were not completed until 1588. Everybody knows the story of that year,

[1] A Spaniard, or possibly a Basque. His real name was Inigo Lopez de Recalde.

and especially of the great week, 21–28 July, and its sequel. But although the immediate cloud was lifted the danger was not yet over. King Philip was a pertinacious person, and his material resources were almost illimitable. He set to work at once to prepare a second expedition and, if his shipbuilders had profited by the lessons of 1588, it might well have succeeded had it sailed. During June 1596 Drake, Howard, and Essex made certain that it never would,[1] and then at last the long strain was ended. England could reckon upon an independent future. It would never become a province of the Spanish empire. Elizabeth would die upon her throne and the resources of the Inquisition would never be applied to the destruction of the Reformed Church.

The reign of Queen Elizabeth is one of the most important epochs in our history. When it began, our national and religious independence were alike precarious. Before it ended both were secure. During the period our Church received the distinctive impress which it has retained with very little alteration ever since. So did our language. We cannot read Chaucer without the help of a glossary of some sort. The Wycliffite version of the Bible would be useless on the lectern of any Church today. If on the eve of Agincourt Henry V had delivered a speech on the lines of the ones which Shakespeare has put into his mouth I doubt whether we should be able to do more than grasp the general sense, if so much, could it be made audible to us now. But Elizabethan English—the Prayer Book, Spenser, Shakespeare and the Authorized Version—presents very little difficulty to anyone who has had any education. It is *our* language. The England we know took shape when Elizabeth was on the throne.

The end of the sixteenth century is therefore a convenient point from which to review the Reformation as a whole and to try to assess its outcome and value. In other words, to find some answer to a question which is often asked, *For what does the Church of England really stand?* or *What is the position of the Church of England?*

To begin with, it may be worth while to refer briefly to three

[1] It is said that the nucleus of the library of Trinity College, Dublin, consists of books captured at Cadiz by this expedition.

views of our Church which are entertained in some circles. The best which can be said of them is that they can be made to appear plausible. They will not stand serious examination.

1. The Church of England is merely one of the forms of Protestantism which made their appearance on the Continent during the sixteenth century. For some reason it never developed as fully as they did, but its real affinity is with them. The attitude of Henry and of Elizabeth towards episcopacy, to which reference has been made earlier in this chapter, is a sufficient answer to this suggestion. We could and did welcome foreign scholars and benefit by their learning without substituting, or proposing to substitute, their system for our own. For much of what follows I am indebted to Creighton's essay on "The Position of the Church of England" in *The Church and Nation*, pp. 248–69. For example, what is said about the Lord's Supper at the end of the Catechism is, almost word for word, a translation of a passage in Calvin's treatise *De Coena Domini* (On the Lord's Supper). It would not be easy to improve upon it. We are not Calvinists and never have been, but we can appreciate the work of a great theologian who, when dealing with a Holy Mystery, was careful to abstain from the over-definition which had worked havoc in the medieval Church.

2. The Church of England is the medieval Church with its system partially mutilated by the steps which were thought necessary in the sixteenth century to get rid of the papal supremacy. That had now gone and the rest of the system ought to be restored.

It is unnecessary to say more than that to speak of restoring the medieval system (not the primitive) without the Papal supremacy is like proposing to build a romanesque arch without a keystone.

3. The Church of England is a compromise between two opposing interpretations of Christianity, roughly analogous with our party system in politics. The Prayer Book holds the balance between them, and the principal duty of an English bishop is to see that this equipoise is not disturbed.

This is not an inspiring view, and if it were true would depict a state of things which could hardly be permanent. The phrase "A bridge Church", which is sometimes used, is not a happy one, if only because no one wishes to make his permanent home upon a bridge. Also, a bridge can be traversed in either direction with equal ease; from "Rome to Geneva"[1] or "from Geneva to Rome", to borrow the phraseology of a bygone age. It does not unite the communities which lie at either end.

A system which appeals to sound learning, and therefore refuses to capitulate to extremists, may at first sight appear to be of the nature of a compromise. *Via media* (a middle path) is a more accurate description, and the two have really nothing in common except upon the surface. A compromise is a working arrangement accepted by two persons or parties who despair of reaching full agreement. Each acquiesces in something which he dislikes because he thinks it impossible to get his own way entirely at the moment. He hopes that he may be more successful at some future time. Meanwhile he will put up with what he has been able to secure.

A *via media* is not an attempt to provide partial satisfaction for two irreconcilables along the lines which they have laid down already. It offers them something positive, which is not identical with the views of either, but may be expected to supersede them by its intrinsic superiority. A simple illustration is a code of coherent, intelligible, and effective law. That might be considered to lie midway between anarchy and tyranny. But it is not a compromise between them. It is something entirely different from either and makes both impossible. To be effective, and to discharge its purpose, it must be understood and accepted voluntarily by those to whom it applies. Coercion can only be applied successfully for as far and as long as it has the support of public opinion; which means sporadically, against a small number of notorious evil-doers.

Of course, anyone to whom the principle of private judgement in religion is anathema will not find himself at home in such a system. The career of John Henry (Cardinal) Newman is a case in point. But it may be worth while to point out that to decide to forgo the exercise of private judgement in future involves an

<hr>

[1] Calvin made Geneva his headquarters.

act of private judgement of the most far-reaching and irrevocable character. A man must decide for himself whether he proposes to continue to use his private judgement or not. If he decides against, he can never reverse or even reconsider that decision. Even to contemplate doing so would mean changing the whole character of his religious allegiance. By admitting, indeed encouraging, the continuous exercise of private judgement as a permanent feature in its system, the Church of England does not exalt it to a position of undue importance. We do not regard the use of it, once for all in one particular way, as the fundamental intellectual prerequisite of religion.

Regarded as a whole, the system of our Church, as far as it is distinctive, is the religious expression of the combined respect for law and respect for individual liberty which is the immemorial tradition of our race.[1] It may be impossible to say whether the tradition was in our remote ancestors before they had begun to cross the North Sea, but certainly it has always been in us here. It has made itself felt in various ways all through our history, and has shaped our development as a nation. Our whole outlook and way of life has been moulded by it for more than a thousand years. It is perhaps the best contribution which we have made and can make now to the general welfare of mankind. If we have much to learn from other nations, they need to learn that from us: never perhaps more than now. It has found expression in the fullest measure and at the highest level in our Church. This goes far towards explaining how it has been possible for what was planned originally as a local arrangement, in view of known needs within a limited area, to become the centre of a world-wide communion. From this it follows that we do not stand primarily for any particular truth peculiar to ourselves, or at least distinctively ours, so much as for a particular conception of the nature of truth as a whole, and of the methods by which we may hope to arrive at a knowledge of it. We do not think that the function of authority is to preclude argument and discussion.

Emphasis is often laid upon the conservative and cautious character of our Reformation compared with contemporary

[1] See Chapter 4.

movements elsewhere. More important, as it seems to me, is its corporate character. It was never identified with a political party, and although naturally it provoked some opposition (and opposition in those days was almost always violent) we were never within sight of anything which could be called civil war. Our Reformation was much more religious than its parallels on the Continent or in Scotland. Besides this, no name has ever been attached to it as have those of Luther, Calvin and Zwingli to the systems which they inaugurated. Thomas Cranmer played an important part, but that was because he held the highest office in the Church. He had been consecrated as Archbishop of Canterbury while the old order of things was still in being. He is believed to have contributed largely to the Prayer Book, an undertaking for which his personal gifts fitted him. But no one knows the exact extent of his personal contribution, and no name, neither his nor that of anyone else, has ever been attached to it. It is, and has always been, the Book of the Church of England. The position of the other great religious and literary monument of the period is similar. The names of the scholars who produced the Authorized Version which appeared in 1611 are of course known. But they are hardly a matter of common knowledge. They are never used in connection with their work, as are those of St Jerome, Wiclif, Tyndale and Coverdale. It does not derive any part of its authority from them. It is, as it has been from the day of its first publication, the version authorized by the Church of England. No further description or guarantee is necessary.

Our reformed Church has never adopted officially any title except the geographical one, which does not do more than state a fact. It is the Church *of England*, and needs no other label. In modern times the adjective *Anglican* has had to be coined, because the words *of England* are not strictly applicable to the offshoots of our Church which have struck root outside our shores. They are in full communion with us, though we claim no authority over them. Therefore a word had to be found to distinguish them from other religious bodies in the countries where they are,[1] and to show that their outlook is in all essentials identical with

[1] In the United States *Episcopal* is used.

ours. *Anglican* makes plain the stock whence they have sprung, without describing its characteristics.

The principal object which the English reformers had in view was the revival of personal religion, which had been brought near to extinction by an over-legalized administration and a mass of largely unintelligible ceremonial.[1] The *Book of Common Prayer* shows how they addressed themselves to this very formidable undertaking.

First, while being careful to retain the framework of the Church they simplified the system which had grown up within it. Many ceremonies were abandoned as unedifying, and by substituting English for Latin, services were made more intelligible.

Secondly, they aimed at something uniform throughout the whole of the limited area with which they were dealing. It was their intention that anyone who went into any church anywhere between Berwick-upon-Tweed and Penzance at service time should be able to understand exactly what was going on, and to take his own part intelligently. If they may be considered to have been rather too rigid, it is to be remembered that for a long time past the Church had been suffering from too much variety in its services. At the present day the demand for more variety seems to be stronger amongst the clergy than amongst the laity.

Thirdly, they intended that their system should give the individual sufficient liberty to be fully educative. It is obvious that a directive system which leaves no room for individual liberty can never be fully educative. In fact, beyond a point which may be reached very soon it must stunt moral and intellectual growth. It is also obvious that to entrust people with more liberty than they have been accustomed to enjoy is to run a risk: sometimes, perhaps, a considerable one. But we believe that in the long run the risk, however real, will justify itself.

Fourthly, they introduced much more, and more systematic, reading of the Bible into the services. They intended Church-goers to have an opportunity of becoming well acquainted with the whole of the New Testament, and with as much of the Old as its greater length allows. Probably no lectionary with which everybody is perfectly satisfied will ever be devised. But it will

[1] See Chapter 10, p. 211.

hardly be disputed that the reformers were right in their deter-
mination to make the Bible as a whole as well-known as possible.
The most serious criticism which can be brought against this
part of their work is that they did less than justice to the deutero-
canonical books[1] which they labelled, rather inaccurately,
apocrypha, and very nearly expelled from the Bible altogether.
They also arranged for the recital of the whole psalter every
month, in the course of Divine Service in every Church.

Fifthly, they missed no opportunity of appealing directly to the
conscience of the individual with all the emphasis they could
command, recognizing the part which the Bible has to play in
this. This principle pervades the whole book from beginning to
end, to such an extent that illustrations of it are hardly necessary.
Mention may, however, be made of the Introductory Sentences
prefixed to Morning and Evening Prayer, and to the Exhortation
which follows them. It reaches its climax in the Communion
Office. By the use of the Ten Commandments we proclaim the
Moral Law in all its majesty before we proceed to the highest
central act of Christian worship. We declare it to be divine (*God
spake these words*) and therefore absolute and directly applicable
to everyone both in his personal life and in his relations with his
fellows. In the same spirit all possible weight is thrown upon the
act of Communion. Communion had almost ceased amongst the
laity by the beginning of the sixteenth century. The hearing of
Mass, a less individual and less exacting alternative, had taken its
place. The eighth rubric appended to the service directing every
parishioner to *communicate at the least three times in the year of which
Easter to be one* was as high a standard as they thought it possible
to set. It represented an immense advance on current practice.

One innovation which has not proved successful was the
attempt to familiarize the nation as a whole with the Athanasian
Creed[2] by substituting it for the Apostles' Creed at Morning

---

[1] The *other books* of *Article* VI.

[2] It will be enough to say here that this document is not in the proper sense
of the word a Creed. It is an *excursus* on the doctrines of the Trinity, and on
incarnation. As such it is of great value. It appears to have originated in the
south of France probably soon after the year 400. St Athanasius, the fourth-
century Archbishop of Alexandria, was not the author.

Prayer on certain days in the year, including Christmas Day, the Epiphany, Easter Day, Ascension Day and Trinity Sunday.

It was hoped, no doubt, that it would give people a more intelligent attitude towards the great central mysteries of the Christian faith. It has, however, proved to be more than the members of an average congregation can appreciate. It is really better fitted to be a guide to Christian *teachers*, which may well have been the purpose which it was intended to serve. But those who object to it most strongly, commonly on account of the emphasis which it lays upon right belief, seem to forget that it lays emphasis upon right conduct, to which the Nicene and Apostles' creeds make no reference.

Lastly, they were careful to secure the right relation between the two great ministries upon which the Christian life, individual and corporate alike, is built, and by which it is maintained. The Church of England does not put the Word either above or below the Sacraments. The two are to be kept together, because if either is exalted unduly at the expense of the other all religious and moral standards will be lowered. This principle, which runs through all the Reformers' work, receives its clearest expression in the *Ordering of Priests*:

> Be thou a faithful Dispenser of the Word of God and of his holy Sacraments

and again

> Take thou Authority to preach the Word of God and to minister the holy Sacraments in the Congregation, where thou shalt be lawfully appointed thereunto.

It has enabled us to produce a distinctive type of piety, deep, pure, sober, unemotional, which will stand comparison with anything to be found in any part of the Christian world.

No one would wish to maintain that our reformers made no mistakes. *The Book of Common Prayer* was necessarily of the nature of an experiment. Possibly none of those who helped to compile it expected that it would stand for so long as it has, with so little alteration. Perhaps it would not have done so, but for the civil war of the seventeenth century. In that struggle it became almost a *palladium*.[1] The Cavaliers were determined to maintain it at all hazards: the Puritans made the possession of a copy a crime in the day of their power. This may have helped to invest it with a sanctity to which it is not really entitled. The time may have come, as was thought thirty years ago, when it should be revised, and could be improved.

No doubt improvement is not impossible, but the starting-point must be a real understanding of what the compilers of the book hoped to effect by it. Then must follow a dispassionate consideration of the measure of success which it has achieved. For both these purposes a background of historical knowledge is more important than proficiency in liturgical studies. Then it may become possible to discern in what respects the book has failed, and for what reasons. Then an attempt to remedy its failures and supply its deficiencies might be made which would command general assent and prove to be of value. This does not, however, appear to have been the temper in which those who were responsible for the abortive books of 1927 and the following year approached their task.

The medieval Church came to ruin because it felt bound to profess to be able to answer any question which could be asked, and because it was too ready to accommodate emotional forms of popular piety. Those dangers can never be eliminated finally. Perhaps they can never even be remote, especially when the clergy are zealous in their work. But in the *Book of Common Prayer*, the *Ordinal* and the *Articles* the reformed Church of England has erected a bulwark against them at least as strong as any to be found anywhere in the world.

It is impossible to leave the reign of Elizabeth without some mention of the Puritan attempt to capture the Church. During Mary's reign a number of English Churchmen had taken refuge on the Continent as some Roman Catholics did at a later date. The Marian exiles went chiefly to Frankfurt or Geneva. But at Frankfurt they found the sacramental teaching of the Lutheran Church was not to their liking. Geneva was their spiritual home,

---

[1] A sacred object believed to be a guarantee of victory to its possessors. Compare the story of the Ark in 1 Sam. 4, 5, 6.

and the ecclesiastical system erected there by Calvin their model.

When they could return after Mary's death they naturally thought that their hour had come. Now they could carry to its logical conclusion what had only been begun by Cranmer and Henry VIII, and refashion the Church according to their own ideas and wishes. The great obstacle was of course the episcopate. That must somehow be got out of the way, or at least deprived of any real power. If it were to be allowed to continue it must be merely as a matter of convenience. The ecclesiastical courts must disappear. Parliament must be supreme.

It would take too long to discuss the struggle in detail here. At times the language and behaviour of what is perhaps best described as the presbyterian party were so outrageous that the Government was compelled to deal severely with them. Elizabeth was alive to the political importance of episcopacy from the standpoint of the sovereign, if she were not particularly interested in its real place in the life of the Church. She was not prepared to see it reduced to an executive instrument for parliamentary purposes.

Neither was Parker, her first archbishop, who held the see of Canterbury from 1559 to 1575. His successor, Grindal, who had been consecrated as Bishop of London in 1559 and translated to the see of York in 1570 and thence to the see of Canterbury in 1576, was more favourably disposed towards the ideas of the returned exiles, and had his reign lasted longer almost irreparable mischief might have been done. His successor, Whitgift, who was translated in 1583 from the see of Worcester, which he had held since 1577, was of a different pattern. When he died in 1604 it was reasonably certain that the reformed Church would continue upon the lines which had been laid down.

There have always been some who for one reason or another have objected to the Church's system, or to some part of it. Possibly if they had been treated with more leniency during the sixteenth and seventeenth centuries they might have disappeared. But a sovereign whose throne is not very secure cannot afford to be very tolerant. Some points to which great importance was attached in the sixteenth and seventeenth centuries—e.g., the wearing of a surplice and the dress of the clergy generally—must seem very trivial to us to-day. The mainspring of all forms of Protestant nonconformity in England has always been social and political rather than religious. They represent the self-assertion of a class which thinks (perhaps with some justice) that it is not receiving as much general recognition as its intrinsic merits deserve.

The vexed question of the relation between the Church and Parliament, which can perhaps never be settled for good, was raised to a higher level by the work of Richard Hooker, who was Master of the Temple in 1585, and died in 1600. His *Laws of Ecclesiastical Polity* in five books, of which the fifth appeared in 1597, has never been superseded. The massive reasoning, and the temper which has earned him the title of *The Judicious* (an uncommon quality amongst the controversial writers of the time, or indeed of most other times), make the book an English classic.

12

From the accession of James I to the Restoration—1603–60

ONE great benefit which we owe to the Reformation is the emancipation of the Church from the State. It was not complete. At the time there was probably no one who would have wished it to be. But so far as it went it was real, if in the opinion of some people at the present day it was not carried far enough. The power of the Crown over the Church had always been considerable in England, and after the middle of the fourteenth century had increased steadily, until by the beginning of the sixteenth it was almost absolute. The revenues of the Church were employed as a matter of course to provide salaries for civil servants of various kinds, including the principal officers of State. If it was impossible to root out the abuse in a moment, it was diminished considerably at once and brought to an end during the next century.

George Abbot, Archbishop of Canterbury, was Treasurer, which was virtually what we understand by Prime Minister,[1] from 1618 to 1620, as was William Laud, 1635–6. Laud was succeeded as Treasurer by William Juxon, who followed him in the see of London and retained the treasurership for five years. He was the last ecclesiastical person to hold it. Since the death of Mary Tudor there has been only one ecclesiastical Lord Chancellor —John Williams, who was appointed in the summer of 1621. He was Dean of Westminster at the time, and pointed out that the deanery house was so conveniently situated in relation to Westminster Hall that if he was allowed to retain it the public funds would be spared the cost of providing him with a suitable

---

[1] The first official title of the Prime Minister, and until after the beginning of this century his only one, is *First Lord of the Treasury*.

residence elsewhere. This proposal commended itself to the thrifty soul of King James 1. Before the year was out Williams was consecrated as Bishop of Lincoln. He retained his other offices, and their demands upon him made it impossible for him to visit his diocese, which was then the most extensive in England. It is, however, only fair to say that he used some of his wealth to found four new scholarships and two new fellowships in his old college, St John's, Cambridge. In earlier days he had, as Dean of Westminster (when Laud was for a time one of his canons), increased the number of King's Scholars by four, and his benefaction to St John's was to make further provision for them. Soon after the accession of Charles I he was compelled to surrender the Great Seal and to betake himself to his diocese. He went to Buckden in Huntingdonshire, where there was a house belonging to the see. (The Bishop of Lincoln continued to live there until the middle of the nineteenth century, and part of the building, which is of red brick, is still to be seen.) There he applied himself to his episcopal duties, and planned a commentary on the Bible which his biographer[1] says was completed with the exception of the Apocalypse. So far as is known it does not exist now. He also projected a collection of the works of Robert Grosseteste, but does not appear to have carried out his intention. This work would probably have been of more interest and value to us than the commentary. On 4 December 1641 he was translated to the see of York, but can hardly be said to have occupied it effectively. Shortly after the outbreak of the civil war he took refuge in his native Wales, where he died in 1650. The later medieval tradition of episcopacy, which may be considered to have flowered in Thomas Wolsey, died with him.

It may be worth while to mention that the Lord Chancellor was originally no more than the King's domestic chaplain who wrote the royal letters in between services. Necessarily he was in Holy Orders, and naturally he became one of the most important personages in the kingdom. When the business became more than he could manage single-handed he had a staff of assistants known

[1] John Hackett, Bishop of Lichfield 1661-70. The title of the book is *Scrinia Reserata*.

as the *Clerks of the Chancery*. They were in Holy Orders too, and each of them was allowed to hold up to eight benefices, none of which he had ever the least intention of visiting, for his maintenance. These clerks really governed the kingdom, and were the original *King's Counsel* before the legal profession annexed the title. The memory of this arrangement is preserved in the fact that the precedence of the Lord Chancellor today is between the two Archbishops. As an ecclesiastic he could not rank before the Primate of All England, but as Lord High Chancellor he could not give place even to the Archbishop of York. He had to have a large amount of ecclesiastical patronage at his disposal in order to man the Chancery, and this he still retains. The Lord Chancellorship is therefore the only great office of state which cannot be held by a Roman Catholic.

The Clerks are represented today by the *College of Chaplains* to the King, who now number twenty-four. They are still, technically, members of the royal household and therefore wear a scarlet cassock and a badge containing the royal cipher. Their only duty is to preach once a year at the Chapel Royal, St James's, and at Buckingham Palace, if so commanded. They receive no emoluments except a small sum to cover the cost of their annual journey to London. The position is regarded as an honourable one, if its long history is not generally known. The last English bishop to hold an important office of state was John Robinson[1] (Bishop of Bristol 1710–14 and of London 1714–22), who was Keeper of the Privy Seal in 1711. He was also the first English plenipotentiary at the Peace Conference at Utrecht in 1712, and the first signature to the treaty, which amongst other things gave us a monopoly of the American slave trade, is his. The memory of an old tradition, or time-honoured abuse, whichever we prefer to call it, is preserved today in the fact that the archbishops and the Bishop of London are always members of the Privy Council. They are not, however, expected to attend it more frequently than they may find compatible with other claims on their time and energy. The accession of James VI of Scotland to the throne

---

[1] From 1697 to 1709 he had been the accredited representative of England at the Court of Charles XII of Sweden.

of England on 24 March 1603 brought us a measure of political security which we had never enjoyed before. The Spanish danger was over, and as there was no place on the Continent of Europe where we were vulnerable, we had nothing to fear from France. The risk of a stab in the back when we were preoccupied elsewhere was ended.

James I is a perplexing figure. In most respects he seems to have been so unlike his predecessors that it is hard to believe that he was a Stuart. But his descendants exhibited the characteristics of the family in unmistakable fashion. It is said that a few minutes before her execution, which took place at Fotheringay on 8 February 1587, when the imminence of Philip's attack, which was made in the summer of 1588, must have been beyond question, Mary Queen of Scots said that she hoped that her son (with whom she had not been on cordial terms) "would remember that she had never said anything to put him out of his fair kingdom of England." It can never be known for certain exactly what she really did say. But if she used these words, or anything like them, it is difficult to see what she meant except that James was not her son. If he were, it was not in her power to prejudice his future. Mary's son was born on 19 June 1566. For some time immediately before that date her life had been that of a hunted fugitive. In view of the long rides which she was compelled to take to escape from her enemies, it is difficult (impossible might be too strong a word) to believe that she could have given birth to a living child. A few years ago the bones of a male infant were discovered in Holyrood House. The body had been wrapped in a scrap of material which might have been part of an altar frontal or an ecclesiastical vestment. Obviously there had been some reason for wishing to dispose of it as quickly and unobtrusively as possible. It is a tempting conjecture, if it can never be more, that this was the child to whom the Queen had given birth, which had died very soon afterwards, if it had ever lived.

In that case, who was the man who succeeded to the throne of Scotland as James VI? Again, we can only guess. But there were living at that time no less than six illegitimate sons of James V. The best known was the Earl of Moray, who was Regent of

Scotland 1567–70. The Earl of Orkney was another, and three others were Prior of Coldingham, Charterhouse, and Whithorn respectively. If a son had been born to one of these at about the same time as Mary's child, he might have been substituted for the dead infant. Very few people need have known what had been done, and it would have been to their interest to say nothing about it. The succession to the throne of Scotland, which was a matter of great importance, would have been secured, and the changeling would have had as much Stuart blood in him as the child whose place he had taken, if it had come through illegitimate channels.

Anyone who has ever inspected a long row of family portraits in a country house must have noticed that it is not uncommon for the family type to be submerged for a generation and then to reassert itself vigorously. There seems, therefore, to be no reason to doubt that James VI was a grandson of James V if, as appears to be upon the whole probable, neither he nor his father was born in lawful wedlock. After Mary's death there must have been very few people who knew the real facts. If the truth were as has been suggested above it was not suspected in England. England was prepared to accept James *faute de mieux*, but closer acquaintance revealed personal characteristics which made it impossible to respect him. He was probably aware of this and sought to strengthen his position by reviving in very extreme form a theory of monarchy which we had discarded in 1399.[1] Probably, also, monarchy had always been more personal and autocratic in Scotland than it ever was in England, and he did not realize how wide and deep was the gulf between the thought and feeling of the two kingdoms. His theory of the divine right of kings may have given him the self-confidence which he was conscious of needing, and did not do him any harm. But it was destined to prove unfortunate for his dynasty and his kingdom. It is not too much to say that it brought his son to the scaffold and drove his grandson into exile. It then led to a schism in the Church[2] and prompted some sixty years of semi-religious, semi-political intrigue which did immense harm to the Church and no good to the nation.

[1] See Chapter 10.   [2] The Non-jurors (see p. 277).

Finally, on 16 April 1746, it sent the Highland clansmen charging heroically to their own destruction at Culloden. It expired with them there.

The accession of James I ended the tension under which England had lived for nearly fifty years, and the sudden relaxation produced the sort of effect which can usually be discerned immediately after a war. Standards of conduct went down, and there was nothing inspiring or elevating about the throne. Parsimony and squalor were its principal characteristics. It is, however, only fair to say that the chronic financial embarrassment of James I and Charles I was not entirely their own fault. The king was still expected to live of his own to a larger extent than we should consider to be reasonable or even possible. Elizabeth was conscious of the great and increasing difficulty of the position, but was very chary of imposing taxation. She did not feel her throne sufficiently secure to risk provoking unpopularity. Accordingly she sold or mortgaged a considerable portion of the Crown lands and spent the money as income. Her successors had to bear the outcome of this policy. It is possible that the nation as a whole never knew what had happened and therefore did not understand why the king was always trying to increase taxation.

Naturally the Church shared in the general decline. Once its existence had become perfectly secure it was not immediately obvious what its future was to be. From 1558 to 1596 the part which it had to play was clear. It had to help maintain the political independence of England, with which its own continuance was linked very closely. Perhaps it was associated more intimately with English national feeling than was to its own highest interests. That danger must always recur whenever the national life is threatened by a foreign enemy. After 1603 there was no enemy, either on our front or in our rear, of whom we need be afraid. There was no one left who remembered the abuses of the medieval system, and not many people who had much recollection of Mary's reign. If there were nothing very particular left for the Church to do, perhaps it did not matter very much how it went on. Besides this, the remarkable success of the Counter-Reformation on the

Continent had reduced many of the Reformed Churches there almost to the position of beleaguered garrisons. They did not understand the fundamental differences between our Reformation and their own (it is not too much to say that they never have yet), and they naturally began to look to England (or Great Britain) as the principal Protestant power. Protestantism was safer here than anywhere else, and we might therefore be expected to lend at least our moral support to our hard-pressed allies. There was a real possibility that we might be drawn into a pan-Protestant federation of some kind which might have compromised us fatally. The personal sympathies of George Abbot (Bishop of Lichfield 1609, of London 1610 and Archbishop of Canterbury 1611–33) were in that direction. But a strange misfortune befell him in the summer of 1621. When shooting with Lord Zouch at Bramshill he accidentally killed a keeper. As he was in fact guilty of homicide the see was put into commission for a time, as some bishops-elect, amongst whom were John Williams and William Laud, declined to be consecrated by him. The incident is worth noting because it shows that (contrary to the view sometimes expressed for controversial purposes) even at that time episcopal consecration was considered to mean no more than the conferring of legal authority. Abbot's legal status was unimpaired, at any rate if the Crown chose so to determine. The point at issue was his spiritual competence. After a time he was restored to his functions by a commission of eight bishops.

The foolish Gunpowder Plot of 1605, which was prompted by nothing more than the continuance of fines imposed for recusancy[1] upon Roman Catholics, which James had rashly promised to remove, naturally produced an outburst of indignation against Popery and all its works, which was not without solid moral foundation. The day was ordered to be observed with a special service which was included in all editions of the Prayer Book down to the year 1859. After 1688 some modifications were introduced to make it applicable to the landing of William III at Torbay on 5 November as well.

Despite the general character of the period two very important

[1] Refusal to attend their parish church, as the law required.

contributions to the life of the Church were made during the reign of James I, if their beginnings belonged to the days of Elizabeth. First the Canons of 1603 and secondly the Authorized Version of the Bible, which appeared in 1611. It is so described because it was intended to supersede various unauthorized versions of Puritan provenance which were in circulation.

1. Mention has been made already[1] of the extraordinary confusion into which the law of the Church fell during the late medieval period. *Canon Law*, as it was called, was really papal law. Opinion differs as to whether the rejection of the papal authority necessarily abrogated the whole body of Canon Law *en bloc* or not, but it certainly brought the production of some simple and more intelligible code within the limits of possibility. An attempt was made during the sixteenth century, but it came to nothing. The complete revision of the whole body of the Church's law proved to be more than could be carried through at that time. But a number of rules and regulations were drawn up from time to time with a view to meeting immediate administrative needs, without pretending to completeness. During the year 1603–4 these were formed into a single coherent code by Richard Bancroft (Bishop of London 1597–1604, Archbishop of Canterbury 1604–10) with the assistance of several distinguished lawyers. This code, which consists of 141 canons, was passed by the Convocation of Canterbury in 1604 and by that of York a little later. It is still in force, and is the only body of ecclesiastical legislation (as distinct from such measures as have been passed in recent times by the Church Assembly) the authority of which cannot be impugned on any ground. Some of its enactments are now obsolete and a comprehensive scheme for its revision was produced in the year 1947.

2. If the Authorized Version must be regarded as a product of Elizabethan learning and scholarship, it was not ready for publication until the year 1611. As a translation it is not always accurate, and in places it is obscure. In both these respects it can, however, stand comparison with two even more famous earlier versions,

---

[1] See Chapter 7.

the Septuagint[1] and the Vulgate.[2] Whatever its defects may be, it has established itself long since as an English classic, and (it is to be hoped) will always remain one. Its wonderful rhythm is probably due partly to the fact that the translators were more familiar with the Vulgate than most English clergy are today, and partly to the influence of what was known as the *Cursus Romanus*. This means the stereotyped and traditional style of the Clerks of the Papal Chancery, whose letters had gone all over Western Europe for centuries. It so happens that English lends itself very readily to the rhythm of post-classical Latin, and it is to this fact that the language of the Elizabethan Prayer Book and of the Authorized Version owes its distinctive quality. The additions made to the Prayer Book in 1662 show that the secret had survived until then, if subtle differences are discernible. Modern attempts to emulate it have not for the most part been very successful: probably because the authors have not looked unto the rock whence it is hewn and to the hole of the pit whence it is digged.[3]

More accurate translation is possible today, partly because some important manuscripts of which the scholars of the sixteenth and early seventeenth centuries did not know, are available now. The Revised Version, which was completed in 1884, is in some respects superior to the Authorised. But it has never laid hold of popular imagination. Since that time a number of modern scholars belonging to various Christian communions have tried their hand with the New Testament. Monsignor R. A. Knox[4] has been, as I think, the most successful of those whose work I know. But from the standpoint of pure scholarship he was handicapped by the supremacy which he is bound to assign to the text of the Vulgate.

The most prominent figure in the Church during the first quarter of the seventeenth century was Lancelot Andrewes. He was

---

[1] The Greek translation of the Old Testament, made probably during the third century before our era for the Jews of Alexandria.

[2] The Latin translation made by St Jerome in the fourth century. It is today the Authorized Version of the Roman Church.

[3] Isa. 51. 1.

[4] A son of Eton and Oxford who has transferred his allegiance to the Roman Church.

born in 1555 and in 1589 became Master of Pembroke College, Cambridge. In 1605 he became Bishop of Chichester. He was translated to the see of Ely in 1609 and to that of Winchester, which he held until his death in 1626, ten years later. His *Preces Privatae* (Private Prayers) are a devotional classic and his name stands first, if only for alphabetical reasons, in the list of the scholars who produced the Authorized Version. He was also a learned controversialist and wrote at length in defence of the position of the Church of England against Cardinal Bellarmine. Some of his arguments were probably more cogent then than they would be today. One short extract is not perhaps as well known as it deserves to be, and may therefore be reproduced here. The reference is to the Eucharist in general and to the doctrine of Transubstantiation in particular.

Praesentiam (inquam) credimus, nec minus quam vos veram. De modo praesentiae nil temere definimus, addo nec anxie inquirimus; non magis quam in baptismo nostro, quomodo abluat nos sanguis Christi: non magis quam in Christi incarnatione quomodo naturae divinae, humana in eandem hypostasin uniatur.[1]

We believe (I say) in a Presence as real as you do. We make no rash definition as to the manner of the Presence, nor, I may add, are we curious to know; any more than we are curious to know how in our Baptism the blood of Christ cleanses us, or how in the Incarnation of Christ human nature in united with the Divine Nature to form the same Person.

It would be hard to find a better example of the attitude of devout reticence in relation to the deepest mysteries of the Christian faith which our Church (it might not be too much to say *alone*) has been wise enough to adopt and strong enough to maintain.

The accession of Charles I on 27 March 1625 brought a promise of better things. The Church was not primarily responsible for the fact that this promise proved illusory.

A notable figure during the earlier part of the reign was George Herbert. He was born in 1593, and was a younger brother

---

[1] *Ad Cardinalis Bellarmini Apologiam Responsio*, § 11.

of the Lord Herbert of Cherbury, who is sometimes regarded as the "father of Deism".[1] After an exceptionally distinguished career at Cambridge he entered Holy Orders, and while still a deacon accepted the rectory of Bemerton, near Salisbury, on the advice, it is said, of Laud. (It would be interesting to know what arrangements he made for the celebration of the Holy Communion until he became a priest.) Bemerton is said to be the smallest Church in England. Other claimants to the distinction known to me are at Wythburn in Westmorland at the foot of Helvellyn, Wastdale Head in Cumberland in the shadow of Scafell Pike, and at Culbone in the woods between Porlock and Oare in the western corner of Somerset. There may be others elsewhere. While at Bemerton he wrote his famous *Priest to the Temple*, in which he draws a picture of the country parson as he ought to be. The pastoral and devotional standards set are of the highest order, but it is remarkable that he makes no mention of any services in the church on week-days, even in Lent or Advent. He may have considered that the duty of saying Morning and Evening Prayer daily imposed by the Prayer Book went without saying and therefore need not be specified as far as he was concerned personally, and that no congregation of any kind could be expected upon a week-day. He also published two volumes of poetry which reach a high level, if the metaphors and diction are sometimes fanciful by our standards. He also wrote some hymns, of which the best known is perhaps *Teach me, my God and King*.[2] He held a prebendal stall in the cathedral church of Lincoln in virtue of which he was patron of the parish of Leighton Bromswold in Huntingdonshire. He found the church in bad condition, and refurnished it throughout in light oak. On either side of the chancel arch he placed two exactly similar pulpits, and directed that service should be read from one and the sermon delivered from the other "to the end that the people should not put praying either above or below preaching." His wishes are observed there to this day.

Woodwork of this period is not common in England, but two fine examples (both dark) are to be seen in the church of St John the Evangelist in Leeds and at Croscombe near Wells in Somerset.

[1] See Chapter 14.   [2] No. 485 in the English Hymnal.

It is many years since I visited Leighton Bromswold, but a photograph of the exterior which I have seen recently suggests that he also built or rebuilt the top story of the tower. The work represents the last flicker of the Gothic tradition, as it may be seen in the chapel of Wadham College, Oxford, and in the church of Low Ham in Somerset. Both these are probably a little earlier. He died in 1633. If it is difficult to estimate his influence during his lifetime, he left to the Church an imperishable legacy.

Leighton Bromswold is not much more than five miles from Little Gidding, and it is probably to this fact that the friendship between George Herbert and Nicholas Ferrar owes its origin.

Nicholas Ferrar was born in London on 22 February 1593. His father was a prosperous merchant, and in due course he proceeded to Clare Hall, Cambridge. He became a Fellow and subsequently travelled widely. In 1624 he was elected a Member of Parliament for Lymington in Hampshire, and to all appearance a brilliant and prosperous career (despite the failure of the Virginia Company, in which his father had invested a considerable sum) lay before him. But his own tastes were of another kind. He wished to restore community life in the Church of England, having, perhaps, observed during his travels how much we had lost by its complete disappearance in the previous century. With the help of his mother he bought the manor of Little Gidding in May 1625. The village had been reduced to a single hut, and there was a large and dilapidated manor house, a few yards from which lay a small and neglected church which was used as a hay barn. He went to work so vigorously that in little more than a year the house and church were fit for use. He was ordained deacon in the chapel of Henry VII in Westminster Abbey by Laud, then Bishop of St Davids, but destined before the year was out to be translated to the see of Bath and Wells. He never proceeded to the priesthood, so while he took the daily offices in the church at Little Gidding the community was dependent for Holy Communion on the rector of Steeple Gidding, who was a near neighbour.

The household consisted at first of Nicholas Ferrar and his mother, his elder brother John with his wife and their three children, and his sister Susanna Collett with her husband and eleven of their children. It was increased subsequently, until with three schoolmasters and some domestic servants it came to number some thirty persons. It was a unique experiment inasmuch as the community included members of both sexes most of whom were closely related by ties of blood or affinity. There was no rule of celibacy; several of the Collett daughters married and left. There was no idea of founding an Order. The object was to create a family life, strictly disciplined and dedicated to devotion and industry. One of the occupations practised was the production of a "Harmony of the Gospels" by the simple process of cutting up copies of the Bible and pasting the slips suitably arranged into other volumes. Naturally, at that day, this was not regarded as a waste of time. Some of these volumes were bound very handsomely and one was accepted by the king.

Despite its isolation the community soon attracted attention, both friendly and hostile. The king visited it more than once, the last occasion being 2 May 1646 on his way from Oxford to entrust himself to the Scottish army near Newark. The field to the southwest of the church is still called *The King's Close*, a name which is believed to record the fact that he came across it then.

Williams, Bishop of Lincoln, whose house at Buckden was not much more than ten miles away, visited Little Gidding four times, and although its ways were not exactly as his, was unstinted in his praise of what he saw and heard there. He refused, however, to accept the vows of lifelong celibacy which some of the ladies wished to tender. He protected the community against Puritan aggression as long as he could, and Dr Richard Busby,[1] the famous headmaster of Westminster School from 1640 to 1695, was another staunch friend.

The king's last visit gave the Puritans their opportunity. The inmates saved themselves by flight, but the house was looted and the church desecrated. Some of them seem to have returned soon afterwards and to have lived there until about 1660. But the community ("The Arminian Nunnery" was the Puritan descrip-

---

[1] Also prebendary of Cudworth in Wells Cathedral and subsequently treasurer.

tion) was never reconstituted. Nicholas Ferrar himself had died in 1637 and perhaps it could not, even in favourable circumstances, have outlived him for very long.

The manor-house has disappeared, but its site is occupied by a farmhouse. The present church dates for the most part from the time of Queen Anne, if some of the furniture belonged to the older building. There is a plain altar-tomb, without any inscription, a few feet from the west door, which is believed to contain the body of Nicholas Ferrar. It may have been just inside the church of his day. When I visited the place some forty years ago, the eagle-lectern had just been discovered at the bottom of a neighbouring pond and replaced in the church. As the beak and claws had disappeared, it may be presumed that they were of some valuable material, such as silver, and that the zealot who threw it into the water had forgotten the story of Achan the son of Carmi which is told in the seventh chapter of Joshua.[1]

The two leading figures amongst the bishops during this period were William Laud and John Williams, of whom the former was translated from London to Canterbury in 1633, and the latter from Lincoln to York in 1641. They were lifelong antagonists, as they represented the two schools of thought which under varying names and in slightly different form have always existed in the Church. Before the Reformation they contributed not a little to the standing opposition between the secular (parochial) and regular (monastic) clergy.[2] Today in England they are usually labelled *Anglo-Catholic* and *Evangelical*, and these titles may be accepted as generally intelligible, without subscribing to their accuracy. All that need be said of them here is that both have made valuable contributions to the Church, and that neither is entitled to deny the right of the other to exist.

Personal considerations tended to increase the hostility between the two bishops. Williams was the younger by some nine years, but in their earlier days he outstripped Laud in the race for

[1] For a further account see *Little Gidding and its Founder*, by Henry Collett (S.P.C.K., 1925), and *Little Gidding*, by J. W. P. Jones (S.P.C.K., No. 50 in a series entitled *Notes on Churches and Abbeys*). There is a novelist's picture in *John Inglesant*, by J. H. Shorthouse.

[2] Monks desired simpler services and resented episcopal control.

preferment. He was also better born, and probably the cleverer of the two, if Laud were the more highly principled. The portrait of him which hangs at Bishopthorpe, the residence of the Archbishop of York, suggests that he had a sense of humour, of which Laud's face gives little indication.

They also differed fundamentally with regard to what was becoming steadily a more important and difficult question—namely, how to deal with the Puritans. Williams did not take them very seriously. They had hardly existed in the Wales in which he had grown up, and were not numerous in the social stratum to which he belonged. He thought that if they were treated with toleration, and a certain measure of ecclesiastical preferment came their way, they would soon disappear. In that world no one would have seen any objection to using patronage of any kind as a bribe to turn an enemy (actual or potential) into a friend. Laud belonged by birth to the class from which the Puritans drew their chief strength, as their descendants have done ever since. He was much more alive to the danger to be apprehended from them, but made the mistake of thinking that they could be crushed by force. When in 1641 Williams was committed to the Tower for protesting against the exclusion of the bishops from the House of Lords (an act which came near to costing him his life at the hands of an infuriated mob), Laud was already there. It was thought wiser that the two Primates should not meet, lest some fantastic charge of conspiracy should be brought against them. But they exchanged affectionate greetings, and it may be hoped that the longstanding breach between them was healed.[1]

It is unnecessary to speak here at any length on the political developments of the reign of Charles I. The outline, at any rate, is a matter of common knowledge. The general situation was extraordinarily difficult in view of the increasingly factious temper which prevailed, especially in matters ecclesiastical. It is not easy to account for this, but it must be recognized as a fact. One illustration will suffice. When Laud held his metropolitical Visitation of the province of Canterbury, with the object of bringing about a higher standard of seemliness and order in the

[1] For some account of Laud see Appendix D.

furnishing and arrangements of churches and in the conduct of Divine Service, he found that in the church of Hingham in Norfolk, about fourteen miles to the west of Norwich, the floor of the chancel was on the same level as that of the nave, and that the altar was on the floor level. He directed that it should be raised at least one step, as is usual. Most people now would think this desirable, if only for the sake of appearances, but would not regard the matter as of the first importance. But the rector felt so strongly that sooner than comply with the archbishop's directions he resigned the benefice and departed to America. The parishioners sympathized so closely with his attitude that a considerable number of them accompanied him, amongst whom was included an ancestor of Abraham Lincoln. It is interesting to speculate as to what course the American Civil War might have taken, more than two centuries later, had he remained at home. As it turned out they might all as well have done so, because the archbishop's orders were disregarded, and the floor of the church presents an unbroken level from end to end today.

Had the king been stronger, and therefore less obstinate, and Laud wiser, and therefore less violent, the catastrophe which came upon the kingdom and overwhelmed them both might perhaps have been averted. Probably they had an unfortunate influence upon each other, as neither seems to have possessed the power, almost indispensable to a ruler, of measuring with some accuracy the extent and quality of the opposition which he is provoking. Besides this, Charles was probably incited by his French queen, in whose eyes a king who was not an autocrat was a king in name only.

Both men are said to have been below middle height, and it is often noticeable that men who are unduly short are prone to self-assertion. This may be due to a suspicion that most other men look down upon them metaphorically as they do physically.

Charles's position was undoubtedly one of extreme difficulty. He was embarrassed financially through no fault of his own,[1] and his opponents were by no means always reasonable. The well-known episode of the ship-money (which was almost a turning-point in his fortunes) is a good illustration.

[1] See above, p. 243.

James I had allowed the navy to decay, though it was obvious that as a nation we were bound to depend increasingly on sea-borne commerce, and a State which needs a large merchant fleet must have a navy adequate to protect it.

Charles found that he must spend a great deal upon the navy, and it was obvious that the whole burden could not be borne by the coast towns. It must fall upon the whole nation. Country squires, many of whom had possibly never seen the sea, and certainly knew nothing whatever about it, resented the new tax. They could recognize nothing beyond their own immediate interests, and did not realize how closely their own well-being was linked with the national fortunes as a whole. It is perhaps fair to say that they did not feel certain that the money would ever reach the navy. When Parliament refused to agree to the tax, Charles tried to impose it without parliamentary consent.

The position went from bad to worse, until on 22 August 1642 the king set up his standard at Nottingham. Perhaps even then each side hoped that the other would not fight. Like all his family (except his eldest son), Charles had a fully adequate sense of his own importance in the general scheme of things, and of the deference which he was entitled to receive. He may have persuaded himself that this display of royal majesty would over-awe his contumacious subjects and move them to return to their duty. The Parliamentary party may well have thought that even Charles would not be so ill-advised as to match himself with the City of London. But now there could be no turning back.

The struggle was really between parliamentary government and royal autocracy, but unfortunately it also became one between the Church and Puritanism (the word *Nonconformity* was not yet in use). It was also to a large extent between the gentlemen of the countryside and the mercantile population of the towns. The issue was hardly in doubt from the outset. The royalists gained some early successes, chiefly through their superiority in cavalry. But experience shows that if cavalry can from time to time win battles, it can never be the decisive factor in a war. It is unnecessary to record the story in detail here. By 1646 the king's plight was so desperate that he threw himself on the loyalty of the Scottish army, which was lying near Newark. He had been born in Scotland, in the ancient royal palace of Dunfermline on the northern shore of the Firth of Forth. He hoped, no doubt, that the Scots would rally round him and that with their help, and with the use of Scotland as a base, he might recover everything which he had lost. On 30 January 1647 the army in which he had placed his trust sold him to his enemies for £400,000. Half the money was paid immediately and the other half in two instalments. Both parties seem to have recognized that the transaction was not creditable, and disingenuous attempts to disguise its real character were made. It ought never to be forgotten. In the light of it the devotion to the Stuart family which was professed in Scotland during the next century, and is perhaps not quite extinct yet, cannot be taken very seriously. Charles was executed on 30 January 1649 on a scaffold erected outside the banqueting hall of Whitehall Palace, now the United Services Museum and the only portion of the palace remaining. Laud's head had fallen on Tower Hill on 10 January 1645.

Both the king and the archbishop died in a manner worthy of their religion, in respect of which they had refused to compromise their convictions, and of their office. They may therefore fairly be accounted martyrs. I do not know of any church dedicated in the name of Laud, but there are five or six in the name of *King Charles the Martyr*.[1] A special form of service for 30 January was added to the Prayer Book at the Restoration, but fell into disuse during the second half of the nineteenth century. The parallel between the king and our Lord is drawn too closely to be consonant with modern taste.

We are compelled to ask ourselves, How did it come about that these two shocking scenes, for such they must be called, were possible? The executions were carried out quite deliberately, after a lengthy trial in each case, and commanded a sufficient measure of support from public opinion at the time. The men who

[1] E.g., at Plymouth, built in 1665; at Tunbridge Wells, built in 1889; and at South Mymms in Middlesex, built a few years ago. Also one at Falmouth, which dates from 1662.

were directly responsible for them were not in the least as the French revolutionaries of the eighteenth century, or their Russian, German, Spanish and Italian counterparts in our own day. They were sober, God-fearing Englishmen, deeply if narrowly religious, who set themselves a high moral standard in their personal conduct. Their leaders included some men of good birth and breeding. How was it that they felt themselves bound to act as they did?

The answer seems to be that they were convinced that the whole fabric of religious and civil liberty would be destroyed if those two men were allowed to continue in power. There was no law which they would not set aside for their own purpose, no person on whom they would hesitate to lay hands. They could not be kept in prison indefinitely. The places where they were detained would become centres of subversive activity, and there might be a revulsion of public feeling, such as brought Charles II to the throne, which would restore them both, and then the last state of the nation would be worse than the first. They could not be exiled to the Continent. If they were, the king at least would be a perpetual source of danger. There was no St Helena to which they could be deported. There appeared to be no solution of the difficulty except that they must die. The important question is not so much, How can these two executions (judicial murders, if we prefer so to call them) be justified? as, How had a situation arisen which seemed to those who had to deal with it to be absolutely intolerable, and to admit of no other remedy?[1] The blame for the unhappy developments of the twenty years which led up to the impasse does not rest entirely with either side. After the king's death some royalist forces remained in the field for some two years and a half. They were scattered at the battle of Worcester on 3 September 1651, and south of the Tweed the triumph of the parliamentary party was complete.

Everything short of torture and mass murder was done to ensure that the Church of England should cease to exist. The whole system was abolished by law. The clergy were driven forcibly from their benefices, and many of them were reduced to

[1] See Appendix D.

absolute destitution.[1] Some sought refuge abroad and some were sheltered secretly in the houses of royalists. But even the possession of a copy of the Book of Common Prayer was a crime. The destruction of windows, screens and the furniture of churches was probably more the work of individual fanatics, such as William Dowsing, who worked much havoc in East Anglia, than the deliberate policy of the Government. But it regarded their proceedings with an indulgent eye.

Cathedrals were desecrated, and at Wells the Chapter House was put up for sale for building material. Fortunately no local contractor of sufficient enterprise to undertake the demolition could be found. If Oliver Cromwell had lived a few years longer, or if Richard Cromwell had been a man of his father's stature, the Church might have disappeared for ever.

Yet the measures taken by the Government were not always as successful as was expected. Two instances which happen to be known to me may be quoted here. At Meltham, a village set high in the hills about five miles to the south-west of Huddersfield, the present church of St Bartholomew was consecrated nine days before the battle of Worcester, by an Irish bishop who was hiding in the neighbourhood. Apparently the services were carried on without interruption until the Restoration. At the village of Melton, some twelve miles north-east of Ipswich, the parish registers were kept all through the Commonwealth period by a churchwarden who made no attempt to conceal his royalist sympathies. For a time there was a succession of "intruded ministers", but after about the year 1655 religious ministrations ceased, and people got married before the magistrates at Woodbridge, a neighbouring market town. A little later there appear to have been no justices of the peace, and the only course remaining was to have the marriage cried in Woodbridge market on three successive market days. This was considered to invest it with as high a degree of legality as was to be had. The picture which the registers give of the gradual breakdown of the whole

---

[1] An account can be found in *The Sufferings of the Clergy*, by John Walker, sometime Fellow of Exeter College, Oxford, published in 1714. A revised edition by A. G. Matthews appeared in 1948.

machinery of government, religious and civil alike, is remarkable. But all the time, it is recorded, there was a priest in hiding in the desolate and marshy peninsula between the estuaries of the Deben and the Orwell, who could be procured to bless these unions in the Church's way. What went on in out-of-the-way corners of Yorkshire and Suffolk may well have gone on elsewhere. But it must have been almost impossible to hold an Ordination anywhere, however secretly. So in course of time the clergy would have died out. If that had happened Roman Catholic emissaries might have succeeded in taking their place in the next generation.

It sometimes happens that the worst outcome of an abuse is the violence of the reaction which follows. The Puritan régime became as intolerable as its immediate predecessor, until on 8 May 1660 Charles II was solemnly proclaimed king at Whitehall and at Temple Bar in the presence of both Houses of Parliament. Three weeks later, on his own thirtieth birthday, he entered London amidst acclamations such as England had not heard since Henry V rode to St Paul's to give thanks for the victory of Agincourt.

During the period of the Commonwealth conferences were held at Westminster between the Scottish Presbyterians and the English Independents, as they were commonly called, in the hope of securing a uniform ecclesiastical organization on both sides of the border. They were not successful, and the details do not concern us now. But at one of them a metrical version of the Psalms was produced which is believed to have been the work of Francis Rous, Provost of Eton College. The Scots seem to have thought highly of it and took some copies home with them. It is used, I believe, in the Established Church of Scotland at the present day. If it was ever used in England it was displaced by the joint work of Tate[1] and Brady[1] a generation later. It is curious that a Provost of Eton, one of the most thoroughly English of all our institutions, should have supplied the Church of Scotland, which

---

[1] Nahum Tate, 1652–1715, Poet Laureate, possibly the author of the well-known hymn *While shepherds watched their flocks by night*, and Nicholas Brady, 1659–1726.

has always been almost fiercely "nationalist" in its outlook, with one of the distinctive elements in its worship.

The best legacy of these dismal days was bequeathed by a little group of men known as the Cambridge Platonists. The most distinguished of them were Benjamin Whichcote, Provost of King's College from 1644 to 1660, and Ralph Cudworth, who became Master of Christ's College in 1654. They revived the philosophy of Plato (428–347 B.C.) and applied it to Christianity. Briefly, they did not look for final authority in matters of religion either to an infallible Book or an infallible Church. They relied upon inner spiritual experience, emphasizing the mystical element, which in one form or another makes its appearance in religion all the world over and has done so from time immemorial. To them the spiritual world was not to be pictured as a remote country to which we may win at some future time. It is here and now, and nothing else is real. Everything which we perceive by means of our senses is no more than a pale and unsubstantial reflection of it. It is our only true home, and we can take possession of it at will. In as far as we do so, the changes and chances of this mortal life come to mean less and less to us. St Paul showed that he understood the fundamental principle of this philosophy, whether he had learned it in one of the Platonic schools, which lasted until the sixth century of our era, or not, when he wrote

> For the invisible things of him since the creation of the world are clearly seen being perceived through the things that are made, even his everlasting power and divinity.[1]

To men who took this view of the nature of spiritual reality the arid and interminable disputations in which the Puritan divines delighted meant little or nothing. They breathed a different air, and their feet were set upon a rock about which there could be no argument. If their disciples have never been very numerous, the tradition which they started has never died out in the Church of England.[2] We owe to it much of what has been best and most distinctive in our religious thought during the last three

---

[1] Rom. 1. 20.
[2] See *The Platonic Tradition in English Religious Thought*, by W. R. Inge, 1926.

hundred years. Whether it will be able to survive the increasing ignorance of Greek which has been spreading over the land like a fog since the beginning of the present century remains to be seen.

Cromwell himself was interested in education and is said to have contemplated founding two new universities, one at York and one at Manchester. But if any scheme was definitely put forward nothing came of it.[1]

The Civil War established the fact that, owing to the development of artillery, the feudal castle or fortified manor house had ceased to be of any military value. Its walls could be breached by cannon firing from a distance outside the range of any weapons of which the defenders could possess themselves. A private person could no longer offer any effective resistance to the forces of the State. This strengthened the position of the Government very considerably and meant that an armed rebellion had very little prospect of success. Artillery was equally effective in the field. The Duke of Cumberland was a more experienced soldier than any of his Jacobite opponents, and his troops were better disciplined than the Highland forces. But it was his cannon which reduced the battle of Culloden to an affair of some twenty minutes.

[1] Manchester has had an independent university for a generation now. The idea of a University of York has been brought forward again within the last few years.

13

Unsettled Weather—2

From the Restoration to the death of Queen Anne—1661–1714

THE restoration of the monarchy naturally meant the restoration of the Church as well. Most of the bishops were still alive, though the sees of Canterbury and York had both been vacant for several years. They were filled by the translation of William Juxon, who had become Bishop of London in 1633 and had attended Charles I upon the scaffold, and of Accepted Frewen, Bishop of Lichfield since 1644. The difficulty which had presented itself at the beginning of Elizabeth's reign[1] did not recur. It is impossible to say exactly how many of the dispossessed clergy were alive, but, having regard to the average expectation of life at the time, about two-thirds is probably a reasonable guess. They were reinstated in their benefices as quickly as possible and the worship of God in the Church's way was resumed throughout the land. Certain constitutional changes were made. The coercive jurisdiction of the ecclesiastical courts over the laity, which had been one of the principal weapons in Laud's armoury, came to an end, and the Houses of Convocation surrendered their immemorial right to tax themselves for the public service. Possibly it had become an anachronism, but it emphasized the distinctive position of the clergy as an estate of the realm, which is now almost universally forgotten or ignored. In future the clergy were to be taxed by Parliament in common with the rest of his Majesty's subjects.

Charles II might fairly be described as a genial cynic. Intellectually he was the ablest of his line, if his character was not such as to command respect. So far as he had any religion his inclination was towards the Roman Church, into which he is believed to

---

[1] See Chapter 11, p. 223.

have been received privately upon his death-bed. His guiding principle was Not to go on his travels again, and he recognized that the Church of England could contribute a great deal towards making his throne stable. In the interests of national tranquillity and dynastic security he was genuinely anxious for a religious settlement, however little he may have known or cared about the causes of the discord which had prevailed.

Accordingly, on 15 April 1661 a conference met under the presidency of Gilbert Sheldon, Bishop of London. It is known as the Savoy Conference, because it was held in the old Savoy Palace in the Strand (nothing of this is to be seen today except the chapel, which has now been assigned to the Royal Victorian Order). Each side had twelve representatives. The leading figure amongst the Churchmen was John Pearson, Bishop of Chester 1673–86, one of the foremost scholars of the time, and the author of an *Exposition of the Creed* which is not yet entirely obsolete. He was seconded by Peter Gunning, Bishop of Chichester 1670–75, of Ely 1675–84, master of St John's College, Cambridge and a professor of divinity. Of the Puritans, the best known is Richard Baxter, author of *The Saints' Everlasting Rest*.

The Conference was really foredoomed to failure from the start, because the two parties took fundamentally different views of what they had come to do. The Puritans thought that there was to be an unrestricted discussion of the form of service to be used in the Church in future. The Churchmen considered that they had come to hear what arguments in favour of any alterations in the Prayer Book could be advanced. Behind these different views lay two different and irreconcilable conceptions of the nature of the Church. To the Puritans then, as to some people today, the system of the Church is of no more importance than the architectural character of a building intended for any form of Christian worship. Within very wide limits it can be determined freely by the taste and convenience of those by whom it is to be used, and the same may be said of its interior furnishing. There can be no permanently valid reason for giving exclusive preference to any design.

To others, the Church's system, of which episcopacy is the

core, is something which we have received, as we have received the Canon of Scripture; or, at least the Canon of the New Testament.[1] The earliest stages in the development of both may be obscure to us now. But we believe that the Holy Spirit has been at work in them. So much may be said without committing ourselves to any disputable opinions in relation either to Inspiration or Apostolic Succession. Since the second century no professedly Christian teacher or community has attempted to impugn the authority of Scripture as a whole, and since the fourth there has been very little doubt as to the contents of the Canon. The Puritans objected to the Apocrypha[2] and could adduce some reasons for doing so, but they would never have dreamed of going further. They could not understand that in the eyes of their opponents to offer an alternative to episcopacy is at least comparable with putting forward some alternative to the Bible. Even now there are many people who do not appreciate that standpoint. The fact that episcopal government has from time to time led to abuses is no more relevant than the fact that many people have from time to time drawn unwarranted and extremely mischievous conclusions from the Bible.[3]

After the failure of the Conference the Church had to go its own way. The Houses of Convocation revised the Prayer Book, making a few additions and some unimportant alterations. A new preface was written, which is believed to have been the work of Robert Sanderson, who was Bishop of Lincoln from 1660 to 1663. It deserves to be studied carefully for the light which it throws upon our standards and our general outlook. The revision was ratified by Parliament and the Prayer Book became as we have received it today. (An attempt to revise it was made soon after the beginning of this century, but the proposals of Convocation [to which the newly constituted Church Assembly had contributed a good deal] were rejected by the House of Commons in 1927 and again in 1928.)

---

[1] All the books of the New Testament as they are commonly received we do receive.—*Article VI.*

[2] *Deutero-canonical* books is a more accurate description.

[3] The defence of negro slavery is an instance (see Chapter 14).

Perhaps the most significant addition made in 1662 was a service for the Baptism of Adults. This is mentioned specially in the preface, as having become necessary owing to the recent disorders which had made it impossible for infants to be baptized in the ordinary way. Then follows a remark of which the full implications cannot have been imagined at the time.

[it] may be always useful for the baptising of natives in our plantations and others converted to the faith.

This is the first recognition of the fact that the expansion of England had begun and that our Church had incurred responsibilities, which would not diminish as time went on, beyond our own shores.

The Prayer Book settled, there remained what were known as the "intruded ministers" to be dealt with. These were Puritan preachers who had acquired, usually by violence, possession of a number of parish churches and were officiating therein in accordance with their own tenets. By an Act of Uniformity passed on 19 May 1662 it was ruled that if they would accept episcopal ordination and undertake to use the Prayer Book in future they should not be molested. If they refused, they would be deprived. This may fairly be regarded as a generous offer. No inquiries were to be made into the title by which they held their benefices and received the income from them. But if they wished to remain, they must obey the law. According to a book which was published anonymously in 1663 with the title *Ichabod*,[1] *or*, *The Five Groans of the Church*, 1,342 ministers are said to have taken advantage of the offer. It remained open until St Bartholomew's day (24 August), when some 1,800–2,000 ministers marched out. They are entitled to the honour which is always due to men who have sacrificed worldly prospects for conscience' sake, but it is not easy to admit that they had a real grievance. Attempts were made to maintain that their expulsion contravenes the declaration guaranteeing liberty of conscience, which the king had issued from Breda before his return to England. This contention cannot, however, stand. Liberty of conscience means that a man may worship God

---

[1] Sometimes attributed to Thomas Ken, afterwards Bishop of Bath and Wells.

whether privately or publicly as he thinks fit, and that he cannot be penalized for refusing to take part in a form of worship of which he does not approve. It does not and cannot mean that he may appropriate buildings and revenues belonging to a Church of which he is not a member, and use them for the propagation of his own private opinions. "Elastic" would describe such a conscience more accurately than "free".

The day was known as *Black Bartholomew* in some circles, and perhaps still is. It made Non-conformity (the word must be introduced now) a factor in English life, which has persisted down to our own day. The real *raison d'être* had always been political and social at least as much as religious. The places of these men had to be filled as best they could be, which meant that in some, perhaps too many, instances the standard of the royalist clergy was low. Much has been made of this from time to time for controversial purposes. But a good deal of the criticism directed against the royalist clergy was in a sense irrelevant. The ministry of the Church does not depend entirely upon the personal qualifications of the clergy. The clergy do not act as individuals, but are as they are because they are the accredited representatives of the Church. This authorization makes their ministrations valid, whatever the precise significance attaching to that word may be. It is desirable that their personal qualifications should be as high as possible, and in the event of grave moral failure the authority by which they act must be withdrawn, at any rate for a time. But to make everything depend upon the person of the individual minister, as the Puritans did, and as some people do today, is a form of sacerdotalism[1] which the Church of England cannot countenance. What was known as the *Five Mile Act*, which was passed in 1666, was harsher and perhaps less easy to defend. The House of Commons insisted upon it, though the king was not in favour of it. It enjoined that any minister who had not subscribed the Act of Uniformity four years before must take an oath against the lawfulness of bearing arms against the king and endeavouring alteration in Church and State. If he failed to do this he was not to

---

[1] I.e., attaching too much importance to the person of the *Sacerdos*, or priest.

come or be within five miles of any town in which he had formerly acted as parson, vicar or curate.

This modified form of banishment may have been unnecessary, and must have caused some hardship and resentment. But the royalist squires who made up the majority of the House of Commons had suffered much at the hands of the Puritans. It is not wonderful if they were nervous as to what might happen if strong nonconformist congregations were allowed to grow up in the towns.

A chapel built very soon after the passing of this Act is still to be seen on Hatfield Heath, a little-known and rather desolate corner of Essex. Five miles plus a few yards separate it from the town of Bishop Stortford across the Hertfordshire border. Its 250th anniversary was celebrated some thirty years ago. There was no church on the heath until after the nineteenth century was well on its way. A few hundred yards away the remains of what must have been an unusually large oak tree were to be seen until about fifty years ago. Local tradition had it that the original congregation held their services underneath its branches until the chapel was ready for use.

Opinions may differ whether the Church at the Restoration missed a great opportunity, or escaped a dire calamity. If the Independents could have found a home within the Church's system, that would have been to the advantage of both. But they do not seem to have contemplated the possibility seriously. They wanted the system of the Church, which we had been at pains to preserve during the previous century, to be remodelled to suit their idiosyncrasies. Had the Church agreed it would have abandoned its national quality. It would have identified itself with something sectional and of recent origin and would have lost its power of guiding and influencing the life of the nation as a whole. Puritanism was never really indigenous. The leaders always looked abroad for guidance and inspiration, and it has always been more influential in America than here. At a turning-point in our national history, when we decided to maintain the continuity of our religious and political life by restoring the Church and the monarchy, the Puritans (or Presbyterians and

Independents, if we prefer so to describe them) did not conform. They accepted the monarchy grudgingly, because they really had no choice. The Church they would not accept. They turned aside and chose the semi-private position which they have held ever since.

The plague of 1665 was not a national catastrophe on the scale of the plague of the fourteenth century,[1] as it was almost restricted to London. Refugees carried it to Witham in Essex, where a long list of deaths may be seen in the church. It also reached Eyam in Derbyshire. The story of the heroic and successful efforts made by the vicar, William Mompesson, to confine it to the village is well known. The insistence of a prayer *In the time of any common plague or sickness* in the Prayer Book shows that such outbreaks were regarded as periodic.

The fire of the following year,[2] of which a vivid description can be found in Pepys's diary, was a more serious calamity. The immense destruction which it caused in the city shook the whole fabric of our commercial prosperity, and recovery was necessarily slow. But the disaster provided one of the greatest of all English architects with a unique opportunity. Sir Christopher Wren (1632–1723) received a general commission for the rebuilding of the city. If all his plans could not be carried out as he would have wished, he left us St Paul's Cathedral and a unique set of other churches. St Paul's was his own work in a very special sense, as he supervised the process of construction more closely than modern architects are accustomed to do. Many of the other churches must be said to have been built "under his auspices." It is impossible that he should have been personally responsible for them all. He broke completely with the Gothic tradition, which had dominated English church-building for almost exactly five hundred years. He employed the style known as Palladian, from an Italian architect named Palladio, who practised during the second half of the sixteenth century. Palladio had reverted to the style of the Roman Empire, with such modifications as were necessary to adapt it to ecclesiastical or domestic use.

The style had been introduced into England during the earlier

---

[1] See Chapter 8, pp. 146–7.   [2] 2–5 September.

part of the seventeenth century by Inigo Jones, but Wren was the first person to employ it on a large scale. Anyone who saw the dome of St Paul's rising above the ruins of the city and marked the smaller churches, such as England had never seen before, which were springing up all round it must have felt that he was watching the birth of a new order of things.

There were originally seventy-two of these churches, in an area of little more than a square mile. In 1939 forty-nine of them were still standing. During the war twenty-one of them sustained damage at the hands of the enemy, and four must now be regarded as beyond repair. St Paul's itself was hit by a bomb twice, and while much less damaged than might have been feared, must be considered to have escaped destruction by a narrow margin. Despite the splendour of Wren's achievement, or perhaps because other architects thought him inimitable, there are few Palladian churches to be seen outside London. Holy Trinity, Leeds, which was built between 1720 and 1730, is a fine example of the style.

The fire was at the time supposed to have been caused by deliberate arson carried out by Roman Catholics. There appears to have been no foundation whatever for the belief, but the fact that it was widely held shows how deeply engrained in the public mind was the conviction that the Papacy was our inveterate enemy and would shrink from nothing which might do us a deadly injury.

The belief was recorded in an inscription on the plinth of the monument erected by Wren to commemorate the fire near the spot where it originated. This drew from Pope the lines:

> Where London's column pointing at the skies
> Like a tall bully lifts the head and lies,[1]

which were justified by the real facts. In modern times the inscription has been removed.

It was during that troubled year 1665–6, when men's minds were occupied with thoughts of war, pestilence and disaster, that Isaac Newton was beginning the great series of mathematical studies which were destined to place him intellectually on a level

[1] *Moral Essays*, Ep. III, 339.

with any Englishman who has ever lived, and in the next generation to exercise a profound if indirect influence upon the religious
thought of England.

Charles II died on 6 February 1685 and was succeeded by his
brother James, whose short reign is one of the most tragic in our
history. He was in his fifty-second year when he came to the
throne, and perhaps we should say now that he had a bad nervous
breakdown in middle life. As Duke of York he had never been
popular, partly perhaps for reasons which redound to his credit.
His religious standards at least were higher than those of his
brother, and of the dissolute society which frequented the Court.
As Lord High Admiral he waged relentless and to some extent
successful war against the corruption and inefficiency which he
found in the administration of the navy. In this he was ably
abetted by Samuel Pepys, secretary to the Navy Board, who in
recent times has been recognized as a really great public servant.
He commanded the fleet in person against the Dutch and displayed
a very high degree of skill and courage. In fact, he was thought
to have risked his life more than the commander-in-chief ought
to do. On the throne he showed himself a very different person.
As king it is not unfair to call him arrogant, irresolute and weak.
He was a sincere and avowed Roman Catholic, and may have
regarded his accession to the throne, which he had had no reason
to anticipate in earlier life, as a divine call to establish Roman
Catholicism in England. To this end he was prepared to use force.
It must always be remembered to the credit of James II and his
descendants that, unlike their ancestor, Henry IV of France, they
refused absolutely to forswear their religion for the sake of a
throne. In little more than four months from his accession he
was challenged. On 11 June, James, Duke of Monmouth, an
illegitimate son (as it was believed) of Charles II,[1] landed at Lyme
Regis in Dorset to make a bid for the Crown. He relied chiefly
on the fact that he was a Protestant. The brief episode is of

[1] After 1746 a number of Jacobite papers found their way to Sweden. A few
years ago they were rediscovered and examined. It is said that among them was
proof of the marriage of Charles II to Lucy Walters. If the marriage really took
place, then the Duke of Monmouth was the lawful heir to the throne. But no
attempt to uphold his legitimacy seems to have been made at the time.

particular interest to a Wells audience because the county of Somerset was the principal theatre of the rebellion and our cathedral and city were both affected by it directly.

The canon-in-residence during the month of June and July was Thomas Holt, Chancellor of the Church. He has expressed his opinions in the record of the proceedings of the dean and chapter, known as *Chapter Acts*. He was a fervent supporter of King James, and the story can best be told in his own words. The original entries are in Latin.[1]

> After this a disgraceful civil war began countenanced by Prince James, Duke of Monmouth, an illegitimate son of the most glorious Prince Charles II, late King of England, who was present with the rebels in person. The most noble Lord Charles, Duke of Somerset, Lord Lieutenant of the County, was despatched to this neighbourhood, but found the military forces which ought to have been the King's defence in a parlous condition for want of money, which is the sinew of war, and not less from the bad disposition of the rank and file, who were deserting their leaders and the royal cause and attaching themselves forthwith to the rebels.

On 18 June the chapter voted £100, which was apparently all they had available at the moment, to the king's cause, and Richard Healy, who is commemorated by a tablet fixed to the wall of the east cloister, was commissioned to take the money to the Duke of Somerset. This minute is signed by four of the five canons— Thomas Holt, Robert Creighton, Edwin Sandys and Henry Dutton. The dean (Ralph Bathurst) and the fifth canon (Richard Busby) were not present. Since Bathurst was also President of Trinity College, Oxford, and Busby Head Master of Westminster School, they were probably occupied with their duties elsewhere. The money was apparently regarded as a gift rather than as a loan. At any rate, there is no record of its repayment.

If Monmouth could have taken Bristol he might well have gained the throne. But the city shut its gates against him, and a formal siege was out of the question. The army was in retreat (and once a

---

[1] The translation reproduced here appeared in my *Story of Wells Cathedral* (first edition, 1934).

rebel army has begun to retreat its cause is lost) when it passed through Wells on 1 July. On that morning the chapter ought to have held a meeting, but circumstances made that impossible. The events of the day are recorded as follows, in another hand, possibly that of Nicholas Niblett.

> On Tuesday 1 July 1685 between 4 & 5 p.m. in the Chapter House of the Cathedral Church of Wells the Reverend Thomas Holt, D.D. chancellor, and Canon residentiary, and president of the Chapter[1] in the presence of Nicholas Niblett, notary public, in view of the increase of the civil war and the fact that this cathedral church has experienced to a lamentable extent the ferocity of the fanatical rebels, who this morning stole all its furniture, all but destroyed the organ, and turned the sacred building into a stable, prorogued the chapter and all the business to the 28th day of July between the hours of 9 and 12 a.m. hoping that before that date the wicked rebellion would have been completely extinguished.

> The prayer of the most worthy president was heard. The happy sixth day of July intervening ended the rebellion and destroyed the rebels at Weston Zoyland in this County so it is possible to return in safety to the charge of the Church which has been established against the violence and hatred of our enemies and the gates of hell.

> God has given us this peace.

The closing words, DEUS NOBIS HAEC OTIA FECIT, which are written in capital letters, are a quotation from Virgil.[2]

The conduct of the rebels at Wells alone was sufficient to discredit their cause in so far as it professed to be a religious movement. The battle, which is usually known as Sedgemoor, was the last fought on English ground. It will be enough to say here that the rebels hoped to surprise the royalist forces at dawn. The "moor" across which they came is a low-lying tract of country which is often flooded in winter. (What are generally termed *marshes* elsewhere are called *moors* in Somerset.) It is intersected

---

[1] The title borne at Wells by the senior canon, who presides over meetings of the chapter in the absence of the dean.

[2] Eclogue 1, p. 6.

by large drains known as *rhines*. These can be serious obstacles; if the depth of water is not very great, the mud is probably bottom-less. If the rhines on Sedgemoor were then as they are now, it is easy to see why Monmouth's army met with disaster. A short distance outside the village of Weston Zoyland for which they were making, there are now two rhines running parallel with each other, and separated by only a few yards. This is an unusual arrangement. The morning is said to have been misty. If the vanguard crossed the first rhine successfully, and was then brought to a stand by the second, of which it did not know, confusion would result immediately. However that may be, the royalist sentry on the tower of Weston Zoyland church detected the presence of the troops, so the surprise which was the rebels' only chance of success became impossible. The battle did not last very long. Monmouth escaped, but was found a few days later hiding in a ditch. He was executed on 15 July 1685, little more than a month after his landing.

A novelist's account of the rebellion can be found in *Micah Clarke*, by Sir A. Conan Doyle.

The rebellion was followed by what has come to be known as the *Bloody Assize*. The presiding judge (George Jeffreys), who subsequently became Lord Chancellor, is commonly represented as a sadistic monster, who revelled in causing prisoners to be hanged in droves, and abused and taunted them from his place on the bench. The matter was investigated very carefully a few years ago by the Very Reverend Prior (now the Right Reverend Abbot) E. Horne of Downside, who published the result of his researches in an article in the *Downside Review*[1] entitled "The Bloody Assizes in Somerset".

The real facts appear to be as follows. Jeffreys was not alone. He was accompanied by four other judges[2] who must at least have concurred. All the prisoners were charged with high treason. They had no defence of any kind. They were bound to plead *Guilty*,

---

[1] Vol. liii, 1935.

[2] Sir William Montague, Lord Chief Baron, Sir Cresswell Lewis of the Common pleas, Sir Francis Withers of the King's Bench, and Sir Robert Wright of the Exchequer.

and the only sentence which could be passed was that of Death. But it does not follow that the sentence was carried out, or even intended to be carried out in every instance. Extenuating circumstances could be taken into account, after sentence had been passed. But that was bound to be a lengthy business which the King's Commissioners could not attempt to deal with personally at the moment. The record of the Taunton Assize exists today in the Record Office.[1] The proceedings did not occupy more than two days—Friday, 18 September, and Saturday, 19, and there were 513 prisoners. It is therefore manifestly impossible that Jeffreys should have made a lengthy speech to each of them, as he is said to have done.

This fact alone obliges us to entertain some doubt as to the credibility of the story as a whole.

In fact, four men—Simon Hamblyn, William Gatchell, William Cooper and Joseph Cooper—were condemned, and there is no doubt that the first three were executed. There is some uncertainty with regard to Joseph Cooper, as the word *reprieved* appears against his name. Then there is an entry *Reprieved by the Judge*, followed by 509 names. The total number of executions which took place in the three counties of Devon, Dorset and Somerset is given variously as between 239 and 251. If we take the higher figure, which is unlikely to be an under-estimate, it does not amount to one in ten of the rebels taken at Sedgemoor with arms in their hands.[2] Besides this, 847 were sentenced to varying periods of transportation. Some escaped from prison and some died of smallpox in gaol before their sentences could be carried out. Probably some more died on the voyage. Few if any can have returned. This cannot be considered unduly harsh by the standards of the time. Punishments were, as we should think, unnecessarily severe, and the gallows was always in evidence. For a moment the rebellion had seemed to be within sight of success and the Crown had been seriously alarmed. Prior Horne has shown that the reason why Jeffreys has been so traduced is that everyone has used without question a tract of 16 pages which

[1] Assizes 1685–97, 23/3.
[2] They are said to have numbered about 3,500.

was published in 1689, entitled *The Protestant Martyrs, or, The Bloody Assize*. It was subsequently enlarged and reached a fifth edition in 1705. It was reprinted by Messrs Blackwood in 1873.

This document was the work of Titus Oates, a man of the worst character. For his activities in relation to the "popish plot" (which never really existed) he was tried by Jeffreys, who sentenced him to be whipped, fined, pilloried and imprisoned for life. He was really fortunate to have escaped hanging. In 1689 William III released him by an act of what must be regarded as misguided clemency. He immediately set to work to revenge himself on Jeffreys by blackening his memory in every way possible. He was abetted by a man named John Tucker, who had taken part in the rebellion but had been let off with a whipping. The printer was named John Dunton. The pamphlet appeared under the name of James Best, but Dunton must have known who the author was, and can hardly have been under any illusions about him. Dunton was subsequently imprisoned for debt and is said to have died insane. If he were not as great a villain as Oates or Tucker, he was not a particularly reputable character.

In the *Dictionary of National Biography* after each name a word or two usually appears to indicate the general nature of the activities of the person whose biography is about to be given, *e.g.*, *ambassador*, *political economist*, *divine*, and so forth. After Titus Oates's name the single word *perjurer* is to be read. An exhaustive examination of the whole dictionary would be an almost impossible task. But as far as I have noticed he is the only person in it to be so described. If his distinction is not unique it is certainly rare.

As soon as James felt himself secure upon his throne (his coronation was a sadly maimed rite) he turned his attention to the task to which he may have thought he had been divinely called, namely: the extirpation of the Church of England and the substitution of the Roman Catholic religion for it. He struck at Oxford first, and endeavoured to force a Roman Catholic president upon Magdalen College. When the Fellows refused to forgo their right to elect, he expelled them and put creatures of his own into their place. For the moment he seemed to have been successful.

One of the most important colleges in Oxford had become Roman Catholic, and it might be assumed that the rest of the University would soon follow suit. A Roman Catholic Oxford would be a big step towards a Roman Catholic England. This was in September 1687. The resistance of the Fellows had, however, won the admiration of England, and they were honoured guests wherever they went. In little more than a year the king had to give way (by that time even he could see that his throne was tottering) and they were restored.

But early in 1688 James thought himself strong enough to take the step which was destined to bring him to ruin. On 4 May he ordered a Declaration of Indulgence to be read in all churches during Divine Service on Sunday, 20 May, which happened that year to be Rogation Sunday. This would have granted complete toleration to all nonconformists, including Roman Catholics, in whom alone James was interested. Charles II had prepared a similar declaration in 1672, but Parliament had declared it illegal, and illegal it remained. For that reason the Church was inflexibly opposed to it. It is important that the real point at issue should be clearly understood. As in the struggle between Henry VIII and the Papacy, it may easily be confused, or misrepresented for controversial purposes. It is not true to say that the Church was opposed to toleration in principle. The abstract merits of the proposed declaration did not really enter in, though opinion might well have differed as to whether the time had yet come when such measure of toleration as we now regard natural in any civilized country was desirable, or even possible, in England. The point was that the king was trying to override the law by his personal *fiat*. The Church took its stand in defence of the law (which is always the only ultimate guarantee of individual liberty) against arbitrary personal rule. The nation understood perfectly well what was happening. Our immemorial respect for law coupled with respect for the liberty of the individual (which it is probable James never understood) was roused, and as on former occasions proved invincible. The rest of the story can be told briefly.

On Friday, 18 May, seven bishops met at Lambeth—William Sancroft (Archbishop), William Lloyd (St Asaph), Francis Turner

(Ely), John Lake (Chichester), Thomas Ken (Bath and Wells), Thomas White (Peterborough), Jonathan Trelawney (Bristol). They would have been nine had Peter Mews of Winchester (who had commanded the royalist siege-train at Sedgemoor) not been ill and had Robert Frampton of Gloucester been able to arrive in time. Late that night they presented a petition to the king setting out their reasons for refusing to publish the Declaration. He recognized the petition as a standard of rebellion (as indeed it was), and ended the audience with the words *I will be obeyed*. He was too much of a foreigner by blood and upbringing to realize that it is dangerous to talk to Englishmen in that strain, especially when they know that the law is on their side. On the next two Sundays the Declaration was read in a very few churches, and in some of them the congregation walked out. It was obviously a complete failure. The king was resolved to punish the bishops by bringing them to trial on a charge of conspiracy to diminish the royal power. Since they refused to enter into their recognizances to appear at Westminster Hall and answer the charge, they were committed to the Tower. This was a very ill-advised step. Their journey thither by water was a triumphal progress and popular feeling in their favour mounted higher daily. The trial came on on 29 June, and at ten o'clock next day the jury, who had sat up all night, returned a verdict of *Not Guilty*, which was received with immense enthusiasm everywhere. The Church was recognized as having saved England from arbitrary rule, and was set on an unassailable (and perhaps for that reason perilous) pinnacle of popularity. Some attempt at a reconciliation between the Crown and the Church was made during the summer, but the situation was obviously an impossible one. Overtures were made to William, Prince of Orange, who had some Stuart blood in his veins, and had married James's eldest daughter, Mary. He landed at Torbay on 5 November, and for a moment it looked as if we were committed to another civil war. But the memory of the last was not dead, and few people in England were prepared to fight for James. The scale was perhaps turned by the action of Lieutenant-General John Churchill (afterwards Duke of Marlborough), who on the night of 23–4 November left James's camp at Salisbury, accompanied by the Duke of Grafton and some four hundred officers and men, and joined William's army at Axminster, some fifty miles to the south-west. James recognized that his position was hopeless, and on 11 December fled the country, having previously thrown the Great Seal into the Thames, apparently with some idea of paralysing the whole machinery of government. There was an interregnum of two months until on 12 February Parliament offered the Crown of England, France and Ireland to William and Mary jointly. A Convention Parliament in Scotland followed suit about a month later. A revolution had been carried out with remarkable speed and without the shedding of a single drop of blood. Probably no one foresaw that it would involve England in sixty years of semi-religious, semi-political intrigue which did immense harm to the Church and no good to the nation.

A number of clergy, headed by Archbishop Sancroft, held that in no circumstances could a nation depose its anointed sovereign, so successfully had the theory of the monarchy put forward by James I been developed. Therefore they could take no oath of allegiance to the new sovereign. They were given a reasonable time for reflection, and as they remained obdurate were deprived of their office. Six of them were bishops, all of whom except Frampton had been members of the famous seven. Some four hundred clergy went with them, and an unknown number of laity. The schismatics (for so they must be termed) are known as *Non-Jurors* (Not-Swearers), because they refused to take the oath. They took from the Church a volume of piety and learning which it could ill afford to lose.

Whatever their personal qualities it is, however, difficult not to think that Dr Johnson was justified in his remark,[1] "I never knew a non-juror who could reason."

When people refuse to accept one solution of a very difficult problem, it is fair to ask what alternative they have to propose. What did the Non-Jurors think ought to have been done? The throne was without an occupant. James had fled from the country which he had shown himself incompetent to govern, after having

[1] Boswell's *Life*, vol. iii, p. 350.

broken every pledge he had given to the Church and having attempted to substitute personal autocracy for constitutional rule. Public feeling was so hot against him that nothing could replace him on the throne except a French army, whose duty it would be to keep him there for as long as suited the plans of Louis XIV. No one in England can really have desired this. It is believed that even the Papacy would not have been over well pleased had it come about. A republic was out of the question, and there were still plenty of people who could recall the days of the Commonwealth. James's son was less than a year old. The business of government had to be carried on. What better course was open than to invite his elder daughter to share the throne with her husband? The attitude of the five bishops who had been numbered amongst the seven is particularly hard to understand. When they withstood James in the matter of the Declaration they must have known that if they were not risking their lives they were risking everything else. A heavy fine and a period of imprisonment were the very least they could expect if they were defeated, and they faced the prospect like valiant Christian men. They must, however, have thought it possible that they might succeed, and must have recognized that then the king's position would be untenable. They drove him from the throne—and then declined to accept the successor whom their own action had made necessary. If they were not prepared for the situation which they brought about, it looks as if they were unable to foresee the probable outcome of their own acts. Men who are without this power are not fitted to hold high office in the Church or the State, especially in difficult and dangerous days.

The best remembered of them is Thomas Ken, author of the two famous hymns "Awake, my soul" and "Glory to thee, my God, this night." He had been nominated to the see of Bath and Wells by Charles II, to whom he had commended himself by his refusal to have Nell Gwyn under his roof for a night when he was living at Winchester. The incident and the sequel do equal credit to both. After his deprivation he lived principally at Longleat, which had passed to Sir Thomas Thynne, first Viscount Weymouth and ancestor of the present Marquess of Bath. He died there on

19 March 1711 and is buried in the churchyard of the parish church of Frome. The words *uncanonically deprived* appear in the inscription which he composed for his tomb. The portrait of him which hangs in the Bishop's Palace at Wells shows a curiously childish face. It suggests that, whatever his devotional and literary gifts, impulsiveness and obstinacy were conspicuous features in his character.

The original Non-Jurors won a considerable measure of support in the universities, if the nation as a whole regarded them with indifference or contempt. Whatever may be said on their behalf, it is less easy to justify their successors, who never had taken any oath to King James. The consecration of bishops who could never have dioceses and existed to keep a schism alive is, to say the least, a dubious proceeding. As the century wore on they quarrelled amongst themselves over matters of ceremonial, called the usages, and sank deeper and deeper into obscurity. Their last bishop is said to have maintained himself by working as a watchmaker, in or near Manchester, and to have died about the year 1780. Some congregations survived until after the nineteenth century had begun.

The movement produced some devotional literature, including a revision of the Book of Common Prayer of real value. Of course, there would be no question of its adoption by the Churches. But as a whole it must be taken as an illustration (others can be found) of the fact that piety and perversity sometimes go hand in hand, and that learning is not always accompanied by wisdom.

During the last ten years of the seventeenth century there was a perceptible reaction against the licentiousness of the Restoration period, which had been a reaction against the severity of the Puritan régime. Religious and ethical societies sprang up, of which the best known is the *Society for Promoting Christian Knowledge*, which was founded in 1697 by Dr Thomas Bray. Its primary purpose was to distribute Bibles and other good books amongst the poor at home. But it soon concerned itself with the provision of lending libraries (of religious books) for the colonists in North America. He followed this up in 1701 by the *Society for the Propagation of the Gospel in Foreign Parts*. This is hardly a private society, as the Archbishop of Canterbury has always been president *ex officio*. Originally it directed its attention chiefly towards the colonists, who were becoming an increasingly important factor in relation to Church and State alike. But in the year 1710 it decided that preference was to be given to the conversion of heathen and infidels. It is therefore the first real attempt on the part of our Church to face its missionary responsibilities.

During the primacy of John Tillotson (1691–4) an attempt was made to revise the *Book of Common Prayer*, perhaps with some idea of making it more acceptable to nonconformists. The Toleration Act of 1689 had removed virtually all restrictions upon their worship, and it may have been thought that they would now be better disposed towards the Church, and that with a little encouragement many of them might be induced to make it their home. We need not regret that the new book never came into use;[1] but it contained two interesting provisions with regard to Communion. There were to be at least four celebrations annually in every parish instead of the three enjoined previously, the additional one to be at the time of harvest. If this practice had been adopted generally it might have led to some form of Harvest Thanksgiving service such as was introduced about the middle of the nineteenth century and is almost universal now. Besides this, there was to be a monthly Communion at "great Churches in towns". This was instituted at the parish church of Leeds by John Killingbeck when he became vicar in 1691. He was a proctor for the clergy in York Convocation, so must have taken part in the discussions which led to the proposal. It would be interesting to know how widely his example was followed. But both provisions show that the Sacrament of the Lord's Supper was beginning to regain its rightful place in the life of the Church. Recovery from the degrading abuses to which it had been subjected during the later Middle Ages was necessarily slow. It was not really complete until our own time.

[1] The draft was reprinted by order of the House of Commons about the middle of the nineteenth century and copies can be had from H.M. Stationery Office.

During the last ten years or so of the seventeenth century the general climate of opinion began to change; especially perhaps in relation to natural phenomena of all kinds. This was no doubt largely due to the influence of the Royal Society which Charles II had inaugurated in 1662: the best legacy bequeathed to the nation by any Stuart. Medicine freed itself from its disreputable associates of earlier days, astrology and magic. It is, however, said that during the last illness of Charles II medicine was administered to him in a cup made from the skull of a man who had been hanged, in the belief that this would make the dose more effective. Executions for witchcraft ceased.[1] Several people have tried to ascertain what really lay behind belief in witchcraft, but without very much success, so far as I know. The commands given in Exodus 22. 18 and Deuteronomy 18. 10 would have been regarded as all the justification required for putting a sorcerer to death, once his guilt had been established. But they do not furnish any grounds of conviction, and these are not always easy to understand. Had these people, of whom the great majority were women, any exceptional (or abnormal or supernatural, whatever adjective we prefer to use) powers of which they made malevolent use? The only certain answer seems to be that their neighbours thought so, as apparently did they; which does not settle the matter. The further question, How far could belief in the existence of such powers produce the results ascribed to them? is outside the scope of these lectures.

One remarkable feature of the period is the number of clergy. In the year 1688 Gregory King published a statistical analysis of the nation.[2] He used the hearth tax, a predecessor of our rates, as the basis of his calculations. He could not, of course, take anything of the nature of a complete census of the population, and of the pursuits in which they were engaged. That was not done until 1801. His conclusions are therefore of the nature of guesses. But they are well-informed guesses, and are probably not

---

[1] They continued for a little time in Scotland. In England a few capital sentences were passed after 1700, but were not carried out. The law was repealed in 1736.

[2] Reproduced by Dr Trevelyan in his *English Social History*, pp. 276–8.

very far from the truth. He did not attempt to include Scotland in his survey. His estimate for the total population of England and Wales is just over five and a half millions. He reckons two thousand *eminent clergymen*[1] and eight thousand *lesser clergymen*. It is not clear exactly where he drew the line. The former category must have included deans, archdeacons, masters of colleges and professors in the universities of Oxford and Cambridge. But the total of these must have been a long way short of two thousand. That is not, however, a matter of importance. The point is that he reckoned that there were ten thousand clergy of one kind and another. This meant, roughly, one to every five hundred and fifty of the population. Today the ratio is about one to every three thousand. The maintenance of so large a ministry must have been a matter of considerable difficulty. A good many of the clergy (more, in all probability, than at the present day) were drawn from the higher social strata, which meant that they could at least supplement their professional earnings from their patrimony, if they could not live entirely "of their own". But many of them were undoubtedly very poor.

So far back as 1655 a society had been founded to make some provision for the widows and orphans of clergy who had been expelled from their benefices by the Puritans. In 1678, when its original purpose had come to an end, it ceased to be a private venture. It was incorporated by Royal Charter under the title of the *Corporation of the Sons of the Clergy*, which explains itself. Since 1727 the Archbishop of Canterbury has always been the president. The first vice-president was Sir Christopher Wren, and subsequent holders of the office have included eight Lord Chief Justices and four Lord Chancellors. Since 1799 there has always been a member of the Royal Family amongst the stewards. The raising of its status in 1678 was a recognition of the fact that the material welfare of the clergy, and especially of their families, is the concern of the nation as a whole.

An important feature of the later Stuart period is the appearance of the ecclesiastical antiquary. In the controversies of the time all parties sought to defend their position by the appeal to antiquity,

---

[1] The bishops are classed by themselves as *Spiritual Lords.*

and this led to the making of many real contributions to learning by members of the Church of England. Some of them were laymen, some were in Holy Orders. It would take too long to enumerate them all now, but special mention may be made of the following:

1. Sir William Dugdale (1605–86). He was Garter King of Arms, and beside various publications which might be considered proper to his office produced *Monasticon Anglicanum* in three volumes. There was, of course, much more in the way of monastic ruins to be seen in his day than there is now.

2. Anthony Wood (1632–95). He spent most of his life at Oxford and wrote on the history of the University and the country.

3. Thomas Rymer (1641–1713). He was a Cambridge man, and in 1692 was appointed historiographer to William III. His great work is his *Foedera* in twenty volumes, which he undertook at the behest of the Government. It consists for the most part of a collection of the public "conventions" between Great Britain and other powers (*Conventiones Literes et Acta Publica*).

4. Thomas Hearne (1678–1735). He was at one time second keeper of the Bodleian library at Oxford, but was expelled for being a Non-Juror. Probably this afforded him considerable private satisfaction, as he seems to have been a quarrelsome person who thoroughly enjoyed a grievance.

After the accession of George II (approximately) interest in studies of this kind died down. The eighteenth century was too urbane to concern itself with anything which could be labelled "Gothick". A hundred years later the Oxford Tractarians cherished a romantic but ill-informed sentiment, to which the novels of Sir Walter Scott probably contributed not a little, for everything medieval. When this fog had cleared it was recognized that the foundations for intelligent and scientific study of our own past had been well and truly laid by the scholars of the Restoration. A very great deal has been built upon it by many master hands.

During the same period Richard Bentley (1662–1742) created in the field of classics what we understand by critical scholarship. As a classical scholar he is at least the equal of anyone whom England has ever produced. It would be difficult to exaggerate the debt which the Church and the nation alike have owed for the last two hundred years to the tradition which he inaugurated. Its disappearance would be an irreparable loss.

For the last forty-two years of his life he was Master of Trinity College, Cambridge. His relations with the Fellows were not harmonious, and attempts were made to deprive him, on the ground that he had violated the statutes. The case came before the Bishop of Ely as Visitor of the College, but soon after the conclusion of the trial he died, on 31 July 1714, before he had pronounced sentence. The judgement was found amongst his papers, and would have deprived Bentley. The question was allowed to rest until 1733, when the Fellows again appealed to the Visitor. Next year he pronounced sentence of deprivation, but it proved ineffective because the Vice-Master, who alone could execute it, refused to do so. All attempts to compel him to act came to nothing, and the old hero (it is difficult to call Bentley anything else) died in 1742 in possession of his Mastership. Undoubtedly his services to the College were very great.[1]

The whole story is very curious reading, and it may be doubted whether such a figure as Bentley could have existed in any other country in the world, or at any other period of our history.

The position of the Church of England has probably never been stronger than at the turn of the century. It had gained immense prestige by its resistance to James II, and the action of the non-jurors had done little to tarnish this. Visitation returns show that round about the year 1700 nonconformists of all kinds were very few. Roman Catholics, Non-Jurors and Quakers accounted for most of them. Roman Catholics were to be found principally amongst the land-owning families. Their strongholds were (and perhaps still are) in Lancashire, in the district between the rivers Wyre and Ribble, which is known as the *Fylde*, in Yorkshire, especially along the upper valley of the Esk, and on the borders of

---

[1] *Cambridge University*, by A. Gray, pp. 219–22.

Staffordshire and Derbyshire. Jews were to be found only in the large towns. London, Bristol, Norwich and York probably accounted for nearly all of them. Quakers were in a few colonies, the most important being in Buckinghamshire, Essex, Norfolk and the Furness district of Lancashire.

Economists tell us that the countryside, with which the Church has always been closely linked, was probably more prosperous during the early years of the eighteenth century than at any time before or since. We seem to have achieved the due balance between town and country, upon which a healthy and stable national economy depends. No one could guess how completely it was to be destroyed during the nineteenth century. Everything seemed to be in favour of the Church. During the next fifty years this commanding position was lost.

Mary II died on 28 December 1694 without issue. James II died on 6 September 1701, and William III on 8 March 1702. Supporters of the Stuart cause welcomed his death, but there could be little doubt that the next occupant of the throne must be the Princess Anne. The son of James II (afterwards to be known in England as the Old Pretender) was not quite fourteen years old. The time had not come for any attempt to place him on the throne. But after the death of William, Duke of Gloucester, at the age of 11, on 30 July 1700 it was fairly certain that Anne would leave no heir. Her reign was unlikely to be long. Her death would give the Pretender his opportunity.

It may be worth while to point out that in the eighteenth century the word *Pretender* had not acquired the opprobrious associations which attach to it now. It was used in its original (Latin) sense, which is *Claimant* and does not imply that the claim is dishonest. The sense in which it is generally used now must be ascribed to the fact that most claims, especially to a great inheritance, have turned out to be fraudulent.

Jacobite intrigue had never ceased entirely at any time since 1688. But after 1702 the climate became more favourable. A general picture of what went on can be found in Thackeray's *Esmond*. It must have been demoralizing in the extreme. Queen Anne herself was well disposed towards the Church and allowed the Houses of Convocation to meet, after an interval of several years. It must, however, be admitted that they did very little to win respect. They quarrelled incessantly and acrimoniously over minutiæ of procedure, so that there was more justification than might appear at first sight for the silencing of them by George I.[1] Queen Anne left the Church one valuable legacy, in what is known as *Queen Anne's Bounty*. Pope Nicholas IV (1288–92) had been compelled to levy certain additional taxes upon the clergy to meet the increasing and probably unforeseen expenses in which Innocent III had involved the Papacy.[2] After the Reformation these payments naturally passed to the Crown. In 1704 Anne surrendered them voluntarily for the benefit of the Church, which must have meant a considerable financial loss for her. A Corporation was formed to receive and administer the money, and it would be difficult to exaggerate the value of what it has done during nearly two hundred and fifty years.[3] On 1 April 1948 the "Bounty" ceased to have a separate existence and was merged with the Ecclesiastical Commission which had been created by Act of Parliament in 1836.

A notable landmark in our recognition of our growing responsibilities beyond the seas was that in 1710 Christopher Codrington left his estates in Barbados to the Society for the Propagation of the Gospel, to found a college there. The constitution shows that he anticipated by at least a century the medical missions of to-day, as it makes provision for

> A convenient number of Professors and Scholars to study and practice Physick and Chirurgery as well as Divinity—that they might have the better opportunity of doing good to men's souls while they are taking care of their bodies.[4]

For some reason the bequest did not take effect fully until 1743.

During the early years of the eighteenth century the system of party politics on the lines to which we are accustomed became established. *Whigs* and *Tories* were the descriptions used, and may

[1] See Chapter 14.   [2] See Chapter 6, p. 111.
[3] See *Queen Anne's Bounty*, by W. R. le Fanu, second edition by F. G. Hughes, 1933.   [4] See also Chapter 15, p. 322.

be considered to correspond roughly to the Liberals and Conservatives of a later day. The immense prestige and influence of the Church made the politicians on both sides anxious to secure it as their ally. In many parishes the parson was the only man who took in any kind of newspaper, except perhaps the squire. Therefore the country clergy could and did play a very large part in the formation of public opinion. In innumerable parishes all that the people could know of the course of public affairs was what the parson saw fit to tell them. Much, too, would depend upon how the story was told. Higher in the social scale there was a great demand for pamphlets, and many of the clergy were well qualified to write them. If there could be only one Jonathan Swift, there were other pens which were not negligible.

Thus the clergy as a body were almost compelled to assume a position in the political world which was unlikely to conduce to the best interest of their real work. In that world no one saw any reason against buying a political friend by bestowing preferment in the Church upon him. The clergy can hardly be blamed if they were not sufficiently far in advance of their time to adopt the view of these transactions which is more usually (if not invariably) held today.

During Anne's reign we began our great march along the road to imperial power. Marlborough's brilliant victories showed that the French armies were not invincible and that we could produce a general to rank with any, anywhere. On 23 July 1704 Sir George Rooke hoisted our flag over the rock of Gibraltar, which meant that our access to the Mediterranean was secure. Our star was everywhere in the ascendant, to a degree which would have seemed inconceivable not many years before. But everyone knew that the reign was, as it were, an interlude. Before Anne came to the throne it was fairly certain that she would have no heir, and whenever she died a formidable crisis would have to be faced. We should have to choose between the son of James II and the Elector[1] of Hanover, who was a great-grandson of James I through the

---

[1] The title borne by seven German princes, two of whom were ecclesiastics, because they elected (at any rate in theory) the Emperor, whose exalted position had become little more than titular.

female line. His title to the throne was as good as that of James I
had been, with the difference that in 1603 there was no one who
had a better. It was obvious that our destiny would be affected
very deeply by our decision. Perhaps the use of the words *Queen
Anne is dead* in a semi-proverbial sense reflects the general feeling
of the time that her death was of more moment than that of most
sovereigns. It really did mark the close of an era.

14

The Skies Clear—1

From the death of Queen Anne to the Peace of Paris—1714–63

IT is still customary in some circles to deprave (in the Elizabethan sense) the Church of the eighteenth century in every way possible. This tradition is one of the less valuable legacies of the Oxford Movement. Naturally, almost inevitably, the Tractarians intensely disliked the eighteenth century and all its ways and works—partly because it had immediately preceded their own day, and each generation is apt to find satisfaction in overturning the gods of its fathers, which its children or grandchildren will probably pick up and piece together again, and partly because it offered no foothold for their sentimental medievalism. The inspiration of a fine classical church and of the "Gothic" revival which swept the land from 1840 (or thereabouts) onwards have really nothing in common.

It cannot be denied that the eighteenth century as a whole was coarse in its speech and dirty in its habits. In the highest and lowest classes drunkenness was rife and sexual morality hardly existed. With regard to the latter, however, a considerable improvement was effected by the numerous Charity Schools, as they were called, which sprang up in the reign of Queen Anne.[1] The Society for the Promotion of Christian Knowledge was very active in promoting these, and also in supplying Bibles and Prayer Books to the army and navy. Standards of conduct seem to have been higher amongst the middle classes, who are always the real backbone of the nation.

Yet, if the aristocracy was as a whole licentious, many of its members were magnificent patrons of art and literature. They

[1] See *English Social History*, by G. M. Trevelyan, pp. 325–9.

travelled on the Continent, and probably saw more of foreign society and learned more foreign languages than most English travellers do today. Their country houses contained well-stocked libraries which were not simply for ornament or ostentation. They did not forget all the Greek and Latin which they had acquired in their youth. They officered and led the armies and (perhaps to a lesser extent) commanded the ships with which we finally fought Napoleon to a standstill.

In every walk of life corruption was rampant. With the exception of the Bench of Judges (which had not, I believe, included a corrupt member since Bacon), it was pretty nearly true to say that, "Every man had his price." Indeed, the whole business of bribery was so blatant and so generally recognized that it almost ceased to be corrupt. But, as is bound to happen when a system of bribery prevails, the standard of duty was, speaking generally, low. The law was harsh, and was harshly if not very efficiently administered. The number of capital offences was very large. The condition of the prisons was such that a considerable proportion of the prisoners often died of what was known as gaol fever before they could be brought to trial. Yet, despite this unpromising background, the national achievement during this period makes the century one of the most notable in all our history.

Marlborough had shown the world that a new power had arisen whose forces were a match even for those of France. Fifty years later, so diligently did we build on the foundations well and truly laid by him, the Peace of Paris in 1763 recognized us as a great imperial power. Fifty-two years after that saw us, despite the loss of the American colonies, in a position of world-wide supremacy such as no other nation has ever enjoyed. There was no enemy anywhere whom we had need to fear, and the natural resources of the globe were available for our needs.

The darkest stain on the period as a whole is the slave trade. By a clause known as the *Assiento* in the Treaty of Utrecht we secured from Spain the privilege, denied to any other foreign power, of a small legitimate trade with her American colonies, and of sending 4,800 negro slaves thither annually. This was regarded in England as a diplomatic triumph. The restricted monopoly was bad enough, and of course it gave rise to a larger illicit traffic which the Government could do little if anything to control. This abominable if lucrative business was not brought to an end until 1807, when William Wilberforce and his friends at last succeeded in rousing the conscience of England. This must be regarded as the greatest achievement of the Evangelical movement, of which more will be said on a later page.

But although the shipping of fresh slaves to America was stopped, slavery continued for another generation in the West Indies under our flag, and in the southern part of the United States for a generation after that. A civil war was needed to bring it to an end.

Slavery is always abominable, if only because no one can ever be good enough to own slaves. In the world into which Christianity was born every relation in life was more or less poisoned by it.[1] But there it was the recognized fortune of war. The slave might be as well born and educated as his master and he sometimes rose to a responsible position in the household. He might hope to receive his liberty at some time, perhaps by his master's will. These "freedmen" (liberti or libertini), as such people and their descendants were called, often played an important part in public life and became extremely rich. As time went on Christian public opinion did a good deal to mitigate the slaves' lot. But, as Bishop Henson[2] has pointed out, negro slavery was worse. It was based on a distinction of race, which was necessarily permanent, and could therefore be regarded as part of the order of nature. Divine sanction was claimed for it on the strength of the curse laid upon Ham by Noah.[3] For the negro slave in the American colonies, whether he had been kidnapped and had survived the horrors of the voyage from Africa across the Atlantic (known as the Middle Passage), or whether he had been born to his lot in life, the future held nothing. He had not had, and could not get, the education which might have fitted him for some position of responsibility. He could not hope to receive his freedom. He was simply the most

[1] See Chapter 1.
[2] *Christian Morality*, pp. 240–2 (Gifford lectures).
[3] Gen. 9. 24–5.

useful of domestic animals, and could never be anything more. If he were sometimes treated with kindness it was little more than the consideration which we should bestow upon a valuable horse.

It is difficult for us now to understand how the conscience of England tolerated such a system for a year, let alone for a century and more. We can only accept the shameful fact, and wonder how much it did to weaken the influence of Christianity, not only in our own country, and to debase all moral standards. The crowning irony is that when attempts were made to give some knowledge of Christianity to the slaves it was found to be necessary to explain carefully that Baptism was not a step towards emancipation. The negroes seem to have recognized more quickly than we did that slavery and the Christian profession are incompatible. How did the Church fare in this strange mixture of squalor and achievement, of intellectual perception and moral obtuseness?

For more than thirty years after the death of Anne, Jacobite intrigue was incessant and the possibility of a rising never very far away. Everyone knows that attempts were made in 1715 and 1745. We need not linger over the details now. It is probably true to say that the former came nearer to enlisting the support from England necessary for success, if the latter was more spectacular. The clergy as a whole, or at least the High Church party, which was very strong, were suspected of Jacobite sympathies. There was certainly some warrant for this, as is shown by the career of Francis Atterbury, Bishop of Rochester and Dean of Westminster 1713–23. He was convicted of treasonable correspondence with the exiled Stuarts, and was committed to the Tower in 1720. He was deprived of his offices in 1723 and banished from the kingdom. For the next ten years, until his death, he did all in his power to promote the Stuart cause.

He was obviously of the nature of a stormy petrel. How many of the clergy shared his view, whether privately or openly, it is impossible to say. To us now their attitude must appear to have been one of almost incredible political fatuity. By this time everybody knew what a promise given by a Stuart was likely to be worth. What would have been the fate of the Church of England, to say nothing of constitutional government, if James III (the "Old Pretender") had reigned from 1714 to 1766? If any remnant of either had survived, how would they have been treated by the Young Pretender, had he reigned as Charles III from 1766 to 1788? And what of the last scene of all, if the throne had been filled from 1788 to 1807 by Henry IX, Cardinal-Bishop of Tusculum (Frascati) since 1761, and of Ostia after 1803? It is interesting to speculate as to whether he would have tried to reign in person, or would have appointed a regent of some kind. Is it conceivable that the Papacy would have given him a dispensation to marry? Probably, however, some years before his death England would have fallen to Napoleon like a ripe pear, so that neither as a Church nor a nation should we have had any future worth considering.

Of course, this development could not have been anticipated in 1720. On the whole, however, it seems probable that the Jacobite clergy did not think politically at all. They had got hold of a phrase, *passive obedience*, which sounded well, and relieved them of moral and intellectual responsibility. That was enough for them. But men who could contemplate sacrificing the religious and civil liberties which the seven bishops had risked everything to maintain[1] to the interest of a dynasty which had proved itself incompetent to rule England were obviously not well fitted to lead the nation as a whole, and could hardly expect to retain its respect.

If it is not unfair to call the first two Georges licentious boors, they were not deficient in shrewdness and common sense. They knew perfectly well that the only reason for their presence in England was that they were not Roman Catholics. Naturally and rightly they regarded the Church of England as the principal buttress of their throne, and being German Lutherans considered that the *raison d'être* of a Church of any kind was to furnish the civil power with a useful tool with which to carry on the business of government. Jacobite sympathies on the part of the clergy, whose political influence was much greater than it is today (especially in the country parishes), were therefore very dangerous. It is therefore, upon the whole, not surprising that in

[1] See Chapter 13, pp. 275–76.

1717 George I silenced the Houses of Convocation. They were allowed to meet, that they might remain in being, but not to discuss anything. It was a high-handed act, if he never realized how unconstitutional it was, and it must be admitted that the record of the Lower House of Canterbury during the previous reign had not been such as to command respect. It had devoted most of its energy to acrimonious squabbles over points of precedence and its relations with the Upper House.[1] The embargo was not lifted for a hundred and forty years: for a century, roughly, after there had ceased to be any justification for it. Its results were serious, as it prevented the clergy from taking council together, during a period of very far-reaching social and political change.

The Jacobite clergy could not be coerced or persecuted. But some of them might be seduced by judicious offers of preferment. No one would have seen any objection to this at the time. Whig clergy, whose loyalty to the throne was undoubted, could be encouraged and rewarded. This was the deliberate policy of Sir Robert Walpole, who, except for a brief interval (1717–21) was First Lord of the Treasury from 1715 to 1742, and he was wholeheartedly supported by Edmund Gibson, who was Bishop of London 1723–48.

Gibson, who had been Bishop of Lincoln from 1716 to 1723, is entitled at least to rank with any bishop who has held the see of London. Besides considerable other activities he produced a monumental *Codex Juris Ecclesiastici Anglicani*, the most comprehensive attempt which has been made since the Reformation to provide the Church with a comprehensive code of law. For some years he was Primate in everything but name, as John Potter, who was Archbishop 1737–47, became almost incapable of acting. If Walpole was a genial cynic who took little real interest in the Church, Gibson was not. He never recommended a man for a bishopric or deanery merely because he was a Whig (this became apparent more than once), but he did take pains to ensure that anyone whom he thought fit for the office on other

---

[1] Less is heard of York Convocation. Probably it was less quarrelsome as being smaller and farther away. It has retained both of these advantages.

grounds should be a Whig. For many years he was almost om-
nipotent in such matters. More will be said of him in connexion
with the American colonies.[1] Such political appointments are,
of course, open to criticism, though as long as the clergy are, or
may be, important figures in the political world it is obvious that
they will be made from time to time. In the hands of Walpole
and Gibson they meant that the bishops were out of sympathy
with a considerable proportion of the clergy, and that they spent
more time in London and in attendance at the House of Lords
than we should think desirable now. (Probably, however, they
spent more time in their dioceses than many of their medieval
predecessors had done.) All this was not good for the parochial
life of the Church, which with some notable exceptions tended
to become lethargic. But before we condemn it out of hand, we
must consider it from the point of view of the two men primarily
responsible. Walpole and Gibson believed that the preservation
of the religious and civil liberty which we had won, inch by inch
as it were, through the centuries was at that time bound up with
the maintenance of the Hanoverian sovereigns upon the throne,
also that the Church could do more than anything else to keep
them there. Can we say that they were mistaken? And if religious
and civil liberty had been destroyed in England by Stuart despotism, backed by French gold if not by French bayonets as well,
where would they have survived? If they had fallen, what could
the future of Christianity or civilization have been? If we take the
long view, the twenty-five years of Gibson's London episcopate
may be considered to have saved the Church of England, and all
that as the Anglican Communion it has come to mean for the
world today.[2] If some of the eighteenth-century prelates deserve
to be called worldly, it would be interesting to know how they
compare with their contemporaries at the Courts of Louis XIV
and XV. If political appointments to the Bench continued after
the justification for them had passed away there is nothing to
surprise us in that. It was, in fact, almost inevitable, in view of
the tradition which had been established.

[1] For a full acount of him see *Edmund Gibson*, by Professor N. Sykes (Oxford
University Press, 1926).   [2] See Chapter 15, pp. 314 ff.

After the Jacobite danger was over, there was something to be said for the view of George III, that the bishops ought to spend sufficient time at Court for him to get to know them, that when a translation had to be made, especially to one of the five[1] great sees, he might be in a position to have some opinion of his own about anyone whom the Prime Minister might recommend.

During the reigns of the first two Georges the Church was by no means dead, nor entirely submerged in politics, as two very important episodes will show. First, what is known as the Deistic Controversy, and secondly, the Evangelical Movement. If the former of these has long been a closed chapter, the effects of the latter are felt in many ways today.

The word *Deism* is derived from the Latin *Deus*, which means *God*. It was not irreligious, which made it all the more formidable. Deists did not dispute the existence of God, and recognized him as the Creator of the visible universe, which rendered his power and beneficence self-evident. This is not far from the position taken up by "Solomon" in Wisdom 13. 9 and endorsed by St Paul in Romans 1. 18–21. They also accepted as equally self-evident the Moral Law, despite the failure of the pagan world in this respect. (It is interesting to speculate how long this belief would have survived, and how soon they would have discovered that moral principles, however lofty, cannot maintain themselves unless provision is made for a continuous supply of moral power.) All this they called Natural Religion and regarded as part of the immemorial inheritance of all mankind. This system left no room for any particular revelation at any special time or place, and such words as "supernatural" or "mysterious" were abhorrent to them. Their ideas had been developed gradually during the seventeenth century. They are traceable in the writings of Lord Herbert of Cherbury (1581–1648), an elder brother of George Herbert, which form to a large extent the background of the religious and philosophical thought of Bacon (1561–1626). The writings of John Locke (1632–1704) also contributed to it, especially his famous *Essay Concerning Human Understanding*, which was published in 1690. Perhaps the strongest impetus of all

[1] Canterbury, York, London, Durham, Winchester.

was given by Sir Isaac Newton, whose *Principia*[1] was published in
1686. By his enunciation of the Law of Gravity he presented a
picture of the universe as an orderly calculable system. It did
not admit of variation within itself, and there could be nothing
in it which was not ultimately intelligible to human reason. On
these premises such phenomena as the Hebrew Prophets, and
still more the Incarnation, are impossible.

This was not a criticism of any particular feature in the
Christian system, such as the books directed specifically against
miracles which have been published from time to time. It
challenged the very foundation of Christianity, by denying the
possibility of the position taken up in Hebrews 1. The attack was
really formidable and for a moment looked as if it had succeeded.
But it was countered by a very remarkable series of apologetic
works which appeared between the years 1714 and 1738.

It would take too long to give a complete list of them here.
The most famous is Butler's *Analogy*,[2] which was published in
1736. The author was Bishop of Bristol 1738–50, during which
time he had a famous interview with John Wesley, and of Durham
1750–2. The story that he refused the Primacy in 1747 because
he did not think himself the man to uphold a falling Church is
legendary. The *Analogy* is one of the most important religious
classics in our language, and few books so small in bulk can have
produced any comparable effect. Except for the belief that the
world had not been in existence for more than about six thousand
years and that the historical character of the Old Testament is on
a level with that of the New, the book stands in very little need of
revision today. Both these assumptions were accepted universally
without question at the time, and neither affects the general
argument in any way.

The following passage from what he calls the *Advertisement* is
worth quoting in full:

It is come, I know not how, to be taken for granted by many
persons, that Christianity is not so much as a subject of

[1] *Philosophiæ Naturalis Principia Mathematica.*
[2] *The Analogy of Religion Natural and Revealed to the Constitution and Course of
Nature.*

Inquiry; but that it is now at length discovered to be fictitious. And accordingly they treat it as if, in the present age their were an agreed point among all People of Discernment, and nothing remained but to set it up as a principal subject of Mirth and Ridicule, as it were by way of Reprisal for its having so long interrupted the pleasures of the World.

(It is not uncommon today to find that what profess to be purely intellectual objections to Christianity are really prompted by the dislike of the moral restrictions which it places on conduct.)

The Bishops of Durham are a distinguished line and Lightfoot, who held the see from 1879 to 1889, must rank with any of them. He always regarded Butler as the greatest of his predecessors.

The next most remarkable figure in the controversy is George Berkeley, who was at one time Dean of Derry, and from 1734 to his death in 1753 Bishop of Cloyne. (More will be said of him lower down in connexion with the American colonies.) He is perhaps the only bishop we have ever had who is unquestionably in the front rank of European philosophers.[1] His best known work is *Alciphron, or The Minute Philosopher*, which was published in 1732. His sermons are contributions to philosophic thought the value of which the lapse of two centuries has done nothing to impair.

Deists were routed on their own ground with their own weapons by thinkers of greater intellectual calibre. The victory was so complete that many people today do not know that the battle had to be fought; still less how doubtful the issue appeared at one time to be. Today the Church is more highly organized and more active. In some respects its outlook is wider and, as many people would say, more Catholic. But it is open to question whether between the years 1914 and 1938 we could have put into the field an army of thinkers comparable with those of two centuries before, had the need arisen. The nearest approach to Deism to be found today is probably in the Unitarian body.

The first stirrings of the Evangelical Movement may be discerned at Oxford as early as 1729. In that year a number of young

---

[1] William Temple, Archbishop of Canterbury 1942–4, has a claim to be considered in this connexion.

men, which included Charles Wesley, then a junior Student of Christ Church, and his elder brother John, who was a Fellow of Lincoln College, decided to form themselves into a little society for the purpose of mutual edification. They aimed at a disciplined life of prayer and study and set themselves to observe carefully the system of the Church with its ordered round of feasts and festivals. It was for this reason that they were nicknamed Methodists. So far as the Church at large is concerned the movement may be considered to have begun in the year 1739, just after the struggle with Deism was over (or had at least passed through its critical phase), when John Wesley began open-air preaching. His name and that of his brother Charles are the best known, but there are many other Evangelical leaders who ought not to be forgotten: Samuel Walker (1714–61), who as Rector of Truro inaugurated a religious revival in Cornwall; Thomas Adam (1701–84), who for fifty-eight years was incumbent of Wintringham in Lincolnshire; and William Grimshaw (1708–63), who in 1742 became perpetual curate of Haworth (a place destined to be made famous by the Brontë family) in the West Riding. He was an eccentric personage, and his last words when on his death-bed are said to have been, "Here goes an unprofitable servant." To them may be added John Berridge (1716–93), who had been at one time a Fellow of Clare Hall in Cambridge. In 1755 he became incumbent of Everton in Bedfordshire, on the presentation of his college, where he remained until the day of his death.[1]

At their best the Evangelical preachers brought into religion a warmth which had been rather lacking. They showed that the Church is more than an august institution to be respected. It has a direct personal message for the individual soul, especially for the soul conscious of its own sinfulness. The difference in thought and feeling becomes obvious if we compare a well-known hymn by Joseph Addison, who died in 1719, with an even better known one by Charles Wesley, who was born in 1707 and lived until 1788. The first and last verse of each will be sufficient to quote here.

[1] For the information given above I am indebted to vol. vii of the *History of the English Church*, by Stephens and Hunt; especially Chapter X.

The spacious firmament on high
With all the blue ethereal sky,
And spangled heavens, a shining frame,
Their great Original proclaim.
The unwearied sun from day to day
Does his Creator's power display,
And publishes to every land
The works of an almighty hand.

What though in solemn silence all
Move round the dark terrestrial ball;
What though no real voice nor sound
Amid their radiant orbs be found;
In reason's ear they all rejoice,
And utter forth a glorious voice;
For ever singing as they shine
"The hand that made us is Divine."

English Hymnal No. 297.

(If Addison's hymn owes something to Psalm 19, the psalmist's religion is the more personal of the two. It is, however, fair to add that his *The Lord my pasture shall prepare*, which is based on Psalm 23, strikes a more personal note.)

Jesu, Lover of my soul;
Let me to thy bosom fly,
While the nearer waters roll,
While the tempest still is high:
Hide me, O my Saviour, hide,
Till the storm of life is past;
Safe into the haven guide,
O receive my soul at last.

Plenteous grace with thee is found,
Grace to cover all my sin;
Let the healing streams abound;
Make and keep me pure within.
Thou of life the fountain art;
Freely let me take of thee;
Spring thou up within my heart,
Rise to all eternity.

English Hymnal No. 414.

The movement laid hold of the nation, as nothing of the kind had done since the coming of the friars some five centuries before. It would be difficult to exaggerate the effect which it produced, especially as the century went on, and the demoralizing effect of prolonged war was increasingly felt. It may not be too much to say that it saved us from some sanguinary outbreak comparable with the French Revolution. It was primarily responsible for the founding of the Church Missionary Society in 1797 and for the abolition of the slave trade in 1807.[1] Its effects continue to this day, and for my own part I should be sorry to see them die out. But the following brief criticisms may be passed upon it without injustice.

1. It laid too much emphasis on emotion. Emotion must have a place in religion as in every department of human life. But the balance between the emotional and intellectual aspects must always be preserved carefully. If emotion is allowed to become dominant moral standards will always decline. The personal conviction of the individual that he is saved (which may carry with it a belief that he can name the exact moment at which his salvation became assured and that his future conduct is irrevelant) is not of first-rate importance. Unfortunately in many people, especially in those of little education, the emotional faculties are stronger than the rational. It is easier to make people feel than to make them think. But the essence of emotion is that it cannot be permanent, any more than a swimmer can remain poised on the crest of a wave.

The open-air proceedings of the Methodists were often marked by outbreaks of hysteria in the congregations. John Wesley came to regard these as the outward and visible signs of the new birth unto righteousness, which was the burden of his message, until he found it difficult to believe that without convulsions, foaming at the mouth and so forth there was no presence of the Holy Spirit.[2] This was in his earlier days. Later he seems to have felt

[1] See above, p. 291.

[2] Such outbursts seems to be really matters for the pathologist, and of very little religious significance. The same should probably be said of what is known as "speaking with tongues" (glossolalia) and the queer stories of levitation and incandescence which are told of some saintly personages in the Roman Church.

more doubt about them. Similar phenomena occurred at some of Berridge's meetings.

2. It was unduly rigid in relation to amusements of all kinds; especially the theatre. Undoubtedly the theatre of the Restoration was licentious, as was the society for which it existed. This was largely a reaction from the unnatural severity of Puritan days and ought not to be regarded as something permanent. Ultimately the moral standards of the stage will be shaped by those of its habitual patrons.

3. It entertained an unreasonable prejudice against the part of the Bible usually called in England *Apocrypha* (*Deutero-canonical* is a more accurate term).[1] This had (and has) apparently no better foundation than that it cannot be reconciled with certain preconceived and ill-founded ideas as to the nature and meaning of Inspiration. The translators of the Authorized Version had certainly stretched their authority to the limit when they printed all these books together, thereby making it easy for subsequent editions to omit them entirely. It has certainly been a serious loss to English-speaking Christianity all the world over that the practice of publishing Bibles without them has made them almost unknown.

It is irrational to pretend that for the last three centuries or so before our era the Jewish Church and nation have no history. Both St Paul and the author of Hebrews were well acquainted with Wisdom.

4. During the second half of the nineteenth century the Evangelical party in the Church lost a great deal of ground by adopting an obscurantist attitude, which has perhaps not been completely abandoned even yet, in relation to biblical scholarship, especially as far as it affects the Old Testament.[2] This may be to some extent a legacy from the unimaginative literalism of their ancestors of the century before. Whatever its source, it has proved extremely mischievous.

---

[1] i.e. *Of secondary rank.* See the latter part of Article VI, *Of the sufficiency of the Holy Scriptures for Salvation.*

[2] It is only fair to say that some of the protagonists of the Oxford Movement were equally unreasonable, e.g. Pusey in relation to the Book of Daniel.

John Wesley (1703–91), who is one of the most conspicuous figures of the time, was a very difficult person with whom to deal. He had extraordinary power as a preacher, and this was combined with a physical energy and endurance hardly less remarkable. His courage was of a high order. It is easy to say now that the Church ought to have been able to retain him and his followers. But he never hesitated to set its rules aside when he found it convenient to do so. The words *I look upon all the world as my parish*, which are to be found in his *Journal*,[1] and may now be read under his bust in Westminster Abbey, may be taken as a lofty expression of missionary zeal. But they reveal complete ignorance of, or indifference to, the system of the Church to which he belonged. The Church which had commissioned him to preach the Gospel, and had put the word *parish* into his mouth, is on a territorial basis. It does not allow its ministers to invade each other's spheres of authority at will. Wesley's failure to appreciate this may be due in part to the fact that he had never had a parish.

As early as 1741 he began commissioning lay preachers, although he must have known that in the Church of England the commissioning of preachers, whether lay or in Holy Orders, rests with the bishop. This was obviously a long step in the direction of schism, whether he realized it or not. About the year 1750 he had his memorable interview with Joseph Butler, who was then at Bristol. The bishop was deeply shocked by his claim (which appears also to have been made by Whitefield on his own behalf) to special private inspiration.

"Sir, the pretending to extraordinary revelation and gifts of the Holy Ghost is a horrid thing, a very horrid thing."[2]

The truth is, there was a very gullible and childishly credulous side to Wesley's character. This appears in his *Journal*. As time went on he became more and more convinced, as gifted enthusiasts are apt to be, that his own methods were the only ones. Anyone who disputed them, or even thought any others worth trying, was the enemy of God. There could be only one end to this. By

[1] 11 June 1739.   [2] Quoted by Stephens and Hunt, vol. vii, p. 93.

1760 his lay preachers, who still professed to be acting in the Church's name and on her behalf, began to take out licences for their chapels, and to administer the Sacraments in them. Lay baptism has always been recognized in an emergency when there is no alternative. But a lay celebration of the Eucharist could only be justified in very special circumstances, such as could hardly arise in eighteenth-century England.[1] Finally, in 1784 Wesley ordained two men to act as bishops in America. He had visited the North American colonies and realized the need. Probably he knew nothing whatever of the difficulties, of which more will be said lower down. Theoretically a good deal may be said in favour of presbyteral ordination, and in Article XXIII, *Of Ministering in the Congregation*, we have been careful not to repudiate it unreservedly, though it is not and never has been our own practice. Wesley knew perfectly well that the Church in whose name he professed to be acting did not authorize him to ordain anybody to any office. Therefore he put himself completely in the wrong and his action must be regarded as invalid. Only a few weeks later Samuel Seabury had been duly consecrated as Bishop of Connecticut at Aberdeen and was on his way across the Atlantic. To the end of his life Wesley considered himself to be in full communion with the Church of England. But it was obvious that as soon as he was in his grave his followers would constitute themselves as a separate body. Fortunately they were only a part of the Evangelical movement.

A noteworthy figure during the first half of the century, if geographically he was on the extreme fringe of the Church, is Thomas Wilson, who held the see of Sodor and Man from 1698 to 1755. He was as firm a believer in ecclesiastical discipline as Laud had been, and the special circumstances of his see enabled him to enforce it to an extent impossible in England. He enjoyed, in fact, all the advantages of establishment without its drawbacks. Some of his penances, especially for sexual offences, may seem to us unduly severe, but they must be judged from the standpoint of the day, which is not ours. In spite of them he seems to have

---

[1] General Gordon is said to have held one when he was besieged in Khartoum in 1885 and had no hope of relief.

been popular in his diocese, for upon one occasion when he came into violent collision with the civil power public opinion was on his side. He refused translation to a wealthier see in England more than once. When pressed by Queen Caroline, who took a lively interest in religious questions and ecclesiastical affairs, he replied, "I will not leave my wife in my old age because she is poor." To us it must seem remarkable that a man so essentially good did not realize that in the long run coercion will never promote the increase of true religion.

The battle of Culloden, which was fought on 16 April 1746, is a dividing line in the affairs of Church and nation alike. It meant the security of the House of Hanover, and the end of sixty years of Jacobite intrigue. It is, however, said that some years afterwards Prince Charles Edward visited England in disguise with an idea of blowing in the gate of the Tower of London and carrying the fortress by a *coup de main*. Apparently he could not secure sufficient support to make the attempt. It is said that during this visit he was received temporarily into the Church of England, probably in St Martin's-in-the-Fields.

Many harsh things have been said about our dealings with the Highlanders, and especially about the Duke of Cumberland, who commanded our forces. The letters of Horace Walpole[1] throw a good deal of light on public opinion at the time. Some extracts from them are worth reproducing here.

1. *To Sir Horace Mann*,[2] 9 *December* 1745:

They (the rebels) got nine thousand pounds at Derby and had the books brought to them and obliged everybody to give what they had subscribed against them. Then they retreated a few miles but returned again to Derby, got ten thousand pounds more, plundered the town and burnt a house of the Countess of Exeter. We are threatened with great preparations for a French invasion, but the Court is exceedingly guarded, and for the people the spirit against the rebels increases every day. Though they have marched thus into the heart of the kingdom there has not been the least symptom of a rising not even in the great towns of which they possessed themselves. They have

---

[1] Vol. ii (Richard Bentley, 1846).   [2] British Minister at Florence.

got no recruits since their first entry into England excepting one gentleman in Lancashire, one hundred and fifty common men and two parsons at Manchester and a physician from York. But here in London the aversion to them is amazing.

2. *To Sir Horace Mann, 3 January* 1746:

His Royal Highness (the Duke of Cumberland) is expected in town every day, but I still think it probable that he will go to Scotland. The country is very clamorous for it. If the King does send him, it should not be with that sword of mercy with which the present family have governed those people. All the world agrees in the fitness of severity to highway men, for the sake of the innocent who suffer; then can rigour be ill-placed against banditti who have so terrified, pillaged, and injured the poor people in Cumberland, Lancashire, Derbyshire and the counties through which this rebellion has stalked?

3. *To Sir Horace Mann, 21 March* 1746:

The Duke complains extremely of the *loyal* Scotch; says he can get no intelligence and reckons himself more in an enemy's country than when he was warring with the French in Flanders. They profess the big professions wherever he comes but before he is out of sight of any town, beat up the volunteers for rebels. We see no prospect of his return, for he must stay in Scotland while the rebellion lasts, and the existence of that seems too intimately connected with the being of Scotland to expect it should soon be annihilated.

4. *To Sir Horace Mann, 15 April* 1746:

The other day an odd accidental discovery was made; some of the Duke's baggage which he did not want was sent back from Scotland with a bill of the contents. Soon after another large parcel but not specified in the bill, was brought to the Captain directed like the rest. When they came to the Custom House[1] here it was observed and they sent to Mr Poyntz[2] to know what they should do: he had them opened, suspecting some trick, but when they did they found a large crucifix, copes, rich beads and books and such like trumpery, consigned from

---

[1] The baggage had been sent by sea.   [2] The Duke's Treasurer.

the titular primate of Scotland, who is with the rebels; they imagine with the privity of some of the vessels to be conveyed to somebody here in town.

5. *To Sir Horace Mann, 25 April 1746* (on receipt of the news of Culloden):

It is a brave young Duke.[1] The town is all blazing round me as I write, with fireworks and illuminations.

6. *To George Montague, 24 June 1746:*

All the inns about town are crowded with rebel prisoners, and people are making parties of pleasure, which you know is the English genius, to hear their trials. The Scotch, which you know is the Scotch genius, are loud in censoring the Duke for his severities in the Highlands.

7. *To George Montague, 2 August 1746:*

The Duke said publicly at his levee that (Lord Kilmarnock) proposed murdering the English prisoners.

Lord Kilmarnock, who was executed on Tower Hill during the month of August 1746, had been Lieutenant-General of the Jacobite army. It was believed that an order dated 15 April, that no prisoners were to be taken, was found amongst his papers. The fact seems, however, to be doubtful, and if the order was made there seems to be no evidence that it was published to the army. It seems also to be doubtful whether on their southward march the Jacobites drove the women and children of the countryside before them as they approached Carlisle, so that it was impossible for the defenders to fire upon the head of their columns. They were, however, believed to have done so.[2]

8. *To Sir Horace Mann, 12 August 1746:*

Popularity has changed sides since the year '15, for now the city and the generality are very angry that so many rebels have been pardoned.

[1] He was twenty-five years of age.
[2] Horace Walpole to Sir Horace Mann, 22 November 1745.

It is possible to throw some halo of romance round the figure of "bonnie Prince Charlie". But nothing can disguise the squalor of the whole enterprise, which as it went on degenerated into nothing but a sordid scramble for loot. It was also impossible to conceal (except perhaps from the prince himself, who seems to have inherited the inability to see the real facts of any situation, which can be discerned in other members of his family) that no one in England would lift a finger to help a Stuart to the throne. And this time the patience of England was exhausted. In 1715 we had done as little as we could. But all the rebels of 1745 had lived under Hanoverian government for thirty years and their leaders at any rate may be presumed to have taken an oath of allegiance to George II. The prince himself had escaped and was still young enough[1] to make another bid for the Crown if he saw any hope of support. We were determined that there should be no third time, and that meant that we must put it out of the power of the Highlanders ever to be troublesome again. The situation justified severe measures. Opinion will differ as to whether those which we employed were unduly severe. English public opinion at the time thought not. They proved successful.

The Scottish nuisance was hardly abated before we found ourselves once more at war with France. This struggle, which began in the year 1755, was destined to last, with a few uneasy intervals, for sixty years. We lost the American colonies in the course of it, but emerged triumphant and more powerful than ever before. We are more familiar than the second half of the nineteenth century could be with the financial stringency and general demoralization which are the accompaniments of war. Both are formidable hindrances to the work of the Church. Besides, from about the year 1800 the effects of the rapid increase in population (due perhaps chiefly to the diminution of the death rate) and the migration into the towns began to be felt. What has come to be known as the Industrial Revolution, which was to change England from a thinly populated agricultural country to a densely peopled manufacturing one, had begun. There is therefore not very much

---

[1] He lived until 1788, but had ceased to be a potential danger for some years before his death.

to be said about the Church as a whole during this period.[1] If some clergy held more than one benefice (partly, perhaps, for financial reasons, as at the present day), and if some were negligent or worse, there were others. One of them, James Woodforde by name, has become well known by means of the diaries which he kept. Some volumes have been made public during recent years. He was born on 16 June 1740 at Ansford in Somerset, of which his father was rector, holding the vicarage of Castle Cary at the same time. He was educated at Winchester and New College, Oxford, of which he became a Fellow. He was ordained in 1763 and for the next ten years held various curacies in Somerset. He then returned to the university for a year. In 1774 he was presented by his college to the living of Weston Longueville in Norfolk, where he remained until his death on 1 January 1803. He was not an enthusiast, but discharged punctually and decorously all the duties which were expected of him by public opinion at the time. Only an exceptional man is ever likely to do much more. He was respected by his parishioners, with whom he seems to have been on intimate terms, and was undoubtedly a quiet power for good. He may be taken as a good example of the better type of eighteenth-century country parson. We happen to know of him. There may well have been many others of whom we do not know. Such men kept the Christian tradition alive in what was in some respects a cloudy and dark day.

The loss of the American colonies affected the Church in two ways. First, it caused an abrupt fall in the value of money, by making a sudden large addition to our national debt. The circumstances which led up to the quarrel are so often misrepresented that it may be worth while to say something about them briefly here.

From 1755 to 1763 we had to undertake expensive operations to defend the colonists against the French. The position of the thirteen colonies was strategically weak. They were not much more than a narrow strip along the eastern seaboard. The French were established to the west of them along the line of the Mississippi and to the north. Conquest would probably have

---

[1] The foundation of the Church Missionary Society will be dealt with in the next chapter.

meant something not far short of extermination, as the French, who had not given up all hope of securing the whole of North America, never hesitated to enrol Red Indians in their forces. After the war was over we found it necessary to maintain an army of ten thousand men for the protection of the colonists. We thought that they ought to make some contribution to the cost of their own safety. George Washington and his fellow tobacco planters thought not. *No taxation without representation* was a useful cry, but it will not stand close examination. It was impossible for the colonists to be represented directly in the British Parliament, three thousand miles away, and there was no authority in America which could levy a general tax for such a purpose. Anti-British sentiment was deliberately fomented during the next ten years by a number of demagogues (possibly in receipt of French pay), of whom a man named Samuel Adams of Boston seems to have been the worst. The methods by which we tried to raise money were not unreasonable, but provoked violent resentment. The first was a stamp duty on legal documents executed in the colonies. This appears eminently equitable and was cheap and easy to collect. But it aroused so much opposition that it was repealed after a year. Then we tried a tax on tea, an imported luxury. This was collected for a time until on 18 December 1773 a number of ships laden with tea appeared in Boston harbour. They were boarded by men disguised, it is said, as Mohawk Indians and their valuable cargoes thrown into the water. This was a piece of piracy pure and simple, and the perpetrators would have had no grievance had they been treated as pirates usually are. Our retaliatory measures, which consisted in closing the port for a time, may have been injudicious, but cannot be considered excessive. From that time onwards war was almost inevitable. It is unnecessary to speak in detail of the course of the struggle. The outcome is a matter of common knowledge. When it was over there was an exodus, to the number, it is said, of some forty thousand, which included many families of the best stock, to the maritime provinces of Canada, where their descendants are to this day. The *United Empire Loyalists*, as they were called, preferred to lose all they had, and to start life over again, to remaining in the republic of which George Washington was the head. Despite our financial straits the British Government made an honest attempt to compensate them generously for their sacrifices.

The loss of the American colonies affected the Church in another way as well, perhaps more profoundly if less directly. It ended the difficulty, of which more will be said in the next chapter, in the way of providing them with bishops. It has also meant that for more than a century and a half there has been an important, if not very numerous, Church in full communion with us and speaking English, which is not under our flag. This is to the advantage of the Christian cause throughout the world, and emphasizes the fact that the Anglican Communion as we are now accustomed to describe it is more than the Church of the British Empire.

A feature in the Church life of the period which ought not to be ignored is the number of musicians which appeared. Handel was a German, but lived in England from 1712 onwards, and for a large part of the time was organist of the parish church of Edgware. Less famous names which can be found in our own anthem books are Samuel Arnold (1740–1802), Thomas Attwood (1767–1838), William Boyce (1710–79), William Croft (1677–1727), William Crotch (1775–1847), Maurice Greene (1695–1755), Philip Hayes (1738–97), James Kent (1700–76 and James Nares (1715–83). Hymns also made their appearance, if many people, of whom Dr Johnson was one, regarded them with suspicion, if not downright dislike, as Methodist innovations, as indeed to some extent they were. But apart from them there had been nothing for the congregation to sing except metrical versions of the Psalms. A Church which can produce good music and hymnody[1] has not forgotten what worship means, whatever criticisms may be directed against it.

One development of the eighteenth century which ought not to be ignored is the Sunday school, which, it is hardly too much to say, was the seed from which the whole modern system of elementary education has sprung.

[1] Most of the more regrettable hymns in use today are products of the nineteenth century.

Sunday schools are commonly supposed to have originated at Gloucester. The two men primarily responsible were Robert Raikes, the proprietor of a Gloucester newspaper, and Thomas Stock, one of the parochial clergy of the city. Raikes's position enabled him to secure a measure of publicity and support for the scheme which it would have been difficult to obtain otherwise.

The year 1780 is the date given for the establishment of the first four of these schools, but there is reason to think that there may have been one in connection with the parish church of Bolton in Lancashire as early as 1774.[1] Twice a day on Sundays (their only free day) the children of the labouring classes were collected into these schools and taught to read. This was the only sort of education, or indeed of social life, within their reach. The Bible was used as a textbook, that they might acquire some knowledge of religion as well as of their letters. Writing was not taught, because in the eyes of many good people this accomplishment was unnecessary for them, and might even prove mischievous. In this connexion it may be of interest to mention that about the year 1905 I was told by an old Lancashire cobbler, who had for many years been a Sunday school teacher in the parish of Swinton (about halfway between Manchester and Bolton), that the reason why Unitarianism was strongly entrenched in the neighbourhood of Manchester was that the Unitarians were the first body to teach writing in their Sunday schools.

As the nineteenth century wore on, and elementary day schools multiplied, the Sunday school became more and more as we have known it. Perhaps the most remarkable feature of the system was the immense volume of devoted lay service which it elicited. The Sunday-school teachers of England must have numbered tens of thousands. If some of them were not very competent, the fact that they were prepared to make a real sacrifice of part of their Sunday leisure, when hours of work were longer than they are now, was very impressive.

It showed that they really cared about their Church, and about the religious welfare of little children. Probably in the long run this counted for more than the teaching actually given. The system

---

[1] See *Church and People,* by S. C. Carpenter, p. 38.

developed most fully in Lancashire and Yorkshire, especially perhaps in the former, where young men and women used to attend Sunday school until they were in the neighbourhood of twenty-five. The tie between teacher and pupil was often intimate and life-long.

Since the beginning of the present century, or at any rate since 1914, circumstances have deprived the Sunday schools of a good deal of their old influence and importance. But they have served the Church and the nation well for more than a century, and their disappearance would be a serious loss.

If the Church led the way the nonconformist bodies soon became very active and energetic in the developing of Sunday schools of their own, especially the Methodists.

15

The Skies Clear—2

From the Peace of Paris to the Battle of Waterloo—1763–1815

THE fourth outstanding event of the eighteenth century is the expansion of the Church beyond our own shores. This deserves to rank at least with the overthrowing of the Deists, the Evangelical Movement and the final removal of the Stuart threat to religious and civil liberty, which had poisoned the life of the Church and nation alike for sixty years.

This fourth event is perhaps in reality the most momentous of all, if that were not suspected at the time. It has already produced results which could not have been foreseen, and the end of them is not in sight yet. For it has compelled and is compelling us to think of our Church in a new way. The Church of England is one thing. The Anglican Communion (a phrase which the eighteenth century never heard), of which it is the centre, is another.

We have never affixed a descriptive label of any kind to our Church. The *Church of England* gives no hint as to any distinctive qualities which it may possess which separate it from the Church of any other region of the globe. The only title we have ever accepted formally is a simple statement of geographical fact, as we might speak in some connections of the *Church of France* or the *Church of Italy*. But it does remind us of some very important facts in our history.

When our Church was taking the shape in which we have it now it was never intended to be more than a local arrangement. The omission of earthquakes (*terræ motus*) from the list of natural calamities from which we pray in the Litany to be delivered is a significant if small indication of this. The Reformers of the sixteenth century set themselves to deal with various abuses

314

with which everyone concerned was only too familiar, within
the provinces of Canterbury and York. The conditions in the area
affected were well known, and it could be assumed that they
would be fairly constant for a considerable time. We were not
concerned with trying to overthrow any other system elsewhere.
Our uncompromising rejection of the pretensions of the Papacy
was inspired by the knowledge that they were the root of
everything of which we wished to get rid. If other countries liked
to put up with them, that was nothing to us. The attempt to
extend our system even to Scotland and Ireland was an after-
thought, and was prompted chiefly by political motives. It never
met with much success. Accordingly, an Englishman could, and
can still if he pleases, accept the Church as part of his national
inheritance, as he may accept the monarchy, parliamentary
government, and many other things. He may regard it as the
legitimate development of Christianity in our climate, as our
system of government is the legitimate development of the ideas
of justice and freedom under the same conditions. This would not
be the highest motive. But it would be perfectly reasonable, and
up to a point adequate. But as soon as our Church has crossed the
seas its position becomes different. At first the change may be
almost imperceptible. If it is the Church of an English colony,
then it may help to remind the settlers in a new land of the rock
whence they were hewn. It may be valued as a link between them
and the island to which they still refer as Home. But with each
generation the strength of this appeal must become less. If the
colonists continue to speak English, or a derivative thereof, as
presumably they will, they will think of themselves less and less as
English. As their own particular history lengthens they will feel
less and less interest in ours. They will know little or nothing of
the abuses with which we had to deal in the sixteenth century, and
will therefore find the steps which we took to remove them and
prevent their recurrence very difficult to understand. Even at the
present time in England there is an almost unbelievable ignorance,
even amongst the clergy, with regard to almost everything connected with the Reformation. And as soon as we come to deal
with natives of Asia and Africa, all these difficulties are aggravated.

As soon as the Church of England ceased to be what its title implies—namely, a compact geographical and racial unit—it entered upon a new phase in its history. Little by little it became imperative that if our position as the centre of a world-wide communion, and the existence of that communion, are to be justified we must find some *raison d'être* which does not depend either upon the accidents of our domestic history during what is already a fairly remote past, or upon our subsequent rise, which has already passed its zenith, to imperial pre-eminence. It is not clear how far we have tried to face the question, "What is the real basis of the Anglican Communion?" Certainly, as far as I know, nothing resembling a full or final answer has been returned to it.[1]

The glib cliché "Catholic and Reformed" will not really suffice. Both words call for a good deal of interpretation, and might be construed in more than one sense. Other communions might claim the title (including the Church of Rome, in view of all that was done by the Council of Trent,[2] and the success of the Counter-Reformation which followed it), whether we could admit their claim or not. Some of them might deny it to us.

The story of the expansion of our Church is not unlike the story of the growth of our empire. To some extent it has been almost fortuitous and the motives by which it has been prompted have not always been of the best. It has gone very much further than was contemplated originally, and we may consider that it has been for the good of the world as a whole. As has been pointed out in Chapter XII, it was not certain until after 1598 that we should be able to preserve our national independence, or that our Church would continue to exist. The question of any extension beyond the seas did not therefore arise. A beleaguered garrison cannot concern itself with schemes of foreign conquest. But after the accession of James I our position became tolerably secure, and Englishmen began to settle abroad on the Continent

---

[1] The nearest approach is resolution No. 11 of the Lambeth Conference of 1888. But this has never become more than a weighty expression of opinion and aimed originally at promoting Home re-union only.

[2] See additional note at the end of the chapter.

of Europe and in India as traders, and in North America as colonists who did not intend to return.[1] The most important of the European settlements were at Delft and Hamburg. The settlers' motives were primarily economic, though political and social considerations (and sometimes religious ones as well) played a part. The trading ports in Europe and India were supplied with chaplains as a matter of course. But these men did not aspire to be missionaries. Indeed, the directors of the East India Company were then, and for a long time afterwards, definitely opposed to any attempt to convert the natives, for fear of the disturbances to which they thought it would give rise.

The position in America was somewhat different. Many of the colonists had gone there with the express intention of escaping from the system of the Church of England, which they regarded as oppressive, and therefore preferred to find ministers of their own way of thinking to any who might be sent to them by authority.

William Laud set on foot an ambitious scheme for extending the Church of England to every part of the world in which the British Government had, or might hope to acquire, any interest.[2] But circumstances prevented its development. In 1633 an Order in Council was issued placing all foreign churches as "Concerning their church government under the Bishop of London as their diocesan." This was not intended to apply to America, as he had another scheme for sending a bishop to New England "to keep the Puritans in order there." Nothing came of this, which is perhaps hardly a matter for regret. But the proposal is perhaps the origin of the undefined authority over "the Plantations" which from the Restoration onwards was considered to be inherent in the see of London. It is presumably due to the Order in Council

[1] Newfoundland had been formally occupied in 1573 by Sir Humphrey Gilbert. A chaplain went out to minister to the settlers, but after a few years he found his position untenable, chiefly owing to lack of support, and came home. He must have been the first person to use the Book of Common Prayer outside England. The whole island did not pass to our flag until the Treaty of Utrecht in 1713.

[2] See *Edmund Gibson*, by N. Sykes, p. 334. I have drawn largely upon Professor Sykes's book for this chapter.

that the English congregations in Northern and Central Europe are to this day within the jurisdiction of the Bishop of London.[1] Their immediate oversight is entrusted to a bishop who now takes his title from Fulham, where the Bishop of London's residence is situated. He is in law a bishop-suffragan of the London diocese.

Then came the Civil War with the virtual destruction of the Church. But as soon as its revival and continuance were assured we did recognize that circumstances had brought us missionary responsibilities which we had not had before. The *Preface* to the Restoration edition of the Prayer Book calls attention to the fact that the new service for the Baptism of such as are of riper years (which was perhaps intended primarily for those who had missed Baptism in their infancy during the dismal days of the Commonwealth) "may always be useful for the baptizing of natives in our plantations and of others converted to the faith." By "natives" it may be presumed that American Indians are meant, not Negro slaves. A definite proposal was made for the consecration of Dr Alexander Murray as Bishop of Virginia, and it is said that letters patent making the appointment were prepared. For some reason which is not apparent the project was abandoned and forgotten.[2] In the reign of Queen Anne there was a suggestion that Jonathan Swift[3] should be made Bishop of Virginia. This may have been prompted by the desire of his political opponents to remove his devastating pen to the other side of the Atlantic. It is interesting to speculate as to the outcome had he accepted the offer.

Henry Compton, who was Bishop of London 1675–1713, accepted the responsibility for the plantations which had attached itself to his see and took a very lively interest in American affairs. But it was obvious that a jurisdiction exercised from a distance

[1] Since 1842 congregations on the shores of the Mediterranean have been under the jurisdiction of the Bishop of Gibraltar (originally Valetta).

[2] Sykes, op. cit., p. 369.

[3] In 1713 he became Dean of St Patrick's, Dublin. Earlier in the year he had applied for the deanery of Wells, which became vacant on 5 January by the death of William Graham. (I am indebted to Mr A. J. Wicks of Monkton Combe School for this information.)

of three thousand miles could never be effective. It was by no means certain that letters despatched from one side of the Atlantic would ever reach their destination on the other. It is said that some of the more important ones were sent in triplicate by three different ships, in the hope that one copy might be delivered safely to the addressee. Commissaries were sent from time to time to exercise disciplinary functions on behalf of the bishop, but even in the most favourable circumstances they were unlikely to be able to do very much. More often than not their presence seems to have been resented by the governor, if the colony were a royal one, or by the proprietor if it were proprietary, because he thought that his rights were being invaded. The "vestries", too, liked to feel that the clergy were under their undisputed control. Still, however incomplete its organization and sporadic its distribution, by the year 1700 the extension of the Church of England to America was a fact, and it was obvious that its development there would be a matter of great and increasing importance.

Many harsh things have been said, and are still believed, about the "refusal" of the Church at home to provide the Church in America with an episcopate. Undoubtedly an opportunity was missed, and the result has been deplorable. It is therefore worth while to remember what was attempted.[1] It is not fair to charge the Church at home with indifference or inertia. More blame attaches to the Government, but before pronouncing any judgement we must consider the problem as it presented itself to the statesmen and politicians of the time. To them it was much less simple than it appears to us now.

During the seventeenth and eighteenth centuries (and even perhaps during the early years of the nineteenth) the Church was regarded as a political force; if not primarily, at least to an extent not easy for us to understand now. This may have been a matter for regret. But it was a fact which could not be ignored. The pulpit was a greater power than it is now, partly because it had fewer rivals, and the objection to political sermons which is entertained in some circles today did not exist. Of course,

[1] See Sykes, op. cit., chapter x, "The Plantations."

politics were politics then, and were not entangled with economics as they are now. Besides this, in many parishes the parson
was the only man who took in any kind of newspaper, and perhaps
almost the only man who could read one. Although his social
status was low (especially during the earlier part of the eighteenth
century) his political influence was very great. He could do more
than anyone else to mould the inarticulate mass of public opinion
before which all sovereigns and parliaments must ultimately bow.

In England the Church has always been linked closely with the
throne. If more closely, as some would say, than has been for its
own good, the fact remains. Civil war made the union closer
than before. And everyone knew that episcopacy was the core of
the Church's system and a principal source of its strength. For a
century after the restoration episcopacy and the monarchy were
regarded as inseparable.

A considerable proportion of the early settlers in America had
no love for the monarchy, and had in fact crossed the Atlantic for
that reason. If they could not escape from it entirely they could
remove themselves to a distance which would make interference
with them much more difficult. They had even less love for the
Church. If a bishop had been sent after them they would naturally
have regarded that as an attempt to strengthen the hold of the
monarchy over them and to force upon them a religious system
which they particularly wished to avoid. They had not taken any
tradition of religious toleration with them, and did not in many
instances regard such a thing as desirable. Maryland had it from
the beginning, because the founder, Lord Baltimore, was a Roman
Catholic and saw that the only possible way of securing toleration
for his co-religionists was to make it general.

Our whole position in North America was none too secure,
and the loyalty of the colonists was not beyond suspicion. The
despatch of a bishop might have led to violent disturbances (the
horror and hatred which Laud had inspired survived him by nearly
a century) of which the French might not have been slow to take
advantage. It would certainly have meant taking a risk of the
kind which the average politician is commonly most anxious to
avoid. It might well have seemed better to put up with complaints

which were unlikely to lead to anything than to hazard our political future in North America.

After 1688 a further difficulty arose. If a bishop necessarily stood for monarchy, which line was he likely to espouse? The question became especially acute after 1714. If the colonial clergy as a whole became Jacobite, there was plenty of French help close at hand, and the position of the Government might well become untenable. If they had no bishop to lead them they would be less dangerous, and such influence as the Bishop of London could exercise would certainly be upon the side of the House of Hanover.

The position was not made easier during the years 1724–6 by the attempt of a number of independent ministers in New England to hold a synod, which was regarded as an infringement of the prerogative of the Crown, however harmless a proceeding it might appear to be in our eyes, and by the visit of two Non-Juring bishops named Talbot and Welton.[1] Writs to return to England were served on both. But Talbot, who had been officiating in America before he received his episcopal orders, was allowed to remain. He seems to have been a man of unblemished character. Welton seems to have been unbalanced and with a penchant for self-advertisement.[2]

It must be remembered that for almost exactly sixty years after 1688 it was the principal preoccupation of his Majesty's ministers to see that the Roman Catholic Stuarts did not make their claim to the throne good. In this long-drawn-out and difficult game the Church was the most important piece. It had to be used in the interests of the game, which, unless a very long view were taken, were not always its own. If we think that the politicians of the time might have shown more courage and insight and might have paid more attention to the purposes for which the Church really exists, it is only fair to remember that the situation was not of their own making. It had been bequeathed to them by James II, and we have good reason to be thankful that they won the game at last.

If it seemed to be impossible to provide North America with a

[1] Sykes, op. cit., pp. 348–9.   [2] Sykes, op. cit., p. 235.

bishop, its religious needs were not neglected, in as far as it lay within the power of the Church *per se* to supply them.

The last quarter of the seventeenth century was prolific in societies for promoting moral and religious purposes. This was to some extent a reaction against the extreme licentiousness of the years of the restoration. The most famous of these, perhaps the only one which has survived, is the *Society for Promoting Christian Knowledge*, which appeared in 1697. It was the work of a Dr Thomas Bray, who has perhaps never received quite as much credit as is his due. He had become well known through the publication of a set of catechetical lectures, and he formed a scheme for providing parochial libraries throughout England for the benefit of clergy and laity alike. The Bishop of London appointed him as his commissary for Maryland, and in the year 1700 he visited the colony. He soon came to the conclusion that be could serve the Church there better from England than on the spot, and in 1701 obtained a charter for what is now known as the *Society for the Propagation of the Gospel*. Since the Archbishop of Canterbury has always been the president, the Society could not be regarded as a private or semi-private venture. It was an attempt on the part of the Church to face its new responsibilities beyond the seas. It was intended originally for work amongst the colonists only. But in the year 1710 it was decided that preference was to be given to the conversion of heathen and infidels. At first, as was natural in view of the circumstances of its origin, the Society restricted itself to the western hemisphere. Today it extends all over the world.

In the year in which it enlarged its scope the Society received a very remarkable legacy. Colonel Christopher Codrington,[1] who happened to have been born in Barbados, his father having been Governor of the Leeward Islands, left his estates in the island to found a college there. The constitution provided for "a convenient number of Professors and Scholars to study and practice Physick and Chirurgery as well as Divinity . . . that they might

[1] He entered Christ Church in 1685 and became a Fellow of All Souls in 1690. He was Governor of the Leeward Islands 1697–1703, and died at Barbados in 1710.

have the better opportunity of doing good to mens souls while they are taking care of their bodies,'' thereby anticipating in a very remarkable fashion the medical missions of our own day. For some reason the bequest did not take effect for more than thirty years.

Another great figure in the missionary world at the time is George Berkeley. Today he is probably remembered chiefly on account of his philosophical writings, which were of great importance in the Deistic controversy.[1] He was a Fellow of Trinity College, Dublin, and in 1724 became Dean of Derry. He did not apparently feel that the deanery involved more than occasional residence at most, but considered that it provided him with an opportunity of doing missionary work in America. He conceived a plan for planting a missionary college in Bermuda. The climate was good and any point on the eastern seaboard of the continent was readily accessible from it. Travel by land from north to south in the colonies was still very difficult. The scheme aroused considerable interest in England, and in 1725 he procured a charter authorizing the foundation and a promise of £20,000 from the Government. He went to America in 1728, but was obliged to return in 1732, when he found that Sir Robert Walpole had no intention of paying the money. Without it the college could not be built, and the whole scheme came to an end.

Berkeley was appointed Bishop of Cloyne in 1734 and died there in 1753. He has received some recognition in our own time, which if less than his due is of the kind he would appreciate most, by the foundation of Berkeley College in the University of Yale by an American member of King's College, Cambridge.

The Peace of Paris made our position in North America secure, at any rate for the moment, and the question of the episcopate might well have been raised again. But successive Bishops of London were not apparently so zealous in the matter as Gibson had been, and as the questions which were destined to lead to the American War of Independence became more acute the Government was less and less inclined to do anything which might stir up more ill-will.

In 1783 the independence of America was recognized, and

1 See Chapter 14, p. 296.

the Church of Connecticut elected Samuel Seabury as their bishop. One of those who worked most actively to bring this about was a son of the famous George Berkeley.[1] Seabury came to England seeking for consecration, but the English Primates did not feel able to act. (Frederick Cornwallis of Canterbury had died on 19 March, and his successor, John Moore, may hardly have been in the saddle when Seabury appeared.) Probably they thought that the American Church was not in a position to support a bishop with adequate dignity, and they may have found it difficult to picture a bishop who had not got the authority of the State behind him, as well as that of the Church. They did not think they could consecrate without a royal mandate, and were reluctant to ask for what they thought would be refused. If we think them unduly timid, it must be remembered that it was not quite a century since the Church had showed itself to be the great champion of constitutional government as against arbitrary personal rule. It had never abandoned that character and it was therefore very undesirable (to say the least) that its two highest officers should do anything which could possibly be construed as illegal. Briefly, if the archbishops deliberately broke the law why should anybody else observe it? Their point of view is not ours. But to do them justice we must try to understand what it was. In the circumstances it was not unreasonable.

Dr Seabury's next idea was to seek consecration in Denmark. At the suggestion it is said of Lord Chancellor Thurlow he went to Oxford to consult Dr Routh, afterwards the famous president of Magdalen College, as to the propriety of such a step. Dr Routh advised against it on the ground that the status of the Scandinavian bishops was doubtful. He suggested that Seabury should turn to Scotland, where there were bishops whose position was beyond question,[2] if their existence was sometimes almost forgotten. Consecration took place in Bishop John Skinner's private chapel at Aberdeen on 14 November 1784, the other two consecrators being Robert Kilgour and Arthur Petrie. (The Scottish bishops at that time did not use territorial titles.)

[1] See above, p. 323.
[2] See Dr Routh, by R. D. Middleton (O.U. Press, 1938), esp. chapter v.

Bishop Seabury naturally took back with him the Scottish Episcopalian Prayer Book, and that has always been the foundation of the American Liturgy. It is not identical with our own, and in some respects may be considered superior to it. It derives from the book of 1549, without reference to those of 1552 and 1662.

In 1786 an Act was passed empowering the archbishop to consecrate to the office of a bishop persons who were subjects or citizens of countries outside his Majesty's dominions. This put an end to all legal difficulties, and on 4 February 1787 William White and Samuel Provoost, both citizens of the new American republic, were consecrated in the chapel of Lambeth Palace as bishops of Pennsylvania and New York respectively. On 19 September 1790 James Madison was consecrated, also at Lambeth, as Bishop of Virginia. In 1792 the American bishops added to their number by consecrating Thomas John Claggett as first bishop of Maryland.

In 1787 Charles James Inglis, a British subject, was consecrated as first bishop of Nova Scotia, and a colonial episcopate had begun. He had been rector of Holy Trinity, Wall Street, New York, but after the War of Independence an organization known as the *Sons of Liberty* (who appeared to think that they could justify their exalted title by refusing to allow anyone to express an opinion with which they disagreed) made his position untenable and he had returned to England.

The last great landmark in the expansion of the Church during this period is the formation of the Church Missionary Society. This was the work of the Evangelical party in the Church, which now included many people of wealth and position in its ranks and was very strongly entrenched in the residential suburban parish of Clapham. The president has always been a layman, and taken as a whole the Society has always represented the "Evangelical" part of the Church more than the Church itself. The preliminary meeting from which it sprang was held in the spring of 1799, when our political fortunes were at a very low ebb and our economic straits dire. The Society did not actually take shape until 1801. The original title proposed was *The Society of Missions to Africa and the East*, showing that its object was to reach parts of the world which the Society for the Propagation of the Gospel had hardly attempted to touch. To the credit of the Nonconformists it must be recorded that they were in the field already. William Carey (a Baptist shoemaker) is the most notable name. The project met with a good deal of objection, partly on the ground that missionary work in India could produce very few converts, if any, and would probably lead to political and social disturbance. There is, of course, a very wide difference between work in countries of ancient civilization such as India and China, and the plantations. If some of the Society's missionaries have shown themselves deficient in tact when dealing with long-established heathen customs, and too ready to regard their ministry as interchangeable with that of continental Protestants, that is no disparagement of the faith and courage which launched the venture, or of the work which it has accomplished since its inception.

In 1814 Thomas Fanshaw Middleton was consecrated as first bishop of Calcutta, so that by the time Napoleon had been beaten to his knees the stage was fairly set, if nobody suspected it, for the astonishing expansion of our communion all over the world, which the next hundred and thirty years were destined to see.

The Church of England as men had always thought of it had really ceased to be. It had become the centre of something world-wide, as England had become the centre of a world-wide empire. The two facts cannot be dissociated. Probably many more people talk and think about the British Empire than about the Anglican Communion and hardly suspect that the latter is extended more widely than the former has ever been. Still less perhaps that it may be expected to outline the political system in which it was, in a sense, cradled and to contribute even more to the well-being of mankind.

NOTE

The Lambeth Conference of 1888. Resolution No. 11, to which reference has been made in a footnote earlier in this chapter, runs:

That in the opinion of this Conference the following Articles supply a basis on which approach may be by God's blessing made towards Home Reunion:

(a) The Holy Scriptures of the Old and New Testaments as "containing all things necessary to salvation," and as being the rule and ultimate standard of faith.

(b) The Apostles' Creed, as the Baptismal Symbol; and the Nicene Creed, as the sufficient statement of the Christian faith.

(c) The two Sacraments ordered by Christ Himself— Baptism and the Supper of the Lord—ministered with unfailing use of Christ's words of Institution, and of the elements ordered by Him.

(d) The Historic Episcopate, locally adapted in the methods of its administration to the varying needs of the nations and peoples called by God into the unity of His Church.

These resolutions are sometimes called the Lambeth Quadri-lateral.

16

*Summer Sunshine—*1

*From the Battle of Waterloo to the passing of the first Education Act—*1815-70

A T Waterloo our march from comparative obscurity to imperial
supremacy, which began when Marlborough turned his back
upon the Rhine and set his face towards the Danube, and was
made possible by a series of incomparable seamen, came to a
triumphant close. The British Empire was destined to receive
many important additions during the century which followed, but
our position had been finally established. We were not only a
Great Power, but virtually the only one. Our maritime strength
brought the resources of the entire globe within our reach, and
the brief heyday of the coal-fired steam engine strengthened our
position still further. We came very near to being "the workshop
of the world," and if as a long-term policy this presented serious
drawbacks, it was immensely profitable for a time. It enabled us
to perfect the manufacturing skill which had been the undoing of
Napoleon, and to accumulate the resources, both at home and
abroad, which enabled us to save the world from Germany twice
during the present century. No nation has ever enjoyed comparable
supremacy, political and economic alike, and perhaps none ever
will. We may also say that none ever abused its power less.

It is true that we had lost the American colonies, but politically
they might almost have been upon another planet. And the
unfortunate, almost accidental little war of 1812, during which
we burned the Capitol at Washington and carried off the frigate
Chesapeake from under the very noses of the astonished and morti-
fied citizens of Boston,[1] had shown the Americans that there was

---

[1] On 1 June 1813, Captain Broke of H.M.S. *Shannon* was severely wounded
and had to hand over the command of his ship to the first lieutenant, whose name
was Wallis. He finished the action and took the *Chesapeake* into Halifax as a
prize. Seventy-four years later I saw him, as Admiral of the Fleet Sir Provo
Wallis, in Queen Victoria's Jubilee procession. He was then in his 97th year.
The entire action was over in twelve minutes.

a wide difference between fighting a defensive war, with abundant French help, on their own territory and meeting us on anything resembling equal terms whether by sea or land. An attack on New Orleans was, however, unsuccessful.

But if the horizon was bright, brighter in fact than anyone suspected at the time, the foreground was very sombre.

The long war had had the usual effect upon all moral standards, and had left us burdened with what then appeared to be an impossible mountain of debt. The migration to the towns (which as far as London was concerned had begun to give rise to anxiety as far back as the reign of Queen Elizabeth),[1] the characteristic of the industrial revolution, was well upon its way, and the conditions under which many of the labouring classes lived and worked were almost indescribable. Things were often not much better in the countryside. The Government had suppressed with very great severity any attempt on the part of labourers to combine in order to secure higher wages and better conditions of work. If this policy can hardly be endorsed, it was not a mere piece of brutality inspired by avarice, as it is sometimes represented. The Government believed that any rise in wages or cost of production, at any rate while the war was in progress, would overturn our whole system of agriculture and manufacture, upon which our prospect of defeating Napoleon depended. They may have been mistaken in their belief, probably in fact they were. But such was their belief, and where our national existence was at stake all other considerations had to give way. Many of the ideas of the French Revolution (at any rate until the Terror) found a considerable number of supporters in England, especially perhaps amongst nonconformists. It was after a dinner given in Birmingham on 14 July 1791, to celebrate the anniversary of the fall of the Bastille, that the mob sacked the house and chapel of Dr Priestley, the eminent Unitarian minister (who had not been present at the dinner), and destroyed a quantity of valuable scientific apparatus. The incident admits of no defence, and it is difficult to justify the leniency with which the rioters were treated afterwards. But it reflects a widespread if ill-founded conviction that a noncon-

[1] *R.H.S. Transactions*, vol. xxx, p. 49.

formist was likely to be as disloyal to the State as he was to the Church.

The Government were afraid of some large-scale outbreak in England, and relied to a very great extent upon the Church to prevent it. In a sense they were justified, inasmuch as the Christian religion is always opposed to any form of violence. But if a Government decides to try to use the Church as an institution to promote its own social and political policy the effect is bound to be almost wholly bad: especially if, as was the case then, a considerable proportion of the clergy are magistrates. It makes religion appear to be an instrument of oppression, and the tradition once established is not easy to live down. During the years 1815–30 the Church in general, and the bishops in particular, became increasingly unpopular, especially when it became known that a number of them had voted against the Reform Bill in the House of Lords. Some of the attacks upon the Church were malicious and without any foundation in fact. *The Black Book or Corruption Unmasked*, which was published in 1831, referred to Ordination as "a gross and beastly absurdity," and the writer affected to believe that all the income of all the benefices in the gift of any bishop formed part of his own income. On this theory it appeared that the Archbishop of Canterbury was in receipt of £70,000 a year and the Bishop of Durham £91,000.

In 1825 Joseph Hume, who might have been credited with at least a modicum of knowledge and common sense, could speak in the House of Commons of "the enormous sinecures[1] called rural deaneries." (It would be interesting to know what he imagined a rural deanery to be. In fact, it is a group of parishes, usually about twenty in number, treated as a unit for certain administrative purposes. The incumbent of one of them is appointed by the bishop as rural dean, and it is his duty to summon the clergy of the other parishes, with, in some instances, representative laity, to meet for consultation and discussion. Sometimes he acts as a channel of communication between bishop and clergy. It also falls to him to inspect periodically the fabric of the churches of

---

[1] A sinecure is a benefice which carries an income but does not involve any pastoral duties.

the parishes in his deanery. If his duties are not very laborious, they are important and unpaid. It would not be easy to point to any part of the Church's administrative system less open to adverse criticism on any rational ground whatever.)

It was, however, true that the administrative system of the Church was in need of reform, if not quite so urgently as that of the State. In a manner perhaps characteristic of England, public opinion became focused upon the inequality of the stipends attached to various offices. This was really a minor point and had come about almost fortuitously. The war had sent up the value of tithe (which depended upon the current price of corn), and in some instances the march of events had increased the value of ecclesiastical lands enormously. The exploitation of the coal measures had brought to the see and cathedral of Durham almost fabulous wealth,[1] while the incumbents of many parochial benefices in many parts of the country received stipends on which they could not live. Accordingly, in 1836 a body called the Ecclesiastical Commissioners was founded by Act of Parliament to deal with these anomalies, which in some instances deserved to be called abuses. It included the two archbishops, all diocesan bishops, the deans of Canterbury, St Paul's, and Westminster, and nine laymen in addition to the five principal officers of state (the Lord Chancellor, the Lord President, the Prime Minister, the Chancellor of the Exchequer and the Secretary of State). There were also five judges, now reduced to two. Of course, in 1836 it was never contemplated that the great offices of state would ever be filled by men who were not at least in name members of the Church of England.

One of the first acts of the Commissioners was to take over the various episcopal estates. The time had gone past when a bishop could be personally a large land-owner, even if he possessed the requisite knowledge. He was bound to be entirely in the hands of his agents, and the temptation to make as much as he could during his tenure was sometimes too strong to be resisted. Besides this, the incomes of some sees had swollen beyond all reasonable

[1] By the generosity of the chapter much of this was used to found the University of Durham in 1832.

requirements,[1] whilst that of others was quite inadequate. It is difficult to arrive at trustworthy figures, but it is probable that Canterbury, York and Winchester at least had more than £20,000 a year each, whilst Exeter and Rochester are said to have had no more than £300 and £1,400 respectively. The Bishop of Exeter was sometimes given a canonry in Durham Cathedral which was reputed to be worth £7,000 a year, and the see of Rochester was held with the Deanery of Westminster. Both these arrangements were probably regarded as scandalous by people who did not know the reason for them. What was really more scandalous was the state of things which made something of the sort necessary.

On paper the richest see was Durham. It is, however, very difficult to say what the income really was, as a large part of it was derived from the fines payable on the renewal of copyhold leases. This form of tenure is now probably almost extinct. It meant that the lease instead of being granted for a definite term of years was for the lifetime of someone (it might be the king) whose name appeared in the "copy". In view of the uncertainty of his tenure the tenant paid a lower rent than would have been required had his lease been for a specified number of years. But whenever the lease terminated he had to pay a sum down for its renewal. This payment was known as a fine. A good deal of ecclesiastical and collegiate property used to be let in this way. The immortal corporation was bound to receive the fine sooner or later, which it could spend on improving its property. Meanwhile, as it had no sons to start in the world, and no daughters for whom dowries might have to be paid, it could put up with some loss of income for a term of years. There was an element of gambling about the business, from the point of view of landlord and tenant alike. If a large part of the property were let on those terms it meant that the landlord's income might fluctuate violently from year to year, and he could never predict accurately what his receipts would be for the next twelve months. This was the case at Durham. Perhaps the average income of the see over a period of

---

[1] The income of London must have been large, for in a letter written in October 1830 describing a visit to Fulham, Dr Hook mentions that upwards of fifty servants assembled in the chapel for evening prayer (*Life*, vol. i, p. 210.)

not less than ten years may have been in the neighbourhood of £40,000. That was not really excessive, in view of the fact that he was earl palatine and responsible for the civil administration of the county. This arrangement was brought to an end in 1836 and the income of the see fixed at £8,000. Bishop Lightfoot subsequently parted with £1,000 of this to help endow the new bishopric of Newcastle.

The bishops of Durham are sometimes said to have been prince-bishops, but this is inaccurate. In England the title *Prince* has always been restricted to members of the royal family. They were, as has been said above, earls palatine.[1]

A palatinate is one of the many legacies of the Roman Empire to Europe. Certain provinces whose situation exposed them to sudden attack were taken out of the ordinary system of administration. They were governed by men directly responsible to the emperor himself and to no one else, whose authority was as if he were acting in person. They were called *comites palatii*[2] (companions of the palace), to indicate their special relation to him, and from this the title of *Count Palatine* is derived. Durham was an important defence against Scottish invasion, and the city and castle, being upon a rock, surrounded on three sides by the river Wear, were virtually impregnable before the days of artillery. The Earls of Northumberland to the north were not perhaps entirely to be trusted and might even try to erect an independent principality of their own. It was to the interest of the Crown to strengthen the bishop's hands in every way. As earl palatine he held all the rights and exercised all the power which could be claimed by the Crown within the area of his bishopric. His position there was at least semi-royal. By 1836 the time for this had gone past and the palatinate rights reverted to the Crown. But the bishop still surrounds his mitre with a ducal coronet and is presented with a sword when he enters his diocese for the first time. Today the railway station at Darlington is

[1] To mark his rank the Bishop of Durham always wore a purple cassock of a peculiar pale shade. Since about the year 1900 English bishops in general have taken to wearing purple cassocks, apparently without any authority.

[2] The original palace was the emperor's house on the Palatine hill at Rome (*Domus palatina*).

usually the scene of the ceremony. Within the walls of Durham Castle (now the headquarters of the university) the proper form of the loyal toast is "The Earl Palatine of Durham, commonly called in England King George VI."

Soon afterwards the Commissioners laid heavy hands upon the cathedrals and stripped them of a large part of their endowments. It is not clear by what principle they were guided in confiscating the revenues which a cathedral requires to do its work efficiently. It is not even certain what they considered the work of a cathedral to be. The property obtained in this way was used for the benefit of the parishes up and down the country, which now receive some £2,000,000 annually from this source. No one disputes that the money has been well and wisely spent. But the cathedrals have been to a large extent crippled for nearly a century. The intellectual life of the nation would not have been strengthened had the colleges of Oxford and Cambridge been plundered in the interests of elementary schools, and it may be doubted whether our religious life has gained by the sacrifice of the cathedrals to the parishes.

Speaking generally, it would be difficult to praise too highly the work which the Ecclesiastical Commissioners have done, and are doing, for the Church, by their skilful management of the property which has passed to them.[1] In one respect, however, they may be considered to have been curiously shortsighted. When they took over the episcopal and capitular estates they gave the former owners annuities of fixed amounts in perpetuity. They left themselves with no power to augment these at any future time should it appear to be necessary. An annuity payable to an individual is one thing, as he probably does not receive it for more than (say) thirty years at the outside. But a perpetual annuity takes no account of any possible fall in the value of money over a longer period. During the nineteenth century the value of money fell steadily, chiefly because the world's supply of gold was increased by the discoveries in California, Australia, South Africa and Alaska. A provision which had been adequate or even generous in 1836 or 1856 had become quite inadequate by 1900, and the

[1] See *Number One, Millbank*, by James Brown, published by S.P.C.K.

position has deteriorated since. Similar considerations apply to many parishes. When the Church Assembly came into being immediately after the first war with Germany warning voices were raised, but no attention was paid to them. Some twenty years later the fact that something not unlike a financial crisis had overtaken the Church could no longer be ignored. The immediate response of the Assembly was to decide that in future no incumbent of any parish may receive more than £750 per annum. Few will get so much. There can be no question that provision for the efficient maintenance of a ministry sufficiently numerous to do the work required is the most urgent problem before the Church at the moment, and that no solution of it is in sight.

From 1836 onwards the organization of the Church became more elaborate. In that year the see of Ripon was created (the first new bishopric since the reign of Henry VIII), to be followed by Manchester in 1848. In both instances there was an old collegiate church with a dean and canons ready to hand which could be transformed into a cathedral without much difficulty or expense. Ripon had, in fact, served as a sort of secondary cathedral to York for some time past. St Albans and Truro came in 1877, Liverpool in 1880, Newcastle in 1882, Southwell in 1884,[1] Wakefield in 1888, Southwark and Birmingham in 1905, Sheffield in 1909, Chelmsford, and St Edmundsbury and Ipswich (for the county of Suffolk) in 1914. Since 1920, Blackburn, Bradford, Coventry, Guildford, Leicester and Portsmouth have been added to the list, making a total of twenty new sees in less than a century. It must, however, be admitted that the religious outcome of this immense and costly activity has been disappointing. The number of clergy has declined steadily since about 1890, and doubts are now (in 1948) being openly expressed as to whether England can be regarded as a Christian country. Some of the new dioceses are said to be proving too small. It does not seem to have occurred to anyone that it might be easier to collect the money with which to make a new diocese than to find a man qualified to be bishop of it, and that there is no surer way of weakening any institution

[1] From which a diocese of Derby was formed in 1927.

than to create posts which require men of first-rate capacity in excess of the number available.

In 1860 the Houses of Convocation were once more allowed to transact business. Since then they have met regularly and have played a useful part in the formation of opinion amongst the clergy, if they have never commanded as much respect as had been hoped in the eyes of the nation as a whole.

In 1870 the office of bishop suffragan, which had lapsed in 1607, was revived, and titular bishops of Dover and Nottingham were appointed to lighten the labours of the two Primates. Since then these useful functionaries have multiplied to an almost alarming extent. At the present time (1948) there appear to be thirty-nine bishops suffragan in the two provinces, beside seventeen assistant bishops.[1] The problem of providing stipends for them without diverting funds intended for other purposes has yet to be solved.

The dominant factor during the whole of the nineteenth century was the rapid and continuous increase of population. Nothing resembling it had been known in the history of the world before. At the census of 1811, the first to be taken, the population of England and Wales was returned as between ten and eleven million. It had perhaps doubled itself in the last one hundred and twenty years.[2] In the next sixty years it rose to twenty-three million, and by the year 1911 the twenty-three millions of 1871 had become thirty-six. No department of our national life was untouched by this, and it has left us a formidable legacy of social and economic problems. But nothing was affected more adversely than the parochial system of the Church, especially in the towns, where the increase was more noticeable and overwhelming than anywhere else. Leeds, for example, multiplied sevenfold during the century (from 60,000 to 450,000), and so did Sheffield. The same might be said of almost any other large town. Now the unit of Church life for at least a thousand years had been the parish. This was, as a rule, rural, and if it covered a large area that meant

[1] An assistant bishop is a man who was consecrated for work elsewhere which he has resigned. The appointment is purely personal. A bishop suffragan has some status, if no authority, and therefore assumes a territorial title. (See above, Chapter 11.)

[2] Since the publication of Gregory King's *Tables* (Chapter 13, p. 281).

that the greater part was almost uninhabited.[1] When parishes were urban the area was usually very small, as may be seen in the city of London or in York or in Cambridge today. Each parish was a real community, with the church as its centre, and in many instances the community sense seems to have been very strong. It was usually possible for the parson to know all his parishioners by sight at least, and to be in a very real sense the father of a family. All this was swept away, almost as it were in a night. The community in which ties of blood relationship had played an important part, and where different social classes and occupations were wholesomely represented, was submerged by a flood of new settlers, and became the suburb of a town. The newcomers had no natural cohesion, no roots and no traditions. Socially and economically they were all upon the same level. They came to work at the new factory, lured by the prospect of higher wages than they could hope for on the land, but still for the most part desperately poor. The rural labourer or craftsman, who had some skill in which he could take a pride, was replaced by the occupant of a dingy hovel, sometimes a cellar in a mean street, whose work in life was to watch and tend a machine.

If the Church was taken by surprise no one can say that it did not make enormous efforts to cope with the new situation. New parishes were formed (the legal procedure having been made less cumbrous) and churches built in all the large towns all over the country. In Leeds, to take a single instance, of which I happen to have first-hand knowledge, fifty new churches were consecrated between the years 1840 and 1890. A few of these replaced older ones which had become too small, but the majority were new foundations. And clergy to man them were forthcoming, even if stipends were not.[2] It is impossible to estimate the amount of money spent on church building during the second half of the century. It is unfortunate that the builders did not as a rule make

[1] The old parish of Halifax measured about 20 miles by 18. But the greater part was moorland.

[2] Frederick John Wood, afterwards vicar of Headingley, served as assistant curate at the parish church of Leeds from 1856 to 1881 for a stipend of £5 per annum. It is impossible to say how many such there were, or how much the Church owes to them.

any attempt to endow their foundations. Money was abundant, and a capital sum of even £1,000, the interest to provide a fabric fund, or part of the stipend of an assistant curate, would have been of immense value a few years later.

If the Church's efforts to overtake the new situation were never fully adequate, they deserve to be called heroic. It may be doubted whether any other Communion could point to a similar outburst of energy and self-sacrifice at any period of its history.

Statistics soon become wearisome, but it may be worth while to give a few from the private journal of Charles Thomas Longley, first bishop of the new see of Ripon. It has never been published in full.

	1836	1856
Number of churches and chapels[1] in the diocese ..	307	432
Incumbents	297	419
Assistant curates	76	146
Parsonage houses	170	301

Longley must have been a man of exceptional energy and ability, as is evinced by the fact that he was translated to the see of Durham, and thence to York and finally to Canterbury. But what he did may be taken as typical of what was going on in many other dioceses at the same time. The story is continued by his successor, Robert Bickersteth. Between October 1836 (the day of Longley's consecration was 6 November) and 31 December 1879 no less than 296 new churches had been consecrated in the diocese. Twenty-four of these were built by private munificence without any public appeal for funds. Archbishop Harcourt of York presented the new bishop with a chapel for his palace. (The house has now been abandoned as too large and expensive.) If such things could go on in a remote part of Yorkshire it is impossible to say that the Church was dead, or the nation as a whole given over to money-making.

When Walter Farquhar Hook became vicar of Leeds in 1837, which meant that he was responsible for the pastoral care of

---

[1] Sometimes called *chapels of ease*. The services conducted in them were those of the Church, but they were not parish churches, and were not licensed for marriages.

almost the whole township, he found that his staff consisted of one
assistant curate and one clerk in Orders. They were at the church
from 8 to 11.30 every morning for marriages. They baptized
twice and churched twice daily. Funerals took place twice a day
in winter and three times in summer.[1] There was really no
possibility of attempting any parochial work as we understand it.
Probably a similar state of things obtained at the old parish church
of Manchester, now the cathedral. By 1844 the population had
risen to a little over 150,000 and a division of the parish was
effected. Twenty chapels of ease became parish churches served
by resident incumbents. The old mother church retains its
dignity and the natural importance of the vicar is enhanced by the
amount of patronage in his hands. Under the new régime Leeds
has been for approximately a century one of the principal strongholds of the Church, and perhaps the place in which the principles
of the Oxford Movement have been translated into the terms of
parochial life more successfully than anywhere else.

Hook himself was not quite a product of the movement, as he
was born in 1798. There were certain features in it of which he
disapproved, if he welcomed much of it. His real background was
the High-Church tradition of the eighteenth century. During his
twenty-two years at Leeds he set a standard for the mother church
of a large town which has been widely imitated. He became Dean
of Chichester in 1859 and died in 1875.

After this brief sketch of the Church as it was during the stormy
years immediately after Waterloo, something must now be said of
the three movements which were destined to affect it very deeply
during the next eighty years. It would hardly be too much to say
that they have changed it out of all recognition, and their influence
is not yet spent. They are first the Oxford Movement, secondly
the Christian Social Movement, and thirdly the contest between
science and religion. So much has been written about the first of
these that a very short summary will be sufficient here.

Most of what was best in the Church during the first thirty
years of the nineteenth century was owing to the Evangelicals.
But without detracting from the moral standard which they set,

[1] *Life*, vol. i, p. 372.

or from their missionary zeal, their presentation of the Gospel was deficient in one respect. They appeared to have overlooked, as many people do today, that belief in the Holy Catholic Church is part of the Creed. Some informal conferences were held at Hadleigh in Suffolk, of which Hugh James Rose, a distinguished scholar (and, as it happened, a Cambridge man), was rector. The publication of some tracts dealing with the nature of the Church was considered, but the movement is usually held to have begun with a very outspoken Assize sermon preached by Keble in the university church at Oxford on 14 July 1833, entitled *National Apostasy*. The immediate occasion was the suppression by the Government of ten redundant bishoprics in Ireland, or, to speak more accurately, their union with other sees.[1]

It had long been obvious that the Reformation had failed in Ireland, and was never likely to succeed. After all, an appeal to conscience was unlikely to be very fruitful amongst the squalid peasantry of the Celtic-speaking part of the island. The bishoprics were not needed, and placed an intolerable tax, in the form of tithe, on a very poor country. The holders had not always been men who deserved respect. If any of these facts were known to Keble they did not weigh with him. All he could see was that sacrilegious hands had been laid upon the Sacred Ark and that the Government had repudiated the Christian faith. His sermon produced a great sensation and was followed by the issue of a number of pamphlets entitled *Tracts for the Times*. They were all by distinguished hands and some by very distinguished ones. They aimed at giving people a juster view of the nature of the Church. The Church of England is not a creation of Henry VIII nor a government department. Its history is longer and more inspiring than was generally supposed at that time. It has more in common with the older parts of the Christian world than many people realized. If much of this is familiar to us now, it needed saying, and with emphasis, then. The immediate and immense success of the Tracts showed how badly teaching of this kind was required. Finally, in 1840 came the famous Tract XC from the pen of John Henry Newman, vicar of the university church,

---

[1] Cashel and Tuam ceased to be archbishoprics.

himself. In this he tried to show that the Thirty-nine Articles can be interpreted or explained in a way to which no Roman Catholic need take exception. The modern reader must judge the cogency of the argument for himself. Naturally this produced a storm. The *Articles* had long been regarded as the sure shield of our national protestantism against the attacks, open or covert, of Rome. If there were really nothing in them in which a Roman Catholic could not acquiesce the very foundations, as it seemed to many, of our Church were undermined. It was clear that this Tract must be the last.[1] Five years later Newman took the step which it must long have been clear to most people (except perhaps himself) he would take sooner or later, and was received into the Church of Rome. A number of less distinguished figures followed his example. The immediate occasion of his secession, as stated by himself, seems trivial and fantastic enough today. His historical studies had led him to turn his attention to the Arians of the fourth century. It will be enough to say that the Arian heresy arose at Alexandria and ultimately destroyed the Incarnation by making Christ no more than the first of all created Beings. It became very popular in the East, but the Church of Rome, which perhaps never really understood what it was all about, rejected it uncompromisingly, and posterity has endorsed the verdict. To Newman it appeared that if in the fourth century, when a dispute arose between the Churches of Rome and Alexandria, the Church of Rome had been in the right, then when a dispute arose twelve hundred years later between the Churches of Rome and England, about something entirely different, it followed that the former (which he believed to be the same[2]) must be in the right again.

Much has been written about Newman, and he will probably always be something of an enigma. Perhaps the explanation is that his character was fundamentally emotional and weak, and that he was very much afraid of the conclusions to which his extraordinarily keen and subtle intellect might ultimately lead him. He could not feel "safe" (a word of which he was fond) until he was

---

[1] It was said once that it ought to have been published in Latin. Then it would have been read only by people qualified to express an opinion about it.

[2] This makes it difficult to believe that he knew much of medieval history.

in a position which enabled him to say that he had no opinions. One thing, however, may be said of him without fear of contradiction. Few greater masters of the English language can ever have lived. His secession was, of course, a severe blow to the Movement, but by this time it had gathered sufficient momentum to continue on its way.

Shortly afterwards another considerable secession was caused by a dispute between the Bishop of Exeter and a Mr Gorham, who had been presented to the benefice of Bamford Speke, in his diocese. The bishop refused to institute him on the ground that he disbelieved in baptismal regeneration. The Judicial Committee of the Privy Council, which if not an ideal tribunal was the only one available, decided that Mr Gorham's utterances were not irreconcilable with our accepted formulæ. This judgement was endorsed by the two archbishops and he was duly instituted, in defiance of his diocesan bishop.

Of course, in some quarters this was regarded as an unwarrantable overruling of the authority of the Church by the State. It seems to be impossible for many people to understand that it is not the function of an individual bishop to try to invest his opinions with the force of law, but to administer the law of the Church as it stands, whatever his private opinion of it may be. To determine what the law really is the help of a professional (lay) judge may be very valuable, if not indispensable. The most prominent of the seceders was Henry Edward Manning, Archdeacon of Chichester. He eventually became Roman Catholic Archbishop of Westminster and a cardinal. (It is believed that he came within a little of being elected Pope, after the death of Pius IX.) On 29 September 1850 it appeared to Pius IX (who two years before had had to fly in disguise from Rome) that the time had come when the Anglican schism (as he probably termed it) might be ended by a bold stroke. Accordingly he "restored the hierarchy"—in other words, divided the map of England into a number of dioceses and placed a bishop with a territorial title (*Birmingham*, *Clifton*, etc.) over each. He had misread the situation as badly as Pius V had done two hundred and eighty years before, when he hoped to cow England by excommunicating Elizabeth and declaring the throne vacant. Our latent hatred of popery and all its works blazed up. In the excitement of the moment people did not see that what the Pope had done was merely a paper transaction. His bishops had no legal status other than that of any nonconformist ministers, and could only exercise authority over those who were already prepared to submit to it. All he achieved was to revive our national dislike of the Roman Church, and to intensify the suspicion with which the Tractarians and their disciples were regarded in some circles.

As the Oxford Movement spread to the parishes and began to affect the parochial clergy, it entered upon a new phase. Originally its adherents, whilst meticulous in the matter of reverence, were indifferent to ceremonial. The clergy who were working in large parishes, especially in the more squalid parts of London, felt that they could make very little impression unless they gave their people something to see as well as to hear. More light and colour must be introduced into the Church's worship. Unfortunately these clergy, who were devoted parish priests, seem to have known very little of the principles of religious ceremonial. If during a holiday on the Continent they saw anything which appealed to them, they imitated it at home without much consideration as to its real meaning or intrinsic suitability. This led to violent outbreaks—some of which were deliberately fostered by outsiders. The nation was puzzled and alarmed by these "innovations in religion", as it did not understand what was happening. The attitude of the clergy concerned was not always conciliatory. They felt that they were being persecuted (as in a sense they were), but did not seem to recognize that persecution would probably cease if they would take the trouble to make themselves understood. Their assertion that they were merely carrying out the instructions of the Prayer Book carried no weight. In any case, it ignored the practice of more than two centuries.[1] Less than justice was done to their real evangelistic zeal. Public opinion against "Ritualism", as it was generally called, became very strong and finally took shape in the Public Worship Regulation Act of 1874,

[1] The importance of custom as an interpretation of law can never be ignored.

which was described as a Bill "to put down ritualism." There are, however, some things which cannot be "put down" (or set up) by Act of Parliament, and the measure was a complete failure. A few clergy, perhaps five or six, were imprisoned under it for contempt of court. But this was rightly recognized as a scandal, and when they had to be released their position was strengthened by the martyrdom which they had undergone.

These unseemly squabbles went on here and there until the beginning of the present century and have done much to bring the whole Church into contempt. With the exception of Bishop Creighton, who died on 14 January 1901 at the age of 58, few of the people concerned seem to have understood the right way of dealing with matters of this kind. It is not legislation or prosecution. The tradition that most clergy spend most of their time in quarrelling with their bishops about details which no sensible man would think worth taking seriously is now very firmly established and very widespread.

The feature of Ritualism which aroused most anger and disgust had nothing strictly to do with ritual at all. It was the belief that ritualist clergy insisted upon private confession, especially from their candidates for Confirmation, and were in the habit of putting very improper questions to them. It is impossible to say how much truth there is, or ever was, in that accusation. Some people prefer not to recognize that our Church makes provision for private confession, while others are equally reluctant to admit that it gives them no right to insist upon it. It is also probable that some clergy try to use what is meant to quiet a troubled conscience as a means of rousing a sleeping one, and do not recognize that confession unless handled carefully will end by weakening character and lowering the sense of sin.

One outward and visible sign of the movement from which there is no escape is the "restoration" of innumerable ancient parish churches which was carried out under its auspices. 1840–60 (roughly) is the period during which the wave of the "Gothic Revival" (as it was called) smote the countryside. No doubt many churches stood in urgent need of repair, but the work called for more knowledge and understanding than were as a rule brought to it. The indiscriminate and uninformed admiration of all things medieval which the movement had done much to foster had led to the belief that a church was not really a church unless its architecture and furniture could be termed "Gothic." All traces of the seventeenth and eighteenth centuries must be eliminated, and the clock put back to some period vaguely known as the "Age of Faith." Anyone who knows anything about architecture will recognize as he contemplates these costly efforts that the authors did not understand the past which they wished to reproduce, and have created something which never did exist anywhere at any time. The prebendal stalls in the Quire of Wells Cathedral are a glaring instance. "Pretentious humbug" is not an unfair description of work of this kind, and as soon as anyone has recognized this he may begin to wonder how far a similar criticism may be brought against the movement as a whole.

In the preface which he contributed some years ago to Dr Yngve Brilioth's[1] book *The Anglican Revival* Dr A. C. Headlam, a very distinguished son of Oxford and from 1923 to 1946 Bishop of Gloucester, has described the movement as a failure. This seems to be too sweeping, if it never laid hold of the nation as its Evangelical forerunner did. For good or ill it has never lost the associations which go with the word "Oxford", and it has affected the clergy more than the laity. This is true of its descendant—some would say degenerate descendant—usually known as "Anglo-Catholicism" today. Anglo-Catholicism can be effective sporadically in large towns where eclectic congregations can be gathered, but parochially it appears to be a failure, especially in the country. There does not seem to be the least likelihood that it will ever be the religion of England. If people like and respect their incumbent they may be prepared to put up with what they regard as his incomprehensible vagaries. But they do not regard them as of any religious significance, and will usually welcome a change if an opportunity of making one arises.

But whatever criticisms may be brought against the movement there can be no doubt that, taken as a whole, its influence upon the Church has been beneficial. It has led to a higher standard of

[1] Subsequently Bishop of Vaxjo.

pastoral duty amongst the clergy. Non-residence is a thing of the past, except where circumstances compel two or more parishes to share an incumbent. Churches are better kept, if not better attended. Celebrations of the Holy Communion are more frequent, and all services are conducted with more care and reverence. It is not too much to say that almost all these things are due ultimately to the Oxford Movement, and there can hardly be a parish in the land in which it has not made itself felt, directly or indirectly.

But when full credit for all this has been given where it is due we cannot forget that the movement has left us some very dubious, not to say mischievous, legacies.

First, its doctrine of Apostolic Succession.

Bishops have always been regarded as the successors of the Apostles, for the very obvious reason that they hold in the Church the kind of position which the Apostles seem to have held during the period covered by the New Testament. But the early history of episcopacy and the process by which the bishop became distinct from the presbyter (in the New Testament the terms are interchangeable) are obscure, and we are never likely to know much more about them than we do now. The phrase seems to have originated with Irenæus, who was Bishop of Lyons from 177 to 199. He uses it in the plural, and in a sense which is not attached to it today. By his time the last living links with any Christians of the apostolic age were gone.[1] The canon of Scripture was not as definite and authoritative as it is now, and many fantastic speculations, corresponding roughly with what is known as "theosophy" today, were rife. His problem was to answer the question, "What is the true Christian tradition, and where is it to be found?" His answer was to point to the apostolic sees. There were certain bishoprics, notably Antioch, Ephesus and Rome, which were known to have been founded by Apostles. Therefore the Gospel which they had received must be the true one. The succession of bishops ever since was known. The period was hardly longer than that which separates us from the Napoleonic

[1] Polycarp of Smyrna, who is believed to have been a disciple of St John, had died in the year 156 at the age of 86.

wars. These men had been elected by the churches over which they were presiding. Therefore their orthodoxy must have been known to be beyond dispute. What they taught must be what the apostolic founder had taught, otherwise they would never have been chosen. They are in agreement all the world over, and the true Christian tradition is safe in their hands. To Irenæus "apostolic succession" meant legitimate succession to an office known to have been held originally by an Apostle, regarded as a sufficient guarantee of doctrinal orthodoxy, and nothing else.

In nineteenth-century England a very different meaning was read into the phrase by the Tractarians and their successors. They were anxious to show that the Church had an inherent authority of its own, which was not derived from the State. But since in England bishops are nominated by the Crown, the view that they derive all their authority from the Crown, and are in fact a species of civil servant, can be made to appear plausible. The Tractarian rejoinder was that they derive it from the Apostles, not merely by legitimate succession but by an unbroken tactual line. In this way a mysterious (almost it would seem magical) power has been handed on from generation to generation. Only the holders of this power can confer "valid" Orders, and only the holders of "valid" Orders can administer "valid" Sacraments. The precise meaning of the word "valid" in this connexion is difficult to define. Nor is it easy to find any test of "validity" which can be applied, except one which the Church of England does not recognize. Of course, the theory *may* be true. But it involves assuming more than we really know. It does not admit of proof (or disproof) and it is not easy to see how it ever can. All that can be said positively is that it is difficult to reconcile with some facts known to us in the early history of the Churches of Rome and Alexandria.[1] If the succession has ever been broken it has been lost for ever, and therefore the very existence of the Church hangs by a very slender and uncertain thread. To regard the bishop as the organ of the whole Body of Christ through which, for certain purposes, the Church functions, as seems to be the view of the Orthodox Churches of

[1] See e.g., Jerome, Ep. 101 *ad Evangelium.*

the East, is much less open to criticism and leads to a precisely similar conclusion. As the century wore on the Tractarian theory became increasingly popular amongst the clergy, for reasons which are readily intelligible. Nonconformists were relieved of certain disabilities because it was recognized that they were not dangerous politically. They were admitted to Oxford and Cambridge. Socially and intellectually their status went up. It was therefore pleasant for the clergy to reflect that whatever the personal attainments of these men might be their ministry was hopelessly vitiated at its source. Whatever success might appear to attend their efforts, sacraments administered by them were nothing. Beside this, as bishops became more numerous and therefore individually less distinguished they tended to lay an increasing emphasis upon the unique purity of their spiritual pedigree. The theory has, however, never been accepted by the Church of England, though attempts are continually made to assume that it has been, or to introduce it as it were by a side-wind. Probably many people regard it now as indisputable.

In his book *The Claims of the Church of England*[1] the present Archbishop of York refers to difficulties in the way of inter-communion with the Church of Finland, due to the fact that that Church "had lost since 1884 its Apostolic Succession" (the Finns' own comment on this assertion might be interesting). The circumstances were as follows.

In 1884 the three Finnish bishops died, so that the episcopate became extinct. The country was then a province of the Russian Empire, and the Russians, it was believed, would not have allowed a Finn to go to Sweden for consecration, or a Swedish bishop to come to Finland to give it. Accordingly, when an archbishop had been nominated the chapter of the cathedral church of Turku proposed that Professor Granfelt, who was not in episcopal orders, should officiate, and the Government con-sented. The circumstances were abnormal and can perhaps never recur in any part of the Christian world. But any theory of the ministry which "unchurches" the Church of Finland on the ground that Archbishop Renval received presbyterian consecra-

[1] Page 253.

tion only is not easy to defend and goes far beyond what the
Church of England authorizes any of its sons to say. We have
declared that episcopacy is our rule and by that we stand. That
may be considered to put our own nonconformists out of court,
because their forebears were all cradled in our Church, and left it
because some part of its system seemed to them intolerable. But
we have never said that no other system can ever be permissible
elsewhere. Indeed, in Article XXIII, *Of Ministering in the Congregation*, we have taken particular pains not to say so. Until that
Article at least has been lawfully repealed no individual member
of the Church of England has a right to say that any foreign
communion is a Church only in name *solely* because it practises
presbyterian ordination, or that apostolic succession, as it has
come to be generally understood, is part of our authorized
teaching.

Secondly, insistence upon fasting Communion.

Everyone would agree that as a general principle it is desirable
to receive the Holy Communion as early in the day as may be, and
that for people who are neither old nor infirm to receive it
fasting is a useful piece of discipline. (It can, of course, be practised
more easily by those who have servants at home to prepare breakfast for them while they are in church.) It is said, however, that
many clergy today teach that the fast is a moral obligation, and as
such absolutely binding. To disregard it is to be guilty of mortal
sin. No dispensation from the rule is possible, any more than (say)
a dispensation to commit adultery.

Now, we know a great deal about the social habits and customs
of the world in which Christianity grew up. The Roman day
began at 6 a.m.[1] Work usually ended at noon, and the first meal
(a very large one) was at 3 p.m. and was known as *prandium*.
Supper (*Coena*) followed at a later hour. The Romans did their
work and took their exercise on an empty stomach. Therefore
originally fasting Communion meant no more than Communion
during the earlier and business part of the day. No religious
significance attached to it. Fasting Mattins would have been
equally common. Our system of three, or even four, smaller

[1] See e.g. Martial IV. viii, written during the latter part of the first century.

meals is probably better for health and more suited to our climate than the two very heavy ones of the Roman world. But the old habit persisted for a very long time. Until near the end of the sixteenth century dinner and supper were the only meals customary in England, if by that time dinner was usually before midday. Samuel Pepys refers to his "morning draught," but that could hardly be called a meal. He took it at his tailor's, or wherever he might happen to be, if he took it at all, and it is not clear whether he had anything to eat with it or not.

Suetonius records as an instance of the disgusting gluttony of the Emperor Vitellius in A.D. 69 that he had three or even four meals a day, in which was included a *jentaculum*, or early breakfast.[1] It is not easy to see on what rational ground a practice which was born of ordinary pagan social custom can have risen to the level of a Christian principle. The arguments sometimes adduced in its favour would appear to require fasting after reception of the Sacrament for at least as long as before, if the conclusion has not yet been drawn in practice.

Thirdly, the theological colleges.

For two centuries or more after the Reformation it was considered that Oxford and Cambridge could provide all the professional training that was needed by clergy of the Church of England. But as time went on it became clear that they were in some respects inadequate and that something on the lines of the seminaries of the Roman Church was required. There is no question that these institutions have done a great deal of very valuable work. But unfortunately, except for the college at Edinburgh and Queen's College, Birmingham, which stand rather apart, they have all come into being since the year 1839 and were all intended originally either to advance or to counteract the teaching of the Oxford Movement. They have therefore helped to split the Church in two, and if the two portions do not regard each other with as much ill-feeling as they used, the division is none the less real and makes the administration of patronage unnecessarily and extraordinarily difficult. It is not easy to see how the breach, which is dangerously wide, can ever be healed if

[1] *De Vita Cæsarum*, vii. 13.

the theological colleges continue as they are. At present many of them are in practice almost completely isolated. Those that are in cathedral cities (e.g. Chichester, Wells, or Salisbury) are theoretically under the immediate eye of their diocesan. At one time this may have meant a good deal more than it does now. In modern times the chief pastor of a diocese is away too much, and too busy when at home to supervise any particular institution effectively, and the colleges sometimes seem to think more of preserving their own distinctive tradition than of their relation to the Church which they exist to serve. There is a system of inspection, but it does not appear to be very effective. The inspectors have no means of ensuring that any attention will be paid to their recommendations. The problem of staffing them does not become easier. The number of clergy qualified for such work is small and does not increase, and many of them appear to be unwilling to undertake it, partly perhaps because much of the teaching which they are required to give is very elementary.

Originally the colleges could count on a fairly high and uniform educational and social standard amongst the students. There was a solid foundation on which they could build. That is not so now. Anyone who has examined for the General Ordination Examination must have noticed how little background of good general education most of the candidates appear to possess. Partly owing to changed circumstances, the theological colleges as they are now are hardly equal to their task. Yet it is difficult to see how they can be strengthened, or what substitute for them could be found. It is often said that one reason why many of the clergy of today fail is that they cannot express themselves in any language which the laity can understand. If this is true the atmosphere of the theological colleges must be to some extent to blame. Archbishop Benson foresaw this danger more than fifty years ago.[1]

It is worth while to remember that Chichester, the oldest of the Victorian colleges, owes its origin to the fertile brain of Henry Edward Manning,[2] then Archdeacon of Chichester. Ten years later he had lost all faith in the future of the Church of England, which perhaps he had never really understood.

[1] *Life*, pp. 185, 348–9, 404.   [2] See above, p. 342.

17

Summer Sunshine—2

From the Education Act to the first German war—1870–1914

MENTION has already been made above of the conditions which the industrial revolution created in the poorer parts of London, and in the manufacturing towns of the north. All this was a long way from the Common Rooms of Oxford. If the fathers of the Oxford Movement knew anything of it they probably regarded it as inevitable. There always had been poverty and squalor, and presumably there always would be. It was for Christian charity to mitigate these evils, even if such mitigation meant no more than casual half-crowns to beggars. But it did not occur to most people that the Church as such was, or ought to be, concerned with such things as housing and conditions of work and rates of wages. Its business was to save souls, and these things must be left to adjust themselves. There were, however, some clergy who took a different view, and in consequence of their efforts the movement which came to be known as Christian Socialism[1] was born. Two of the principal leaders were distinguished London clergy, Frederick Denison Maurice[2] and Charles Kingsley.[3] The former had been a Unitarian, and was a professor at King's College, London, beside holding other important positions. He was dismissed from his professorship on grounds of unorthodoxy in matters of doctrine, and eventually became incumbent of St Edward's, Cambridge. In respect of ability and character he ranks very high amongst the clergy of his time. The latter is perhaps remembered today more as a novelist than as a social reformer. He was at one time a lecturer at Queen's

---

[1] The phrase seems to have come into use about the year 1850.
[2] 1805–72.
[3] 1819–75.

College, London, and for many years rector of Eversley in Hampshire. Two years before his death he was appointed a canon of Westminster. The year 1848 saw violent revolutions in most countries of Europe, and for a moment we seemed to be in sight of one in England. On 10 April a large crowd assembled at Kennington Common with the intention of proceeding to Westminster and laying their grievances before the House of Commons. They were informed that they would not be allowed to cross the Thames and that the bridges were held by soldiers, but that a petition might be presented by a representative deputation in the ordinary way. The meeting was the only direct appearance in London of a movement that had many adherents in the midlands and the north. It was known as Chartism because the members had put forward a "Charter" in which they called upon Parliament to redress their grievances. Most of their demands would be regarded today as entirely reasonable, and have in fact been conceded long since. But at the time they were considered by most people to be dangerously revolutionary. Probably inflammatory speeches were made at Chartist meetings up and down the country, and some Chartists may have been prepared to resort to violence. But the crowd at Kennington Common dispersed quietly after listening to some speeches. This seems to have been due chiefly to the courage and resolution of Mr Mayne,[1] the Commissioner of the Metropolitan police, who had taken the measure of the Chartist leader (Feargus O'Connor) very accurately. After that day it was clear that there would be no repetition of the events of 1381.[2] But it needed no little courage for any clergyman to avow himself a Chartist, as Kingsley did. He saw no less clearly than Maurice that social reform would come to very little unless it had moral and religious foundations, and that Christianity and Socialism were not necessarily hostile forces, as most people believed then and some do still.

The visible results of the movement so far as the Church was concerned were attempts to bring to the artisan population of the

[1] Afterwards Sir Richard Mayne, K.C.B.
[2] See Chapter 8, p. 159.

towns educational opportunities and amenities of various kinds which had hitherto been beyond their reach. The Working Men's College in Great Ormond Street and Toynbee Hall were two of the earliest of these ventures. The latter was founded by the Rev. Samuel Barnett,[1] vicar of the parish of St Jude, Whitechapel, which the then Bishop of London (John Jackson) is said to have described as the worst in the diocese. The Oxford House in Bethnal Green and the Cambridge House in Camberwell are two of the best-known of the subsequent "settlements". Several colleges followed suit, St John's, Cambridge, who planted a mission in Walworth, being the first in the field.

Whatever these settlements did or failed to do, they provided points of contact between poor and well-to-do. They showed that if the Church as a whole was lethargic with regard to social problems, some members of it at least were not. That is a service the value of which it would be difficult to over-estimate. It is probably one of the things, and not the least, which has prevented the development of the bitterly anti-religious temper which has often been conspicuous in continental socialism.

It must, however, be admitted that the social gospel has not as yet proved very effective. It was, and is, intended primarily to reach the urban artisan. Yet there is probably no class in the community to whom everything for which the Church stands means less. It is not a question of active hostility (of which there was probably more fifty years or so ago), but of complete indifference. The idea that religion is intended as an opiate, which seems to be a commonplace on the Continent, is not yet extinct in England.

Moreover, the preachers of the social gospel need to be careful lest they give the impression that the primary function of Christianity is to produce an economic concise paradise of high wages for short hours of light work, and that it must stand or fall by its success or failure to achieve this amoral purpose. Also, lest they forget that (as Creighton used to point out) wealth must be produced before it can be distributed. Ecclesiastical orators appear at times to be strangely ignorant of the real facts of

[1] Subsequently a canon of Westminster.

industry, and to do less than justice to the knowledge, foresight, courage and intelligence which the head of a firm must possess if he is not to fail. These are the real capital of the business, and harder to procure or replace than capital in any other form. The moral value of these qualities is not in dispute, and there is therefore no reason why they should be denied or grudged their due reward. To demand far-reaching economic changes in the name of Christ usually means linking Christianity very closely with some particular scheme or legislation, which means with the fortunes of some political party. All that need be said of this is that it is a very dangerous course to adopt, and appears more likely to lead to a thoroughly secularized Church than to an even partially Christianized society. The Church cannot be and ought not to wish to be indifferent to the social order by which it finds itself surrounded. It must strive continually to permeate that order with its own principles, to an ever-increasing extent. But its spokesmen ought to know that neither they nor anyone else will ever see a perfect social order on this side of the grave, and that the history of attempts to make Christian principles effective by means of legislation is not, upon the whole, encouraging. Legislation often seems to offer the reformer a convenient short-cut to his goal, especially if it be legislation by which he personally will be unaffected. But it is not uncommon for people who yield to the seductions of tempting short-cuts to wish that they had kept to the road before they reach their journey's end.

The third important episode in the life of the nineteenth-century Church was the conflict between religion and science.

It may be difficult for many people now to believe that until the middle of the last century the date 4004 B.C., which used to appear at the top of the pages of Genesis, was generally accepted as the year of the creation of the world. We owe the figure to James Ussher, who became Archbishop of Armagh in 1625, and he is said to have reached it by the simple method of adding up the recorded ages of the patriarchs. Its appearance "in the Bible" invested it, in many eyes, with the inerrancy attaching to the rest of Holy Writ. But presently Sir Charles Lyell, the geologist (1797–1875), and Sir Richard Owen, the naturalist (1804–92), began to point out that the earth must have existed and have been inhabited by beasts and men for a very much longer period. It might be possible to maintain that they were mistaken, at any rate for a time, but Darwin's *Origin of Species*, which was published in 1859, could not be overlooked. His theories, which if not entirely true were much nearer the truth than anyone had got before, could not possibly be reconciled with the picture drawn in the early chapters of Genesis. He held that all existing forms of animal life are derived from a much smaller number of much simpler forms by a process of gradual development which has been going on for thousands of years, if not for millions. The suggestion that we are descended from any form of ape, or even that apes and men have a common ancestor, proved particularly unpalatable in religious circles. Preachers asked their congregations scornfully whether they would prefer to look for our first parents in the garden of Eden or "in the gardens commonly called Zoological". It appeared to many people that if Darwin was right the title of the Bible to be counted inspired could not be maintained and that the entire structure of Christianity must fall to the ground. Nobody seemed to have recognized two important factors in the situation. First, that the Church has never attempted to define "inspiration": consequently its relation to historical inerrancy can be only a matter of opinion. Secondly, that what "Darwinism" made impossible was not belief in Inspiration in itself or as a whole, but only belief in an arbitrary theory of its nature, which was not much more than two centuries old. More than sixteen hundred years before Origen of Alexandria,[1] perhaps the most diligent student of the Bible who has ever lived, had written as follows:[2]

What reasonable man will think that there was a first, second and third day and evening and morning without sun and moon and stars? And what was the first day like without even a heaven? And who is so silly as to think that God planted a garden in Eden towards the east, as a human husbandman might do, and placed a tree of Life in it which could be seen and touched, so that a man who had tasted of the fruit with his

[1] C. 185–251.   [2] *Philocalia*, C. 1, n. 17.

physical teeth could receive life? And if God is said to walk in the garden in the cool of the day and Adam to hide under the Tree, no one, I think, will doubt that such things, which are figurative, convey certain deep religious truths by means of what seems to be history, but did not in fact take place. . . . And what need is there to say more, since anyone who is not absolutely blind can collect thousands of similar instances of things which are written as if they had happened, but did not happen as they are said to have done.

The allegorical method of interpreting Scripture which was characteristic of the scholars of Alexandria did not commend itself to those of Antioch. To us it must sometimes seem almost fantastic. But it was a way of dealing with the moral difficulties which the Old Testament must present to anyone who has no conception of a progressive revelation, which meant until very modern times Almost Everyone. It also recognized that the Holy Spirit can use other material beside facts to convey religious truth. In this respect its theory of Inspiration was better than the unimaginative literalism which dominated English thought until near the end of the last century, and was perhaps the worst legacy of the Reformation. Had it been generally known in England that such teaching as that of Origen was being given in the third century, as much of the conflict between science and religion as was concerned with Genesis need never have arisen.

If it would be too much to say that there are no matters with regard to which science and religion appear to be at variance, it is worth while to call attention to three factors which are sometimes overlooked:

1. The study of any form of natural science rests on the assumption that the physical order is at bottom rational. Otherwise it would not be intelligible, and to study it would be as futile as trying to make sense of combinations of letters which do not make real words in any known language, or to extract the square root of a surd. The further we go the more fully does the assumption appear to be verifiable by experiment. But in the nature of things it cannot be verified completely. It must always remain an

assumption. To stake a life's work upon its truth is an act of faith at least equal to anything demanded by the Christian creed.

2. The function of natural science is to observe processes as closely as possible and to describe them as accurately as may be. This is a difficult undertaking, and the whole world owes to the students of natural science a debt of gratitude for the standard of perseverance and laboriousness which they have set.

3. To describe a process is not, however, to explain it, and if students of natural science begin to speak of "causes" or "values", they have quitted their legitimate province for one in which their methods do not apply and their conclusions are likely to be open to criticism.

To us now the whole episode seems to have been born of unwarrantable assumptions by both sides and to do very little credit to anybody.

At about the same time another attack on Christianity developed. It was more formidable than its forerunner (which was for the most part concerned with part of the Old Testament only) and came from Germany. A group of German scholars set themselves to rewrite the early history of the Church on the assumption that SS Peter and Paul lived and died in irreconcilable hostility. The only foundation for this theory is the dispute to which St Paul refers in the second chapter of Galatians, with reference to the terms on which Gentiles could be admitted to the Church. The New Testament (it was asserted) was written about the middle of the second century to cover up this discreditable episode of nearly a hundred years before. It followed, therefore, that very little of it was what it professed to be. Acts was pure romance. These views were widely accepted in England, especially in intellectual or pseudo-intellectual circles. Respect for German scholars had not yet been shaken by the discovery that a German can combine learning and perversity in a way which no one else can rival.[1] And it is fair to say that up to this time German

---

[1] Nearly fifty years ago Dr Walter Headlam, whose pupil I had the good fortune to be, used to impress upon me that if a German was generally right in his facts he was almost invariably wrong in any conclusion which he drew from them. This was apropos of *Æschylus*, but the principle seems to apply in other fields as well.

work on the New Testament had been more thorough than ours.

In this controversy the historical value of the New Testament as a whole was at stake—a more important matter than the details of the Pentateuch. Three Cambridge scholars—Professors Lightfoot, Westcott, and Hort, of whom the first two were destined to become in succession bishop of Durham—were primarily responsible for its vindication and what may be called the rehabilitation of the several books (if not of their traditional authorship) has gone on ever since. A few years ago a scrap of papyrus was discovered which shows that the fourth Gospel was in circulation in Egypt before the year 120. This means that a good many opinions as to the date at which it was written and as to the personal relation of the author to the story which he tells have had to be revised.

An outcome of the Tübingen school (as it was called, from its headquarters in Germany), if not a direct product of it, was the "Liberal" views which obtained considerable currency during the second half of the century. Matthew Arnold[1] may be regarded as a typical exponent of them. These "Liberals" held that the Hero of the Gospel was primarily, if not solely, an ethical Teacher. Like many such, he aroused more opposition than he had anticipated by going further than he intended originally, and so his life ended in disaster. What the Church needs to do now is to clear away the cloud of legend which has gathered round him and so see him as he really was. We can admire his courage, insight and singleness of purpose without going further, and the more diligently the world tries to live by his teaching the better, even if it should turn out that he never really existed. This plausible theory overlooked two facts, either of which is fatal to it:—

1. Some of the epistles in the New Testament are considerably older than the Gospels. We must turn to them to see what the earliest Christians of whom we know anything thought of Christ. It is remarkable to see that there[2] during the lifetime of those who

---

[1] 1822–88; son of Thomas Arnold of Rugby.
[2] E.g. in Galatians and in 1 and 2 Thessalonians.

had known Him the "legend" appears full-fledged. Periodically ever since men have tried to reduce the story to something more commonplace. But their attempts have never been successful.

2. There is not the least likelihood that Christian moral principles will survive apart from the faith which gave them birth and sustains them from day to day. This is clearer to us now than it was even half a century ago. After all, the world does not need ethical instruction so much as moral powers. We all know well enough what we ought to do. Our real need is to find some inspiration sufficient to enable us to try honestly to live up to the best we can see, and to renew the effort after every failure. For this we must depend upon the influence of a living Person.

However, these "liberal" notions lingered on until after the beginning of the present century; principally, perhaps in academic circles. They could not survive the German invasion of Belgium in the summer of 1914, which showed how negligible is the moral restraint which civilization can impose on human savagery.

It has been said above that the most remarkable feature in the history of our Church during this period is its expansion beyond the seas. Two notable landmarks in the process are, first, the inauguration of the Colonial Bishoprics Fund in 1841, and, secondly, the holding of the first Lambeth Conference in 1867.

The former of these was set on foot by a letter from the Bishop of London (Charles James Blomfield) to the Archbishop of Canterbury (William Howley), who presided in person over the inaugural meeting held on 27 April at Willis's rooms, King Street, St James. It may therefore be regarded as a corporate act of the Church. Hitherto our work overseas had depended upon the energy of individuals. Now the Church as a whole was trying to meet its new responsibilities. Before the end of the year six new bishoprics had been established—New Zealand (now Auckland), Valetta[1] (moved to Gibraltar), New Brunswick, Cape Town, Van Diemen's Land[2] and Ceylon (now Colombo). Never before

[1] The capital of the island of Malta.
[2] When the name of the island was changed to Tasmania the title of the see was altered to correspond.

or since have we carried through so large a piece of overseas work in a single year.

The idea of the Lambeth Conference originated in Canada. Or, if that is an overstatement, the first definite step towards the summoning of it was taken there on 20 September 1865, when at a provincial synod the Bishop of Ontario moved that the Archbishop of Canterbury and the Convocation of his Province should be urged to adopt some means

> by which the members of our Anglican Communion (perhaps the first use of the phrase) in all quarters of the world should have a share in the deliberations for her welfare and be permitted to have a representation in one General Council of her members gathered from every land.

The resolution was adopted unanimously and was sent to Archbishop Longley together with a more personal appeal. He felt that it behoved him to act with caution, as there was a strong suspicion, or more than a suspicion, that the real purpose of the Conference was to obtain an endorsement of the action which Bishop Gray of Cape Town had taken against Bishop Colenso of Natal, whom he had excommunicated and deposed from his see for heresy.[1] That story is too long and intricate to be retold here, and belongs to the history of the Church of South Africa rather than to that of the Church of England. Two types of question were involved, theological and ecclesiastical. On the theological issue, especially as regards the historical accuracy of the Old Testament, most people today would say without hesitation that Colenso was right. On the ecclesiastical issue, where the question was what jurisdiction could be claimed by the see of Cape Town over the see of Natal, as the constitution of the Church in South Africa then stood, it is less easy to speak positively.

Colenso did not appear before Gray's "court", so was sentenced in his absence. He ignored the judgement, which was quashed by the Judicial Committee of the Privy Council, an authority which Gray refused to recognize, and is said to have described as "that masterpiece of Satan", an outburst occasioned apparently by the

[1] Colenso died in 1883.

fact that it had ruled in effect, if not in so many words, that he was not above the law nor Colenso outside its protection. The result was a schism which lasted until 1891 and, in very attenuated form, has lingered on until our own day. For fear lest the issues should be still further confused and the scandal aggravated if the Conference were to discuss the matter in any way, several of the English bishops, including the Archbishop of York[1] and the Bishop of Durham,[2] refused to come. But of the 144 invitations sent out 76 were accepted, and 72 bishops appear to have been present. The meetings lasted for three days, and the Conference was considered to have been so successful that it was decided to repeat it at intervals of years. This has been done as far as circumstances have allowed. The eighth was held in 1948 and lasted for five weeks: 325 bishops are said to have been present. We probably owe it to the astuteness of Archbishop Longley that the first Conference was not induced to put out some statement as to the nature of Inspiration and the inerrancy of Holy Writ which would have become untenable in a few years' time.

The period 1860–90 may be regarded as the culmination of what Dr Inge has called "the most wonderful century in human history".[3] The worst horrors of the industrial revolution were over and it was a period of readjustment and reform. High hopes for the future were entertained, if they were tainted by an almost superstitious belief in progress, which was not infrequently confused with material comfort. If the days of excessive privilege were ended, the domination of the half-educated had not begun. As at Athens after the deliverance from the Persians, there was a great flowering of art and literature. In poetry it is only necessary to mention Tennyson (1809–92), Browning (1812–89) and Coventry Patmore (1823–96); Wordsworth, Shelley and Keats belong to an earlier generation.

In prose there are Dickens (1812–70), Kingsley (1819–75), Ruskin (1819–1900) and Stevenson (1850–94). Today we think of Ruskin first as an art critic who made people see that Turner, who had died in 1851, was a very great painter, and second as a

---

[1] William Thomson.   [2] Charles Baring.
[3] *The Victorian Age*, p. 7 (C.U. Press, 1922).

social reformer to whom too little attention was paid. But whatever we may think of some of his theories and prejudices there can be no question that he was a great master of the English language. Thackeray, who died in 1863, may just be included. Mention must also be made of Meredith (1828–1909) and of Carlyle (1795–1881), if Bishop Creighton was justified in saying that if you take away his insolence and his Scotch accent there is not very much left.

In painting there are no rivals to Romney, Gainsborough and Reynolds, but the two Richmonds, George (1809–1906) and his son William, Leighton (1830–96), Millais (1829–96) and Watts (1817–1904), are not negligible figures. Mention must also be made of Samuel Cousins (1801–87), the greatest master of mezzotint we have ever produced. If architecture and music lagged behind as a whole, Pearson (1817–97) rises very high.

Before 1860 zeal for education had led to the carrying out of much needed reforms in the universities of Oxford and Cambridge as well as to the foundation of two new universities, Durham in 1832 and London in 1836 (many others have appeared since). The older public schools were also reformed in various ways and a number of new ones were founded on similar lines. Of these Marlborough has perhaps been the most successful and distinguished. The public school system is certainly not beyond criticism, but it has served the nation well upon the whole for nearly a century now. The new foundations seem to have been fortunate enough to secure very remarkable men as head masters in their early days, who gathered round themselves a distinguished company of assistants. So long as public schools can continue to do this they will flourish. But if their general standard should show a marked decline, parents in a less prosperous age may begin to doubt whether they are worth the money.

In 1870 a step of the greatest importance was taken when the State made itself directly responsible for the education of the poorer classes. Hitherto this had been left to voluntary effort. The religious bodies provided schools at their own cost, towards the maintenance of which the State since about the year 1830 made cautious contributions. The immense majority of these schools were the property of the Church, and the religion of the Church was taught in them in the Church's way. But the task had become more than voluntary effort could undertake successfully. Where the need was greatest, which meant in the poorer quarters of the large towns, the resources of the religious bodies were at their lowest. Accordingly the State decided to fill the gap (originally it did not aspire to attempt more) by building schools at the public expense. Nonconformists objected to the teaching of religion as the Church understands it in these schools, and while it was intended that religion should be taught in them it was decided that no formula "distinctive of any religious denomination" must be employed. In other words, religion must not be taught in the way which anybody really believed to be the best. Curiously this provision was not considered to exclude the Apostles' Creed. (Possibly Parliament thought that it really is the work of the Apostles. The fact that it is in substance the old baptismal creed of the Roman Church, and that it has never been accepted in regions in which the authority of the Papacy runs or has run, can hardly have been realized.) It was inevitable that undenominational religious teaching should prove ineffective, partly because it is impossible to find an undenominational teacher to give it, and partly because any presentation of Christianity which does not rest upon membership of a worshipping community will never make any deep or lasting impression upon those to whom it is offered. However good the syllabus provided may be (and it is only fair to say that some of those which have appeared in recent years are very good indeed), it can be worth very little divorced from the common Christian life and worship, which are only to be had by membership of the (or at least of *a*) Church.

It soon appeared that many of those who stood in most need of some education were least anxious to be educated, and it was thought advisable to make school attendance compulsory. Shortly afterwards fees in elementary schools were abolished. Both these steps were taken with the best intentions, but have proved mischievous. The life-blood of any system of education is the amount of interest taken in it by outsiders, especially by the parents of the children directly concerned. A system which is compulsory and free will command very little interest, especially when the parents are not ratepayers,[1] and no expenditure on equipment can make this loss good. If the results of the system of elementary education which has been in force for the last seventy years are disappointing, that does not detract from the credit due to the intentions of those who provided it. Their ideals were high if, largely on account of the two well-meant mistakes to which reference has been made above, the former of which was made by a Liberal Government, the latter by a Conservative, they have been very imperfectly realized.

By the end of the third quarter of the century we had given to India a measure of unity and peace which it had not known since the days of Akbar. In 1877, on the advice of Disraeli, the Queen assumed the additional title of Empress of India. Some people questioned the wisdom of this at the time. But it probably helped the nation as a whole to form a juster view of the greatness of our achievement. No one foresaw how soon the new title would have to be abandoned.

Ten years later the Queen celebrated the completion of fifty years upon the throne. She emerged from the seclusion in which she had immured herself since the death of the Prince Consort in 1861. The unpopularity in which this had involved her disappeared like a morning mist, and the remaining fourteen years of her reign were like a splendid sunset. The celebrations were mainly of a domestic character and emphasized the Queen's position as a matriarch. But they undoubtedly quickened national consciousness.

Ten years later a "Diamond Jubilee" was kept. The note struck was imperial rather than domestic, and London was filled with strange-looking warriors who had come from places of which many of those who stared at them had probably hardly heard. Taken as a whole, however, this function was less successful than its predecessor. Keen eyes could detect ominous cracks in

---

[1] Or are not ratepayers directly. When the rateable value of a house is below a certain amount the rates are payable by the landlord. He adds them to the rent, so the tenant who pays them ultimately is unlikely to be aware that he is doing so.

the imposing structure. On 20 June 1897 Dr Jex Blake, Dean of Wells preached a very remarkable sermon in the cathedral church from the text "A little one shall become a thousand, and a small one a strong nation."[1] He did full justice to the achievements of the Victorian age, but called attention to the inherent weakness of our position despite our very sudden rise to unparalleled prosperity and power. A few years were destined to make that plain to everyone. But unusual foresight and courage were needed to say it in the summer of 1897. One sentence may be quoted: "We may once again be standing on the brink of a great European war".

In little more than a year (September 1898, to be exact) we had delivered the Sudan from the bloodstained tyranny of the Khalifa who had succeeded the Mahdi, which meant that the peace and security of Egypt were assured. We regained possession of Khartoum and General Gordon was avenged. He had perished on 26 January 1885, when the city was captured by the Mahdi's forces. His peculiar combination of military prowess and religious fervour had caught the imagination of the public, and his death (which was due to the fact that the Government at home failed to give him adequate support) was felt to be a national disgrace. A Gordon Memorial College for the benefit of the natives was opened shortly afterwards, and the city is now the seat of a bishop.

After the decisive victory of Omdurman it seemed to many people, principally perhaps in academic circles, that the forces of the Crown had become virtually an anachronism. The Guards, and some other troops, would have to be retained in England for ceremonial purposes, and there would have to be a small army in India, chiefly to undertake punitive expeditions on the North-west Frontier. But it was regarded as axiomatic that we should never again be at war with a civilized power, and there was no savage one left which could put fifty thousand men into the field. A navy sufficient to undertake hydrographic work, and to suppress piracy and slave dealing as need arose, would meet all possible requirements. In less than thirteen months we found ourselves

[1] Isa. 60. 22.

obliged to declare war upon the Dutch republics in South Africa. At the time opposition to the war was strong at home. A foolish filibustering expedition known as the Jameson Raid, in 1896, which had come to complete disaster in four days, had done much to discredit us in the eyes of the world. It appeared to mean that we were set on war and were not sincere in any negotiations into which we might enter with Kruger, the President of the Transvaal. If portraits are to be trusted, his facial resemblance to Brigham Young, the Mormon "prophet" who established his adherents in what is now the State of Utah, was curiously close. The likeness between them seems to have been more than super-ficial. Both were religious fanatics,[1] and therefore entirely un-scrupulous in their policy. Both were ignorant of any world out-side their own immediate surroundings. Kruger refused point-blank to concede any political rights to the non-Dutch immigrants into his country, who in a generation had rescued it from bankruptcy and made it one of the wealthiest in the world per head of the population. English settlers in other parts of South Africa watched anxiously to see whether we could be trusted to stand by our fellow-countrymen should need arise. The campaign cost us more in men and money than had been expected. Possibly we looked for a second Omdurman. Our principal difficulties arose from the area of the theatre of war and from the mobility of the Boer commandos. As they did not wear any recognizable uniform they could disappear without difficulty when they were hard-pressed. At the beginning they outnumbered us considerably and their field artillery was superior. We made mistakes and they gained some victories which they were unable to exploit. At the end of two years organized resistance on the part of the Boers was over. Kruger took refuge in Portuguese territory and the Trans-vaal was formally annexed. A long period of guerrilla warfare ensued, which was finally brought to an end by Lord Kitchener. The British Empire had now reached its fullest extent, but Queen Victoria, who died on 22 January 1901, did not live to see the

---

[1] Kruger was nominally a Christian, if his religion owed more to the Old Testament than to the New. Young was the repository of a new revelation which made use of a few phrases borrowed from the Old Testament.

latest additions. There can be little doubt now that if the two
Dutch republics had not passed to our flag South Africa would have
been German before many years had passed. As it was, the German
flag might well have been hoisted at Cape Town in 1915 if Von
Spee's squadron had not been destroyed at the Falkland Islands
on 8 December in the previous year.

As a comparison between Kruger and Brigham Young has been
drawn, it may be worth while to mention that the Americans had
to fight a Mormon war, which proved much more troublesome
than they had expected, before the territory occupied, or at least
claimed, by the Latter Day Saints (as they termed themselves)
was incorporated into the Union as the State of Utah. This
episode does not seem to have attracted any attention in Europe.

Among the many valuable lessons which we learned from the
South African war was that we were extremely unpopular on the
Continent. How far this was a legacy from the bullying tactics of
Lord Palmerston half a century before, and how far it was due to
envy of our position in the world, is hard to say. But the fact was
beyond question. If either Germany or France could have intervened forcibly on behalf of the Boers they would certainly have
done so, and could have counted upon at least the goodwill of
Russia. The determined bid for sea power made by Germany from
1900 onwards, to which many people in England seem to have
been curiously blind, showed us that the days in which no one
could dream of disputing our maritime supremacy were passing
quickly, if they were not quite over.

If the period 1860–90 may be regarded as the climax of a
wonderful century, it was a golden age of the Church, as far as any
age can be considered to deserve that epithet. Speaking generally,
churches seem to have been better attended than they are now,
and the pulpit was a real power. When Henry Parry Liddon was a
canon of St Paul's (1870–90) his sermons, none of which took
him less than an hour to deliver, were an event in the life of
London. Many of the bishops were men of real distinction, and the
affairs of the Church attracted much more general attention,
especially amongst the educated classes, than they do now. Solid
religious books were read and discussed with very real interest

by the laity as well as by the clergy. It will be sufficient to refer very briefly to three such here:

1. *Essays and Reviews*, which appeared in 1860 and was condemned formally by Convocation. The best-known of the seven contributors were Frederick Temple, Head Master of Rugby,[1] who wrote on "The Education of the World," and Benjamin Jowett, Master of Balliol College, Oxford, who dealt with "The Interpretation of Scripture." His essay contained the sentence, "Interpret the Scripture like any other book." In many eyes this seemed to amount to a denial of its title to anything which could be called inspiration. It was, and perhaps is still, forgotten that he went on to say, "There are many respects in which Scripture is unlike any other book; these will appear in the results of such an interpretation." Few people would have much fault to find with most of the book now, and the excitement and interest which it aroused are not easy for us to understand. But it seems to have been read much more widely than any similar publication would be today.

2. *Supernatural Religion*. This work appeared in 1872. It was published anonymously, and rumour ascribed it to Connop Thirlwall, who had recently resigned the see of St David's. The author was in fact a Mr W. R. Cassels, who appears to have no other title to distinction. Briefly, he set himself to show, with an immense parade of learning, that early patristic literature is quite untrustworthy, so that its value for the light which it throws upon the general condition of the Church and the Canon of Scripture is virtually *nil*. It was, and was meant to be, subversive of the origin of traditional Christianity. It had an extraordinary vogue until Lightfoot,[2] who was then a canon of St Paul's, wrote a series of articles about it which appeared in the *Contemporary Review* between December 1874 and May 1877. He exposed the author's pretensions by showing that he had borrowed the work of others without acknowledgement and had not always understood what he was reproducing. This killed the book immediately. It is doubtful whether any work of this kind would attract so

---

[1] Afterwards Bishop of Exeter, then of London, and finally of Canterbury.
[2] Afterwards Bishop of Durham.

much attention now, and whether there would be any considerable public capable of appreciating the cogency of Lightfoot's
arguments.

3. In 1889 there appeared a volume which perhaps means more
to the present generation than either *Essays and Reviews* or *Supernatural Religion*. It was entitled *Lux Mundi*: *A Series of Studies in the
Religion of the Incarnation*. It was a collection of essays by a number
of men who were engaged in teaching at Oxford between the
years 1875 and 1885, and found themselves compelled by circumstances "to attempt to put the Catholic Faith into the right
relation to modern intellectual and moral problems." The contributors were all distinguished. Some of them in later years
achieved very high distinction indeed. The editor was Charles
Gore,[1] then Principal of the Pusey House at Oxford. The purpose
of the authors as expressed in the sentence quoted above would be
regarded now as almost a commonplace, or as stating a perennial
problem to which each generation must apply itself, if it cannot
hope to find anything approaching a final solution. Then it was
regarded as subversive, or at least as dangerous, and a good deal
of excitement seems to have been aroused. The editor seems to
have thought it not unlikely that he would be dismissed from
his post at the Pusey House. No similar book which has appeared
since (e.g. *Foundations* or *Essays Catholic and Critical*) seems to have
attracted nearly so much attention. The general interest taken in
such matters then was very real, if not always very well informed.
There does not seem to be anything like it now.

An important development in the life of the Church during the
second half of the nineteenth century was the foundation of
religious communities both for men and women. The first of
these, and perhaps the best known, is the Society of the Mission
Priests of St John the Evangelist, Oxford (commonly called the
Cowley Fathers), which began in 1866. The Community of the
Resurrection, now at Mirfield in Yorkshire, followed in 1892, and
the Society of the Sacred Mission at Kelham near Newark, in
1894. Others besides communities for women have arisen since.

---

[1] Afterwards in succession Bishop of Worcester, Birmingham and Oxford,
and one of the most influential figures of his time.

It was perhaps inevitable that such things should disappear completely, at any rate for a time, when the monasteries vanished in the sixteenth century, but lack of them has certainly impoverished the Church (the community at Little Gidding[1] can hardly have been intended to be permanent). As the monasteries were once the spearheads of the advance of Christianity in Saxon England, and subsequently strongholds of education and learning, it seems reasonable to hope that their modern representatives may have a great part to play, not only in our own country, in the near future. They have already done more than most people know, and are not likely to founder on the rocks which proved fatal to their medieval predecessors; or (if we prefer a different metaphor) to drift on to the shoals on which they stranded.

The same period may be regarded as the heyday of the country parsonage. If few of the country clergy were wealthy, most of them were not entirely dependent upon their professional earnings. Even when the tithe rent-charge, which was their main source of income, fell to little more than two-thirds of its nominal value[2] the parson still enjoyed a reasonable competence and could give his children the kind of education which he had himself received. Sometimes he was a scholar, and produced books of real value. When the village school depended upon him more than it does now, he was well fitted to take an active interest in it. Very often he was country bred and could take part in the general life of the countryside. He knew all his parishioners, whether they came to church or not, and was respected by them. If he knew less of liturgical matters than his successors today, and had never heard of psychology, his general influence for good, to which the well-ordered Christian household of which he was the head contributed not a little, was probably at least equal to theirs, and he never seems to have complained of not having enough to do. The quality of the family life of the Victorian parsonage is attested by the numbers of its sons and daughters who have served their generation well in Church and State,

[1] See above, Chapter 10.
[2] Due to the general decay of English agriculture and the importation of cheap corn from America and Australia.

sometimes rising to very high distinction.[1] The almost complete disappearance of houses of this type, brought about by a combination of economic and social factors for which no one can be held directly responsible, has been a loss to the nation which cannot be made good.

There are two more outstanding events belonging to this period which must be described briefly here. If many people today have hardly heard of either, each produced results of lasting—perhaps it would hardly be too much to say permanent—importance. Both fell within the primacy of Archbishop Benson (1883–96).

First, the Lincoln Judgement.[2]

By the year 1880 or thereabouts the ritual prosecutions had died down. They had proved futile and had brought no credit to anyone. The Public Worship Regulation Act of 1874 was obviously a dead letter. The Church Association, which had been the principal instigator of the prosecutions, found its funds declining and thought that it must make an effort to re-establish its power and prestige. It had not yet learned that its methods were foredoomed to failure, because religious ceremonial, so far as it is or may be considered to be a genuine expression of religious belief, cannot be dealt with in a purely legal way. Accordingly the Association, which had restricted itself hitherto to parochial clergy, decided to attack a diocesan bishop. The choice fell upon Edward King.[3] It was a bold one, because while he was what was then regarded as an extreme High Churchman, he was a man of saintly character and much beloved by his diocese. It was, of course, expected that the case would come before the Judicial Committee of the Privy Council. It was, however, certain that a large number of people would not respect any decision the committee might give on the ground that the court was not a spiritual one, which meant that the prospect of peace in the Church would not be improved.

Eventually the archbishop decided to hear the case himself. He

[1] See *D.N.B. passim.*

[2] For a summary of the proceedings see the *Life* of the Archbishop by A. C. Benson (one-volume edition, pp. 384–424).

[3] Bishop of Lincoln 1885–1910.

displayed a very high degree of courage in reaching this conclusion, for many people, including some of his closest friends, questioned the authority of any court which he could summon, and feared that any judgement which it might pass would be invalid in point of law. He was urged to veto the prosecution outright, as undoubtedly he had power to do. But this would have amounted to little more than "daubing a wall with untempered mortar."[1]

It so happened that Archbishop Benson was personally exceptionally well fitted to try a case of this kind. His interest in liturgical matters had always been keen and his knowledge of them was both wide and deep. He had as assessors the Bishops of London,[2] Oxford,[3] Rochester,[4] Salisbury,[5] and Hereford,[6] the last-mentioned taking the place of the Bishop of Winchester,[7] who was too ill to attend. Council for the prosecution were Sir Horace Davy, Q.C., Dr Tristram, Q.C., and Mr Danckwerts; for the defence, Sir Walter Phillimore, Mr Jeune, Q.C., and Mr A. B. Kempe.

A very important preliminary decision, on which the whole case was bound to turn, ran as follows:

> The Court is of opinion that when a Bishop ministers in any office prescribed by the Prayer Book he is a Minister bound to observe the directions given to the Minister in the Rubrics of such offices.

The case came on on 4 February 1890, and was heard by the archbishop sitting with his assessors in the library of Lambeth Palace. The actual charges brought had been reduced from ten to seven, and were as follows:

1. Mixing water with the sacramental wine during the Service and subsequently consecrating the Mixed Chalice.

The Mixed Chalice can be justified on purely historical grounds. In the world into which Christianity was born wine was habitually diluted with at least its own bulk of water, as spirits are amongst ourselves. To read any symbolism into the act is fanciful.

---

[1] Ezek. 13. 10–16.   [2] Frederick Temple.
[3] William Stubbs.   [4] Anthony Wilson Thorold.
[5] John Wordsworth.   [6] James Atlay.   [7] Edward Harold Browne.

2. Standing in the "Eastward" position during the first part of the Communion Office.

It may be necessary to explain to a later generation that the rubric which directs the priest to stand "at the north side of the Table" goes back to the time when the Table was usually placed east and west, so that it had north and south sides. Now it is habitually placed north and south (sometimes known as "altar-wise"), which means that it has east and west sides only. Ends are not sides. It is usually impossible for the minister to stand at the east side facing the congregation across it,[1] which would be perhaps the ideal position, and therefore to stand at the west side seems to be the most dignified and convenient position now. It does not imply any idea of sacrifice in any sense which the Church of England rejects.

3. Standing during the prayer of Consecration on the west side of the Table in such manner that the congregation cannot see the manual acts performed.

It is not easy to make them visible when the "eastward position" is adopted. Apart from the general principles of the Prayer Book that the whole service should be as open as possible, there seems to be no particular reason why they should be visible. Probably few people now care whether they are or not. The more recent practice of saying the Lord's Prayer at the beginning of the service in a voice so low that it cannot be audible to the congregation is a deliberate and more serious departure from the intention of the Prayer Book.

4. Causing the hymn *Agnus Dei* to be sung after the Consecration Prayer.

If a hymn is to be introduced into the service at this point this one is as suitable as any other which could be found.

5. Pouring water and wine into the paten and chalice after the service and afterwards drinking such water and wine before the congregation.

[1] As is the custom of the Pope at the high altar in St Peter's.

Considerations of reverence demand some simple and inconspicuous form of temporary cleansing before the vessels are removed from the church.

6. The use of lighted candles on the Table or on the retable behind it during the service when not needed for the purpose of giving light.

Their psychological value as a focus for the eye of the worshipper is obvious, and no particular doctrine need be associated with them.

7. During the Absolution and Benediction, making the sign of the cross with upraised hand facing the congregation.

This ceremony is hardly noticeable from the body of any but a small church.

The trial ended on 25 February 1890 but judgement was not delivered until 21 November. On the first charge it was against the bishop. Charge No. 2 was dismissed, as were charges 4, 5 and 6. With reference to charge 3, it was decided that not only is the minister not to conceal the acts of set purpose, but must do what he can to make them visible. The practice referred to in charge 7 was described as a "ceremony" not retained since it had not previously existed, but an innovation which must be discontinued.[1]

An appeal to the Judicial Committee of the Privy Council was heard during the months of June and July 1891 and dismissed on 2 August 1892, so the Archbishop's judgement was upheld. If as a whole it was to be accounted a victory for the High Church party it displayed a combination of learning, charity and common sense against which little could be said. It was as well received as it deserved to be, and certainly did a good deal to promote peace within the Church. But the archbishop was too clear-sighted not to discern how pitifully trivial were most of the points in dispute, and to recognize that a Church which appeared to consider such

[1] If the practice is not very common, this decision is not obeyed universally now.

minutiæ of primary importance would be unlikely to command the respect of the nation for long.[1] The generation upon whose horizon they loomed large did not suspect that the next would not only see the fundamental truths of Christianity denied and the moral law flouted openly, but would have to fight to preserve our national existence, knowing that if we fell the Church would fall too.

Secondly, the decision of the Papacy with reference to Anglican Orders.

To make the events of the years 1894–6 intelligible it is necessary to go back rather more than a generation. By the year 1880 or thereabouts it had become obvious that the "restoration of the hierarchy" carried out by Pius IX thirty years before had been a failure.[2] So far from disintegrating, the Church of England was showing unmistakable signs of new and increasing vitality. Accordingly the Pope found himself in the position of a sovereign who had annexed a foreign country with much circumstance only to discover after a generation had gone past that his troops were not within measurable distance of occupying it effectively, and that it had retained its own government, and intended to do so, without reference to his views or wishes. The position of the papal bishops who had been sent into England, in lieu of the former vicars apostolic who had shepherded the Roman Catholic congregations prior to 1850, was more awkward still. No one who professes any regard for catholic principles or the unity of the Church can acquiesce in the existence of two sets of bishops side by side, each laying claim to territorial jurisdiction in a country which has been Christian for centuries. Either the new-comers must return to the place whence they came, or they must be able to show that the bishops whose places they aspired to fill are bishops in name only, so that the country in question, despite its past history and present state, is as legitimate a field for missionary work as (say) India or China. Naturally the Papacy was not very anxious to adopt either alternative. But the question could not be allowed to slumber indefinitely. It was brought to a

---

[1] Op. cit., pp. 404–6.
[2] See above, Chapter 16, p. 342.

head almost by chance. It happened that Lord Halifax, who for many years past had devoted his wealth and his leisure (both of which seem to have been virtually unlimited) to advancing what he believed to be the highest interests of the Church of England, when paying a visit to the island of Madeira met a French priest, the Abbé Fernand Portal, belonging to the congregation of St Vincent de Paul, and afterwards a professor in the theological seminary at Cahors. The two men fraternized and discussed the question of possible reunion between the Churches of England and Rome, a matter which had long been of interest to the party of which Lord Halifax as president of the English Church Union[1] was the recognized leader. They came to the conclusion that the difficulties if great were not insuperable. The first requisite was to find some point of *rapprochement*, and it appeared to both that Anglican Orders might serve. Hitherto the Papacy had merely ignored their existence. Accordingly M. Portal published a pamphlet entitled *Les Ordinations Anglicanes* under the pseudonym of "Fernand Dalbus". He did not make clear, perhaps intentionally, what conclusion he wished his readers to draw. It created considerable interest abroad, and the Abbé Duchesne,[2] head of the French School of Archæology at Rome, whose name stood high in the world of learning, if it were not quite as distinguished as it was destined to become, reviewed the pamphlet in the *Bulletin Critique* and decided definitely in favour of Anglican Orders. Shortly afterwards M. Portal visited Rome and was received by the Pope and by Cardinal Rampolla, the Secretary of State. Omens seemed to be favourable, and in the month of September he visited Archbishop Benson in company with Lord Halifax at Dulverton, on the edge of Exmoor. The archbishop was wary and declined to commit himself to anything which might appear compromising. He knew that anything short of a personal letter from the Pope could be disavowed by the Vatican if convenient, and he could not appoint anyone to act on his behalf as the Pope could. The justice of his suspicion soon became apparent. Cardinal Vaughan delivered at Preston a speech which was remarkable chiefly for its vigour. He was neither

---

[1] Now known as *The Church Union*.   [2] Subsequently a cardinal.

a theologian nor a historian, but he could understand that any recognition of Anglican Orders must be fatal to his pretensions. On 22 April 1895, Leo XIII issued an encyclical letter *Ad Anglos* (To the English) which showed how little he understood the real state of affairs in England. The very existence of the Church of England was ignored, which meant that no idea of Reunion had ever crossed his mind. The absorption of English Christians into the Roman Church was all he had in view. This was followed in June 1896 by the bull *Satis Cognitum* (It is a matter of common knowledge), which merely repeats the familiar, not to say threadbare, statement about St Peter and his successors. On 13 September followed the bull *Apostolicæ Curæ*, in which Anglican Orders were dismissed as *absolutely null and entirely void*. The grounds of this sweeping assertion are *Deficiency of Form and Lack of Intention*. The older attempt to impugn the consecration of Archbishop Parker was wisely abandoned.

The *Answer* of the English archbishops was published on 29 March 1897. Its appearance had been delayed by the death of Archbishop Benson in October. It is believed to have been the work of Mandell Creighton[1] and John Wordsworth.[2] It shows that by *form* was meant no more than certain picturesque ceremonies which were not generally adopted until the fifteenth century and for that reason alone cannot be regarded as essential. *Intention* relates to the fact that at one time we did not after the words *Receive ye the Holy Ghost* add *"for the office and work of a priest"* (*bishop*). It may be held desirable that they should appear to make plain exactly what is being done. But as all Holy Orders must depend on the Divine Commission to the Apostles recorded in St John 20–23, the words used by our Lord there must be counted sufficient for the bestowal of any ministry which can be exercised in His name. To assert that they need amplification to become effective is certainly presumptuous, if not profane.

These documents were reprinted in Latin and English in 1932 by the S.P.C.K. for the Church Historical Society, and may be commended to any Englishman who has any qualms as to the

[1] Bishop of Peterborough 1891–3, of London 1897–1901.
[2] Bishop of Salisbury 1885–1911.

position of his own Church or any illusions as to that of the Church of Rome.[1]

About the year 1890 the religious climate of England began to change. It is hard to account for this; probably there was no single cause, but a number of factors contributed, amongst which the gradual secularization of education (especially in the elementary schools provided by the State) must be reckoned. General interest in Church matters began to wane and an ominous decline in the number of candidates for Ordination set in. In or about the year 1885 the figure had stood at about 870 per annum. By 1900 it had fallen to about 700, or little more, and the bishops of the populous urban dioceses began to lament the impossibility of obtaining an adequate number of assistant curates for work in the parishes. Hitherto the clergy had been drawn chiefly, if not entirely, from the professional classes and smaller landed gentry. As these sources seemed to be running dry, it was decided that recruits must be sought from lower social strata. The Society of the Sacred Mission at Kelham and the Community of the Resurrection at Mirfield gave a notable lead, and before long most dioceses had boards of their own for the purpose. If the vocations discovered were fewer and the quality of the men who offered themselves lower than had been hoped, a considerable number of very useful recruits was secured. It was not, however, sufficient to arrest the decline. By the year 1914 the figure was little more than 600, and it has never stood so high since. For more than a generation now the pastoral work of the Church has not been done as it used to be for lack of men, and the evil results of this neglect become steadily more apparent.

It is, of course, desirable that the ministry should as far as possible be recruited from every social stratum (as in fact it always has been), provided that its general level remains that of a liberal profession. But if a young man finds that as candidate for Holy Orders he can secure a better education than would otherwise be within his reach, and knows that admission to Holy

---

[1] For a further account of what passed see *A Roman Diary*, by T. A. Lacey (Longmans, 1910), the *Life of Archbishop Benson* (one-volume edition, pp. 492, 591), and the *Life and Letters of Mandell Creighton*, vol. ii, pp. 176–80.

Orders will mean immediate and permanent enhancement of his social status, it becomes additionally difficult for him to be sure of his own motives. Moreover, it seems to have been forgotten that men who could not pay for their own education would have very little if anything beyond their stipends on which to live afterwards, and would probably expect to marry at an earlier age than their predecessors had been in the habit of doing. Therefore, for every pound raised to educate them for the ministry, at least an equivalent sum should be set aside as capital to provide for their maintenance afterwards. If it should come about that most of the clergy were entirely dependent on their professional earnings, something not unlike a financial crisis would come upon the Church. Warnings to this effect were given from time to time, but no attention seems to have been paid to them.

It has become the fashion in some circles to disparage the Victorians in every way possible. Like all other generations, they made mistakes, for which their successors had to pay. But they had high ideals, and both preached and practised a gospel of integrity, industry and thrift. This enabled them to raise England to a position of pre-eminence such as no other nation has ever enjoyed. The Church kept step with the national advance.

Here I must bring these lectures to a close. No one knows better than I how much has been omitted which might have been said with advantage, and how much of what has been said might have been said better. I have tried to give you a series of pictures of our Church in relation to the national life as a whole and to show how and why it has come to be as we know it now.

My aim has been to give you a better understanding of the real character of our unique spiritual inheritance, and a deeper appreciation of its value. It is the best thing which we have to offer to the world today, and there can never have been a time when there was greater need of it.

Epilogue—1914–47

ON 4 August 1914 we declared war on Germany in fulfilment of our undertaking to come to the help of Belgium should need arise. The Germans could never understand why we felt bound to honour our pledge.

In any event, it is not easy to see how war between the two countries could have been averted for much longer.

Germany had climbed from obscurity to power by means of three short and successful wars—against Denmark in 1864, Austria in 1866 and France in 1870. A fourth might be expected to give her the supremacy she coveted and had come to regard as her due. Besides this, William II, who had succeeded to the throne very young, had lived in an atmosphere of flattery for so long that he regarded himself as an almost supernatural personage, at the head of an invincible nation. He was also anxious to make trial of his new fleet. It may not be known generally that the construction of the heavy German ships was such that they could never have been used at more than a few hours' steaming from their bases. This left no room for doubt where and against whom they were intended to be employed. The men did not live in them, but in barracks on shore, and they could therefore be divided into a larger number of separate compartments than ours, a fact which stood them in very good stead at the Battle of Jutland on 31 May 1916.

The struggle lasted until 11 November 1918, which was much longer than most people had expected at the outset. The Church lost a good deal of ground during those years, partly because the gradual dislocation of ordinary social life, and the inevitable increase of Sunday labour, especially upon the land, after the German submarines had brought us within measurable distance of starvation, interrupted the habit of church-going.

Besides this, in the eyes of many people moral problems are

quantitative, so that the unprecedented scale upon which the war was being waged seemed to place additional and almost insuperable difficulties in the way of believing in the goodness of God. In their own language, they "lost their faith." It would be nearer the truth to say that they found out how feeble and unreflecting it had always been. The situation was not improved by the assertions of some highly placed ecclesiastics that the war would lead to a great revival of religion. It did not seem to occur to these prophets that if they were right it would become very difficult to deny that war is a spiritual tonic which a nation needs from time to time.

During the years 1911–13 Archbishop Davidson had maintained an amicable correspondence with some well-known German divines, and seems to have accepted their protestations of friendliness at their face value. One of them, Professor A. Harnack, afterwards became distinguished even amongst his fellow-countrymen for the rancour with which he assailed England. Speaking in London on 25 March at a meeting of the British Council of the Associated Churches for fostering friendly relations between the British and German peoples, Archbishop Davidson said: "When people talk lightly of inevitable war they are creating the mischief which they profess to deplore. It is a notion absolutely untrue. We believe the thing to be morally impossible in view of our home responsibilities both in England and Germany."

The extent to which his wonted political sagacity had deserted him is shown in a letter which he wrote to Dr Dryander, Court Chaplain to the German Emperor, under date 11 June 1913: "At this moment everything is happily tending to a true understanding of the essential brotherhood of Germany and Great Britain."[1]

It must be presumed that these words represented his real opinion. But was it likely that the German High Seas Fleet would be left to rust at its anchors?

When the storm broke he was taken by surprise. Neither by temperament nor tradition was he the man to deal with a sudden emergency. It seems to have taken him, and the episcopate generally, nearly two years to grasp the character of the struggle

[1] *Life.* by G. K. A. Bell, vol. ii, p. 661.

and the magnitude of the effort which we should have to make to escape destruction. In the autumn of 1916 a *National Mission of Repentance and Hope* was launched, which does not appear to have produced very much effect. A large number of clergy were out of the country serving as chaplains to the forces, and most of the "Messengers" who were despatched to strange parishes probably felt that they would have been better employed at home amongst their own people. The events of the preceding months had been so harrowing that few people could respond to any additional emotional stimulus. By this time there were few families which had not lost a father, or a son, or a husband, or a brother, and the message which they needed was of another character. "Spiritualism" received a considerable impetus during these years.

For some years past the difficulty in the way of getting ecclesiastical Bills through Parliament had been very great and was not likely to diminish. However well disposed the Government of the day might be, the pressure of other business made it almost impossible for the House of Commons to find time for the discussion of Church affairs, which it was becoming less and less well fitted to undertake. Some modification of the relationship between the Church and the State had become desirable. During the later stages of the war a vigorous agitation was set on foot to secure such changes as its supporters thought necessary. In the early summer of 1917 it assumed the pretentious title of the *Life and Liberty Movement*, and its object was said to be "to win for the Church the liberty essential to fullness of life." This convenient phrase could be made to bear almost any construction which anyone might feel inclined to put upon it.

Many supporters of the movement were men of high repute, if the future prominence of some of them was hardly guessed. Their sincerity was beyond question. But for one reason or another most of them had had very little experience of ordinary parochial work, and had not seen active service. It was therefore doubtful how far they understood the situation with which they felt themselves competent to deal. They indulged freely in such expressions as " having reached the boiling point " and " going over the top " (the latter metaphor being derived from the trench warfare, in which most of them had taken no part), which were difficult to reconcile with the kind of temper by which the conduct of Church affairs ought to be directed.

The years 1917–18 were not favourable to dispassionate or careful consideration of anything. The general demoralization of war was being felt increasingly, and the whole atmosphere was feverish. Many of those who might have had much of value to say about any alterations in the relation between the Church and the State were serving their country overseas.

Archbishop Davidson was very well fitted to act as a restraining influence in such circumstances, and it is in all probability mainly due to him that the agitation did not lead to something like disaster. When far-reaching proposals, for many of which there was much to be said, were put forward, he warned the over-ardent that " it is obvious to everyone that it is impossible to make this a *fait accompli* during the war," as in all probability they had hoped and expected. Finally, on 23 December 1919 the Enabling Act received the Royal Assent.

By this Act, which owed its passage through Parliament chiefly to the patience and skill of the Archbishop and Lord Wolmer,[1] a fundamental change in the constitution of the Church was made. A new statutory body known originally as the *National Assembly of the Church of England*, and afterwards more briefly as the *Church Assembly*, came into being. It consists of three Houses, of Bishops, Clergy and Laity. The composition of the first two presented no difficulty. It was necessary only to take the Upper and Lower Houses of the Convocations of the two Provinces, after making some alterations in the system by which the Lower Houses were elected, which secured that the parochial clergy should always be in the majority. The House of Laity was less easy to provide. There had been a House of Laity in the Representative Church Council which had been in existence since 1903. But this body was no more than a debating society. It had no statutory authority, and it was difficult to see how it could be invested with any. Eventually it was decided that in every parish there was to be an " Electoral Roll " on which parishioners were invited to

---

[1] Afterwards Earl of Selborne.

inscribe their names. Each signatory had to state that he (she) "had been baptised,[1] was over 18 years of age, a member of the Church of England and not a member of any Body not in Communion with the Church of England." These electors were to meet annually and choose a Parochial Church Council. The Council was in its turn to elect representatives to the Diocesan Conference (now also a statutory body), the number being determined by the number of names on the parochial roll. The Diocesan Conference in its turn was to elect members to the House of Laity, the number being determined by the total number of names on the electoral rolls[2] of the Diocese.

It may have been impossible, partly on grounds of expense, to devise any more direct form of election to the Church Assembly. But it was fairly obvious that a method so indirect and cumbrous as the one adopted was unlikely to prove very successful. After more than twenty years' experience this part of the scheme has to a large extent been a failure. People have shown themselves reluctant to enter their names on the electoral roll, which is therefore untrustworthy as an index of the real strength of the Church, and in the large urban parishes in which the population changes continually the task of keeping the roll accurate is almost impossible. Little interest is taken in the Annual Church Meeting, and in many parishes the Council can hardly be said to have an effective existence. The parishes in which it is a real help to the incumbents seem to be few.

Two points seem to have been overlooked by the promoters of the scheme, who were intent on securing new administrative facilities, the importance of which they probably overrated:

1. They had transferred the Church from its immemorial territorial basis to a congregational one, thereby coming at least very near to making it one denomination amongst many, instead of the Church of the land. It is impossible to say yet what the outcome of this will be.

[1] Many thought that Confirmation ought to have been made the necessary qualification.
[2] It is said that they were very commonly called *electrical*, a word which at any rate meant something to most of those who inscribed their names.

2. If something like 80 per cent of the members of the Church of England are to be found today in populous urban parishes, something like 70 per cent of the parishes are small rural ones. Yet each parish, however large or however small, is a unit in the Church's system. Whether new administrative arrangements or legislation equally suitable to both can be devised remains to be seen. The Church Assembly hardly seems to be aware of the difficulty. Naturally most of the members of the House of Laity belong to urban parishes in "residential neighbourhoods."

In place of the Ecclesiastical Committee of the Privy Council an Ecclesiastical Committee of both Houses of Parliament was created, to consist of fifteen members of the House of Lords nominated by the Lord Chancellor and fifteen members of the House of Commons nominated by the Speaker. When a measure has been passed by the Assembly it has to lie upon the table of the House of Commons for forty days. At the end of that time, if the Committee so advise, it receives the Royal Assent and acquires the force of an Act of Parliament. Parliament can pass or reject it *in toto*, but cannot introduce any amendment.

If Archbishop Davidson was not fitted to lead the nation in a time of crisis, he was in his element during all the negotiations and discussions which led to this result. Speaking in the House of Lords on 3 June 1919, he said:

> "My Lords, I ask your Lordships to give a Second Reading to a Bill to enable the Church of England to do its work properly,"

and added:

> "Its opponents—and there may be some of them in this House—descry in it perils which I think are quite imaginary or are no greater than those which attend all brave and adventurous legislation. These fears I altogether repudiate. As to its friends, I find a little difficulty in making my own all the hopes and ambitions which have found eloquent expression in the fine body of men and women who have advocated it."[1]

Bell, op. cit., vol. ii, p. 975. For a further account of the general proceedings see pp. 956–80.

It was perhaps unfortunate that the Church Assembly began its career amid a chorus of eulogies from most members of the episcopate which many people thought extravagant. The clergy, who knew much more of the real facts of parochial life, were less sanguine. They recognized that the elaboration of ecclesiastical organization has very little to do with the increase of true religion, with which alone they are concerned, and foresaw that the business of the electoral rolls, etc., would mean a considerable addition to the kind of administrative work which is continually thrust upon them to the detriment of the duties which they were ordained to discharge. They also feared that they would become more deeply immersed in the raising of money, a task of which the Church Councils were supposed to relieve them. But they hoped for the best and tried loyally, for the most part, to work a system in which they did not really believe.

The attempt to revise the Prayer Book came to an ignominious end in 1928, when it was defeated for the second time in the House of Commons by a small but sufficient majority. Probably few people really desired it very much, but many members of Convocation or of the Church Assembly felt bound to vote for it, because most if not all the bishops thought they ought. It is probable that most of the bishops were more intent on securing a disciplinary instrument than upon anything else. For that purpose it might or might not have proved effective.

It would be out of place to attempt to give an account of the Church Assembly here. From the year 1922 onwards some information as to its doings can be gathered from the Prefaces to the annual issue of *Crockford's Clerical Directory*. A selection from them was published in 1947 by the Oxford Press under the title *Crockford Prefaces: The Editor looks Back*. It will be enough to say that, speaking generally, the Assembly's record for intelligence, wisdom, foresight, and grasp of the real nature of any problem with which it has had to deal between the years 1921 and 1945 will stand comparison with that of the House of Commons during the same period.

APPENDIX A

Persecution

NO one to-day would wish to defend the persecution of heretics: that is to say, of one set of Christians by another on the ground that their interpretation of the Gospel is erroneous. Nor can anyone deny that such persecution has taken place in the past, or that it is a dark stain upon the history of the Church. But the truth of the matter is so often misunderstood, and the facts are so often misrepresented, that it is worth while to say something about it here.

There can be no question that Christianity is entirely opposed to all forms of persecution;[1] but it is not always recognized that in this respect it is unique. When we condemn persecution in principle we are, in fact, influenced by the Christian spirit, whether we know it or not. Our condemnation cannot therefore be extended to the Church as a whole. It can only cover those occasions on which the Church has departed from its own principles; and whenever such departures have been made voices of protest have always been raised within the Church itself.

The common belief that paganism was naturally tolerant and that the Church originated persecution is entirely untrue. Plato (428–347 B.C.) may be regarded as standing at the apex, morally and intellectually, of the pre-Christian civilization of Europe. In the *Republic*, in which he draws a picture of an ideal State, he shows himself no friend to liberty in any form. In the *Laws*[2] he goes further, and lays down that persecution ought to be a permanent feature in the working of any well-ordered State. No one must refuse to practise the religion of which the State approves, nor practise a private one concurrently. Disobedience to this rule must be punished: if it is persistent, with death.

The tenor of the *Twelve Tables*, which date from about the

---

[1] The *locus classicus* is Luke 9. 55–6.   [2] 908–10.

388

middle of the fifth century B.C., and were regarded by the Romans as the foundation of their whole system of jurisprudence, is similar. Only such religion as the State sanctioned was allowed.[1] As the Roman State extended its frontiers it found that it had to acquiesce in a variety of cults, side by side with the religion which it approved. These "allowed religions" (*religiones licitæ*) eventually became numerous. The ground of permission was usually that of race. This admitted Judaism, but not Christianity. There is, however, a very wide difference between licensing a number of subsidiary cults for certain specified reasons, and religious toleration as Christianity understands it. The truth is that mankind as a whole has always regarded persecution as natural and necessary. (Witness the relations between Hindus and Moslems in India at the present day.) Christianity alone has taken a different line, partly because it does profess to be concerned with truth, and it is almost a matter of common sense that truth can only make its way by persuasion and voluntary acceptance.

The real question therefore is, How did it come about that from time to time any part of the Christian Church sank to the level of the world sufficiently to readmit the immemorial and universal practice of persecution? The answer (which does not amount to justification) is not entirely simple. It is to be found in the relation between the Church and the civil power. It is sometimes forgotten that persecution can never be undertaken without the consent, at least, of the civil power. Usually the civil power has contributed very active assistance.

In the long run government is possible only by consent. If a ruler cannot make his authority respected, he will find that he cannot rule. Violence, which sometimes appears to be a tempting short-cut to success, is foredoomed to failure. The larger and the more diversified the region to be governed, the more acute the difficulty of finding a basis for authority which will command sufficient respect to make the business of government possible.

For nearly three hundred years the Roman Empire, which

---

[1] *Separatim nemo habessit deos.*

extended from the Atlantic Ocean to the south-western corner of the Caspian Sea, and from the line Tyne—Rhine, Danube—Crimea—Caucasus as far south as the fringe of the Sahara and the Cataracts of the Nile, found the basis which it needed in the person of the emperor, who was to be accounted divine—at first only after his death, subsequently during his lifetime. The system worked extremely well, until the Christian population of the empire became sufficiently numerous to render it impracticable. After the failure of Diocletian's policy of persecution,[1] Constantine took the Church as the basis of his authority. He saw that to be completely effective the Church must be united. He found it divided by a dispute which had originated at Alexandria, known as the Arian heresy. (It will be enough to say here that as it related to the Person of Christ it went to the very heart of Christianity.) Accordingly in the year 325 he summoned a council of bishops, over which he presided in person, with a view of composing the dispute. The Council was not successful, but it was momentous. The absolute master of the world, who had been born and brought up in the tradition of a totalitarian State, recognized that the right way to deal with religious differences is by discussion and argument, and not by violence. Nicæa set a standard for all time. That standard owed its existence to Christianity.

The emperor Theodosius (378–95) found the dispute still alive. Despairing of other methods, he banished the Arians from the empire. It does not appear that he molested them personally in any other way. But his need for a united Church was so great that he felt that he could not tolerate them within his dominions. He was the last man to attempt to rule the whole empire. The task had become impossible. After his death it was partitioned formally between his sons.

In the sixth century Justinian, who reigned over the eastern empire (the western had ceased to exist) from Constantinople, took a further and still more momentous step. His difficulties were very great. His heterogeneous dominions had no natural cohesion and were threatened by the rising power of Persia, as

---

[1] See Chapter 1, p. 21.

well as by internal factiousness. A united front was necessary if the empire were to survive, and nothing could provide this except a united Church. Accordingly he encouraged the bishops to seek out heretics and bring them before the civil authorities for punishment. This made them a species of police, and laid the responsibility for the stability of society and the efficient working of the machinery of government upon the Church.

It might have been better had the bishops refused the responsibility. But the emperor had appealed to them to save the State, as they alone could. Can they be blamed for having responded to the call?

When the barbarous kingdoms which arose on the ruins of the western empire became Christian (Saxon England among them) and developed sufficiently to be termed States, the rulers of them found that the authority of the Church was more august than their own. Naturally they relied upon it for the support which they needed, and bishops and other ecclesiastics were employed more and more in the functions of civil government. The fact that they were almost the only people who could read or write naturally contributed to this. And so the Church became, inevitably (as far as any historical development can be considered inevitable), the foundation of the State to an extent difficult for us at this distance of time to understand. All law and order depended upon respect for its authority. A heretic did not respect the authority of the Church, and it might therefore be assumed that he was unlikely to respect any other. He was a public enemy, potential if not actual, and had to be treated as such. The executive power was weak and therefore could not run the risks which a modern State, possessing a standing army and artillery, need not fear.

In England toleration, religious and political, established itself pretty firmly during the seventeenth century. The last issue of the writ *De heretico comburendo* was in 1612, when Edward Wightman was burned for heresy at Lichfield on 11 April. The statute had been provoked by the extravagances of the Lollards during the reign of a weak sovereign whose title to the throne was questionable. It was passed in 1401, and repealed in 1677.

During the reign of William III toleration became general, if it was not so complete as in our own day. This was not due so much to any moral or intellectual advance as to the fact that government came to rest more upon ideas of other kinds, so that the interest of the State in religion became less intimate and direct. A State has to be very sure of itself before it can afford to be tolerant in matters of religion or politics. Between the years 1939 and 1945, when the existence of the British State was imperilled, a number of people were imprisoned without trial, under regulation 18B, because they were reputed to hold political opinions which the Government thought dangerous. This was persecution. If no one liked it, almost everyone admitted that in the circumstances it was justified. The events of the last thirty years have shown us that even in Europe the edifice of toleration which has been built up, stone by stone as it were, during more than a thousand years, is not as stable as we used to suppose.

If we condemn the Church for having lent itself to persecution, it is only just to take into account the extent to which the evil prevailed. Popular imagination has exaggerated it very considerably.

The Inquisition, which we are justified in regarding as odious, never existed in England. It had the approval and support of the princes within whose territories it worked because it made the business of government easier. It amounted to a form of secret police. Its operations were never so widespread or so merciless as is commonly supposed. Sometimes the sentence imposed no more than a mild penance, such as wearing a cross of brightly coloured cloth on the back for a time. (*The Scarlet Letter*, by Nathaniel Hawthorne, describes a similar "penance" in New England at a much later date.)

Bernard Gui,[1] who worked in France during the early part of the fourteenth century, was a vigorous and efficient inquisitor. Between the years 1308 and 1323 he passed six hundred and thirteen sentences upon heretics. Of these only forty-five, an average of three annually, handed the offender over to the

1 *Mediæval History and the Inquisition*, by A. S. Turberville, p. 227.

secular arm, which meant death, probably by burning alive at the stake. We may think that a total of forty-five death sentences was forty-five too many, but such would not have been the view of the time. The humanitarian ideas of our day were not current in the fourteenth century.

St Thomas Aquinas had argued that if a coiner was put to death (as he was in England until after the beginning of the nineteenth century), how much more ought a heretic to be, because to adulterate the truth which God has revealed is obviously worse than to adulterate the coin of the realm. We need not endorse his conclusion. But there is something to be said for the view that religion is at least as important as money.

The conclusion of the whole matter amounts to this:

Persecution has never been a Christian principle. Deeply as we are bound to deplore its existence within the Church, truth compels us to recognize that its appearances have been fitful and sporadic. They have been due to the fact that the rulers of the Church have sometimes gone further than they ought in the direction of lending to the State the support which it demanded of them, without which it believed that it could not continue to exist.

A national Church will probably always need to be on its guard against compromising its principles through over-anxiety to help the State; especially during a national crisis, such as war.

The substance of what has been written above appeared in four articles which I contributed to the *Ripon Diocesan Gazette* during the years 1943–4.

For further study of the question the reader may be referred to the *History of the Inquisition of the Middle Ages*, by H. C. Lea, and to Bishop Creighton's Hulsean lectures, *Persecution and Tolerance*. These were delivered during the years 1893–4 and were republished in 1906.

APPENDIX B

The Monasteries

A sermon preached in the Abbey Church of Pershore on 4 July 1946, with the title *Lessons of the Past*. The occasion was the annual festival of the "Friends of Pershore Abbey".

Much of it is applicable to monasteries in general, whether their Churches have been preserved for parochial use, as at Pershore, Hexham, Tewkesbury, Bolton and Bath (to mention a few well-known instances), or whether they have become entirely ruinous, as at Glastonbury, Kirkstall, Furness, Rivaulx and elsewhere.

My debt to a sermon preached at Pershore on 29 June 1889 by Mandell Creighton and published subsequently in *University and Other Sermons* is large and obvious.

"Hearken to me, ye that follow after righteousness, ye that seek the Lord: look unto the rock whence ye are hewn, and to the hole of the pit whence ye are digged." (Isa. 51. 1.)

FEW Churches in England can look back over a longer history than this.

Pershore Abbey was founded 689, some years before my own church at Wells, to be a missionary outpost in south-western Mercia, which was still a heathen land. It would not be easy to exaggerate the debt which we owe to the monasteries. The western Roman empire broke down in the fifth century, and as its ruins crumbled Western Europe sank deeper and deeper into barbarism. During that period the monasteries were almost the only lights in a very dark world. They were centres of religion and of civilization. As much of the older civilization as was preserved, perhaps as much as could be preserved, was kept alive within their walls. Almost all the Greek and Latin books which have come down to us are those which monks thought worth reading and copying.

And the monasteries were not only centres of learning, religion and education. They were even more than that. They put work into its proper place. In their view regular work, whether with the hands or the head, or with both, is not only or even primarily our means of gaining a livelihood. Still less is it something which must be got through with as little trouble and for as much pay as possible. It is a man's offering to his Maker, and must therefore be as perfect as it lies in him to render it. In that view of work there is an inspiration which can help drudgery from becoming intolerable, and rouse us to the very best of which we are capable. It has disappeared from our world. I need not labour the difference which its restoration would make.

In England our debt to the monasteries is especially large. When Christianity came to our shores, at the end of the sixth century and the beginning of the seventh, monastic institutions were firmly established in Western Europe. St Augustine, the apostle of Kent, was a monk, as were all his companions. St Aidan, the apostle of Northumbria, to whom we owe perhaps even more, came from the monastery of Iona. As Christianity spread west-wards and southwards over our land monasteries sprang up— indeed, they were the very spearhead of the advancing hosts. The Danish invasions brought them very low. They were easy to find and worth the plundering. But after King Alfred's victories in the ninth century they renewed their youth in the tenth.

There are few sadder or more perplexing chapters in our history than the gradual petrification (there is really no other word for it, unless we like to borrow from the vocabulary of medicine and say "arterio-sclerosis") of the monasteries after about the year 1200. Somehow there seemed to be less and less for them to do. When Henry VIII laid violent hands upon them, they had been growing steadily more and more unpopular for some three hundred years. Perhaps they were ruined by the weight of their own success. At the final dissolution in 1536 there were about six hundred of them, and there had been more. They are believed to have owned at least one-quarter of the soil of England, and that at a time when the land was a much larger part of the whole wealth of the nation than it is today. They had become more than either the Church or the nation could bear. They were not, as is sometimes represented, hotbeds of vice, if there were black sheep to be found here and there. But it was hard to see what good they were doing, or to justify their continuance on such an enormous scale. The nunneries had really ceased to be religious in any but the technical sense. They had become not unlike the residential clubs in which some unmarried women live today. But if far-reaching changes were overdue, it is difficult to deny that they could not have been carried out in a worse way. The measure of an abuse may sometimes be the violence of the reaction which it provokes. And the reaction may prove to be almost as mischievous as the abuse.

The plundering of the religious houses was often quite shameless. No one can tell how much that was beautiful and interesting was destroyed. At least the libraries could have been preserved, and have found permanent homes with the cathedral chapters, the episcopal palaces and the colleges of Oxford and Cambridge.

Something, however, was saved from the wreck. Five new and needed bishoprics were founded and endowed with monastic property. Five great monastic churches became cathedrals. The colleges of Oxford and Cambridge also received something. They were now serving learning and education, as the monasteries had ceased to do long since. But much cruel wrong was done, and the disappearance of groups of kindly landlords and genial country gentlemen dislocated the economic life of many a countryside. If a moral is to be drawn, it would appear to be that it is impossible to live for ever upon a tradition, however venerable and august. It is the equivalent of living on capital. The process must end some day, and the end may come very suddenly. Institutions which cannot find room for new ideas, or adapt themselves to new climates of thought and feeling, will surely perish like the huge prehistoric beasts whose fossilized remains can be seen in our museums. Apparently they died because a changed world could support them no longer. We who are sons and daughters of an ancient nation, heirs and trustees of an ancient church, can never afford to forget that. Many monastic churches were pulled down and sold for whatever the materials would fetch. Some were preserved and passed to parochial use. This is one of them. I believe this noble building was threatened with demolition, but the people of Pershore would not suffer it. They bought the church or at least a part of it, from the Royal Commissioners. I do not know whether the price they paid has been recorded. But the effort must have been great, and the sacrifice real. In this way it became their very own. Many of our parish churches have been the gift of pious and wealthy individuals, to whom honour and gratitude are due. But such gifts can never be quite as what has been won by the common effort and sacrifice of a community. It may be that there are some here today who are descended lineally from the very men who rose up more than four hundred years ago to save the abbey church of Pershore from the destruction with which it was threatened and to start it upon a new and wider career of service to God and man.

For my own part I think that architecture is at least the equal of any art—partly because the architect has more difficulties to overcome than the poet, or the painter, or the musician. No community can have a more precious possession than a great building. And if that building has been designed for the worship of God, the highest activity of which the human spirit is capable, it can lay every other art under contribution. In a great church every art by and through which the spirit of man can express his effort to reach upwards to his Maker can be brought together and blended into one inspired and inspiring harmony. Here form, colour and sound can combine to the glory of the Most High.

Bishop Creighton has said that the real history of England is provincial history. Despite its size and wealth, London has never dominated England as Paris has always dominated France. We have never had anything resembling the city status of ancient Greece or medieval Italy. Our political structure, and until very recent times our social and economic structure as well, has been founded on the small, self-governing, mainly rural community. As Christianity conquered the land the unit became, as a rule, the parish. Our forefathers met together informally at first to discuss and settle their own affairs. In this way they learned little by little to listen to different opinions and to weigh them. They found out that the business of government is seldom quite as simple as it appears to be to those who have never tried their hand at it. And so gradually, not without mistakes and failures, we developed that respect for law and respect for freedom which is characteristic of our race, and perhaps the best contribution which we have to make to the common welfare of mankind.

We know that if law is not respected freedom will disintegrate into anarchy, and that if freedom is not respected law will harden into despotism. Neither danger is ever very remote. The Christian religion is our only safeguard against them, because it declares that anarchy and despotism alike are utterly alien from the mind of God.

This respect was born in our small self-governing communities. It grew up there and will, I think, always have to be kept alive principally by them.

No doubt some future generation will regard the nineteenth century as one of the great flowering periods of our race, comparable with the thirteenth and the sixteenth centuries. But there are certain features presented by it which we cannot but regret. One is the concentration of more than half the population into towns so large that they cannot really be styled "communities." Where the population is numbered by many hundreds of thousands what may be called "community sense" cannot develop. Worse than that, it is almost bound to be destroyed. It is always noticeable that in very large towns respect for law and respect for freedom tend to sink to a low ebb. People are becoming aware of that, and various remedies are being proposed. Most of these are rather artificial. It is impossible to create a community at will, though quite easy to build a new town and stock it with people. A community has to be a slow growth, like a woodland. And it is therefore to the small communities which escaped the steam roller of nineteenth-century urbanization, and can look back over a history of many centuries, upon places such as this, that we must rely for the preservation of the tradition upon which our national life has been built. A number of people do not become a community until they have some object of common interest, and some source of common pride—above all, until they are conscious of some common purpose. And what can provide all this more effectively than a great and noble building which is the visible centre of their common life? Any piece of great architecture will serve. But obviously none can be comparable with a church. A church focuses and promotes our highest aspirations and least selfish interests as nothing else can. It is the common concern of all, the one place where differences of age or station, occupation or temperament, cease to have any meaning, because all who come there come on equal terms as children in their Father's house.

You here are especially fortunate. There can be few places indeed which possess a parish church so noble, which after various vicissitudes is so entirely your own. Still fewer which can look back over a longer history. As this church was saved from destruction four hundred years ago by men who understood its value, so now it is preserved with jealous and loving care, not merely as a survival from the past. What better focus for its common life, and inspiration for its daily tasks, could any community desire? I can express no higher hope than that you may continue to show yourselves worthy, increasingly worthy, of this building, this ancient and splendid inheritance.

APPENDIX C

England and the Papacy 1547–1929

From the death of Henry VIII to the Restoration of the temporal power

THE defection of half of Europe stung the Papacy into action, and the Council of Trent, which sat at intervals from 13 December 1545 to 3 December 1563, carried out considerable reforms. It did not, however, attempt to go deeper than administrative abuses. Meanwhile a very remarkable movement known as the Counter-Reformation, in which the recently formed Order of Jesuits took a very active part, regained for the Roman Church large territories which looked as if they had been lost for ever.

The relations between England and the Papacy, which had been resumed on the old footing during the reign of Mary Tudor, remained undefined for a few years after her death. "Armed neutrality" is perhaps a fair description of them. Eventually Pius V considered (possibly the fact that the King of Spain had one viceroy at Naples and another at Milan helped him to make up his mind) that the time had come for a decisive step to be taken. By a bull *Regnans in excelsis* (He who reigns on high), which was published on 25 June 1570, he declared Elizabeth to be a heretic and deposed her from her throne, leaving it open to any prince of the Roman allegiance to add her kingdom to his own dominions. Only Philip II of Spain was in a position to take advantage of this permission, and he considered that England ought to be his in right of his wife. It is doubtful whether the King of France would have welcomed this arrangement, for, as Spain already ruled in northern Italy and the Netherlands, if England had passed into Spanish hands France would have been surrounded on every side and all but debarred from access to the vast lands which were beginning to be recognized as important sources of wealth and power on the other side of the Atlantic.

Everybody knows the sequel. The Pope and the King of Spain were the first two continental potentates, if not the last, to discover that England cannot be intimidated, and that while its conquest by force of arms is obviously not impossible, the undertaking is likely to present a number of unforeseen and formidable difficulties.

During the seventeenth century the chief fear of the Papacy was Gallicanism—that is to say, lest France, which was taking the place of Spain as the most powerful State in Europe, should break away and form a national Church. It is said that the accession of William III to the throne of England was viewed with favour at Rome, because it was thought that if James II were kept upon his throne, or restored to it, by Louis XIV, England might become Roman Catholic in faith, but in conjunction with France would reject the papal supremacy. The combination of the two would be overwhelming.[1]

During the eighteenth century the Papacy sank to a very low ebb. Any hopes which it may have entertained in relation to the later Stuart princes were destroyed at Culloden (16 April 1746), and as the century drew to a close some people thought that it would cease to exist. During the second half of the nineteenth century it recovered remarkably in the course of the two longest reigns in its history—that of Pius IX from 16 June 1846 to 7 February 1878, and that of Leo XIII from 20 February 1878 to 20 July 1903. During this time direct contact with England was restored after an interval of two hundred and seventy-eight years.

On 16 November 1848 a revolution broke out at Rome and Pius IX fled for his life. The story goes that he quitted the city disguised as a footman behind the carriage of an English lady. From Gaeta he wrote on 4 December to Queen Victoria to the effect that it would be a gracious act on her part to restore him

[1] About the year 1525 there had been a proposal to make Wolsey Patriarch of Gaul and to detach the Churches of England and France from the Papacy. (Acton, *Historical Essays and Studies*, p. 20.)

to his throne. She sent him a civil letter beginning "Most Eminent Sir".[1]

In and about the year 1845 several men who had been prominent in the early stages of the Oxford Movement became Roman Catholics. John Henry Newman, who had been vicar of the university church at Oxford and was destined eventually to become a cardinal, was the most distinguished of them. The importance of this was probably exaggerated at Rome, and Pius IX thought that the Church of England, which he would probably have described as the *Anglican Schism*, was dying a natural death. Accordingly in 1850, when he had been happily re-established on his throne by Napoleon III (who was anxious to conciliate the catholic and royalist parties in France) and was maintained there by a French garrison in the castle of St Angelo, he thought that the time had come to administer the *coup de grâce*. In somewhat flamboyant language (at any rate to English ears) he "restored the hierarchy".[2] That meant that he divided the map of England into a number of dioceses, and set over each a bishop with a territorial title, Westminster, Clifton, Portsmouth, Nottingham, and so on. He had misjudged the situation as completely as Pius V had done. His action provoked an explosion of resentment in England which appears to us now to be out of all proportion to its importance. The act amounted to no more than a paper transaction. The new bishops had no legal status and could exercise no rights or powers which the ordinary principles of religious toleration as recognized by our laws did not allow already to any ecclesiastics not in communion with the Church of England.

Time went on, and the position of these bishops and their successors became anomalous, because the Church of England did not die. It is contrary to every principle of Church Order to have two sets of bishops in the same country independent of each other, and both professing to represent the ancient Church of the land. It can be justified only if one of them must be considered to consist of bishops in name only, who do not exercise the

---

[1] *Letters of Queen Victoria*, ed. A. C. Benson and Lord Esher, vol. ii, pp. 204, 210.

[2] See below, Chapter 16, p. 342.

episcopal office as the Church Catholic has understood it at least since the second century, if not for longer.

In the year 1894 a small group of English and French theologians met to see whether it would be possible to get the Pope to recognize the "validity" of Anglican Orders.[1] Such discussions are not likely to be very fruitful unless the two parties can agree on some standard and test of "validity." "Valid" can mean either "authorized" or "effective" or both, so that the questions arise immediately, "What authorization can be regarded as adequate?" and "What degree of effectiveness is essential, and how can its presence in any given instance be determined?"

Before the discussions had been carried very far the Pope decided that they had better be brought to an end. On 22 April 1895 Leo XIII issued an encyclical letter *Ad Anglos* (To the English), in which he ignored the existence of the Church of England. This was followed on 29 June 1896 by the bull *Satis Cognitum* (It is a matter of common knowledge) on the Unity of the Church, in which he merely repeated the well-worn statements about St Peter and his successors. On 13 September of the same year another bull was published, *Apostolicæ curæ* (Apostolic Solicitude), in which Anglican Orders were condemned as *absolutely null and entirely void*, on the grounds of *Deficiency of Form* and *Lack of Intention*. The *Answer* of the archbishops of England appeared on 29 March 1897. Its publication had been delayed by the sudden death of Archbishop Benson in the previous October. Both these documents were republished, with English translations, in 1932 by the Society for Promoting Christian Knowledge, so are readily accessible to anyone who wishes to examine them.

Thirty years later there were some meetings between English and Roman Catholic theologians at Malines, under the presidency of Cardinal Mercier, whose courage and dignity during the occupation of Belgium by the Germans during the years 1914–18

[1] For an account of what passed see the *Life of Edward White Benson*, by A. C. Benson, pp. 492–591 (one-volume edition); *Life and Letters of Mandell Creighton*, by L. Creighton, vol. ii, pp. 176–80; and *A Roman Diary*, by T. A. Lacey (Longmans, 1910). Also see above, Chapter 17, p. 377 ff.

had won the admiration of the civilized world. Unfortunately, however, he had already shown that he knew nothing whatever about the real state of religion in England,[1] and he misconceived the attitude of the Englishmen altogether. He appears to have been criticized by some of his fellow-countrymen for having consented to meet them, as in a semi-apologetic letter issued to the people of his diocese he justified his conduct by saying that it was not for a bishop to turn a deaf ear when suppliants knocked at the door of the Roman Church.

These meetings were not in any sense negotiations. They were called *conversations*, and aimed at talking over differences, as scholars do. The Englishmen were all scholars of distinction, and bore the highest personal character, but they could not be considered to represent the Church of England as a whole. An ill-advised attempt to keep the whole business secret inevitably failed, and naturally provoked considerable suspicion, and even alarm, in England. Eventually the Papacy declared that it saw no value in such discussions and forbade the resumption of anything of the kind at any future time. It is fair to say that Pius V, for political as much as for religious reasons, declared war on us in 1570, and that his successors of the nineteenth and twentieth centuries do not want peace. They have made it plain that they are not prepared to discuss anything, because they will consider nothing but unconditional surrender. The possibility of any corporate union of the Church of England with the Church of Rome has never been more remote than the Papacy has made it in our own day.

In 1929 the quarrel between the Papacy and the Italian Government, which had been going on since 1870, and had become rather ridiculous, was ended by the creation of a sovereign state of about a hundred acres, to be known as the Vatican City. Thus the Papacy has recovered temporal power, and we can maintain diplomatic relations with it as with any other foreign Government. This may help to promote a better understanding of England at Rome. At that time Mussolini was at the head of the Italian Government, and he was said to have stated

[1] See *Mediævalism*, by G. Tyrrell, p. 19 (Longmans, 1908).

that he had promoted the arrangement because it would ensure that the Pope would always be "a good Italian". Presumably he hoped to secure some measure of moral support for his own policy. Apparently he had neither sufficient education nor intelligence to recognize that the papal claims can be justified only if the Pope is a supranational figure.

At present it is difficult to judge whether the restoration of this minute instalment of temporal power to the Papacy has affected its prestige or its policy in any way.

APPENDIX D

William Laud

A sermon preached in the Cathedral Church of Wells on 7 January 1945

"And it came to pass, when the time was come that he should be received up, he stedfastly set his face to go to Jerusalem, and sent messengers before his face: and they went, and entered into a village of the Samaritans, to make ready for him. And they did not receive him, because his face was as though he would go to Jerusalem. And when his disciples James and John saw this, they said, Lord, wilt thou that we command fire to come down from heaven, and consume them, even as Elias did? But he turned, and rebuked them, and said, Ye know not what manner of spirit ye are of. For the Son of Man is not come to destroy men's lives, but to save them. And they went to another village." (Luke 9. 51-6.)

NATURALLY the two Sons of Thunder wished to avenge the affront which had been offered to their Master. It was the more intolerable as the authors were Samaritans—half-Jews at best, and with no proper respect for Jerusalem and the Sanctuary which God had chosen there. If this churlish village were blotted out, that would be a lesson to all Samaritans which they would never forget.

There was scriptural authority for what they wished to have done. Was it not written that Elijah, the greatest of all prophets, had destroyed in this fashion soldiers sent by Ahab to seize his person, thereby vindicating the honour of the God of Israel and the dignity of his own office?

But by word and act our Lord showed that such methods are not His. Then and there He made clear to all men for all time that His work cannot be done by violence or destruction. Men, even very good men, have found this lesson very hard to learn ever since. Had it been laid to heart the course of history would have been very different.

I have taken this episode for my text, because Wednesday next, 10 January, is the three hundredth anniversary of the execution of Archbishop Laud on Tower Hill. The event is memorable; and as he was at one time bishop of this diocese it is appropriate that something should be said about him in this church today.

The principal authority for his life is the biography which was written by Peter Heylyn, for many years one of his chaplains, and perhaps as intimate with him as anyone ever was. It was published under the title *Cyprianus Anglicus* ("The English Cyprian")[1] in the year 1668, a few months after the author's death. Heylyn had a sincere admiration for the archbishop, and was a whole-hearted supporter of his policy.

William Laud was born at Reading in 1573. His father was a clothier, and sufficiently well-to-do to send his son first to Reading school and then to St John's College, Oxford, of which he afterwards became President. In due course he took Holy Orders. It is unnecessary to dwell on his early efforts to secure place and power. They must be judged by the standards of that day, not of this. If he was no better in this respect than most of his contemporaries, he was no worse.

In 1621 he became Bishop of St David's. In 1626 he was translated to this see. He held it for less than two years, and as by that time he seem to have decided that the Court was his proper sphere, his visits to Wells must have been few and brief, if indeed any were paid. In 1628 Charles I, who was perhaps the closest approach to a real friend he ever made, appointed him to London. From then until his imprisonment in 1641 he was the most powerful personage in the kingdom. Abbot, the Archbishop of Canterbury, was growing old and had withdrawn almost entirely from public life, as he had been unfortunate enough to kill one of Lord Zouch's keepers while shooting deer with a crossbow. In 1633 Laud succeeded him at Canterbury.

Laud was what would be called today an "Anglo-Catholic".

[1] Bishop of Carthage. Martyred 14 September 258.

He represented a party or school of thought, whichever we prefer to call it, which has held a legitimate place in our Church for more than three centuries and has contributed much of value to the religious life of the nation, which it has never dominated. It has probably always been stronger amongst the clergy than amongst the laity.

He appreciated the historic continuity and structure of the Church, and saw more clearly than many of his contemporaries that at the Reformation we had been careful to preserve both these. We had reformed our part of the Church Catholic. We had not brought it to an end and founded a new religious society on different lines to take its place, as most of the continental reformers did. He recognized that as our protest was (and is) against the errors and abuses of the Roman Church only, there is much ground common to us and them. But the mirage of reunion with Rome—"as Rome now is", to quote his own words—never dazzled his eyes. Not unnaturally he was accused of trying to bring in "Popery". This was entirely unjust. But it is probable that he never understood the feelings of horror and detestation with which the Roman Church was generally regarded. The fact that the feeling was largely irrational did not make it less formidable. Rather, more: because what is irrational is not open to argument. It is not extinct today.

He also attached great importance to the ordering of Divine Service: the position of the Communion Table, the dress of the clergy, and so forth. There was need for a higher standard of reverence and decency in such matters. To him these minutiæ were probably of almost divine, or at least semi-divine, authority, and charged with deep and sacred significance. Perhaps he never understood that to some people they are primarily matters of custom and common sense, and related only remotely at best to the knowledge of God, which is life eternal.

His energy was inexhaustible and his power of work almost superhuman. When Archbishop of Canterbury he was also for a year Lord Treasurer, which meant virtually Prime Minister, as far as that office could be considered to exist. At the present day *First Lord of the Treasury* is the first official title of the head of the

Government. Until the beginning of the present century it was the only one. *Prime Minister* is a colloquialism.

He was also a diligent attender at meetings of the Privy Council and (for a time) a member of what was called "The Foreign Committee", the embryo of our Foreign Office. When he relinquished the Treasurership he continued as Chancellor of the universities of Oxford and Dublin, and intervened in their affairs much more than a modern Chancellor is expected to do. He took an active interest in the Church in Scotland and Ireland, more active indeed than was to the liking of the bishops of those countries. He concerned himself closely with English congregations at trading posts abroad, insisting that they should not conform to the Church of the country in which they had settled. At the same time he tried to prevent the congregations of Dutch and French refugees in England from continuing the form of service to which they were accustomed.

He also held a metropolitical Visitation of the Province of Canterbury: a task which, I believe, no archbishop has attempted since. This must have demanded an enormous expenditure of time and energy, especially in view of the conditions of travel. Besides all this he was continually disputing by tongue and pen with Papists and Puritans, and trying to raise the standards of parochial worship throughout the country.

He was the principal and most trusted adviser of the King in all matters, and as Charles's affairs went from bad to worse the archbishop's unpopularity increased. The two were an unfortunate combination, as neither of them seems to have been able to estimate accurately the strength and quality of the opposition which he was provoking. Rulers who cannot do this are likely to end either upon the scaffold, as they did, or in exile, as Pope Gregory VII and James II.

Eventually he was imprisoned by order of Parliament in the Tower for three years, and then condemned to death on a charge of treason. The substance of the charges against him was that he had tried to subvert the laws of the Church and land by arbitrary action. How much truth there was in this it is hard to say. In the allegation that he had tried to reinstate "Popery" there was none. During his imprisonment and trial he bore himself with great dignity. He met his death with the unfaltering courage which he had displayed throughout his life.

"When Laud fell," writes Heylyn, "the Church fell with him." That is true. All that he had done was swept away by Acts of Parliament, and much more besides. Bishops, deans and chapters, and archdeacons were all formally abolished. Cathedrals were closed, except perhaps for an occasional sermon in the nave, and their property confiscated. Some of them, notably St Paul's, were almost laid waste. Here the chapter library was almost entirely destroyed, and the chapter house put up to auction as building material. Fortunately no one attempted to pull it down. Clergy were driven from their parishes. The use of the Book of Common Prayer was prohibited. Even the possession of a copy was a crime. Short of torture and mass murder, little was left undone to ensure that the Church of England as men had known it should cease to exist. When it reappeared at the Restoration it was not as Laud would have had it.

All this is common knowledge. What concerns us today is, Why did it happen?

Of course, as almost always in great upheavals, the revolution got beyond control. Much was done of which Parliament would not have approved. But why was it determined to destroy the archbishop and his works?

The men who brought Laud to trial and execution were not as the Germans of today or the leaders of the French revolution in the eighteenth century. They were Christian men, and as zealous for their form of Christianity as he was for his. Many of them were of high moral character, and well born and bred. How did it come about that they acted as they did?

There cannot be a short and simple answer to this question. In fact there is no single answer. But a number of contributory causes can be discerned, at which we must now glance briefly:

1. Laud's lot was cast in difficult times. For the first forty years of Elizabeth's reign the danger of a Spanish invasion, with all the support which the Papacy could give it, was never remote, and sometimes imminent. After the destruction of the second

Armada in 1598, which, if it had got to sea, might well have succeeded where the first had failed, Spain was no longer to be feared. It was certain that the Queen would die upon her throne, and the continuance of our existence as an independent nation was assured, and with it the survival of our Church.

Five years later our position was strengthened when a chapter of accidents made the tincture of royal blood which ran in the veins of the Stuarts sufficient to place James I on the throne of England. Unfortunate in many ways as that was destined to prove, it did increase our national security. We had no longer to expect a stab in the back whenever we engaged in warfare on the Continent.

The sudden transition from a long period of tension and peril to one of unassailable security was not good for the national character. Moral and religious standards were lowered (despite the appearance of the Authorized Version in 1611) and a spirit of factiousness was displayed, which tended to increase as time went on. Much the same is discernible during the twenty years immediately after the battle of Waterloo. Anyone who casts his mind back over the years 1919–39 will recognize the symptoms.

The Church was affected more adversely than anything else. During the reign of James I it sank to a low ebb. Divine Service was often conducted in slovenly and irreverent fashion. Preaching was feeble and perfunctory where it existed. There was need for a revival. But that could not be effected in a moment. And Laud was not the man to acquiesce readily in anything slow or gradual.

2. He seems to have aroused violent personal animosity in many of those with whom he was brought into contact. This emerges very clearly at his trial. It is impossible for us to account for it. Heylyn hints at an asperity of temper induced by the immense pressure of business which came upon him as arch-bishop. But it seems to have been a life-long characteristic. When he was a candidate for the Presidency of St John's College the proceedings became so stormy that the matter was referred to King James for his decision. He gave it in favour of Laud.

3. The mental qualities which gave him his extraordinary

interest in, and mastery of, detail seem to have debarred him from grasping principles. At any rate, he never seems to have stated his fundamental principles in any way sufficiently intelligible and comprehensive to command respect, if not assent. He declared that the Church of England was not Roman or Calvinist. But he never seems to have said what he thought it was, or ought to be. He quoted Canons, Articles and Acts of Parliament as final authorities, but made no attempt to elucidate the principles which they aimed at expressing. At his trial he affirmed that he had been born and bred "in the protestant religion established during the reign of Elizabeth," but seems to have ignored the two principal points at issue: First, What exactly did that mean? Secondly, Had his policy been inconsistent with it?

His nearest approach to anything fundamental was when he asserted that as England, Scotland and Ireland were united under one crown it was necessary in the interests of stable government that the Churches of the three countries should be uniform.

As a political theory there may be something to be said for this. As a religious principle there is very little. It has never come within measurable distance of success.

4. Lastly, uniformity was his passion: not as a means of allowing differences of opinion, but as a method of securing agreement. When he could not persuade, he was always ready to coerce. The ecclesiastical courts possessed much more power than they do now, and he never hesitated to make full use of it. Hundreds of instances might be cited. One will be sufficient as an illustration.

At Beckington in this county the Communion Table stood in the middle of the chancel, with its length east and west, as was not uncommon in those days. The archbishop required it to be placed against the east wall with its length north and south, as we are accustomed to see it—"altar-wise", as the phrase went. To-day probably almost everyone would prefer this arrangement. The people refused to comply, whereupon the archbishop excommunicated them, as the law allowed. After a year (which it is only fair to say was a longer interval than the law required) he sent them to prison, as the law enabled him to do. As the only method of regaining their freedom, they promised to comply with his requirements. The archbishop had carried his point. But what, we may ask ourselves, was the ultimate outcome? We can only guess the answer. But is it not probable that they emerged unconvinced, and filled with hatred for the archbishop and almost everything for which he stood?

It is never advisable to try to appraise a historical character without reference to his portrait if one exists. There is one of Laud in the bishop's palace here, and others I imagine elsewhere. The high cheek-bones, narrow eyes and sloping eyebrows give a curiously un-English, semi-Mongolian appearance. But most remarkable is the extraordinary immobility of the face. It has the rigidity of a mask. It is hard to say what is to be read there. But there is certainly little indication of sympathy or imagination. One wonders whether he ever read a line of poetry in his life. In short, the portrait is as baffling as its original.

William Laud has always been one of the most enigmatic figures in English history.

He died valiantly and Christianly for his convictions, and must therefore be counted amongst the martyrs. But the utter ruin which he brought not only upon himself—for that he would perhaps have cared little—but upon the Church which he lived and died to serve suggests that, like James and John, he knew not what spirit he was of, and is therefore an outstanding exemplification of a truth which is too easily forgotten or ignored.

No personal piety, no sincerity of purpose, no ability, no courage, no energy can avail to redeem any attempt to do Christ's work by methods which He has taught us plainly are not His.

APPENDIX E

Crown Appointments in Theory and Practice, with Special Reference to the English Episcopate[1]

I. THERE are only two methods by which a man can be appointed to any office: some form of nomination or some form of election. Neither is perfect because no nominator or body of electors is infallible. They may always turn out to have been mistaken in the man of their choice.

The chances of making a mistake are increased if the appointment is a promotion. A man ought only to be promoted for having done something well; and the fact of his promotion makes it virtually certain that he will never have an opportunity of doing that particular thing again. The authority which advances him says in effect: "You have shown proof of good character and general capacity. We therefore hope that you will be successful in the discharge of different, more arduous and more important duties." As a rule this hope is realized, but not always. It is a matter of common knowledge that from time to time there are failures in the higher ranks of any calling, in the Cabinet, in the Services, on the bench of Judges, as well as on the bench of Bishops. Sometimes appointments which were greeted with general acclamation prove unsuccessful, and sometimes unexpected and unwelcome ones justify themselves completely.

Each method of appointment has its peculiar weakness. The individual nominator may be unduly influenced by personal considerations, not always of the best kind, and may be imperfectly informed as to the qualifications demanded by the position to which he has to appoint. Experience has shown again and again that a body of electors seldom has one candidate so out-

[1] Written by the Dean of Wells for the Radcliffe Liturgical Library in Liverpool Cathedral. (Reprinted by the kind permission of the Dean of Liverpool.)

standing that everyone can accept him without hesitation. Usually there are at least two, both well qualified for the position, if not for quite the same reasons. Neither can command a sufficient majority (a majority of one usually is, and ought to be, considered insufficient) to secure election. In dioceses which elect their bishop there is always a House of clergy and a House of laity, and the two Houses very seldom seem to want the same man. After several fruitless ballots have been held both the original candidates have to be dropped and a third has to be found whom everyone will agree to accept, although nobody really wants him.

Appointments made in this way are more likely to be safe than bold or brilliant, and *safety first* is not a very exalted maxim, especially for a Church.

II. For more than a thousand years bishops in England have been appointed by a combination of the two methods. Naturally from time to time the centre of gravity has shifted. Sometimes it has been in the nominator; sometimes in the electors. Prior to the Norman Conquest, a nomination was usually made by the king and confirmed by the Witenagemote. The chapter of the cathedral church seems to have taken little part. Probably it was seldom sufficiently organized to do so. William the Conqueror observed the old form of nominating at a meeting of the Great Council; but he would have been a bold man who dared to dispute the king's choice. Probably he would not have been in a position to do so twice. The struggle between Henry I and Anselm secured the right of election to the cathedral chapters, but as the election did not take place in the cathedral church but in a national Council or in one of the Royal Chapels before the justiciar of the kingdom, it would have been difficult and dangerous to refuse the royal nominee.[1]

King John gave the chapters right of free election, as an inducement to the clergy to support him against the barons. This is the meaning of the often-quoted and commonly misunderstood phrase in Magna Carta, *Ecclesia Anglicana Libera Sit*. It was never really effective in practice. Probably few people would desire to

[1] See Stephens and Hunt, *A History of the English Church*, vol. ii, p. 283.

see it become so now. The attempts made by Henry III to influence the chapters led to an increasing flow of appeals to Rome and so augmented the power of the Pope. This reached its height during the next century. In 1349 Clement VI brushed aside the canonical election of Simon Islip to the see of Canterbury and issued a bull which professed to make the appointment. Yet four years earlier he had told his cardinals that if the King of England were to beg for an ass to be made bishop he must not be denied.[1] The distinction between a petition which must not be refused and a command which must be obeyed is principally one of terminology. Papal pretensions were curbed by the strong hand of King Edward III with the statutes of Provisors (1351) and Præmunire (1353). It is open to question whether the Church gained or lost by these measures, but the rights of the Crown were made more secure. When the Reformation put a final end to all foreign interference with our affairs, it merely meant that the power of the Crown became in theory what it had been in practice for the best part of a couple of centuries, and that the need for disguising it with complimentary verbiage lapsed.

III. Today a *Crown Appointment* means an appointment made by the sovereign acting on advice tendered to him by the Prime Minister of the day. When advice has been tendered formally, the sovereign is bound to accept it. How much informal discussion may have taken place between them first is of course not known. The published letters of Queen Victoria show that in her time there was often a good deal. But it is of course true that the ultimate decision rests, in fact, with the Prime Minister. Some people regard this method of appointing bishops as undesirable, because the Prime Minister need not be a member of the Church of England, or indeed profess any religion of any kind. The objection is not entirely frivolous but cannot be considered to carry much weight, because it ignores the fact that he does not act in his personal but in his representative capacity. Besides bishoprics, appointments are made in the same way to all deaneries and to some of the canonries in some cathedrals. Also to some of the most important professorships in the Universities of Oxford,

[1] Stephens and Hunt, vol. iii, pp. 86–7.

Cambridge, St Andrews, Edinburgh, Glasgow, and Aberdeen, as well as to the mastership of the most important college in Cambridge[1] (if not in the world) and to the headship of one of the largest and most famous of English schools. The Prime Minister cannot be a member of all these great institutions and may never have had any close connexion with any of them. The principle underlying Crown appointments outside its own immediate service is that certain positions are sufficiently important to be matters of national concern. It matters to the nation as a whole by whom they are filled. Therefore the filling of them cannot be left to any local authority, which (human nature being as it is) is only too likely to mean local jealousy and local intrigue. The sovereign and the Prime Minister together represent the nation as no other men can pretend to do. They embody the two sources of authority which we recognize (and it is not easy to see how there can be a third, unless we admit Violence): Hereditary Right, and Power derived ultimately from the electorate.

The first prerequisite of making good appointments in any walk of life is to survey the whole field of choice adequately. The sovereign and the Prime Minister are obviously better placed for doing this than anyone else can be and also are in a position to consult with anyone they choose to any extent they please. Probably they are the last two men in the kingdom who would lay claim to infallibility.

The Crown appointment has the further advantage that the nominee does not have to take up the duties of his diocese or professorship or whatever it may be with the full knowledge that a considerable number of those with whom he will have to deal did their best to get somebody else, and that his unsuccessful rival is probably among them.

It is observable that bishops who have been appointed to dioceses overseas by free election are usually quite ready to return to our "degrading bondage" after a few years should an opportunity present itself.

[1] Also to the largest college in Oxford, where the mastership is attached to the deanery of the cathedral.

It may be added that whenever a see has to be filled the needs of the Bench of Bishops ought to be taken into account, as well as those of the diocese concerned. In what respect does the episcopate need reinforcement at this juncture is a really important consideration. It is, however, unlikely that it would occur to any body of diocesan electors, or that they would be in a position to deal with it if it did.

IV. The process by which a diocesan bishopric is filled in England today is as follows:

1. The chapter clerk informs the Crown (in this connection the Prime Minister's Patronage Secretary) of the vacancy and asks that licence may be given to the dean and chapter to fill it. This licence is the *congé d'élire* and is accompanied by a *letter missive* containing the name of the person recommended by the Crown.

2. Within twelve days after the receipt of these documents the dean summons the chapter to meet in the chapter house to carry out the election. For this purpose (and for some others) the chapter is now usually understood to include the honorary canons, or non-residentiary prebendaries as well as the residentiaries. It is usual to hold this meeting immediately after divine service in the quire, and for the electors to go from quire to chapter house in procession.

3. When the electors have taken their seats in the chapter house they are preconized by the chapter clerk and the dean declares all absentees to be *contumacious*. This does not expose them to any penalty but precludes any subsequent attempt to invalidate the proceedings on the ground of their absence. The dean then asks the chapter by what method they wish to proceed. Traditionally there are three:

(a) *Per scrutinium*. By ballot. In the event of a tie the dean has a second or casting vote.

(b) *Per compromissum*. This is a form borrowed from Roman law. The electors choose some of their number to act for them, pledging themselves to accept their decision whatever it may be. The number of *compromittores* must not be more than one-seventh of the number of members of the chapter present and must always be an even number (two, four, or six) so that when they act with the dean a tie is impossible. Probably this method is seldom followed.

(c) *Per inspirationem*. By acclamation. The dean asks the electors whether they think that the person who has been recommended to them as bishop is worthy of election to the see. If they agree they stand up in their places and say *He is worthy*.

Sometimes the question is put in Latin and the answer returned in that language. English can, however, be employed throughout.

4. When the chapter have decided upon their method of procedure the election is carried out accordingly. The electors then leave the chapter house in procession and return to their stalls in the quire. The dean then declares the election publicly, first from the steps of the high altar and then from the entrance to the quire.

Such election is not a farce. The electors cannot reject the nominee of the Crown merely because they think they know of someone whom they would prefer. But if they believed that he was unfit for the episcopate on grounds of faith or morals, and could adduce sufficient reason for their belief, they could refuse to elect. They could not substitute another name, but could request the Crown to do so. Theoretically such refusal would expose them to very severe penalties under the Statute of Præmunire. But as the precise nature of these penalties seems to be uncertain it is doubtful whether any of them could be enforced. In any case, if the chapter were obviously in the right they would certainly win. Public opinion would be upon their side so overwhelmingly that no Government would dare to touch them. The Crown would be compelled to withdraw its first nominee and put forward a better one. Thus the election is a real and effective safeguard against any abuse of the royal supremacy. Moreover, whatever the previous steps had been, there would have to be a formal meeting of the dean and chapter, as representing the clergy of the diocese, to ratify solemnly a decision which had been reached elsewhere: as treaties have to be ratified by plenipotentiaries representing the nations concerned before they can take effect, after their provisions have been determined exactly elsewhere.

Election is followed by confirmation. This is a purely legal ceremony at which representatives of the Crown satisfy themselves that the election has been duly carried out, that the person before them who professes to have been elected by the dean and chapter of the cathedral church of X really has been and is the person whose name appears in the letter missive.

When a bishop-elect has been confirmed he can exercise all the jurisdiction of the see, whether he is in episcopal orders or not— e.g. present to benefices.

Consecration is performed by the archbishop of the Province, who must be assisted by at least two diocesan bishops of the same Province. If the archbishop cannot act for any reason there must be at least four bishops. The position of the consecrators is closely analogous with that of the electors at an earlier stage. They could refuse to act, if there were adequate grounds for refusal. Here again there is a real and effective safeguard against any abuse of the royal supremacy.

After consecration the bishop does homage. This is not considered to mean that his episcopal character and spiritual authority are derived from the Crown. They have been transmitted by the Church, through the channels of election and consecration. Homage relates to the possessions of the see. Originally each bishopric had its own estates. When the see became vacant they reverted to the Crown for safe custody and were granted again to the next bishop as soon as he was qualified to receive them. More than a century ago all the episcopal estates were transferred to the Ecclesiastical Commissioners. But the ancient form is maintained; and the new bishop cannot receive from the Commissioners the income to which he is entitled until homage has been done.

Last of all comes enthronement (*Inthronization* is probably the correct form) in the cathedral church. In the Northern Province this is done by the dean. In the Southern Province this is done by the Archdeacon of Canterbury. This ceremony is probably unnecessary as it does not appear to possess any legal significance.

It is, however, of long standing, and may be regarded as the formal public presentation of the new bishop to the people of his diocese.

At the same time he is installed by the dean in the chapter house. This ceremony, which is attended by members of the chapter only, is probably essential as it constitutes the bishop Visitor of the chapter. In some cathedrals Latin is used for part of this.

V. The process by which diocesan bishops are appointed in England has a thousand years or more of history behind it. Each step has a real and peculiar significance. The process has developed as is natural in a country which has become increasingly accustomed to act through representative persons and institutions. The system is not perfect; nor is any other. It must be a matter of opinion whether any alternative would serve the Church of England more effectively. Those who are inclined to cavil at its results should perhaps remember that no less than twelve new dioceses have been created since the beginning of the present century and that it may be easier to create additional bishoprics than to find men adequate to fill them.

They may also recall the opening words of Hooker's *Ecclesiastical Polity*:

> "He that goeth about to persuade a multitude that they are not so well governed as they ought to be shall never want attentive and favourable hearers; because they know the manifold defects whereunto every kind of regiment is subject, but the secret lets and difficulties which in public proceedings are innumerable and inevitable they have not ordinarily the judgement to consider."

BIBLIOGRAPHY

The following list includes only the books of which I made use when preparing the lectures. Most of them are well known and easily accessible to any one who may wish to consult them for further study.

The following abbreviations have been employed:—

R.H.S. *Royal Historical Society.*
S.A.S. *Somerset Archæological Society.*
S.P.C.K. *Society for Promoting Christian Knowledge.*
S.R.S. *Somerset Record Society.*

ACTON, LORD: *Historical Essays and Studies* (Macmillan).
AMBROSE, St: *De Excessu Fratris sui Satyri.*
ANDREWES, Bp.: *Resp. ad Card. Bellarmin.*
Anglican Communion. Ed: Bp: Wand (O.U. Press, 1948).
AQUINAS, THOMAS: *Summa.*
AUGUSTINE, St: *De Civitate Dei.*
                Encheiridion ad Laurentium.
AUSONIUS: *Ordo Nobilium Urbium.*
AYTOUN: *Lays of the Scottish Cavaliers.*

BARNARD and SHEPPARD: *Arms and Blazonry of the Colleges of Oxford* (O.U. Press, 1929).
BECKINGTON, Bp: *Register* (S.R.S. 49 and 50).
BENSON, A. C.: *Life of E. W. (Abp) Benson* (Macmillan).
BENSON, E. W.: *Cyprian: His Life, His Times, His Work* (Macmillan).
BERKELEY, G., Bp: *Alciphron.*
BOSWELL, J.: *Life of Dr Johnson.*
BRILIOTH, Y.: *The Anglican Revival.*
British Chronology, Handbook of (R.H.S., 1939).
BROWN, J. R. C.: *Number One Millbank* (S.P.C.K.).
BUTLER, Bp: *Analogy.*

CALVIN: *De Coena Domini.*
CARPENTER, S. C.: *Church and People* (S.P.C.K., 1933).
CHAUCER: *Canterbury Tales.*

CLAUDIAN: *De Laudibus Stilichonis.*
  De tertio Consulatu Honorii.
CLEMENT OF ALEXANDRIA: *Stromateis.*
CLERKE, Bp: *Register* (S.R.S. vol. 55).
COLLETT: *Little Gidding and its Founder* (S.P.C.K., 1925).
CREIGHTON, L.: *Life and Letters of Mandell Creighton* (6 volumes, Longmans).
CREIGHTON, M.: *History of the Papacy* (6 volumes, Longmans).
  Historical Essays and Reviews (Longmans).
  The Church and the Nation (Longmans).

Dates, Handbook of (R.H.S., 1945).
DOWNSIDE REVIEW: *The Bloody Assizes in Somerset,* E. Horne (vol. liii, 1935).
DOYLE, A. CONAN: *Micah Clarke.*
DUGDALE: *Monastican Anglicanum.*

ELVIRA, COUNCIL OF: *Canons.*
EUSEBIUS: *Historia Ecclesiastica.*

FOX, Bp: *Register* (S.R.S., vol. 52).

GARBETT, Abp: *The Claims of the Church of England* (Hodder and Stoughton, 1947).
GASELEE, S.: *Anthology of Mediæval Latin* (Macmillan, 1925).
GIBBON: *Decline and Fall of the Roman Empire* (7 volumes, ed. J. B. Bury).
GIBSON, Bp: *Codex Juris Ecclesiastici Anglicani* (1713).
GLASTONBURY: *Chartulary.* Ed. A. Watkin (S.R.S. 1944–8).
GRAY, A.: *Cambridge University.*
GREGORY THE GREAT: *Dialogues.*

HACKETT, Bp: *Scrinia Reserata.*
HADRIAN, Bp: *Register* (S.R.S., vol 54).
HARBIN, E. H. B.: *The Black Death in Somerset* (S.A.S., vol. lxiii).
HAVERFIELD, F.: *The Romanization of Roman Britain* (Clarendon Press, 1923).
HEADLAM, A. C., Bp: *Preface* to *The Anglican Revival.*
HENSON, H. H., Bp: *Christian Morality* (Gifford Lectures 1935–6, Clarendon Press).
HERBERT, G.: *The Priest to the Temple.*
Historical Monuments, Royal Commission on. Vol. i (H.M. Stationery Office, 1924).

IGNATIUS, Bp of Antioch: *Smyrnæans* (ed J. B. Lightfoot).
INGE, W. R.: *The Victorian Age* (C.U. Press, 1922).
      The Platonic Tradition in English.
      Religious Thought (Longmans, 1926).

JALLAND: *The Church and the Papacy* (S.P.C.K., 1942).
JEROME, St: Ep. 101, *Ad Evangelum.*
JUVENAL: *Satires.*

KEN, T., Bp: *Ichabod.*
KING, GREGORY: *Tables.*
KING, O., Bp: *Register* (S.R.S., vol. 54).

LACEY, T.: *A Roman Diary* (Longmans, 1897).
LAMBETH CONFERENCE OF 1888: REPORT (S.P.C.K.).
LEA, H. C.: *History of the Inquisition.*
LE FANU: *Queen Anne's Bounty* (Macmillan, 1890).
LIGHTFOOT, J. B., Bp: *Historical Essays* (Macmillan).
               Leaders in the Northern Church.
LOCKE: *Essay concerning Human Understanding.*

MACAULAY, LORD: *Essays.*
MALDEN, H.: *Origin of Universities* (Taylor, London, 1835).
MARTIAL: *Epigrams.*
MIDDLETON, R. D.: *Dr Routh* (O.U. Press, 1938).
MOORMAN, J.: *English Church Life in the Thirteenth Century* (C.U. Press, 1941).

NEWTON, I.: *Principia.*
NICÆA, COUNCIL OF, *Canons of.*
Notes and Queries for Somerset and Dorset.

ORIGEN: *Philocalia.* Ed J. A. Robinson (C.U. Press, 1893).

PAPAL BULL: *Satis Cognitum* (S.P.C.K., 1896).
          Apostolicæ Curea (S.P.C.K., 1896).
PAPAL ENCYCLICAL: *Ad Anglos* (S.P.C.K. 1896).
PAUSANIAS: *Description of Greece.* Ed J. G. Frazer.
PEPYS, S.: *Diary.*
PLINY (C. SECUNDUS): *Letters.*
POPE, A.: *Moral Essays.*

Queen Victoria: *Letters of.* Ed A. C. Benson and Lord Esher.

RECORD OFFICE: *Assizes,* 1685–977.

ROBINSON, H. WHEELER: *The Bible in its Ancient and English Versions* (Clarendon Press, 1940).

ROBINSON, J. A.: *Somerset Historical Essays* (British Academy Publications).

The Times of St Dunstan (Clarendon Press).

Two Glastonbury Legends (C.U. Press).

RYMER: *Fœdera.* 20 vols., 1704–35.

Sæpius Officio: *The Answer of the Archbishops of England to Pope Leo XIII* (S.P.C.K., 1906).

SENECA: *De Ira De Clementia.*

SHAKESPEARE: *Richard II.*

SHORTHOUSE: *John Inglesant.*

SMITH, A. L.: *Church and State in the Middle Ages* (Ford Lectures, O.U. Press, 1913).

STEPHENS and HUNT: *A History of the English Church* (9 vols., Macmillan, 1899–1910).

STEPHENS, W. R.: *Life of W. F. Cook* (Bentley, 1878).

STERRY: *Eton College Register 1441–1698* (Spottiswoode, Ballantyne and Co, 1943).

STILLINGTON, Bp: *Register* (S.R.S., vol. 52).

SUETONIUS: *De Vita Caesarum.*

SYKES, N.: *Edmund Gibson* (O.U. Press, 1926).

TACITUS: *Agricola.*

TERTULLIAN: *Adv. Iudaeos.*

De Anima.

De Pallio.

De Pudicitia.

Passio S. Perpetuae.

THACKERAY. *Esmond.*

THOMPSON, A. HAMILTON: *The English Clergy* (Ford Lectures, Clarendon Press, 1947).

THOMPSON, B. HAMILTON: *Glastonbury: Truth and Fiction* (Mowbray).

THUCYDIDES: II. 45.

TREVELYAN, G. M.: *England in the Age of Wycliffe* (Longmans, 1899).

English Social History (Longmans, 1944).

History of England (Longmans, 1926).

History of Trinity College, Cambridge.

TYRRELL, G.: *Mediævalism* (Longmans, 1908).

VIRGIL: *Eclogues*.

WALKER, JOHN: *The Sufferings of the Clergy*, 1714. Revised by A. W. Matthews (Clarendon Press, 1948).
WALPOLE, H.: *Letters*.
WELLS: *Chapter Acts*.
William Cousyn's MS. Ed. A. Watkin (S.R.S., vol 56).
WOLSEY. Bp: *Register* (S.R.S., vol. 55).

YORK: *Books of Acts*.

INDEX

Printed in Great Britain by
Billing and Sons Ltd., Guildford and Esher
G2650